DAVID O. MCKAY LIBRARY

3 1404 00719 1189

OPEN...
AVID O. McKAY LIBRARY
YU-IDAHO
EXBURG ID 83460-0405
460-0405

WITHDRAWN

MAR 0 1 2023

DAVID O. McKAY LIBRARY
BYU-IDAHO

JUN 4 2002

X

CHAPTERS ON THE HISTORY

OF THE

SOUTHERN PACIFIC

LIBRARY OF
EARLY AMERICAN BUSINESS AND INDUSTRY

"The Golden Gate"

CHAPTERS ON THE HISTORY
OF THE
SOUTHERN PACIFIC

By

STUART DAGGETT, Ph.D.

Professor of Railway Economics and Dean of the
College of Commerce, University of California;
Author of "Railroad Reorganization"

REPRINTS OF ECONOMIC CLASSICS

AUGUSTUS M. KELLEY · PUBLISHERS
NEW YORK · 1966

First Published 1922

Library of Congress Catalogue Card Number

66 - 22621

Printed in the United States of America
by Sentry Press, New York, N. Y. 10019

PREFACE

So far as the author knows there is no published study which discusses in detail the important business problems connected with the history of the Southern Pacific Railroad lines. Most of the books which contain references to the Southern Pacific or to the Central Pacific limit themselves to a few chapters upon the romantic aspects of their construction. The few works which treat of the later period confine themselves chiefly to particular episodes in Southern Pacific history, often with the deliberate attempt to discredit the railroad company. The truth is that most writers upon the Southern Pacific have relied upon the reports of the United States Pacific Railway Commission or on Bancroft's "History of California," and very few have done original work from source material.

Yet the usable material dealing with the subject of Pacific railroads is abundant. The Southern Pacific has left a broad trail in California. The record of its doings is to be found in court reports; in state, city, and federal records; in the public testimony, or still better, in the private letters of owners or managers of company enterprises; in the reports of the company itself and of its engineers or other representatives; in pamphlets without number; in files of newspapers. It is true that much of the data is partisan and unreliable as to details. Yet a partisan statement is serviceable if one knows it to be partisan, and, if one has reliable information with which to check the unreliable, the extent of partisan exaggeration in a given case becomes itself a fact of no insignificant importance.

Most of the documents used in the following pages have been consulted in one or another cf three large collections: that of the Bancroft Library of the University of California; that of the Hopkins' Railway Library of Stanford University;

and that of the State Library at Sacramento. Use has also been made of data in the office of the Secretary of State of California and of the State Railroad Commission. In certain cases the manuscript has been submitted to officials of the Southern Pacific Company for their comment, or to shippers or business men who were believed to be well-informed. The work has been more or less actively in progress over a period of eight years so that there has been more than usual opportunity for checking, comparison of views, and the testing of material. It is the author's hope that he has at least examined all the significant classes of information on the particular subjects which he has discussed. With a subject so extensive it is rarely, if ever, possible to reach all the fugitive literature, or to consult all the living men from whom opinions or scraps of information might be obtained. The most that can be said is that there has been a diligent search, with good facilities, through a number of years.

The conclusions which the writer has himself reached with respect to the political and business activities of the Southern Pacific in California, he has explained in the book at length and will not now repeat. There is claimed for them no more conclusiveness than the facts presented in each particular case may justify, although the conclusions are free from conscious bias, and the author's own interests are engaged on neither side.

Acknowledgment is hereby made of the courtesies extended by the libraries of Berkeley, Palo Alto, and Sacramento, and of the patient attention which individuals have given to particular portions of the book.

STUART DAGGETT

Berkeley, California,
February 1, 1922.

CONTENTS

ILLUSTRATIONS

CHAPTER I

INCEPTION OF THE PROJECT

Significance of the History

The history of the Southern Pacific and the railroad companies connected with it affords one of the many examples in American economic life of a great industrial organization built up from small beginnings within the lifetime of one group of men. It is a story full of the interest which attaches to constructive achievement in any line. When we remember that as late as 1870 there was no railroad west of the Mississippi-Missouri River except the Northern, Union, Kansas, and Central Pacific railroads, which possessed a mileage as great as 300 miles, and when we recall that in 1860 the total railroad mileage of the states in this same territory amounted to only 6,000 miles, we are able to form some idea of the successful energy which created a system of 861 miles of railroad in the course of six and one-half years, across an unsettled country, in the face of obstacles due to climate, altitude, and distance from centers of traffic and of finance.

The history of the Southern Pacific is significant, however, for still other reasons than because it illustrates what men can do in spite of serious difficulties. The company's record is important to the student of transportation problems because there is embodied in it much of the experience of the Pacific Coast with respect to railroad construction, railroad finance, railroad rate-making, and the relation of railroad corporations to the public at large, as represented by local, state, and national governments. What the Pacific Coast, and what in particular the state of California know, first hand, of the habits and policies of railroad corporations, is mainly derived from contact with the Southern Pacific Railroad and its auxiliary companies.

The narrative that follows is offered as a contribution from the far western portion of the United States which may help to explain the attitude of that section toward transportation matters; as well as an account of some phases of the earlier development of a railroad system which is now one of the most powerful in all the country, whether we compare this system with the railroads of the East or with those of the West.

The Southern Pacific system today embraces lines from Ogden and New Orleans on the east, to Portland, San Francisco, and Los Angeles on the west. The part of the system first built, however, and at all times the most important part of it, is that section reaching from a few miles west of Ogden, Utah, to the cities of Sacramento and San Francisco. This portion of the larger system was built and is owned by the Central Pacific Railroad Company.[1] It is therefore to the circumstances attending the construction of this portion of the line that attention will first be directed.

Early Activities of Theodore Dehone Judah

The promoter of the Central Pacific Railroad was a young engineer named Theodore Dehone Judah. Judah was born in Bridgeport, Connecticut. He obtained his first experience in railroad building on the Troy and Schenectady Railroad in New York. Later he built a railroad down the gorge of the Niagara River to Lewiston, served as resident engineer on the Erie Canal, and in 1854 had charge of the Buffalo and

---

[1] The statement in the text is sufficiently accurate as a preliminary generalization. As will appear later, the road between Sacramento and Oakland was not built by the Central Pacific, but by certain other companies of which the Western Pacific and the California Pacific were the most important. It may also be important for some purposes to observe that the Southern Pacific system enters Ogden over Union Pacific tracks, and New Orleans over the tracks of the Illinois Central Railroad Company.

New York Railroad then building to connect with the Erie. This was a responsible position for a man with so brief a period of training. When Judah came to California in 1854 he was only twenty-eight years of age. He was soon to make it evident, however, that he possessed more than respectable engineering ability, while he also displayed a capacity for sustained enthusiasm in connection with the project for a transcontinental railroad which eventually overcame all obstacles and resulted in the formulation of definite and successful plans for a transcontinental line.[2]

Judah began work in California as engineer of the Sacramento Valley Railroad. He left the service of the company, however, before the road was finished to Folsom. Subsequently he made a survey for a railroad from Sacramento to Benicia, and also one for a short branch on the California Central Railroad. Still later he was employed by the trustee of the Sacramento Valley Railroad, J. Mora Moss, and the superintendent, J. P. Robinson, to explore the Sierra Nevada Mountains for wagon road routes north of the south fork of the American River, and at the same time to act as agent for the Sacramento Valley Railroad in soliciting freight.

Details of Judah's activities between 1854 and 1860 are difficult to obtain. We know that he visited Washington in order to procure the passage of a bill making grants of land to California for railroad purposes. In 1859 he was the delegate from Sacramento to the Pacific Railroad Convention, where he urged the importance of a thorough survey before any decision should be made regarding the route of a transcontinental railroad. When the convention adjourned he was sent to Washington at his own expense to urge the passage of a

---

[2] On the early history of the Central Pacific, see a document printed by order of the Nevada Senate, entitled "Evidence concerning projected railways across the Sierra Nevada Mountains from Pacific tide-water in California, etc., procured by the Committee on Railroads of the First Nevada Legislature" (Carson City, 1865). This document contains several valuable reports and some interesting testimony.

bill such as the convention favored. He returned in 1860 without having accomplished his purpose, but convinced that Congress was in favor of granting federal aid to a railroad to California from the East, and that it would act when more important matters had been disposed of.[3]

Discovery of Transcontinental Route

It was after Judah's return from Washington in 1860 that he undertook the explorations for the Sacramento Valley Railroad to which reference has been made. Doubtless while engaged on this work he visited Dutch Flat, and doubtless also his enthusiasm for a transcontinental railroad became generally known. Judah was no mountaineer, but he could readily profit by the knowledge of men acquainted with the country. Such a man he found in Daniel W. Strong, a druggist at Dutch Flat, who accompanied him on his explorations. We have Strong's statement that he himself conceived the idea that immigrant travel could be diverted through the Dutch Flat country by the construction of a railroad, and that he hired assistants, made a reconnaissance, and found a continuous divide over which he thought a road could pass. Knowing that Mr. Judah was trying to find a pass over the mountains, he wrote to him, and Judah came from Sacramento to Dutch Flat. Strong says that he showed Judah the route he had discovered, and that Judah thought well of it.[4]

Such is Strong's testimony given years afterwards, when the Central Pacific had proved a success, and it was a distinction to have been connected with it. It is possible that Strong overestimated his contribution to the work. Yet the essential

---

[3] Judah's report of his mission to Washington as a delegate of the Pacific Railroad Convention is printed in full in the *Sacramento Union* for July 25, 1860.

[4] Testimony taken by the United States Pacific Railway Commission, appointed under an Act of Congress approved March 3, 1887, entitled, "An act authorizing an investigation of the books, accounts, and methods of railroads which have received aid from the United States, and other purposes." (50th Congress, 1st Session, Senate Executive Document No. 51, pp. 2838–39, testimony D. W. Strong.) Hereafter referred to as United States Pacific Railway Commission.

Theodore Dehone Judah

fact is that Judah was in the mountains in August, 1860, and that he or Strong, or both of them hit upon a route which Judah pronounced practicable. One may hazard the guess that Strong pointed out a pass and Judah tested it with instruments.[5] Mrs. Judah repeats the story as she heard it:

> It was in the drug store of Dr. Strong at Dutch Flat that the first profile was marked out from notes taken by them (Judah and Strong). Judah could not sleep or rest after they got into town and the store, till he had stretched his paper on the counter and made his figures thereon. Then, turning to Dr. Strong, [he] said for the first time, "Doctor, I shall make my survey over this, the Donner Pass, or Dutch Flat route, above every other."[6]

Appeal for Funds

Judah drew up articles of association for a company late in 1860, and endeavored to get subscriptions for stock, but without much success. Meanwhile, the publication in the newspapers of information relating to the Dutch Flat route cost him his position with the Sacramento Valley Railroad, for the trustee of the company, J. Mora Moss, took the position that the information acquired by Judah while an employee of the Sacramento Valley belonged to the railroad company, and should not have been published without its consent. It is said that Judah was very indignant, but to no avail.[7]

By October or November, 1860, the record thus shows that Judah had satisfied himself of the existence of a railroad route across the Sierras, and that he was intensely interested in having this railroad built. He was not personally a man of capital, although not entirely without means, and success in

---

[5] The expenses of this preliminary investigation were provided by small subscribers around Dutch Flat. 'A paper dated at Dutch Flat, June 26, 1860, contains 47 names, including that of D. W. Strong. No subscription was for over $15, and only nine were for as much as $10 apiece. (United States Pacific Railway Commission, p. 2959.)

[6] Judah manuscript, letter of Mrs. Anne Judah.

[7] Evidence concerning projected railways across the Sierra Nevada Mountains, *sup cit.*, testimony L. L. Robinson.

transforming his bare project into an actual operating line depended entirely upon the financial support which he could obtain. In November, accordingly, we find Judah endeavoring to give wide circulation to the results of his discoveries.

Under date of November 1, 1860, a circular letter was issued directing the attention of the public to "some newly discovered facts with reference to the route of the Pacific Railroad through California." This letter asserted that a practicable line had been discovered "from the city of Sacramento upon the divide between Bear River and North Fork of the American, via Illinois Town and Dutch Flat, through Lake Pass on the Truckee River, which gives nearly a direct line to Washoe, with maximum grades of 100 feet per mile." The estimated length of line in California was 115 miles. It was said that if the Pacific Railroad bill then pending in Congress should be passed, providing an appropriation of $13,000 per mile from the navigable waters of the Sacramento River to the base of the Sierra Nevadas; thence $24,000 per mile to the summit; thence an additional $3,000 per mile for each degree of longitude crossed until the 109th degree was reached, the entire road could be graded without appeal to private investors, leaving only the iron, rolling stock, etc., to be provided from private means. The projected railroad might connect with the Sacramento Valley Railroad at Folsom, or with the California Central Railroad at Lincoln. Subscriptions were asked to an amount of $1,000 per mile for 115 miles, with 10 per cent paid in, to allow the organization of a company under the state law; and it was promised that the money subscribed would be used to make a thorough, practical railroad survey.[8]

In a letter dated the previous day, and addressed to John C. Burck, member of Congress from California, Judah added a few details:

---

[8] United States Pacific Railway Commission, pp. 2960–61, testimony D. W. Strong.

We go out of Summit Valley through what I call Lake Pass, while Fremont's route, or the old Emigrant road, goes over Truckee Pass, which is about 700 feet higher, and a few miles off my route. We strike the foot of Truckee Lake, or the cabins of the Donner party, nine miles from the summit, and from there it is an easy grade down the Truckee River, descending about 40 feet per mile, over a smooth country. The elevation of the pass is 6,690 feet. There are two other passes leading out of Summit Valley, which I had not time to explore, but either of them are practicable, although a little higher. This route is at least 150 miles shorter than the Beckwourth route; crosses the state at the narrowest point, and is on a direct line to the Washoe mines. I will undertake to build a railroad over this route in two years, for $70,000 per mile, from Sacramento City to the state line or Washoe. Thus the question of crossing the Sierra Nevada, I consider solved.

After the tentative organization of his proposed railroad, and the publication of the news of his discoveries in the newspapers, Judah went to San Francisco. He managed to get in touch with some capitalists, but was unable to secure their support. If Congress did not pass a Pacific Railroad bill, they said, no railroad could be built; if a bill was passed, the road still could not be completed for ten or twenty years. They had other interests, and were disinclined to consider a scheme of this sort, however technically feasible. If we may believe the newspapers of the time, no inconsiderable reason for the reluctance of the men approached was the provision of the constitution of California making stockholders liable for their proportion of all the debts and liabilities of any company in which they held stock.[9]

Sacramento Meetings

When he failed to secure support in San Francisco, Judah went to Sacramento. The city of the plains, as it was then

---

9 *Sacramento Union*, January 9 and 10, 1861.

affectionately called by its inhabitants, was less wealthy than San Francisco, but for that very reason might be expected to take an interest in a project which promised her, for some years at least, a position of relative advantage with respect to the trade of the interior. The leading newspaper in that city, the *Sacramento Union,* could be counted on to support any plausible Pacific railroad scheme for political reasons. The citizens had further the advantage of first-hand experience with the workings of the Sacramento Valley Railroad, which had been opened from Sacramento to Folsom in 1856, and was still the only railroad in the state.

It does not, however, appear that these various factors stirred the people of Sacramento to any extraordinary enthusiasm over Judah's scheme, or that they regarded him in any other light than that of an engineer with a risky plan, which it was very desirable to have someone other than themselves finance. Judah, however, called a meeting at a local hotel, and people came. He told them he had made twenty-three barometrical reconnaissances over the Sierras, and had found a line. He needed money to carry the project further, in particular to make a thorough instrumental survey, and he asked them what they would subscribe. Nobody subscribed very much. Huntington says that some gave a barrel of flour, and some a sack of potatoes. Still, the additional subscriptions necessary to the legal organization of Judah's company probably amounted to as much as $56,500 [10] on the 115 miles of line contemplated, and small miscellaneous offerings were not likely to carry the promoter very far.

Collis P. Huntington

It is at this juncture that we first hear the names of Collis P. Huntington, Leland Stanford, Charles Crocker, and Mark Hopkins, all prosperous business men in Sacramento. Hunt-

[10] *Sacramento Union,* January 4, 1861.

Sketch of train on the Sacramento Valley Railroad, 1860

ington and Hopkins ran one of the largest hardware stores in the town. Stanford and Crocker were merchants, and in addition, Stanford had dabbled in California politics to the extent of becoming a candidate for the position of state treasurer in 1857 and for that of governor in 1859, getting badly beaten on both occasions. It is difficult, even at this late date, to estimate the qualities of the four men with confidence. Beyond question, Huntington had the greatest genius for business of the four. Born in Connecticut, and self-supporting from the age of fourteen, he was a trader *par excellence*. In his youth he peddled watch findings from New York to the Missouri River. Later, it is related of him that he started for California with a capital of $1,200, which he increased to $4,000 during an enforced stay of three months on the Isthmus of Panama. He was cool, calculating, unscrupulous, a tireless worker, and a man with few interests outside of work. Enterprise for the public good interested him little. He had few friends, and some of these he lost in later years. Narrow in his sympathies, vindictive, sometimes untruthful, sarcastic, and domineering, he gained his success through the keenness of his mind and the energy and persistence of his character, and also through qualities of courage and imagination which were not absent from his business plans.

Leland Stanford

Stanford was a New York lawyer, who had practiced four years in Wisconsin between 1848 and 1852, and had emigrated to California in the last-named year to seek his fortunes in that state. Stanford came to California poor as the proverbial church mouse. Bassett, who was later his secretary, and who was likely to know the facts, says that two of Stanford's brothers set him up in business in El Dorado County, near Latrobe, with a stock of miners' supplies. Here Stanford remained a while, in partnership with a man named Smith.

Stanford and Smith were said to have done a good business. They thought they were making money until they found that the San Francisco firm with which they dealt was charging them interest on unpaid balances; whereupon they promptly closed up, retiring with their debts paid, but with very little cash.

From El Dorado County Stanford went to Michigan Bluffs, in Placer County, still trading, and in 1855 he moved to Sacramento to take over the business which his brothers had established there. Presumably his operations in Michigan Bluffs had provided him with a little capital. What was quite as much to the point, he had made a number of friends in the mining district, and it is not unreasonable to suppose that his attention had been directed toward politics. In 1857 and 1859, as has been mentioned, he ran for office, but without success. About this time a prospector in the vicinity of Auburn struck a rich pocket of decayed quartz. He knew Stanford, and put his name down for an interest in the claim. From this mine Stanford is reported to have cleaned up about $60,000, a sum which put him in comparatively easy circumstances. In 1861 Stanford ran again for the office of governor, and this time was elected on the Republican ticket. He cannot be said to have yet shown any talent for statesmanship, but he was known as a staunch Union man and a faithful Republican, and he had a local popularity besides, which could be trusted to bring in some votes. After his term of office as governor, Stanford held no political position until 1885, when he was elected United States senator in place of A. A. Sargent. This office he retained until his death. He appears at one time to have had aspirations towards the presidency of the United States, though his candidacy could hardly have been considered seriously. Certainly he served with distinction neither as governor nor as senator.

Stanford's most marked traits were tenacity of purpose, and a certain rude energy in execution. His associates credited him with great solidity of judgment. Like Huntington, he was unscrupulous in the methods which he employed to reach his ends, but, unlike him, he showed ambition if not capacity outside of the business field. In private life, Stanford was distinguished by his love of horses, and by his donations to the university founded in memory of his son. One must hold him inferior to Huntington in business affairs, vain and extravagant. Yet not only his political influence, but the virile power of the man, the attitude of mind which once led an enemy to say of him that "no she lion defending her whelps or a bear her cubs, will make a more savage fight than will Mr. Stanford in defense of his material interests," were invaluable to the transcontinental railroad project in the years of its development.[11]

Crocker and Hopkins

The other two members of the quartette may be dismissed with fewer words. Charles Crocker had no more education than Huntington. He had been peddler, iron maker, gold miner, and trader. In 1855 he was alderman of the city of Sacramento. First and last, his strong point was the handling of men. It was Crocker who drove the work of construction, roaring up and down the line, as he put it, like a mad bull. In deciding the larger problems of policy which arose later, there is no evidence that he had an important part. Indeed, Crocker endeavored to sell his holdings to his associates in 1871, and only continued in the organization because the others proved unable to buy him out.[12]

---

[11] Stanford's election to the United States Senate was resented by Huntington, and led eventually to an open breach between the two men. It is not improbable, however, that Stanford's friends, and not Stanford himself, were responsible for the latter's candidacy. It would not have been difficult to persuade a man of Stanford's temperament that he was performing a public service in allowing his name to be used.

[12] Crocker said of his own personal appearance during the sixties: "While I was building the road, I weighed nearly all the time 264–5 pounds; at one time, in China, I weighed about 274 pounds; the Chinaman who weighed me called me a 4-*picul* man—a '*picul*' being 66 ⅔ pounds. . . . While I was building the road, I weighed the first year, 244, which increased to 265, and when I finished the work, was weighing that. I am 5 feet 10 ¾ inches tall." (Crocker manuscript, p. 63.)

Last of all, we have to mention Mark Hopkins, the "inside man." Hopkins died in 1878, so that his connection with railroad work lasted only fourteen years, and during part of this time he was ill. Less is known of him than of any of his associates. He was the man of detail, the careful scrutinizer of contracts. He was Huntington's partner in the hardware business for twenty-four years, and yet in all that time, according to Huntington, he never bought or sold as much as $10,000 worth of goods.[13] That is to say, he was no trader. Bancroft speaks of him as the balance wheel in the business. We hear of him later as objecting to personal indorsements by the partners of Central Pacific notes. Mr. Crocker once said of him that he was a long-headed man without much executive ability but a wonderfully good man for an executive officer to counsel with. Possibly such a man played a useful part in the Central Pacific organization.

Survey Financed

Huntington, Stanford, Hopkins, and Crocker knew each other as merchants will. Crocker and Stanford may also have met in a political way. The four of them seem to have been friends, at least as early as 1860. Now it appears that Huntington and Crocker, and possibly Stanford and Hopkins also, attended one of Judah's meetings in Sacramento, and were somewhat impressed by his statements. This was the second stage in the Central Pacific enterprise, when the promoter was in the presence of capitalists, and was seeking to convince them that a probability of profit lay in his plans. Huntington says that he spoke to Judah after the public meeting, and that Judah came to his house the following evening.

---

[13] Huntington manuscript, p. 36. The Bancroft Library of the University of California possesses notes of interviews with a number of men prominent in California history collected by H. H. Bancroft or his representatives. In some cases these notes are very full and informing. They will be referred to in the present volume as "Huntington manuscript," "Crocker manuscript," etc. See also Redding, "Sketch of the Life of Mark Hopkins" (San Francisco, 1881).

He adds that subsequently he, Huntington, talked with Hopkins and Stanford, and persuaded them to join him in contributing the money necessary to finance an instrumental survey across the mountains. Other persons who agreed to share in the expense were Charles Marsh, James Peel, L. A. Booth, and Judah himself—each assuming one-seventh of the cost.[14] Charles Crocker was brought in a little later.

The attitude of all these men was of course cautious. Judah had caught their attention, but as yet they would not commit themselves very far. The survey might cost them fifteen or twenty thousand dollars apiece, and they might never go further with the scheme. They thought they could build a railroad if anyone could, and there might be money in it, yet they knew that even to finance surveys involved considerable risk.[15]

Likelihood of Government Aid

Although we have no direct evidence to this effect, it seems very probable that the chance of profit to be secured in building a transcontinental railroad under government auspices stood out more prominently in the eyes of Huntington and his friends than any consideration of the ultimate earnings of the railroad, once it should have been built. What should two dry goods merchants and two dealers in hardware, who knew nothing first hand about railroad operation, have cared about the administration of a railroad 800 miles long? If they wanted interest on an investment, why money commanded 2 per cent a month in Sacramento itself. Only the prospect of still greater gains was likely to attract a speculative trader like Huntington, and the source of such profit could be found only in construction of the road. If this was the real inducement, and if the likelihood of a government subsidy was kept in mind

---

[14] Huntington manuscript, pp. 9–10.
[15] Crocker manuscript, pp. 28–29. See also Hittell, "History of California," Vol. 4.

from the first, it was fortunate for Mr. Judah that, owing to his familiarity with conditions both at Washington and in California, he was in a position to inform his prospective clients of the likelihood of government aid no less fully and authoritatively than he could advise them concerning routes over the Sierras.

Indeed it was only on the question of government assistance that Judah could supply business men of Sacramento with information of a definite sort. He really knew little about the probable cost of a transcontinental line. In his original report of November, 1860, he had declared that the Central Pacific could be built for an appropriation ranging from $30,000 to $72,000 per mile, varying with the difficulty of the ground; but this was an estimate based on a very cursory examination of the line, and could pretend to no exactness. Possibly he was influenced by the fact that the Sacramento Valley Railroad had been contracted for in 1854 at $45,000 per mile, payable 44 per cent in capital stock of the company, 39 per cent in 10 per cent bonds, and 17 per cent in cash. This was equivalent to perhaps $33,000 in cash. The contract price in this case did not include, however, the cost of right-of-way, depot grounds, and engineering expenses, for which additional stock was reserved.[16] Only one year later, when the first instrumental survey of the Central Pacific was completed, Judah was forced to change his estimate to $88,428 per mile for the first 140 miles of that railroad, including 51 miles estimated at $1,000,000 per mile or above. Even these figures were later revised.

Estimating Probable Earnings

Nor was Judah's information about probable earnings a great deal more trustworthy than that relating to probable

---

[16] Report of a committee of the board of directors, Sacramento Valley Railroad Company, August 7, 1855.

costs. There are various ways of estimating the earnings which a new railroad is likely to secure—yet all of them may give curious results when applied to territory which has never enjoyed the benefits of any rail transportation at all, as was substantially the case with California before the Civil War. In general, engineers in California had to reckon with the facts that the population of the state was small; that it had only three cities of importance—San Francisco, Sacramento, and Stockton; that there was but one important business, mining; and that a dense traffic could accordingly be expected only in the distant future after the development of the country served. As a practical expedient most engineers in California who desired elaborate data had some more or less careful count made of the business moving over their projected route by pack train, wagon train, stage, or boat, and then made the broad assumption that this same volume, or this volume increased by an assumed factor, would move over a railroad during its early years. Such was the nature of the estimate made by the incorporators of the Sacramento Valley Railroad in 1853,[17] of the Stockton and Copperopolis in 1862,[18] of the Placerville and Sacramento Valley Railroad in 1863,[19] and of the North Pacific Coast in 1873.[20] Judah had no greater facilities than other engineers of the time, and in his own estimates followed the prevailing custom.[21]

Estimates of this nature were not accurate, and it was unreasonable to suppose that they should be accurate. Judah

---

[17] Articles of association and by-laws of the Sacramento Valley Railroad Company, together with an estimate of the gross receipts of the road when in operation, New York, 1853.

[18] Engineer's report of a preliminary survey of the Stockton and Copperopolis Railroad with estimates of cost and traffic, October, 1862.

[19] Report of the chief engineer on the survey, cost of construction, and estimated revenue of the Placerville and Sacramento Valley Railroad of California, San Francisco, 1863.

[20] Report of President Moore to stockholders, 1873.

[21] Report of the chief engineer on the preliminary survey, cost of construction, and estimated revenue of the Central Pacific Railroad of California, etc., October 22, 1862; report of Acting Chief Engineer Montague, October 8, 1864. Reprinted in "Evidence concerning projected railways across the Sierra Nevada Mountains," *sup. cit.*

in 1862 put the probable gross receipts of the Central Pacific on the first 160 miles out of Sacramento at $4,654,240, or $29,-089 per mile. Mr. Montague, who succeeded him, estimated the annual receipts as far as Dutch Flat at $27,209 per mile and for the whole road, as far as Nevada Territory, he named the figures of $5,456,050, or $34,100 per mile. These were very optimistic figures. As a matter of fact, the earnings of the Central Pacific never much exceeded $14,000 a mile, and during the early period, up to 1870, were as often below $10,000 a mile as they were above it. If it had not been for an operating ratio which in 1866 and 1867 touched the extraordinary figure of 23 per cent, and which did not reach 50 per cent until 1877, the owners of this road could scarcely have kept it out of receivers' hands, so great was the miscalculation.

Organization of Company

We may assume, then, that Huntington and his friends went into the Central Pacific project as a speculation from which they hoped to retire with a profit derived largely from construction paid for out of government funds. Adopting this assumption, the next steps in advancing the enterprise may be briefly described. The meetings in Sacramento which have been mentioned took place in the winter of 1860-61. No progress in surveys could be made at that time, while the Sierra passes were covered with snow. In April, however, a meeting of subscribers to the stock of the Central Pacific Railroad was held in Sacramento, and on the 28th of June, 1861, a company was organized under the general law of the state, to be known as the Central Pacific Railroad of California. The capital of this corporation was set at $8,500,-000, divided into shares of $100 each. The railroad contemplated was to run from Sacramento to the eastern boundary of California, over an estimated distance of 115

miles. Huntington, Hopkins, Stanford, and Crocker subscribed to 150 shares each, as did James Bailey and Theodore
Judah.   Charles Marsh took 50 shares, and other parties
varying, but lesser amounts, to a total of 1,245 shares, or more
than the $1,000 per mile required by the law.   Leland Stan-
ford, Charles Crocker, James Bailey, Theodore D. Judah, L. A.
Booth, C. P. Huntington, Mark Hopkins, D. W. Strong, and
Charles Marsh were the first directors.

Instrumental Survey Made

As soon as the season permitted, Judah was sent back into
the mountains, and in October, 1861, the directors had before
them the substance of his second report, this time based on
an instrumental survey.   Judah now thought that a railroad
from Sacramento to the state line would cost $12,380,000, or
$88,428 per mile.   He did not push his surveys beyond the
point at which he reached the Truckee River, but from his
general knowledge of the country he estimated that the 451
miles between Lassen's Meadows and Salt Lake could be built
for $45,000 per mile, and that the whole road of 733 miles
could be constructed for $41,415,000, or an average of
$56,500 per mile.[22]

In every way this second report was a more careful piece
of work than the one which had preceded it.   The new route
differed from that recommended in November, 1860, mainly
in that it ran from Sacramento through Lincoln and Centralia
instead of through Folsom, and also in the greater detail of
its location.   The principal characteristics of the line were
two: (1) that it followed a nearly continuous ridge from
Lincoln to the summit of the mountains, and (2) that east of
the summit the road wound down the side of the mountain
to Lake Truckee, following the Truckee River from the lake

---

[22] Report of the chief engineer on the preliminary survey, cost of construction, etc.,
October 22, 1862 (October 1, 1861), *sup. cit.*

in the direction of Humbolt Sink, and entirely avoiding the second summit of the Sierras and the crossing of the Washoe Mountains.

This is substantially the line of the Central Pacific today. The maximum grade which Judah allowed himself was 105 feet to the mile. Judah did not at this time re-examine alternative routes via Georgetown and via Henness Pass, which he had considered and rejected the previous fall. Nor did he refer to the line via Beckwourth's Pass, the present route of the Western Pacific, which he later admitted to be easier in grade, if longer in distance, or to the possibility of a route directly east from Folsom via Placerville around the south end of Lake Tahoe. It is probable, however, that these two last-named routes were familiar to him in a general way, as considerable quantities of freight consigned to the Nevada mines were already moving over them.

Emphasis should be laid upon Judah's survey of October, 1861, because the continuance of the Sacramento capitalists in the enterprise depended upon its favorable outcome. After it was completed Huntington and his friends became, on the whole and except during certain intervals of weakness, inclined to see the project through even at the risk of their personal fortunes, provided reasonable government assistance could be secured. It was with this understanding that Judah went back to Washington in 1861 to procure the passage of needed legislation, and it was in this spirit that a formal beginning of construction upon the Central Pacific was made at Sacramento on January 8, 1863.

CHAPTER II

RESOURCES FOR CONSTRUCTION—
STATE AND LOCAL AID

Source of Funds

Some years after the Central Pacific and Western Pacific railroads were completed, Leland Stanford laid before a committee chosen by Congress the following memorandum showing the receipts of these two roads from all sources up to December 31, 1869:

MEMORANDUM SHOWING THE RECEIPTS OF THE CENTRAL
AND WESTERN PACIFIC RAILROADS FROM ALL
SOURCES TO DECEMBER 31, 1869

Source of Funds	Par Value	Approximate Sum Realized
United States bonds issued to Central and Western Pacific	$27,855,680	$20,735,000
Central and Western Pacific first mortgage bonds	27,855,560	20,750,000
Central Pacific convertible bonds	1,483,000	830,000
Central Pacific state aid bonds	1,500,000	980,000
City and County bonds:		
San Francisco to Central Pacific	400,000	300,000
Sacramento to Central Pacific	300,000	190,000
Placer County to Central Pacific	250,000	160,000
San Francisco to Western Pacific	250,000	175,000
San Joaquin County to Western Pacific	250,000	125,000
Santa Clara County to Western Pacific	150,000	100,000
Land sales, balance Central Pacific		107,000
Profit and loss balance, January 1, 1870		1,610,000
Total		$46,062,000
Company owed Contract and Finance Company		1,827,000
Grand total		$47,889,000

We have in the foregoing table a summation of the resources on which Judah and the Huntington group were able to draw in order to build a transcontinental road. It will be noticed that there is no mention in the table of the personal fortunes of the associates, unless the contribution of these gentlemen appears in the profit and loss balance, or in the debt to the Contract and Finance Company—none of the earnings of the railroad during construction, and none of the proceeds of the sale of Central Pacific capital stock. Under these categories some slight addition to Stanford's list must probably be made, though the importance of the addition will not be great.

Collectively the fortunes of the associates, while considerable, were not sufficient to cover more than the preliminary expenses of the work. Judah had but little capital, while, according to Huntington's own statement some years later, the combined assets of Stanford, Crocker, and the firm of Huntington and Hopkins, amounted to something like $1,000,000 when the construction of the Central Pacific was begun.[1] Other estimates put the figure at $160,000,[2] or even as low as $109,000.[3] We do not know, as a matter of fact, how much property the associates possessed, but we do know that it was slight compared with the undertaking which they had in hand.

Earnings and Stock Issues

Probably, indeed, the earnings of the Central Pacific Railroad during construction were more important than the contributions of the partners. Between 1863 and 1869, according to the calculations of the United States Pacific Railway Commission, the gross earnings of the Central Pacific amounted to

[1] United States Pacific Railway Commission, p. 3774, testimony C. P. Huntington.

[2] Complaint of Samuel Brannan, June 21, 1870.   Filed in the case of Brannan v. Central Pacific Railroad, in the District Court of the Fifteenth Judicial District of the State of California.

[3] Bancroft, "History of California," Vol. 7, p. 545, note.   The assessed value of the associates' property in Sacramento County in 1861 was $118,035.

$10,807,508.76, its operating expenses to $4,700,625.56, and its net earnings to $6,106,884.20. The surplus after the deduction of interest and taxes for this period amounted to $2,427,533.80.[4] Most of these earnings came from local business, although an attempt was made to provide facilities for through travel before 1869, by arranging stage accommodation for stretches not yet covered by rails.

If we add three or four million dollars to the receipts listed in Stanford's table, we shall have made liberal allowance for railroad earnings and partnership contributions up to 1869. This allowance would not be materially increased if account were taken of sales of Central Pacific stock. The authorized stock issue of the Central Pacific Railroad in 1862 was $8,500,000. In 1864 this was raised to $20,000,000, and in 1868 it was made $100,000,000. In spite of these large issues, the evidence is perfectly clear that there were substantially no cash subscriptions to Central Pacific stock, nor any market for this stock when issued. It is on record, for example, that one M. D. Boruck opened an office at the corner of Bush and Montgomery streets in San Francisco on behalf of the company, and kept it open, off and on, for about twenty-two days in November and December, 1862, and in February, 1863. He secured three subscriptions to an aggregate of twelve or fifteen shares.[5]

We know also that Crocker went personally to Virginia City to sell stock, but without success. He says of this experience:

> They wanted to know what I expected the road would earn. I said I did not know, though it would earn good interest on the money invested, especially to those who went in at bed rock. "Well," they said, "do you think it will make 2 per cent a month?" "No," said I, "I do not." "Well," they

---

4 United States Pacific Railway Commission Report, p. 87.
5 United States Pacific Railway Commission, p. 3421, testimony M. D. Boruck.

answered, "we can get 2 per cent a month for our money here," and they would not think of going into a speculation that would not promise that at once.[6]

Stanford says that he bought 2,300 shares of Central Pacific at ten cents on the dollar at one time, in order to accommodate a stockholder,[7] and it appears that Charles and A. B. Crocker transferred their stock to Huntington, Hopkins, and Stanford in 1873, for $13 a share.[8] No attempt to sell Central Pacific stock generally was made until 1873, and it was not listed on the Stock Exchange until 1874.[9]

Bond Sales

As a matter of fact, there was no sale at the beginning even for Central Pacific mortgage bonds. Huntington went to New York to get these securities started among the moneyed men there, and after a while he had some small success. But D. O. Mills gave it as his deliberate judgment on a later occasion that there was the greatest difficulty in securing loans on the bonds the Central Pacific had to offer—including government, county, convertible, state aid, and first mortgage bonds— to as much as 75 per cent of the face value of the issues.[10] Iron for the first 50 miles out of Sacramento was delivered to the associates only after they had given their own personal obligations secured by deposit of the company's bonds. An agreement was entered into, besides, that Huntington and his friends would be responsible, as individuals, for ten years, for the payment of interest on these bonds.[11]

[6] Crocker manuscript, p. 32.

[7] United States Pacific Railway Commission, pp. 2630–31, testimony Leland Stanford.

[8] *Ibid.*, p. 2652, testimony Leland Stanford. Stanford and his associates bought stock in 1871 for which they paid $400 or $500 a share, but Stanford says that this was to quiet litigation which he described as blackmail.

[9] Ellen M. Colton v. Leland Stanford *et al.*, in the Superior Court of the State of California in and for the County of Sonoma, 1883. Hereafter referred to as "Colton case." The record in this proceeding contains much valuable information relative to the history of the Southern Pacific and the activities of the Huntington–Stanford group.

[10] United States Pacific Railway Commission, p. 3493, testimony D. O. Mills.

[11] Crocker manuscript, pp. 29–30.

After 1864 conditions improved somewhat, and first mortgage bonds were disposed of at about 75, while convertible and state aid bonds brought 56 and 65 respectively.[12] Yet at the time when the construction of the Central Pacific Railroad was finished the private property of every one of the directors of the company was mortgaged up to the limit of all his individual credit would possibly allow and bear. The notes of the four associates were outstanding everywhere, many of them bearing interest rates as high as from 10 to 12 per cent, and the statement is made that Leland Stanford alone upon one occasion had his account at the bank overdrawn to the extent of $1,300,000.[13]

The consideration of possible Central Pacific Railroad receipts, other than those derived from government aid and perhaps from the sale of the company's first mortgage bonds, brings us back to Stanford's list as containing substantially all the assets upon which the promoters of the Central Pacific were able to rely. Almost half of these assets were derived directly from political bodies of one type or another, and the value of the remainder of those assets was dependent for the most part upon the security which was afforded by the government donations made to the company.

State and Local Grants

Let us now consider with more care the circumstances under which the local and federal authorities extended such generous aid to the transcontinental project, and the extent and quality of the aid given. We may begin with the state and local grants, and in order to assist the reader, a portion of the table which was printed on page 21 will be set forth again at this point in slightly changed form. As thus presented the table is as follows:

---

[12] United States Pacific Railway Commission, p. 2731, testimony Leland Stanford.
[13] *Ibid.*, p. 2399, testimony A. Cohen; p. 2767, testimony Leland Stanford.

Aid Derived by Central and Western Pacific Railroads from State and Local Governments in California

Source of Aid	Par Value	Approximate Sum Realized
Aid by Cities:		
San Francisco, donation to Central Pacific	$400,000	$300,000
Sacramento, subscription to Central Pacific	300,000	190,000
San Francisco, donation to Western Pacific	250,000	175,000
Aid by Counties:		
Placer County, subscription to Central Pacific	250,000	160,000
San Joaquin County, subscription to Western Pacific	250,000	125,000
Santa Clara County, subscription to Western Pacific	150,000	100,000
Aid by State:		
Assumption of interest for twenty years on $1,500,000 7 per cent bonds.		

Arguments for Local Aid

Aid from local political bodies was considered legitimate in the early sixties, and was extended freely to a great number of corporations. Voters were told that the construction of railroads increased land values. Until transportation should be improved, it was argued, agriculture could make but little progress, because the products of agriculture could not be brought to market. The mining interest was depressed in 1870, and in partial explanation publicists pointed out that freight charges to the mines ranged from $50 to $180 a ton. Nor was even more precise calculation lacking. An advocate of subsidies in 1870 stated:

> It costs for passage to San Francisco from Visalia $25 and consumes generally a day and a half. By rail the trip could be made in eight hours, at a cost of $10, thus saving $15 and nearly

a day in time. If on the average, each adult makes one visit per annum to the upper country, and taking 1,300, the number of registered voters, as the adult population, it costs every passenger for the round trip $50 in cash and three days in time—excess over railway fare, $30; board for two extra days, $4; value of time at $2 per day, $4; total excess, $38; total loss to 1,300 passengers, $49,400. I contend, therefore, that the people of Tulare County are now actually paying, in addition to the loss or inconvenience resulting from isolation from market, the sum of $77,780 per annum, for the privilege of being without a railroad.

There was little that was novel in this sort of argument, or in the further contention that the increase of the tax roll of the counties, due to railroad construction, would yield a revenue more than sufficient to cover the taxes incident to the granting of a subsidy. Better transportation meant wider markets, denser population, higher values. Increasing values and volume of sales meant larger profits, higher wages, lower prices, and generally growing prosperity. These things were matters of reasonable anticipation, so that hard-headed business men had quite as much ground as usually underlies business action to approve of even a considerable pledge of state and county property in order to hasten the building of a railroad system. It could not be known whether or not railways would be constructed without subsidies. As we look at the situation today it seems probable that this would have been done, and that railroad building would not even have been greatly delayed. The risk in waiting was, however, great, and the difficulties of a conservative policy were enhanced by the competition of towns, each seeking priority of railroad connection.

Playing Towns Against Each Other

There is evidence that the promoters of the Central Pacific were perfectly aware of the possibilities of securing local subsidies by playing one California town against another.

Huntington wrote David D. Colton in 1871 that the company ought to get a large amount of land and other good things from parties having interests along the line between Spadra and San Gregorio Pass, if it would build them a railroad on which to get out.[14]   T. G. Phelps, president of the Southern Pacific, speaking in the same vein, told Colonel Baker, of Tulare, that it was his private opinion that if that county would donate $100,000 to the company, it would run its road through the town of Visalia.   We also know that pressure was brought to bear upon the city of Stockton, to induce that city to grant a right-of-way, as well as other privileges, to the Western Pacific,[15] and it is notorious that the fears of San Francisco were played upon in order to obtain terminal facilities on San Francisco Bay.

How this policy appeared from the point of view of the opponents of the Central Pacific, may be gathered from a description offered by a member of the Constitutional Convention of 1878:

> They start out their railway track and survey their line near a thriving village. They go to the most prominent citizens of that village and say, "If you will give us so many thousand dollars we will run through here; if you do not we will run by," and in every instance where the subsidy was not granted, that course was taken, and the effect was just as they said, to kill off the little town. Here was the town of Paradise, in Stanislaus County; because they did not get what they wanted, they established another town 4 miles from there. In every instance where they were refused a subsidy, in money, unless their terms were acceded to, they have established a depot near to the place, and always have frozen them out. As stated by the gentleman from Los Angeles, General Howard, they have blackmailed Los Angeles County $230,000 as a condition of doing that which the law compelled them to do.

---

[14] Colton case, pp. 948-49, Huntington to Colton, October 8, 1874.
[15] Tinkham, "History of Stockton," p. 356; San Francisco Chronicle, June 13, 1874.

County Stock Subscriptions

Perhaps the earliest California statute in aid of railway construction was the act approved May 1, 1852, granting to the United States a right-of-way through the state for the purpose of constructing a railway from the Atlantic to the Pacific oceans.[16] In 1857 the supervisors of Yuba County were authorized to submit to the electors of that county a proposal to subscribe $200,000 to a railroad between Marysville and Benicia.[17] And during the following two years the San Francisco and Marysville Railroad not only received a land grant,[18] but secured an enactment, making it the duty of the Board of Supervisors of Sutter County to submit to popular vote the question of a $50,000 subscription to its capital stock,[19] and the duty of the supervisors of Solano and Yolo counties to call elections in those counties with similar intent.[20] No subscriptions were made under these acts.

It seems to have been the intention of the legislature to treat the Central Pacific and the Western Pacific railroads after the same general fashion as other railroads had been treated—that is to say, to allow counties and cities interested to subscribe freely to their stock. By virtue of an act dated April 16, 1859, any county could so subscribe up to 5 per cent of its assessment roll when popular approval had been secured.[21] This was not, however, enough. Between March 21, 1863, and April 4, 1864, the legislature passed eight acts granting special concessions to the Central Pacific and to the Western Pacific. Mr. Stanford had become governor of the state in January, 1862, and this legislation had of course his cordial approval.

In March, 1863, the supervisors of San Joaquin County were authorized to hold a popular election on the question of

---

16 Laws of California, 1852, Ch. 77.　17 Ibid., 1857, Ch. 243.
18 Ibid., 1858, Ch. 300.　19 Ibid., 1859, Ch. 241.　20 Ibid., 1859, Ch. 263, 264.
21 Ibid., 1859, Ch. 262.

subscribing $250,000 to the capital stock of the Western Pacific.[22]   In April, Placer County was authorized to consider a subscription of equal amount to the stock of the Central Pacific.[23]   Next, Santa Clara County was authorized to hold an election and to subscribe $150,000 to the Western Pacific, if it so desired.[24]   Sacramento received the same privilege in April, to the extent of being permitted to take 3,000 shares of the Central Pacific,[25] and was in addition allowed to give away rights-of-way and certain rights of construction of considerable though indefinite value;[26] while San Francisco was permitted to subscribe $400,000 to the stock of the Western Pacific and $600,000 to that of the Central Pacific, making $1,000,000 in all.[27]

Invariably subscriptions contemplated in the acts were to be made in bonds running twenty or thirty years, and bearing 7 or 8 per cent interest.   Counties were to enjoy the usual privileges of stockholders, but were protected by special clauses against the proportional liability for debts of the corporation resting upon the ordinary stockholder by virtue of state law. The proceeds of county bonds issued in subscriptions were to be used for construction of the road, and it was provided that at least an equal amount of other funds obtained from stockholders was to be so used.   It was thus the intention of the legislature that funds for construction should not be entirely derived from county subsidies.

Direct State Aid

In addition to the acts permitting county subscriptions, mention should be made of two important acts by which the state granted direct assistance.   The first of these laws was dated April 25, 1863.   It authorized the comptroller of the

---

[22] Laws of California, 1863, Ch. 77   [23] Ibid., 1863, Ch. 125.
[24] Ibid., 1863, Ch. 207.   [25] Ibid., 1863, Ch. 310.
[26] Ibid., 1863, Ch. 209.   The value of these privileges has been estimated at $200,000.
[27] Ibid., 1863, Ch. 291.

state to draw warrants in favor of the Central Pacific to the extent of $10,000 per mile, the warrants to be issued when the first 20 miles, the second 20 miles, and the last 10 out of 50 miles were finished. These warrants were to bear 7 per cent interest if not cashed, because of lack of money in the treasury to pay them.[28]

The second act, dated April 4, 1864, repealed the act just quoted, and proposed that the state government, instead of drawing warrants, should assume interest on 1,500 of the company bonds, bearing 7 per cent, and running for twenty years. This grant, like the earlier one, was made on certain conditions, such as that the company should transport free of charge public convicts going to the state prison, material for the construction of the state capitol, troops, munitions of war, and the like, that it should construct at least 20 miles of line annually, and in the case of the Act of 1864, that it should deed over certain granite quarries in Placer County.[29]

On the face of it this grant was illegal, because of clauses in the state constitution which forbade the legislature to create liabilities in excess of $300,000 without submitting the proposal to popular vote, or to loan or give the credit of the state in any manner, in aid of any individual, association, or corporation.[30] But it was sustained on the theory that the act amounted to an appropriation in anticipation of revenue, and so did not create a debt at all. Thus the company was able to draw its first interest money in January, 1865.[31]

Opposition to Aid in San Francisco

The various acts just referred to were of course permissive, yet in general the counties seemed very willing to give up to the limit of their legal power. The two exceptions were the

---

[28] *Ibid.*, 1863, Ch. 314.
[29] *Ibid.*, 1864, Ch. 320. Twenty years later the quarries were still undelivered.
[30] Constitution of the State of California, Arts. VIII, XI, Sec. 10.
[31] People v. Pacheco, 27 Cal., 176 (1865).

county of Placer and the city and county of San Francisco. In Placer County there was a very active campaign against the bonds, supported by newspapers such as the *Placer Herald* and the *Advocate*. The proposal for a bond issue was carried, but only by a majority of 409 in a total vote of 3,810.[32]

In the case of San Francisco, the city delegation in the legislature divided five to five on the proposal to authorize the city to subscribe. When the law was finally passed, a long and interesting struggle ensued. The first step after the passage of the act was to hold an election in San Francisco in order to ascertain whether the people would approve of a subscription to railroad bonds. This election took place in May, 1863, and the necessary popular consent was secured. There is reason to believe, however, that illegitimate means were employed to carry the election. We have affidavits that Philip Stanford went to the polls at San Francisco in a buggy, carrying a bag of money; that the said Stanford put his hand frequently in the bag of money and took money, some $20 pieces and some $5 pieces, to a considerable amount therefrom, and scattered the said money among the voters at the said polls, at the same time calling on them to vote in favor of the said subscription. Another eyewitness confirmed this account, adding that while the sum of money spent by the said Stanford was considerable, he could not tell how much as the crowd around the buggy of the said Stanford was so great. Still another testified to having received a written order on Stanford and others for $20, in return for which he and a man named Ross were to endeavor to influence voters at the polls to vote for the subscription.[33]

These affidavits were later supported by the assertion of Hon. William A. Piper, on the floor of the House of Repre-

---

[32] Angel, "History of Placer County," 1882, p. 280.

[33] "The Great Dutch Flat Swindle!—An address to the Board of Supervisors, Officers and People of San Francisco," 1864.

Henry P. Coon

sentatives at Washington, to the effect that he, Piper, was an eyewitness at the election, and saw the brother of Leland Stanford openly going about the polling places, scattering gold and silver to influence and buy votes for the municipal subsidy. Statements of this sort are too detailed and circumstantial to be brushed lightly aside.

Resort to Court

Whether or not the election of 1863 was tainted with corruption, as soon as it was concluded, San Francisco became bound, on or about the 25th of May, 1863, to subscribe $600,-000 and $400,000 to the stock of the Central Pacific and Western Pacific railroads, respectively. The fight against subscriptions, however, did not stop at this point. In an attempt to prevent action, suit was brought by a man named W. N. French against the Board of Supervisors, in the case known as "French v. Teschemaker." French was a resident of San Francisco and a taxpayer. Teschemaker was a member of the Board of Supervisors. The suit alleged certain irregularities in the city election, but rested mainly on the contention that the act authorizing the city and county to subscribe was void and of no effect, because it provided that the city and county should not be liable for any of the debts or liabilities of either the Central Pacific or the Western Pacific railroads beyond the amount subscribed, and that this provision as to liability should be a part of all contracts made by the companies for the construction and equipment of their roads. According to counsel, this was an attempt to create an exemption from the proportionate liability imposed on all stockholders by the state constitution, and was not only void in itself, but its lack of force invalidated the whole subscription, since it was not to be supposed that the legislature would have passed the other clauses of the act without the section in question.

On the 23d of May, 1863, Judge Sawyer of the Twelfth Judicial District granted a temporary injunction. On appeal to the Supreme Court, however, this injunction was overruled. The court said:

> True, the legislature cannot exempt the city and county from liability, but it can authorize the corporation to refuse to contract with persons who do not waive the proportionate liability established for their protection. How the individual liability of a stockholder of a corporation can be a matter of public concern any more than the liability of a copartner, we are unable to perceive, and we are not aware that it has ever been claimed that the latter liability had its foundation in public policy. It is merely a liability created by law, as it might be by contract, and is intended only for the benefit of those who may deal with corporations. It is but another fund to which the creditor may look when the social fund has been exhausted, and whether he chooses to look to it or not is a matter of no concern to the public. . . . There being, then, only a question of private right involved, there can be no question but that the party interested in the enforcement of the right may contract to waive it.[34]

Compromise Plan

The opponents of municipal subscription now turned to the legislature, and secured the passage of an act authorizing the Board of Supervisors of San Francisco to compromise and to settle all claims upon the part of the Western Pacific Railroad and the Central Pacific Railroad for cash or other security, in place of bonds claimed by the companies, provided the power to make such compromise should rest in the Board of Supervisors only after and in case said board should be compelled by final judgment of the Supreme Court to execute and deliver the bonds specified in the act.[35]

Pursuant to this act of April 14, 1864, the Board of

---

[34] French v. Teschemaker, 24 Cal. 518 (1864).
[35] Laws of California, 1864, Ch. 344.

Supervisors appointed a special committee from among their number to consider and report a plan for a compromise. This action was taken on May 23, and the mandamus requiring the supervisors to subscribe $600,000 to the stock of the Central Pacific, which was essential to the adoption of any compromise, was issued on June 7.[36] The committee met with Stanford, reported back to the board, and on June 20 the board passed order No. 582 providing that the city of San Francisco order, execute, and deliver to the Central Pacific 400 bonds for $1,000 each, in full discharge of all obligations on the part of the city and county to make any subscription to the capital stock of said company.

Order No. 582 was duly approved by the mayor on June 21, and became law on that day. On June 29 the acceptance of the Central Pacific was signified to the board, in due form, and on June 27 the supervisors appointed Messrs. Torrey, Bell, and Titcomb a committee to deliver to the Central Pacific the 400 bonds, with interest coupons attached. Nevertheless the mayor, Henry P. Coon, the auditor, Henry M. Hale, and the treasurer of the city, Joseph S. Paxon, constituting the Pacific Railroad Loan Fund Commissioners, refused to issue the bonds. The result was a petition for a mandamus directed against these persons individually, which developed into the case of People v. Coon.

Agreements in Mandamus Proceedings

The main legal points raised in this new litigation were three:

1. The conditions precedent to the issuance of the bonds under the act of 1864 had not been fulfilled, said the petitioner, in that the board of supervisors had not been compelled by final judgment of the Supreme Court to execute and deliver the bonds.

---

36 California Supreme Court Records, Vol. 38, case of People v. Coon.

2. The second contention was that the railroad company could not call upon the supervisors to issue bonds on the city's subscription unless the railroad should call in from other subscribers the whole amount of their respective subscriptions, or until, under the Act of 1863, a sum at least equal to the amount of the bonds should have been expended on the road from other sources. That either of these things had been done, the defendants vigorously denied.

3. It was also declared by defendants that the Act of 1864 had been misconstrued—that it did not relieve San Francisco from her subscription, but simply authorized the city to liquidate that subscription "in cash or other security" instead of in bonds. "We claim," said counsel, "that the act authorized no more than the reduction of the amount of subscription and a change of the mode of payment to cash or other security in place of bonds. It does not authorize a donation of $400,000 or any other amount. In other words, it authorizes a subscription for any amount less than $600,000, payable in cash in place of bonds." [37]

One has the feeling that at this stage of the proceedings, the first and third of these propositions were not well taken. It was too plainly the intention of the legislature to allow the city of San Francisco to withdraw from its subscription for a consideration, to permit weight to be given to technical points like these. On the other hand, it is very doubtful if the railroad had at this time either called in from other subscribers the whole amount of their respective subscriptions, or had expended on the road from other sources a sum equal to the amount of the bonds. The Supreme Court, however, did not make even this concession, but promptly issued a mandamus against Coon, Hale, and Paxon, commanding and requiring them to execute and deliver without delay, to the Central Pacific Railroad of California, the 400 bonds of the city and

---

[37] California Supreme Court Records, Vol. 38. p. 98. *sup. cit.*

county of San Francisco, described in the ordinance before referred to.[38]

Further Litigation

Upon the issue of this mandamus, Coon, Hale, and Paxon signed the 400 bonds. According to a subsequent complaint by the railroad, the bonds so signed were presented by the president of the Board of Supervisors to William Loewy, clerk of the city and county of San Francisco, at a meeting at which a quorum of the supervisors was present. Loewy refused or failed to countersign. On September 27, 1864, a regular meeting of the supervisors was held, at which resolutions were offered requesting Loewy to countersign the bonds, and providing for the affixing of the seal of the city and county to the bonds when countersigned. These resolutions failed of passage, and instead a resolution was adopted requesting the clerk to deposit the 400 bonds with the county treasurer, which he did forthwith. The treasurer then refused to deliver the bonds to the railroad, and fresh proceedings were instituted before the Supreme Court, this time asking for a writ of peremptory mandamus commanding Loewy or his successor to obtain possession of the bonds, and to countersign and assist in delivering them to the Central Pacific; commanding the Board of Supervisors or their successors to call a meeting of the board, to notify the clerk of a time and place at which he might complete the countersigning in the presence of a quorum of the board; to cause the seal of the city and county to be affixed to the bonds; and to appoint a committee to deliver the bonds to the Central Pacific; and commanding the members of the Board of Supervisors who might be appointed such a committee, to deliver the bonds to the Central Pacific. It was obviously hoped to tie things down so that no further delay would be possible.

---

[38] People v. Coon, 25 Cal. 635 (1864).

There seems to have been a split in the Board of Supervisors at this time. Six of the twelve members made individual returns to the complaint, and alleged that they had no part in the refusal to deliver the bonds. The other six and the mayor voted to employ counsel and to defend the suit.

Contentions of Defendants

The case came to a hearing January 7, 1865. In some respects the defense now rested on new ground; in some new emphasis was given matters previously brought forward.

The supervisors in January alleged that the election in San Francisco held May 19, 1863, at which the electors of San Francisco had approved the subscription to the stock of the Central Pacific, had been carried by corruption and bribery. This assertion was given great prominence in the answer of the supervisors, though less in briefs of counsel. Nine instances were cited where A. P. Stanford had given sums ranging from $5 to $40 apiece to electors, or had thrown handfuls of money among the electors "and thereupon they scrambled among themselves for the same." It was urged that these bribes had had great influence upon the vote and that the election was void. These facts had not been known to the supervisors on June 20, 1864, when order No. 582 had been passed, and defendants believed that knowledge of them would have prevented the passage of the ordinance.

Besides this, the supervisors declared that the passage of ordinance No. 582 had been procured by false and fraudulent representations by the railroad company. More important, it was now contended that the Act of 1863 was unconstitutional, in that the legislature was without power to "impose on a municipal corporation of the state the burden of exclusively building or aiding to build a work of general interest to the state, which is in no sense a work of local interest to the corporation on which the burden is imposed."

It was pointed out that the Central Pacific was a work of general interest to the Pacific Coast. It did not come within 100 miles of San Francisco. It had received large subsidies from the federal government on the ground that it was of national importance. Counsel declared that:

> The true test of whether a tax can be exclusively laid on a municipal corporation, is to be found in the purpose for which municipal government is confined within local limits. Citizens living within those limits are exposed to exclusive taxation because, and only because, a peculiar benefit is conferred upon this locality. When the benefit is shared in by the rest of the state, then a state tax is levied, because the citizens of San Francisco received advantage, not in their character as citizens of San Francisco, but as citizens of the state. The state government is as much a benefit to San Francisco as its own municipal government. Yet no one would contend that she could be compelled to support the entire expenses of the former, or that any other city should be compelled to contribute towards the expenses of the latter.

City Compelled to Subscribe

These and other more technical objections were considered by the Supreme Court and were swept aside in a decision rendered at the April term of 1865. The court now held that the legislature had imposed no burden on San Francisco by the Act of 1863, because under that act the city got a consideration, namely, the company stock, for its subscription. The court added:

> Nor does it make any difference as to the validity of the compromise whether the bonds were payable in instalments or in gross, nor whether a legal assessment has been laid on the capital stock of the company, for irrespective of the time the bonds under the Act of 1863 might become due, the company held a claim against the city which was a proper subject of and formed a good consideration for a compromise.[39]

---

[39] People v. Supervisors, 27 Cal. 655 (1865).

This ended the case. It may perhaps be pertinently inquired why it was, if the subscription required by the Act of 1863 imposed no burden on the city of San Francisco as the Supreme Court said, that the city could afford to give $400,000 to get rid of the obligation. Yet, perhaps it would be fruitless to follow too closely the windings of the judicial mind. Stanford later declared that the litigation had injured the Central Pacific very much,[40] while E. H. Miller, secretary of the company, estimated that the suit cost the Central Pacific not much less than $100,000. Of the bonds issued, 315 were sold at $751.60 each, amounting to $236,754, while 85 were paid out at par for rolling stock.[41]

Subscribing Counties Embarrassed

The reluctance of San Francisco to subscribe was not typical of the general attitude toward the Central Pacific in 1865. But it became more typical as the years went on. For this, there were several reasons.

In the first place, the state was much disappointed by the fact that the completion of the Central Pacific did not inaugurate a period of prosperity. The year 1870 was not a particularly good one in California, and the panic of 1873, with the intense depression which resulted, was soon to occur. Among the first effects of the two rail connections with the East, was an influx of eastern manufactures, unemployment, lower prices, and dissatisfaction. This in no way meant that the construction of the Central Pacific had not benefited California, but it gave evidence of a serious though temporary maladjustment.

Moreover, the bonds which had been so lightly voted, proved a real burden on the scanty population of the counties, which was in no adequate way offset by increases in the assess-

---

[40] United States Pacific Railway Commission, pp. 3610–11, testimony Leland Stanford.
[41] Ibid., p. 3464, testimony E. H. Miller.

ment rolls. Indeed, the railroads in early years were assessed at figures that were remarkably low. In Placer County, for instance, the Central Pacific insisted that its road should be assessed at $6,000 per mile, and succeeded in carrying its point in 1865, 1866, and 1867. In 1868 the assessment was raised to $12,000 per mile. The railroad protested, and when forced to submit, increased the rate of freight to all points in Placer County about 40 cents a ton.[42] Nor were taxes even on such modest valuations easily collected. Between 1866 and 1887 railroad tax cases were almost constantly before the courts. At times the Central Pacific refused to pay any taxes at all, on the ground that it held a "federal franchise," and at other times it objected to the terms of the law or to the amount of the assessment.[43] The result was to throw the local tax system into complete confusion.

Experience of Placer County

Let us refer again to the experience of Placer County. In 1863 the Central Pacific asked for a subscription of $250,000, promising to add $9,000,000 to the taxable property of the county. The county tax rate as fixed in February, 1863, for the following year, was 35 cents on $100, and the assessed valuation of the county was $3,071,911.78, yielding a revenue from county taxes of $10,751.69. The railroad company issued an address while the matter of a subscription was under consideration, pointing out that 8 per cent on a bond issue of $250,000 would amount to $20,000, while a tax rate of 35 cents on $9,000,000 of increased valuation would yield $31,500, or a clear excess of $11,500, to the county without considering the effect of the railroad in increasing the valuation of real estate.

These were the results which voters were led to expect.

[42] Angel, "History of Placer County," pp. 158–65.
[43] Fankhauser, "Financial History of California," p. 299 ff.

What happened was that the assessed valuation of the property of the Central Pacific in Placer County was $6,000 per mile as late as 1870, when the county sold its railroad stock; that the total railroad valuation was therefore $553,500, and that the county tax rate rose from 35 cents to $1.73½. Moreover, the railroad taxes for 1868 and 1869 were still unsettled and in dispute in 1870 and remained so until 1873. The total receipts of the county from all sources in 1869 were $127,492.54, of which $46,499.66 were for the state. Against the $80,992.88 remaining, the $20,000 of interest on the subsidy bonds was evidently a material charge.

It was probably not true in general that the financial embarrassment in which many of the counties of California were plunged late in the sixties was due to the pressure of interest charges on bonds issued in aid of railroad construction. The highest rates of taxation for county purposes uncovered by the special legislative committee of 1868 which investigated this matter, were $36.70 per $1,000 for Tuolumne County, and $40 per $1,000 for Calaveras County, neither of which counties had issued bonds in aid of railroads. Extravagance in assistance tendered to railroads was only one of the financial sins of which the counties had been guilty. Nevertheless the burden of outstanding indebtedness for railroads was often severe on communities of declining industry and population, and contributed to the later severe revulsion in popular sentiment with regard to the desirability of local aid to railroad enterprise.

Opposition by Other Transportation Interests

It is proper to mention at this point, also, as throwing light upon popular sentiment, the opposition of the smaller transportation interests of the state to the development of the Central Pacific project. These interests included the stage companies, the express companies, the toll roads, and the Pacific Mail

Steamship Company. In the aggregate their influence was considerable, and it was constantly thrown against the granting of aid to the Central Pacific.

It is a curious commentary upon the effect of government subsidies, that the Huntington-Stanford group brought part of this opposition upon themselves by a deliberate refusal to buy up the Sacramento Valley Railroad for the reason that it was cheaper to build at the expense of the federal government from Sacramento to Auburn than to buy a railroad already in active operation for most of the distance between these points. In cold figures, it would have cost $400,000 to build a new line out of Sacramento, and $285,000, according to Central Pacific engineers, to put the Sacramento Valley Railroad in thoroughly good physical condition. But under federal legislation, to be described in a later chapter, only $250,000 out of the $400,000 would have to be paid by the Central Pacific in cash, leaving a clear gain of $35,000 if the policy of construction were pursued.[44]

The result of this decision was to cause the backers of the Sacramento Valley project to denounce the Central Pacific enterprise as a fraud.[45]

End of Local Subsidies

In the year 1868, a resolution was introduced into the California State Senate urging the appointment of a committee to investigate the use of moneys contributed by the state toward the construction of the Central Pacific Railroad. This resolution was indefinitely postponed by a vote of 18 to 17. The same year notices began to appear in the press, urging the legislature to oppose further railroad-aid legislation. In 1869,

[44] Report of the chief engineer upon recent surveys, progress of construction, and an approximate estimate of cost of first division of 50 miles of the Central Pacific Railroad of California, July 1, 1863.

[45] Letter of L. L. Robinson, chief engineer, to Chas. A. Sumner and Henry Epstein, Chairmen Committees on Railroads, Legislature of Nevada, Sacramento, February 3, 1865. Printed in a pamphlet entitled "Evidence concerning projected railways across the Sierra Nevada Mountains," *sup. cit.*

the *Sacramento Union,* while in favor of a grant to the Stockton and Tulare Railroad, urged the counties to go slow and to secure an amendment to the general railway law, reducing maximum transportation charges to 10 cents per passenger per mile, and 15 cents per ton per mile, before voting aid.

These were but symptoms of a profound dissatisfaction with the results of railroad subsidies. In the fall of 1869 both political parties pronounced against grants of state aid to railroads, but this could not prevent the passage of the so-called "Five Per Cent Act" of 1870, authorizing counties to subscribe to railroad stock up to 5 per cent of their assessed valuation; although it did encourage Governor Haight to veto two bills in March, 1870, the one authorizing the voters of certain counties in the San Joaquin Valley to donate their bonds to the San Joaquin Railroad Company at the rate of $6,000 per mile,[46] and the other providing for the construction of a railroad by the Southern Pacific through Monterey and San Luis Obispo counties, and permitting the counties interested to grant aid. The governor took the position that the proposed subsidies were not only unwise, but that they were unconstitutional for the reason that a donation to a private corporation was not a use of funds for a proper purpose.[47] After a fight which attracted much popular attention, the vetoes of the governor were sustained.

In 1871, Governor Haight was defeated for re-election by Newton Booth, the Republican candidate. In the following year, however, the Five Per Cent Act was repealed, and the period of local subsidies in California came to an end.

---

[46] Stanislaus, Merced, Fresno, Tulare, and Kern counties.   In Kern County the bond issue was limited to $480,000 and in Stanislaus to $180,000.

[47] Letters of Governor Haight, on the constitutional power of the legislature to authorize cities and counties to donate bonds to railroad corporations, Sacramento, 1870.

CHAPTER III

FEDERAL LAND GRANTS AND SUBSIDIES

Government Aid Deemed Necessary

Serviceable as local subsidies were, there is no question that the most important aid granted to the Central Pacific Railroad came from Congress.[1] It was perfectly well understood on the Pacific Coast that no transcontinental railroad could be built without the assistance of the national government. This was the attitude of the California legislature in 1852, when it instructed its senators in Congress, and requested its representatives, to vote for an act providing for the construction of a railway from the Missouri or Mississippi River to the Pacific Ocean, the cost of which should be borne by the general government.[2] It was also the position of the Railroad Convention of 1853, which sat at San Francisco under the presidency of Governor Bigler, and of that better advertised gathering known as the Pacific Railroad Convention of 1859, the resolutions of which concerning routes and state bond issues in aid of railroads gave rise to so much heated discussion.[3]

---

[1] Persons who desire details of the controversies in Congress prior to the outbreak of the Civil War may consult Haney, "Congressional History of Railways," or Davis "History of the Union Pacific."

[2] Laws of California, 1852, p. 276. See also resolutions passed May 17, 1853 (Laws of 1853, p. 315); May 13, 1854 (Laws of 1854, p. 224); February 25, 1854 (Laws of 1854, p. 227); March 19, 1857 (Laws of 1854, p. 370); April 1, 1859 (Laws of 1859, p. 390); April 15, 1859 (Laws of 1859, p. 394). In 1859 the legislature adopted a memorial to the same general effect (Laws of 1859, p. 395).

[3] The proceedings of the Pacific Railroad Convention of 1859 were published in the *San Francisco Alta*, September 21-26, 1859, and in a special supplement of the same paper. See also *The Pacific*, October 6, 1859, and other California papers. The convention was attended by delegates from Oregon and Washington. It thought that the Pacific Railroad should run from the city of San Francisco through the counties of San Mateo, Santa Clara, and Alameda, to the city of Stockton, thence over the Sierras by a central route. It favored also a branch to Puget Sound. Resolutions were adopted contemplating an issue of $15,000,000 in bonds by the state of California to cover the cost of railroads within that state, and an issue of an unspecified amount, presumably $5,000,000 by the state of Oregon. In February, 1860, an adjourned meeting of the same convention was held at Sacramento. Considerable opposition developed at this meeting to the proposal to bond the state for

Judah's Activities in Washington

Not only was it the attitude of the Pacific Coast that federal aid was necessary, but, still more important, Judah was able to advise his associates that Congress looked with favor upon the plan. He was convinced of this of his own personal knowledge, for he had been in Washington both on his own account and as a delegate of the Convention of 1859, and had reported to his constituents that only the pressure of more important matters arising out of the Civil War prevented favorable action upon the bill which they had sent him east to support. Upon this information, indeed, much of the plans of the Huntington-Stanford group was based.

Late in 1861, the Central Pacific Railroad sent Mr. Judah to Washington to solicit whatever aid the federal government might be disposed to give. We have in Judah's report upon this visit, dated September 1, 1862, a very full account of his negotiations. Judah sailed for the Atlantic states on October 10, 1861. During the trip he busied himself in talking with Mr. Sargent, Congressional representative from California, who was his fellow passenger, and in writing up the results of the survey which he had made during the summer of 1861. On his arrival in New York he completed this report, caused 1,000 copies of it to be printed, and distributed the copies widely where he thought they would do most good. Late in November, after conference with Senator McDougal, of California, chairman of the Senate Pacific Railroad Committee, he proceeded to Washington.

From the time of his arrival there to the following July, Judah was engaged in energetic lobbying. His brief previous visits to the capitol had acquainted him with the routine of business there, as well as with the personalities of a considerable

---

$15,000,000. The vote taken at San Francisco was reconsidered, and a new resolution passed, recommending state aid to a transcontinental railroad to the extent of not more than $15,000,000, but proposing that security be taken for the advances made so that the sum should not become a state charge. In other words, this idea of a loan was substituted for that of a donation. (*Sacramento Union*, February 7–11, 1860.)

number of Congressmen. He was aided, also, by the fact that Sargent, at the opening of the session, was assigned to the Pacific Railroad Committee of the House, and by the further circumstance that, with questionable propriety, he, Judah—interested in the outcome of the pending legislation as he was—was made clerk of a subcommittee of the House Committee on Pacific Railroads and secretary of the Senate Pacific Railroad Committee, with the privilege of the floor of the Senate and of the House, and charge of all the papers of the Senate committee.

From this position of advantage Judah was able to watch the progress of the Pacific Railroad bill which Mr. Sargent presently introduced, and to guide it to a certain extent. We know that it was Judah who procured the assent of the Kansas company mentioned in the bill to a change which required its road to meet the Union Pacific at the 100th meridian instead of at the 102d meridian. It was Judah also who secured the passage of the amendment retaining for the Central Pacific the timber on mineral land. Mineral lands were excepted from the lands granted to the Pacific railroads, and Judah was afraid lest this clause should deprive the Central Pacific of all benefit from a large part of the lands nominally given it. It was probably Judah, also, though this is less certain, who secured a change in the terms of the government subsidy increasing the amount and altering the distribution so that the largest payments were made for the road across the Sierras and not for the section east of the California state line, where the difficulties of construction were less. These were important matters, and Judah should not have been permitted to urge them from the vantage point of an official position.[4]

---

[4] Report of the chief engineer of the Central Pacific Railroad Company of California, on his operations in the Atlantic states, Sacramento, 1862. It should be added that Huntington himself was in Washington while the Act of 1864 was being debated. Cornelius Cole, one time senator from California, says of Huntington's activity at this time: "During the pendency of this legislation [Act of 1864], C. P. Huntington spent much of his time in Washington. Many of the amendments were suggested by him, and it gave me much satisfaction to forward his views. In former years in Sacramento we had been in close political fellowship, besides . . . I had been associated with him and others in the organization of the Central Pacific Railroad Company . . ." (Cornelius Cole, Memoirs, pp. 179-80.)

It is perhaps natural to ask whether there is any evidence of improper methods used by the Central Pacific to obtain the passage of the Pacific Railroad bill beyond that just referred to. The weight of the record is in the negative. According to Stanford, Judah had $100,000 in Central Pacific stock at his disposal to cover his expenses in the East. This stock was not worth much, and Judah did not use all of it. Besides this, Judah made an agreement with Hon. S. A. McDougal and Hon. T. G. Phelps, according to which he assigned to certain parties representing the interests of the San Francisco and San José Railroad, the rights, grants, and franchises of the Central Pacific for the portion of road between Sacramento and San Francisco. This looks like an attempt to quiet opposition in California, from which some of the California delegation may have profited. There is no further evidence, however, of any improper bargaining in connection with the passage of the bill, and it is probable that no money was corruptly used. If there had been, Campbell and Sargent would hardly have been naïve enough to send a letter to Judah in behalf of sixty-three senators and representatives, thanking him for his valuable assistance in aiding the passage of the Pacific Railroad bill.

The Pacific Railroad Act

Let us now consider the terms of the federal legislation of 1862 and 1864. The Pacific Railroad Act in its first form was signed on July 1, 1862,[5] and accepted by the company by letter dated November 1.[6] Bancroft says that the company was aware that the assistance offered in this act was not sufficient. The subsidy alone would not build the road, and capitalists would not subscribe on the security offered. However this may be, Judah arranged for the purchase of locomotives, cars,

---

[5] 12 United States Statutes 489 (1862).
[6] United States v. Southern Pacific Co., Record, pp. 1654-57.

and railroad iron before he left the East, and took measures
also to secure early action by the President on the question of
gauge, and on the establishment of the western base of the
Sierra Nevada Mountains.[7]

In December, after Judah's departure, a bill was introduced
to amend the Act of July, 1862. This measure passed the
Senate but was not acted upon by the House. A year and a
half later, however, a new act was passed by both houses, and
became law on the 2d of July, 1864, amending the Act of
1862, and materially increasing the aid which the Central
Pacific was to enjoy.[8] To all intents and purposes the Acts
of 1862 and 1864 were one piece of legislation, and will be
treated as such in the analysis which follows.[9]

Grant of Right-of-Way

What now were the advantages secured to the Central
Pacific by the Acts of 1862 and 1864, and what were the
obligations placed upon that company? We will take up first
the advantages, not necessarily in order of importance.

The first concession which the Central Pacific received
under this legislation was the authority to complete its line
from Sacramento to the eastern boundary of the state of
California and thence eastward 150 miles, provided that the
Union Pacific had not by that time built west to a connection
with it. The company was also authorized to build west and
south from Sacramento to San Francisco, or to a point near-
by. The Act of 1862 had contained no limitation on construction eastward beyond the reference to a Union Pacific
connection. Huntington said later that the restriction of 150

---

[7] Report of chief engineer, Central Pacific Railroad of California, on his operations in
the Atlantic states, 1862.

[8] 13 United States Statutes 356 (1864).

[9] For a full digest of the Acts of 1862 and 1864, and for an account of the Congressional
history involved, the reader is referred to Haney, "A Congressional History of Railways."
Senator A. A. Sargent asserted in 1878 that he, Sargent, wrote the acts himself. (45th Congress, 2d Session, Congressional Record, Vol. 7, p. 2024.)

miles should not have been inserted in 1864. He added, however:

> I said to Mr. Union Pacific when I saw it, I would take that out as soon as I wanted it out. In 1866 I went to Washington . . . I saw probably every member of Congress and the Senate except a few men who were interested in the Union Pacific, or had a direct interest in the Credit Mobilier . . . We passed it through the Senate; I think we got thirty-four against eight opposed to it. I took it over to the House and old Thad Stevens attended to the bill for me, and it went through the House with a vote, I think, of ninety-four for the bill and thirty-three against it.[10]

Judah said of the clause as it stood in 1862, that it virtually conceded to the company the right to construct at least one-half of the line of the Pacific Railroad. He was positive that it would be found advisable to undertake construction for about 300 miles easterly from the state line of California.[11]

In addition to the authority to build, the Central Pacific was given a free right-of-way 400 feet wide across all government lands, besides necessary grounds for stations, machine shops, etc., with the privilege of taking earth, stone, timber, and other materials from the public lands adjacent to the line of said road for purposes of construction.

Land Grant

The company was also granted ten alternate sections per mile of public land on each side of the railroad on the line thereof, and within the limits of 20 miles on each side of the road. The government undertook to extinguish Indian titles, but did not include in its grant mineral lands except coal and iron lands, or lands sold, reserved, or otherwise disposed of

---

[10] Huntington manuscript, pp. 78–79. The act referred to appears in 14 United States Statutes 78–79.

[11] Report of the chief engineer on the preliminary survey of the Central Pacific Railroad, etc., October 22, 1862.

by the United States, or lands to which a pre-emption, home-stead, swamp-land, or other lawful claim might have attached at the time the line of the road should have been definitely fixed. The grant was thus not of a specified number of acres, and no compensation was provided to the company for lands which might prove to be occupied; but in order to prevent speculation and in a measure to safeguard the company's interests, it was provided that at any time after the passage of the act, and before July 1, 1865, without waiting for definite location of the road, the company might designate the general route and file a map, whereupon the Secretary of the Interior should cause the lands within 25 miles of said route to be withdrawn from pre-emption, private entry, and sale. When any portion of the route should be finally located, the Secretary of the Interior should cause the granted lands to be surveyed and set off so far as might be necessary. As a matter of fact, Judah filed his map and general designation before he left Washington in 1862. Lands were to be conveyed to the company on completion of stretches of 20 consecutive miles. A special clause, never enforced, provided that all granted lands not sold or disposed of by the company within three years after the entire road should have been completed, should be subject to settlement and pre-emption like other lands, at a price not exceeding $1.25 per acre to be paid to the company.

Government Subsidy

In the way of a subsidy, Congress ordered the Secretary of the Treasury to issue to the Central Pacific, United States 6 per cent 30-year bonds, in amounts varying from $16,000 to $48,000 per mile. The subsidy of $48,000 was granted for the 150 miles east of the western base of the Sierra Nevada Mountains, this being the most mountainous and difficult portion of the road. East of this section of line the Central Pacific bond subsidy was to be $32,000 per mile, but west of it, it was to be only $16,000 per mile. It was the understanding of the company that these bonds were not redeemable by the government before maturity, and that until that time the interest charges were to be taken care of by the government. This last point was later the subject of litigation in which the company's contention was sustained.[12] The subsidy offered by the government inured to the company on the completion of sections of 20 consecutive miles over the greater part of the road, except that bonds might be issued up to two-thirds of the value of uncompleted work when the chief engineer of the company should certify that a certain proportion of the work required to prepare the road for its superstructure had been done.

Company's Obligations

In return for these very considerable privileges, the demands made upon the Central Pacific do not seem to have been excessive. First and foremost, the company was required to build its road at the rate of 25 miles each year after filing its assent to the provisions of the act, and to reach the state line within four years. The track upon the entire line was to be of a uniform width, to be determined by the President of the United States, so that, when completed, cars could be run from the Missouri River to the Pacific Coast. The grades and curves were not to exceed the maximum grades and curves of the Baltimore and Ohio Railroad, and the whole line of railroad and branches, Union Pacific and Central Pacific included, was to be operated and used for all purposes of communication, travel, and transportation, so far as the public and the government were concerned, as one connected, continuous line.

In the second place, demand was made that the company should pay the principal of the government bonds at maturity,

---

[12] United States v. Union Pacific, 91 U. S. 72 (1875).

and should meanwhile make certain payments on account of principal and interest. The following section taken from the Act of 1862 shows that there is no basis for the contention sometimes made that the government originally expected no repayment of its loan.

> *And be it further enacted* that the grants aforesaid are made upon condition that said Company shall pay said bonds at maturity, and shall keep said railroad and telegraph line in repair and use, and shall at all times transmit dispatches over said telegraph line, and transport mail, troops and munitions of war, supplies and public stores upon said railroad for the Government, whenever required to do so by any department thereof, and that the department shall at all times have the preference in the use of the same for all the purposes aforesaid (at fair and reasonable rates of compensation, not to exceed the amounts paid by private parties for the same kind of service), and all compensation for services rendered for the Government shall be applied to the payment of said bonds and interest until the whole amount is fully paid. Said Company may also pay the United States, wholly or in part, in the same or other bonds, treasury notes, or other evidences of debt against the United States, to be allowed at par, and after said road is completed, until said bonds and interest are paid, at least five per-centum of the net earnings of said road shall also be annually applied to the payment hereof.[13]

In 1864 this section was changed by requiring only one-half of the compensation for services rendered to the government to be applied to the payment of bonds issued by the government in aid of construction, but the declaration that the bonds should be paid was not altered. Not only was this true, but the government demanded security for repayment. In 1862 it declared that the issue of said bonds and delivery to the company should *ipso facto* constitute a first mortgage on the whole line of the railroad and telegraph, together with

---

[13] 12 United States Statutes 489 (1862), Sec. 6.

the rolling stock, fixtures, and property of every kind and description. In 1864 the lien of the United States bonds was subordinated to that of a second mortgage, but the idea of some security was preserved.

Third, the government reserved the right to reduce the rates of fare upon the Central Pacific, as well as upon the other railroads provided for in the Act of 1862, as unreasonable, when net earnings should exceed 10 per cent upon cost, exclusive of the 5 per cent to be paid to the United States.

Fourth and last, an annual report was asked for, which was to set forth earnings, expenses, indebtedness, the amount of stock subscribed, a description of the lines of road surveyed, and the names and residences of the stockholders.

Amounts Granted

It is evident that these demands were very moderate indeed. Under the provisions of the Acts of 1862 and 1864, the Central Pacific and Western Pacific railroads received $27,855,680 in government bonds, and 10,081,945.18 acres in public lands (up to June 30, 1920). From the bonds the companies realized $20,735,000, or $24,092 per mile. From the lands, the Central Pacific received, up to June 30, 1919, the approximate sum of $17,430,000, about equally divided between receipts from sales and receipts from other sources, including leases, stumpage, timber, and miscellaneous. The expenses of the land department may be estimated at $7,000,-000, and the net return therefore was $10,000,000. The yield of the bond subsidy not only exceeded the returns from the granted lands, but the subsidy was ten times the aid received from the state and counties put together, and of course many times the contribution of the partners themselves. What was almost as important, the grant of this federal assistance at once raised the company's credit, so that it could sell its own first mortgage bonds. The sale of company bonds yielded

$20,750,000, or a total of $41,485,000, for government and company bonds together, directly attributable to federal aid, and almost immediately available.

From the point of view of serviceability, the land grant referred to in the Pacific Railroad legislation was much less important than the subsidy in bonds. Government lands along the line of the Central Pacific had no value until the road was completed, nor even then until the slow process of settlement had filled up in a measure the territory through which the railroad ran. Nor was the amount of the grant so definite as to make it a satisfactory basis for credit, although land grant bonds were sold in and after 1870. The theoretical grant was twenty sections, of 12,800 acres to the mile. The grant did not, however, follow the sinuosities in the track, so that in the mountain sections it was quite possible for two miles of railroad to be constructed and yet only one mile of land grant to be obtained.

Not only was this true, but the exceptions provided for in the legislation were important. The records show that the saving clauses in the statutes, coupled with the inaccessibility of some of the lands within the nominal grants, and the differences between the actual mileage of the railroad and the mileage upon which land was awarded, reduced the area passing to the railroad by many hundred thousand acres. In California the Central Pacific was entitled to a nominal grant of 1,843,000 acres, at the rate of twenty sections per mile for a mileage of 144 miles. At least 887,000 acres of this amount were known to be lost to the grant as early as 1895, while the final adjustment will scarcely secure for the company more than half the amount originally expected. In Nevada the company's losses approximated one-ninth and in Utah one-quarter of the nominal grant. The losses on the California and Oregon up to 1897 were 962,703 acres out of a total grant of 3,266,729 acres, but in this case the law permitted the company to select additional lands within "indemnity" limits.

Delays in Transferring Title

How far the government lands failed in providing the Central Pacific with funds with which to build its road, however, can best be understood when attention is paid to the delays incident to the transfer of title. The general procedure in transferring title from the government to the company was as follows:

Under the Act of 1864, the Central Pacific was entitled to receive its lands upon completion of stretches of 20 consecutive miles in a fashion acceptable to commissioners appointed by the President of the United States. Upon acceptance by the government, the sections of land to which the company was entitled were listed and mapped and sent to the United States Land Office in the land district in which the land was located. The lists were examined there by registrars and receivers, and when declared cleared, the railroad company paid for the surveying, selecting, and conveying. Upon the payment of the fees, the lists were certified by the Surveyor-General of the state, and forwarded to the General Land Office at Washington for further examination. If found correct by the office in Washington, patents were issued. If there was doubt, the questionable cases were held for further examination.

In all this procedure delays were frequent. The initiative in the process of conveyance of land lay with the railroad company and not with the government, so that failure to file lists with the local land office or failure to pay into the United States Treasury the cost of surveys of listed lands prevented progress in the distribution of the grant. On the other hand, the slowness of the government in making surveys hindered the railroad in its selections. Still another reason for delay was the fact that within the mineral belt the Commissioner of the General Land Office required the railroad to file affidavits defining the mineral or non-mineral character of lands by 40-acre tracts. This requirement arrested the selection and patenting of lands, because the government survey did not subdivide tracts of 640 acres, and there was no way of identifying any particular sixteenth section of a tract. There were delays also in determining the title to lands claimed by homesteaders and pre-emptors, and there were delays due to the faulty organization of the Federal Land Office.

Land Office Responsible for Delays

Opponents of the Central Pacific freely charged that the company refrained from patenting its land in order to avoid the payment of taxes. This the company denied, pointing to the fact that the lands listed to June 1, 1887, exceeded the lands patented by 622,612.54 acres, and that the cash deposited with the United States Land Department to cover the cost of surveys exceeds the amount charged against the company up to January 15, 1886, by $28,771.92.[14] Mr. Stanford declared that it was the policy of the company to select its lands and present lists as promptly as possible, in order that lands might be disposed of to settlers, and it does appear that it was to the advantage of the Central Pacific to secure title as quickly as it could in the mineral belts, because the company was protected in its possession of land, which later turned out to contain minerals, if at the time of patenting no minerals had been discovered.

The evidence is clear enough that the delay in the patenting of lands to the Central Pacific Railroad was due mainly to the inadequacy of the staff in the General Land Office at Washington and not to the policies of the railroad itself. This is shown by the wide disparity between listings and patents. The excess

14 United States Pacific Railway Commission, p. 2562, testimony W. H. Mills.

of lands selected over lands patented averaged 57,000 acres during the five years ending June 30, 1869. During the next five years the average excess was 64,000 acres, and during the five years ending June 30, 1886, it rose to 248,000. In 1887, as has been pointed out, there was a difference of 622,612.54 acres between the amount of acres which had been listed and those which had been passed to patent. Between 1887 and 1897, there was no year in which the Central Pacific had less than 300,000 acres of land listed and selected and the selections on file in the General Land Office for land in California alone. Yet it is not so important to fix responsibility in this matter, as to observe that the contruction of the Central Pacific was not aided to any material degree by the lands offered to it under the legislation of 1862 and 1864. Up to the beginning of 1870, the company had received only four patents, totaling 144,386.63 acres,[15] which if sold at $2.50 per acre would have brought it $360,966.57. As a matter of fact, less than this was disposed of in the early years, and what was sold was on terms, not for cash in hand. In the later period, land-grant bonds with a lien on the land grant were sold to investors. The first issue of such bonds was, however, in 1871.

The bearing of these conditions on the land-grant policy of the United States is very plain. Congress was legislating in order to get a transcontinental railroad built. Every form of assistance which could be immediately transmuted into funds facilitated construction to the full value of those funds. In contrast with this, assistance which could be realized on only after a lapse of years, served not as an aid to construction, but as a reward to promoters for having taken risks. While to some extent the land grant to the Central Pacific may have aided the sale of Central Pacific first mortgage bonds, in the main its effect was to give a grossly excessive and

---

[15] The Western Pacific had received in addition two patents conveying 27,505.93 acres, but these lands were assigned by the Central Pacific to outside parties.

unnecessary profit to a few persons who held most of the stock of the company, without having invested any considerable capital of their own. Such a policy needs only to be understood to be condemned.

Fixing Western Base of Sierras

Both the subsidy and the land-grant clauses of the Acts of 1862 and 1864 were to receive interpretation by the courts. The subsidy provisions will be discussed again in a later chapter, so that the provisions designated to secure repayment of the government loan need not be considered at this time. Mention may be made, however, of President Lincoln's action in fixing the western base of the Sierras at the point where the line of the Central Pacific crossed Arcade Creek in the Sacramento Valley, a location 7 miles east of Sacramento, in a country which a casual observer would not be likely to call mountainous.

It is not at first sight evident why this point was chosen. The junction of Arcade Creek and the Central Pacific Railroad happens to be at about the edge of the alluvial plain of the Sacramento River, and so is marked by a slight rising of the ground. The rise is not, however, great. The beginning of the Sierra granite is at Rocklin, 22 miles east of Sacramento, and this spot rather than the one selected has the better right to be considered the real beginning of the mountains, so far as any single point can be fixed. As a matter of fact, the advisers of the President, who were in this instance the political authorities of the state of California, made their recommendation on the strength of what they conceived to be the purpose of the federal act rather than on scientific grounds. Mr. Whitney, state geologist, told the government that the intent of Congress was clearly to give a subsidy of $48,000 per mile over the most mountainous section of the road. If, therefore, he said, a distance of 150 miles measured east from the point in the Sacramento Valley where the ascent commenced would clear the most difficult and mountainous portion of the Sierra Nevadas and reach the valley on the eastern slope, then it seemed reasonable that the base of the Sierra Nevadas should be taken as beginning at that point. He recommended the place where the line of the Central Pacific crossed Arcade Creek as such a point.

The same place was selected by the Surveyor-General of the state of California, on the principle that the two extremities of the 150 miles upon which the maximum subsidy was to be given should rest upon corresponding grades, the one to the west, the other to the east of the mountains. These two recommendations seem to have been controlling, although the United States Surveyor-General for California suggested a location further east, where the ascending grade of the Sierras became plainly perceptible to the naked eye.[16] Since this interpretation of the act increased the bond subsidy which the Central Pacific was to receive, the company naturally made no objection.

Conditions of Land Grant

In regard to the land grant, the Land Office was called on for a great many decisions after 1864, mostly in interpretation of the exemptions carried in the federal legislation. The cases were not all brought by or against the Central Pacific, but they nevertheless affected its rights.

In general, the grant of land to the Central Pacific was held to be an absolute unconditional present grant. The route not being at the time determined, the grant was in the nature of a float, and the title did not attach to any specific sections until they were capable of identification. When once identified, however, the title attached to specific sections as of the date of the grant, except in the case of sections which were

---

[16] United States Pacific Railway Commission, pp. 3569–70.

specifically reserved.[17] While the grant was a present grant, it conveyed only land which was public land, that is to say, portions of the public domain which were open to sale or other disposition under general laws at the time the grant was made. This definition did not include lands which became public subsequent to the date of the grant, or lands reserved by competent authority for any purpose or in any manner, whether or not the reservations were mentioned in the granting act.[18]

It followed from the theory that the land grant was a present grant, that a valid homestead entry existing at the date of the passage of the Land Grant Act excepted the land covered from the area granted to the railroad even though the entry were canceled prior to the definite location of the railroad line.[19] The same effect was produced by an uncanceled and unexpired pre-emption claim, or by any other valid claim or reservation which was alive at the date of approval of the granting act. In cases like these the cancellation of the claim restored the land in question to the public domain, but did not operate to replace it within the railroad grant.[20]

Yet, although the theory that the grant took effect as of the date of the granting act was strictly applied against the railroad, the settler enjoyed the protection of a milder rule laid down in the statute itself. Section 7 of the Act of 1862 required the railroad company to designate the general route of the road within a stated time, and instructed the Secretary of the Interior thereupon to withdraw lands within 15 miles (changed to 25 miles in 1864) of the route designated from pre-emption, private entry, and sale; and Section 3 provided that the land grant to the railroad should not include lands to which a pre-emption or homestead claim might have attached

---

[17] United States v. Southern Pacific Railroad Co., 146 U. S. 570, 593 (1892).
[18] Newhall v. Sanger, 92 U. S. 761 (1875).
[19] Kansas Pacific v. Dunmeyer, 113 U. S. 629 (1885).
[20] Hastings and D. R. Co. v. Whitney, 132 U. S. 357 (1889); Whitney v. Taylor, 158 U. S. 85, 92 (1895); Bardon v. Northern Pacific, 145 U. S. 535 (1892).

at the time the line of road was definitely fixed. Pre-emption or homestead claims might therefore be established after the passage of the land-grant statute, provided that this was done before the lands were withdrawn from settlement.[21] Indeed, the Secretary of the Interior ruled that settlement and occupation exempted land from the grant even though the settler failed formally to assert his claim.[22] After the lands embraced in the grant were withdrawn from pre-emption, private entry, and sale, a settler could not secure acreage by subsequent occupation, although he settled prior to the time when the Central Pacific acquired actual title.

Losses Due to Spanish and Mexican Grants

A class of cases distinct from those of ordinary settlers arose in connection with Spanish and Mexican grants. It appeared that when California became a state, the Spanish and Mexican grants were both indefinite and unrecorded, so that it was not known just what lands were public domain and what lands were private. On March 3, 1861, Congress passed an act creating a Board of Land Commissioners in California, and provided that all persons claiming land in California by virtue of any right or title derived from either the Spanish or Mexican governments, should present the same to the board within two years for adjudication, with privilege of appeal to the United States courts.[23]

Following this act, many claims were presented. The United States Supreme Court held that land within the boundaries of alleged Spanish or Mexican lands which were *sub judice* at the time the Secretary of the Interior ordered the withdrawal of lands along the route of the road, were not embraced in the land granted to the company. There were

---

[21] Menotti v. Dillon, 167 U. S. 703 (1897).
[22] Central Pacific Railroad case, 3 L. D. 264.
[23] 9 United States Statutes 631 (1851).

many sections of California lands which were *sub judice* on August 2, 1862, and this fact caused serious loss to the Central Pacific in its grant in California. In addition to losses from the cause just mentioned, the company suffered from the indefiniteness of the Spanish and Mexican grants, and from the delay in determining the extent and boundaries of the Spanish and Mexican claims.

Policy Toward Settlers

It was the policy of the company to invite settlers upon its lands before the lands were patented, and then to select and apply for patents on lands which settlers desired to buy.[24] Sometimes, indeed, the company leased unpatented land to cattlemen at low rates, in spite of its lack of title. Actual transfers were made by bargain and sale deed warranting to the purchaser the entire title acquired by the company from the federal government. The prices ranged from $2.50 to $20 per acre, but little was sold at a price above $5. Usually land covered with tall timber was held at $5, and that covered with pine at $10. The actual cost to the purchaser was slightly greater, because he was compelled to pay for the acknowledgment of three signatures to the deed, and for the recording, amounting in all to perhaps $5.50 or $6. On the other hand, the company granted as much as five years' credit, and through the practice of selling land seekers' tickets from San Francisco, Sacramento, San José, Lathrop, and Los Angeles to points along the line of railroad, which were accepted as cash on the purchaser's first payment for his land, it practically furnished free transportation for California terminals to the sections bought. This last practice, at least, was in force on the Southern Pacific in 1880, and presumably on the Central Pacific also.

All in all, the Central Pacific does not seem to have at-

---

[24] United States Pacific Railway Commission, p. 2412, testimony W. H. Mills.

tempted to withhold its lands from the market, and there is no evidence that the settlement of the coast was retarded by the inability of prospective settlers to get land. The price which the Central Pacific could exact was held in check by the retention by the government of alternate sections, while the large sums which the company spent for advertising redounded to the advantage of the government as well as to that of the railroad. To the general statement that the Central Pacific was not unreasonably grasping in its capacity as landed proprietor, exception must be made of its treatment of timber lands in the North, of which mention will be made elsewhere.

The land-grant policy of the government was a mistake, but it was a mistake because it unnecessarily enriched a few men by securing to them an extravagant share in the unearned increment due to the development of the state of California, without aiding them materially in the task which the government most desired them to perform—not because the grantees endeavored to build up landed estates or to discourage the growth of population. Compared with the land grant, the bond subsidy was distinctly the better policy.

CHAPTER IV

PROGRESS OF CONSTRUCTION—CONSTRUCTION COMPANIES

Commencement of Construction

The construction of the Central Pacific Railroad of California was begun at Sacramento on the 8th of January, 1863. The day the work started was rainy and calculated to damp the most cheerful of spirits. There was, however, a brass band, banners, flags, speeches, and a crowd standing on bundles of hay near the levee to keep its feet dry. Two wagon-loads of earth were driven up before the platform on which were gathered the dignitaries present, and Stanford, then governor of California, seized a shovel and deposited the first earth for the embankment. The enthusiastic Charles Crocker promptly called for nine cheers. The sun smiled brightly, and everybody, for the moment at least, felt happy that after so many years of dreaming, they now saw with their own eyes the actual commencement of a Pacific railroad.[1]

It was fortunate that Mr. Crocker was enthusiastic, for the difficulties which the Central Pacific had to overcome were serious. The chief difficulties were as follows:

Gradients. Some reference has been made in the previous chapter to the elevations which the Central Pacific had to surmount. The highest point which the company had to reach was Summit Station, 105 miles from Sacramento, at an altitude of 7,042 feet. Since Sacramento lay only 56 feet above sea level, to reach this point required an ascent of 6,986 feet

---

[1] 1863 to 1913 "An Account of the Ceremonies Attending the Inauguration of the Work of Construction of the Central Pacific." Interesting details of the course of construction of the Central and Union Pacific railroads are given in Carter, "When Railroads Were New," and in Sabin, "Building the Pacific Railway."

in a distance of 105 miles, more or less, according as the route chosen was longer or shorter. The company's engineer said in 1864 that if it had been possible to maintain a continuous ascending grade, the maximum grade, from the foothills to the summit of the Sierras could have been reduced to 80 feet per mile.

In the attempt to approach this ideal condition the Central Pacific surveyed and resurveyed continuously until its rails were actually on the ground. Barometrical reconnaissances were made in 1862 and 1863 on lines via Downieville and Yuba Gap, and via Oroville and Beckwourth's Pass, in addition to the surveys via Georgetown, Dutch Flat, and Henness Pass, to which earlier reference has been made (page 20).[2] Location surveys reached Alta in 1863, the state line in 1866, and Ogden in 1868.[3] After Mr. Judah's death almost an entire relocation of the line from the 31st to the 48th section was made in 1864 in order to avoid tunneling, and to reduce cost,[4] and still later it was found desirable to shift the whole route between Dutch Flat and Emigrant Gap from the Bear River side of the ridge, up which the Central Pacific was proceeding, to the American River side. This change avoided some 20 miles of 116-foot grade, together with a great deal of curvature.[5]

The final result of these various surveys was a line with maximum grades of 116 feet to the mile. This does not compare unfavorably with most of the transcontinental routes subsequently built. It is interesting to observe, however, that the Central Pacific summit is some 2,000 feet higher than the altitude of Beckwourth's Pass, and that the maximum grade of the Western Pacific Railway, built years afterwards through that pass, is only 52.8 feet to the mile, or one per cent. Neither

---

[2] Report of the chief engineer upon recent surveys of the Central Pacific Railroad of California, July, 1863.

[3] *Ibid.*, December, 1865, and July, 1869.   [4] *Ibid.*, October 8, 1864.

[5] *Ibid.*, December, 1863.

Judah nor his immediate successors, therefore, discovered the best route across the Central Sierras.

Temperature. A second physical difficulty incident to mountain construction was found in the mountain climate. The summer climate of the Sierras is delightful, at least at altitudes of about 6,000 to 7,000 feet. At lower elevations the temperature is often uncomfortably warm. But the winter climate is quite different. As early as August the nights begin to get cold, the first snows come in November, while in January the trails become impassable, and the high levels are unvisited by man until the following year. The official record shows that the greater part of the mountain construction on the Central Pacific occurred between July, 1866, and July, 1868.

Mr. Stanford has testified that both the winter of 1866-67 and that of 1867-68 were unusually severe, and his engineers have dwelt in great detail upon the consequent impediments to their work. Not only did the frozen earth resist pick and shovel, but there were snow banks from 30 to 100 feet deep. It was necessary to remove this snow to permit excavation, and to keep clear the space to be occupied by embankments in order to prevent settling. When the summit was approached tunnels had to be driven through the snow to the rock face. As the whole working force could not be employed in the tunnels, the surplus labor, with all its supplies, was hauled beyond the summit and put to work, at great expense, in the cañons of the Truckee River. The first snow sheds were built in the summer of 1867, and in the following years it was decided to cover all the cuts and points where the road crossed the paths of the great avalanches beyond the summit. The total length of sheds and galleries built by the fall of 1869 was 37 miles, and the cost was $2,000,000.[6]

---

[6] United States Pacific Railway Commission, pp. 2581-82, testimony Arthur Brown, superintendent of bridges and buildings.

In addition to the difficulties caused by snow, it must be remembered that the frozen earth, though uncovered, was difficult to work. Not only was it necessary to blast out material which could have been cheaply moved at a more favorable time, but, when piled into embankments, the ground settled in the spring as the frost was leaving, and required constant attention.[7]

All the various obstacles raised by climate would have been minimized if construction had proceeded more slowly. Indeed, Mr. Hood and Mr. Strobridge, engineers in charge of construction, agreed that if the Central Pacific had been built at less speed, and as such railways are usually constructed, the expense would have been from 70 to 75 per cent less than the actual cost. The saving would not have been due altogether to the abandonment of winter construction, but this would have been an important factor. The Central Pacific, however, preferred speed to economy, in the hope of outstripping the Union Pacific in the race for the business of Nevada, and for the subsidies and land grants offered by Congress.

Supplies. A further obstacle in the way of successful construction of the Central Pacific lay in the difficulty of getting supplies. Wood and stone could be procured in the mountains, but iron, coal, and manufactured articles of all sorts, including rails, locomotives, and cars, were brought from Sacramento or from the East. Prices in general were high, in part because of the war. The first ten locomotives purchased by the Central Pacific Railway cost upwards of $191,000; the second ten upwards of $215,000. Iron rails cost $91.70 per ton at the mills. The price of powder increased from $2.25 to $6 during the period of construction. The cost of food was exorbitant. Hay was worth $100 a ton out upon the line, and

---

7 United States Pacific Railway Commission, p. 2579, statement William Hood; pp. 2580–81, 3150, statement J. H. Strobridge; pp. 2576–77, statement L. M. Clement; p. 3055, testimony E. H. Miller; pp. 2581–82, statement Arthur Brown.

oats about 14 or 15 cents a pound.   Stanford says he sold one potato for $2.50.[8]

In the cases cited, high cost of transportation often played an important part in determining the final prices, and in general, indeed, the expense of moving supplies was comparable with the initial cost.   Among many possible illustrations one may mention the fact that shipments of rails via the Isthmus of Panama as late as 1868 cost, for transportation alone, $51.97 per ton, making the total cost of the rail delivered at Sacramento, $143.67, not including charges for transfer from ships at San Francisco, nor for transportation up the Sacramento River.   Nor was this freight rate high when compared with the cost of wagon hauls in the mountains, when material had to be transported away from the finished track.   Mr. Huntington tells of meeting some teams with ties in the Wahsatch Mountains.   He continues:

> They had seven ties on that wagon.   I asked where they were hauled from, and they said from a certain canon.   They said it took three days to get a load up to the top of the Wahsatch Mountains and to get back to their work.   I asked them what they had a day for their teams, and they said $10. This would make the cost of each tie more than $6.   I passed back that way in the night in January, and I saw a large fire burning near the Wahsatch summit, and I stopped to look at it.   They had, I think, some twenty to twenty-five ties burning. They said it was so fearfully cold they could not stand it without having a fire to warm themselves.

Fortunately for the company, the cost of labor on the Central Pacific and transcontinental lines does not seem to have been excessive.   The total number of men employed ranged from 1,200 in 1864, to 14,000 or 14,500 in 1867, when construction was at its height.   White men, of whom there were

8 United States Pacific Railway Commission, p. 2523, testimony Leland Stanford.   On the other hand, there were abundant supplies of timber along the line, and the price of machinery declined after the war.

some 2,500 or 3,000 in 1867, received $35 a month and board as common laborers, and from $3 to $5 a day as skilled mechanics. Most of the track laborers, however, were Chinamen, who were paid $35 a month, and boarded themselves.[9] These Chinamen proved reliable and willing workers, and, because of his experience with them, it was with distinct reluctance that Mr. Stanford in later years allied himself with the friends of Chinese exclusion.[10]

Letting of Construction Contracts

Such obstacles as these made the task upon which the Huntington-Stanford group had entered a formidable one indeed. Just how the difficulties should be met, Mr. Huntington himself did not know. Arrangements were first made with small contractors for the building of stretches of road from Sacramento towards Newcastle. Charles Crocker resigned his directorship in 1862 and took the first contract for 18 miles. Then Cyrus Collins and Brothers got a contract which they did not complete, and other contracts were let to Turton, Knox and Ryan, C. D. Bates, and S. D. Smith. Mr. Crocker says the people raised a hue and cry saying that he was a favored contractor, so that the directors told him that he could not have more than two miles of the road between the 18th and

---

[9] United States Pacific Railway Commission, pp. 3139–41, testimony J. H. Strobridge. The following table is prepared from Mr. Strobridge's testimony:

NUMBER OF MEN EMPLOYED IN CENTRAL PACIFIC CONSTRUCTION, 1864–69, AND RATE OF PAY

Year	Number of Chinamen	Rate of pay	Number of White Men	Rate of pay
1864	Very few		1,200	$30 a month
1865	7,000	$30 a month	2,500	35 " "
1866	11,000	35 " "	2,500–3,000	35 " "
1867	11,000	35 " "	2,500–3,000	
1868	5,000–6,000		2,000–3,000	
1869	5,000		1,500–1,600	

[10] Huntington was always openly in favor of unrestricted Chinese immigration. He said that exclusion deprived the United States of tractable and cheap labor, which was needed to build up the desert places of the country. He believed the fanatical hostility to the Chinese was limited to California, where, he asserted, the Irish Catholics swung the balance of power. (*San Francisco Examiner*, January 4, 1889.)

30th sections.[11] He adds that the independent contractors got to bidding against each other for laborers, and thus put up the price. Huntington was told that the smaller contractors quarreled with each other, and tried to "scoop" labor from each other;[12] while Mr. Stanford says that the small contractors did not finish their sections in consecutive order, that they did not hurry, and could not be sufficiently controlled.[13]

At any rate, after the completion of section 29, no more contracts were let to anyone except Charles Crocker and Company. According to the associates, it was not so much a question of price as one of organization and control. This may be true, or it may be that the associates finally decided that it would be easier to make a satisfactory profit out of government subsidies by doing the building themselves, than by beating down subcontractors to the lowest possible contract price. It should be noticed that the change in policy referred to did not take place until 1864, when the federal Act of 1862 had been passed and that of 1864 was imminent, and that the Central Pacific did not select any single contractor, but gave all its work to Charles Crocker, one of the original associates.

Contracts with Crocker

The first contract with Charles Crocker, covering sections 1 to 18, provided for a lump sum payment of $400,000, of which $250,000 was to be in cash, $100,000 in bonds of the company, and $50,000 in capital stock. This was also the type of contract made with other contractors up to section 30, although the amounts paid varied. At least one bill for extras

---

[11] United States Pacific Railway Commission, p. 3642, testimony Charles Crocker. A letter from Mr. Judah to Dr. Strong, dated July 10, 1863, suggests that it was Judah's influence which prevented Crocker from building sections 19 to 30. Judah wrote: "I have had a big row and fight on the contract question, and although I had to fight alone, carried my point and prevented a certain gentleman from becoming a further contractor on the Central Pacific Railroad at present." (*Ibid.*, p. 2966, testimony Strong.) This was probably only one of a number of differences of opinion between the Stanford-Huntington group and the original promoters of the Central Pacific, led by Judah. It was only after Judah's death that the first-named interests were able to dominate the situation completely.

[12] United States Pacific Railway Commission, p. 3769, testimony Collis P. Huntington.

[13] *Ibid.*, pp. 2621-26, testimony Leland Stanford.

was allowed Mr. Crocker. Sections 30 and 31 were built by Crocker, and after these were completed he was permitted to continue without a written contract.

In June, 1865, Mr. Hopkins made a report to the president and directors of the Central Pacific upon the general subject of contracts. In this report Hopkins dwelt upon the necessity of rapid construction for the purpose of capturing the passenger traffic between Sacramento and Virginia City; and also in order to comply with the acts of Congress and the state legislature, which required rapid construction of the road. Persons of large capital, he said, seemed unwilling to bind themselves to construct the road as rapidly as necessary. Charles Crocker and Company, on the other hand, had pushed and were pushing the work with extraordinary vigor and success, and had in all cases complied with the orders and directions of the officers of the company. He recommended, therefore, that arrangements be continued with that firm, at rates specified in an accompanying resolution.[14] The directors thereupon adopted this report, and resolved as follows:

> *Resolved and ordered* that Charles Crocker and Company be allowed and paid for all work done and material furnished, or which may hereafter be done and furnished, until the further order of the Board of Directors, in the construction of the railroad of the Company, from section 43 eastward, subject to and in accordance with the terms, conditions and stipulations set forth in the contract with said Charles Crocker and Company, dated September 19, 1863, except so far as the same are modified or changed by this order, at the following rates and prices, and in accordance with the following classification, to-wit:
>
> [Here are inserted the rates for clearing and grubbing, and excavation in various kinds of rock, etc.]
>
> The payments to be made monthly, according to the monthly

---

[14] United States Pacific Railway Commission, p. 3048, testimony E. H. Miller. For a general discussion of the relative advisability of construction by contract as opposed to construction by the Central Pacific itself, see an earlier report by Stanford, Hopkins, and Miller. (*Ibid.*, pp. 3045-46.) This report made the point that the letting of contracts to a responsible contractor would raise the credit of the railroad.

Summit Valley.   Altitude 6,960 feet.   Emigrant Mountain and Railroad Pass in the distance

estimates, five-eighths thereof in gold coin, and the remaining three-eighths in the capital stock of the Company, at the rate of two dollars of capital stock for each one dollar of said three-eighths of said estimate, with the privilege of paying said three-eighths in gold coin in lieu of said stock, at the election of said Company, to be made at the time of such payment.

Payments in Cash and Stock

The essence of this arrangement was that Mr. Crocker was to go ahead indefinitely and that he was to be paid not a given sum per mile, but at a given rate of so much per unit for each class of work which he might find it necessary to do. Payments were to be made in cash, and also up to a certain per cent in stock, taken at a valuation of 50 cents on the dollar. Under date of April 16, 1866, Mr. Crocker requested that stock be given him at a valuation of 30 cents on the dollar, instead of 50 cents, and this was agreed to.[15]

The change from a 50-cent to a 30-cent valuation was made ostensibly because Crocker and Company could not realize more than 30 cents on the stock which they were receiving. As a matter of fact, Crocker could not sell Central Pacific stock at any price, so that the alteration of the contract merely increased his chance for a speculative gain, to be realized after construction should have been completed. Mr. Stanford has said that the directors did not care very much what the prices were, so long as the work was done. Under the contract, the Central Pacific Railroad itself, through Mr. Huntington, purchased locomotives and cars for Crocker and Company, and charged for them at cost.[16] Bonds were also sent from San Francisco to Huntington, but it was Huntington's impression that they were sold for the company, not for the contractors. In any case, Huntington rendered an account every month of what he had done, and Hopkins settled with the company or

---

[15] United States Pacific Railway Commission, p. 3436.
[16] Ibid., p. 3157, testimony J. H. Strobridge.

with the contractors, as the case might be.[17] Describing the situation at a later date, Crocker said, "It was decided that I should go on immediately and see what I could do. I did go on until we got tied up in suits and I had to stop. I could not get any money. They had all the money I had, and all I could borrow. That was the time that I would have been very glad to take a clean shirt, lose all I had, and quit."

The total payments made to Charles Crocker or to Charles Crocker and Company, under the various arrangements just described, were as follows: [18]

TOTAL AMOUNT PAID CHARLES CROCKER AND COMPANY ON HIS CONTRACT AND FOR EXTRA WORK

Cash, or its equivalent, including material furnished him	$ 8,853,117.93
Bonds, taken at par........................	100,000.00
Stock, taken at 50 cents on the dollar........	2,696,200.00
Stock, taken at 30 cents on the dollar........	11,947,530.00
Stock, taken at par value..................	57,980.22
Total	$23,654,828.15

If we take the cash payments at par and the bonds at 75, this would make the tidy sum of $69,210 per mile on 129 miles. When we bear in mind that Crocker accepted the contract for the first 18 miles out of Sacramento at a price including a cash payment of only $13,800 per mile, and that the arrangements with the small contractors who followed him were distinctly less favorable, it is possible to say with some confidence that the profits on the Crocker contracts were considerable. Whatever they were, Mr. Crocker shared them with his associates by

---

[17] The actual cost of the whole work to the Central Pacific depended upon Mr. Crocker's reports upon the work which he did.   There is no evidence that the company exercised any supervision over these reports, although it was to the advantage of the construction company to describe as much of the work as possible as heavy; but on the other hand, Mr. Crocker's engineers testified that Crocker never attempted to influence them in their estimates. (United States Pacific Railway Commission, p. 3207, testimony L. Clement.)

[18] United States Pacific Railway Commission, p. 3511, testimony Richard F. Stevens.

depositing at a later date $14,000,000 in Central Pacific stock in the treasury of the Contract and Finance Company, (discussed in the next section) for the benefit of the stockholders of that organization.   Inasmuch as Stanford was one of the principal stockholders in the Contract and Finance Company, his later categorical denial before the United States Pacific Railway Commission that he had participated in the profits of the Crocker contracts makes interesting reading.[19]

"Contract and Finance Company"

When the Central Pacific approached the state line of California in the latter part of 1867, the associates told Mr. Crocker that they did not think it best for him to go any further.   They said they wanted more capital—they wanted to engage heavy men in the enterprise.[20]   Crocker had not been successful in persuading capitalists to go in with him, while it was believed that investors were deterred from taking stock in the Central Pacific by reason of the liability which would be thereby incurred under California law.   Either Huntington or Stanford—both claim the credit—conceived the idea that there would be an advantage in organizing a corporation to undertake the construction work.   The subject was mentioned on the occasion of one of Huntington's visits to California, although the company was formed while Huntington was in the East.[21] The name finally decided upon for the new corporation was that of "Contract and Finance Company."   Articles of association were filed in October, 1867.   W. E. Brown, Theodore J. Milliken, and B. R. Crocker attended to the details.   Milliken was a merchant in Sacramento, and the other two were connected with the Central Pacific.

According to its articles of incorporation, the Contract and

[19] United States Pacific Railway Commission, p. 2636, testimony Leland Stanford.
[20] *Ibid.*, p. 3661, testimony Charles Crocker.
[21] Colton case, pp. 266–68, deposition of Collis P. Huntington.

Finance Company was formed for the purpose of engaging in and carrying on the business of constructing, purchasing, leasing, selling, holding, maintaining, operating, and repairing railroads, wagon and transit roads, steamboats, vessels, telegraph lines, and rolling stock of railroads; the purchasing, holding, hypothecating, and selling of bonds and stocks issued by railroad and other companies or corporations; the purchasing and using of iron and other materials for railroad and telegraph lines; the borrowing and loaning of money; the conducting of an express and stage business, and any and all other kinds of business connected with or pertaining to railroads and telegraph lines; the transportation of persons and property, on land and water; and the purchasing, holding, leasing, and selling of real estate of all kinds. The capital stock was set at $5,000,000.

Failure to Attract Outside Capital

It is the unanimous testimony of the associates that the real and only reason for forming the Contract and Finance Company was that outside capital might be induced to come in. Huntington says that when the company was organized, he went with new energy to capitalists in the East to induce them to take a share in the risks and profits of construction. Yet from the point of view of attracting outside capital, the Contract and Finance Company was a complete failure. William and Commodore Garrison, of New York, A. A. Selover, Moses Taylor, and William E. Dodge, among others, considered the matter, but all concluded that the risk was too great. In California, Stanford applied to D. O. Mills, W. C. Ralston, Haggin and Tevis, Michael Reese—in short, to everybody whom he thought he might possibly induce to take an interest—but in vain.[22] The result of the failure to secure outside subscriptions to the Contract and Finance Company was that

---

[22] United States Pacific Railway Commission, p. 2640, testimony Leland Stanford.

the associates had to take up the stock of that company themselves. Crocker was made president at an early date, and
apparently took the bulk of the stock in the first instance.
Then, when it was evident that no outside investors would
come in, he put the stock back, and Stanford, Hopkins, Huntington, and E. B. Crocker took equal shares with him—each
subscribing for 10,000 shares out of the 50,000 outstanding.[23]
Later a little stock was disposed of to outsiders, but when the
Contract and Finance Company got into the courts the associates bought this back.

Throughout the whole life of the Contract and Finance
Company the stockholders were the same men who held the
bulk of the stock of the Central Pacific Railroad. Contracts
between the finance company and the railroad company were
therefore made by the associates in one capacity, with themselves in another capacity, a situation unfortunately not unique
in the history of American railroad building. An unusual
feature of the arrangement, however, which was common to
arrangements with other construction companies formed by
the associates, was that the funds of the Contract and Finance
Company, over and above the sums received from the Central
Pacific, were derived from loans to the company by its stockholders and not from payments on the stock subscribed. There
is no evidence that Hopkins, Stanford, Huntington, or either
of the Crockers paid a cent in cash on their subscriptions.
Instead, they gave their notes. To provide the Contract and
Finance Company with funds, they deposited money, sometimes more and sometimes less, paying interest on their notes,
and receiving credit for interest on their balances, each partner
as a rule putting in all the funds which he could spare, and
having an individual account kept of his transactions. The
Contract and Finance Company was, therefore, always heavily
in debt, although the debt was owed to its own stockholders.

---

[23] *Ibid.*, p. 3661, testimony Charles Crocker; p. 2637, testimony Leland Stanford.

The advantages of this arrangement would seem to be two: first, that it concealed effectively the profits which the company was making; and second, that it did not limit any stockholder to a proportionate share in the burdens and gains of the under- taking. If any of the associates desired to participate more heavily than his friends, or less heavily, he could do so. Such a privilege was probably not important before 1869, but it be- came so later.

Contracts with Construction Company

A word may now be said about the contracts which the Contract and Finance Company secured. Under date of December 3, 1867, Mr. Stanford, as president of the Central Pacific, reported to his directors that he had made a contract for the construction and equipment of the railway and tele- graph line of the company lying east of the eastern boundary of the line of California, and presented a draft of the contract, which the directors approved.[24]   Leland Stanford, E. B. Crocker, Mark Hopkins, and E. H. Miller, Jr., were present and voted. Mr. Miller explains that he did not understand at the time who the owners of the Contract and Finance Company were, and that nothing was said about it at the meeting. The contract provided that the Contract and Finance Company should build the road of the Central Pacific from the state line, eastward, 552 miles. It was to grade the road, build the bridges, lay the track, build and complete a telegraph line, furnish telegraph offices and instruments, furnish rails, ties, buildings, roundhouses, turntables, and a specified number of engines and cars and running material per mile. On its part, the Central Pacific agreed to pay $86,000 per mile, half in cash and half in Central Pacific stock, and in practice the Central Pacific provided the equipment and the iron, charging them to the Contract and Finance Company at cost. This statement

[24] United States Pacific Railway Commission, pp. 3436–37.

relative to the terms of the contract with the construction company is made on the strength of the recollections of parties interested,[25] for the actual contract is one of the missing documents characteristic of Central Pacific history. Stanford describes the contract as an exhaustive one. That is to say, the Central Pacific turned over all it had and the Contract and Finance Company built the road and got the profits, if there were any.

The apparent advantages of an arrangement with a construction company as compared with those of construction by the Central Pacific itself, were those connected with specialization of the work. A company which does nothing but construction and which does that all the time, may be expected to have a force more highly trained in this particular grade of work, and a more abundant supply of tools and material than an organization which builds railroads only occasionally. The unfortunate necessity of hiring men for each new job and discharging them at the completion of the job is avoided. In the case of the Central Pacific this advantage was somewhat illusory, it is true, for the reason that the Contract and Finance Company on its first contract, whatever might have been the fact later, could scarcely have had an advantage over the railroad; and as for tools, the Contract and Finance Company had no machine tools at all at the beginning, and had to rely on the railroad not only for cars and engines to transport its men, but for equipment for large construction of any sort. The real reason for using a construction company in this case was a financial and not an operating one.

Profits of Construction

Much has been said about the profits of the Contract and Finance Company. Here, again, books are missing, having

---

[25] United States Pacific Railway Commission, p. 2897, testimony W. E. Brown; p. 3062, testimony E. H. Miller; pp. 3511–20, testimony R. F. Stevens.

been packed into boxes by the industrious Mark Hopkins in 1873, and never again produced.[26] A man named John Miller, one-time secretary of the Contract and Finance Company, and defaulter to the alleged extent of $900,000 at a subsequent period, was in possession of transcripts from these books, if we may believe his statement; but even these transcripts disappeared, if indeed they ever existed.[27] We do not know, therefore, how much construction cost the Contract and Finance Company, and we cannot calculate with any accuracy the profit obtained.

It does appear that the work done by the Contract and Finance Company cost the Central Pacific, in all $23,736,000 in cash and the same amount in capital stock.[28] If we add to this $100,000 in cash and $2,900,000 in bonds paid to the Union Pacific for the stretch of land from Promontory Point to a point five miles west of Ogden, and $1,072,874.79 for snowsheds and other extra work performed in 1870, we have a total of $51,544,874.79, of which $24,908,874.79 was in cash. Taken in connection with the Crocker contracts, this makes an aggregate of $33,761,992.72 in cash, $3,000,000 in bonds, and $38,437,710.22 in stock. It was the judgment of the United States Pacific Railway Commission that the total cost of building the 690 miles from Sacramento to Promontory Point, and of purchasing from the Union Pacific 47½ miles of road from Promontory Point to the end of the Central Pacific line, 5 miles west of Ogden, did not exceed $36,000,000, and this included 9 miles built by small contractors, the payment for which is not included in the figures just given.[29]

In a word, if the conclusions of the United States Pacific

---

[26] United States Railway Commission, pp. 2712–17, testimony D. Z. Yost.

[27] Ibid., pp. 2875–92, testimony John Miller; pp. 3028–33, testimony N. Greene Curtis.

[28] There is some evidence that $6,000,000 of this cash was not strictly cash, but took the form of notes of the Central Pacific Railroad which were ultimately settled in land-grant bonds at $86.50. (United States Pacific Railway Commission Report, p. 75.) Mr. Crocker says that the interest on a portion of these bonds paid his expenses on a trip to Europe. (Ibid., p. 3668, testimony Charles Crocker.)

[29] United States Pacific Railway Commission Report, pp. 74–75.

Summit tunnel (altitude 7,042 feet) before completion—Sierra Nevada Mountains

Railway Commission are to be relied upon, and they were made by engineers relatively soon after the completion of the road, the builders of the Central Pacific were able to accomplish their contracts with the cash and the proceeds of the company's bonds that were turned over to them, and to retain their Central Pacific stock as a clear profit. If we compare this stock surplus with the probable cash investment in the road, taking the shares at any reasonable valuation, say at $15 or $20 per share, the profit does not seem excessive. If we compare it with the contributions of the associates, however, and this is the more reasonable because the associates received the full benefit of the difference between cost and receipts, it represents, on the most conservative calculation, 500 or 600 per cent for an investment which probably did not exceed $1,000,000, over a period of six years. To this should be added the proceeds of the land grant and of the local subsidies.

The federal government seems in these matters to have assumed the major portion of the risk, and the associates seem to have derived the profits. Nor is this point of view vitiated by the fact that the federal government was ultimately repaid its loan in full, for the reason that the repayment was not at the expense of the associates, but was made possible by a credit arising out of the earnings of the road, and represented merely a shifting of the burden of the debt due the federal authorities to the communities along the line.

Besides the completion of the main line of the Central Pacific, the Contract and Finance Company built a portion of the California and Oregon Railroad, part of the Western Pacific, and the entire San Joaquin Valley branch of the Central Pacific from Lathrop to Goshen. The arrangements between the Contract and Finance Company and Central Pacific for this work varied, but substantial additional profits were secured. In 1874, the Contract and Finance Company was dissolved. There is some dispute as to whether its assets were divided into four or five parts, but both Stanford and Crocker have testified that their dividend consisted of approximately $13,000,000 in Central Pacific stock, at par.[30]   At the same time the stockholders of the construction company assumed its debts, amounting to perhaps $1,600,000.[31]

[30] United States Pacific Railway Commission, pp. 2655–56, testimony Leland Stanford; p. 3668, testimony Charles Crocker.   Mr. Huntington said in 1873 that he thought his dividend amounted to about $1,000,000, but in 1887 he admitted that he had earlier mistaken the facts.   (*Ibid.*, pp. 4026–28, testimony C. P. Huntington.)

[31] United States Pacific Railway Commission, pp. 2977–88, testimony W. E. Brown.

CHAPTER V

THE SEARCH FOR A TERMINAL

Progress of Construction

Under its various construction contracts, the Central Pacific steadily progressed, between 1863 and 1869, from Sacramento to a junction with the Union Pacific near Ogden. The official statement of the progress of construction is as follows: [1]

Broke ground at Sacramento............ January 8, 1863
Laid first rail....................... October 27, 1863
Sacramento to Roseville (18 miles)...... Constructed in 1863

Road opened as follows:

To Newcastle	31	miles	January, 1865
" Auburn	36	"	May 15, 1865
" Clipper Gap	42	"	June 10, 1865
" Colfax	54	"	September 4, 1865
" Secret Town	66	"	May 8, 1866
" Alta	78	"	July 10, 1866
" Cisco	94	"	November 9, 1866
" Summit	105	"	July, 1867
" State Line	278	"	January, 1868
" Reno	294 ·	"	May, 1868
" Wadsworth	329	"	July, 1868

(362 miles constructed in 1868)

" Monument Point	667	"	April 15, 1869
" Ogden	743	"	May 10, 1869

Driving last spike, and opened
for business from Sacramento;
distance San Francisco to
Ogden, per time card...... 883   "   May 10, 1869

---

[1] 1863–1913. An Account of the Ceremonies Attending the Inauguration of the Work of Constructing the Central Pacific. *Scribner's Magazine* for August, 1892, contains an article describing the completion of the Central Pacific and also a reproduction of the well-known painting, "The Joining of the Central and Union Pacific" ("The Last Spike").

Relations with Western Pacific

It has already been noted that the line from Sacramento via Stockton to San José was not part of the original plan, and that the rights, grants, and franchises of the Central Pacific in it were assigned to other parties in the course of the Congressional fight. The original assignment of December 4, 1862, was to a group of men which included Timothy Dane, the original projector, and president of the San Francisco and San José Railroad, Charles McLoughlin, and A. H. Houston. In 1864, the first assignees having waived their rights, the Central Pacific Railroad made the same assignment to the Western Pacific Railroad of California.[2] The Western Pacific Railroad in turn let contracts for construction to Houston and McLoughlin, but by 1867, McLoughlin had become involved in litigation regarding his contracts and asked that all arrangements between himself and the Western Pacific be canceled.[3]

This led the Western Pacific to enter into a contract with the Contract and Finance Company, with the result that substantially all the stock of the first-named corporation came into the hands of the Huntington group. McLoughlin retained the federal land grant; the federal subsidy, however, of $16,000 per mile, reverted to the Western Pacific as did the local subsidies, and through it passed to the Contract and Finance Company. The railroad from Sacramento to San José was opened September 15, 1869; on June 22, 1870, the Central Pacific and the Western Pacific filed articles of consolidation.

Lack of Terminal Facilities

In September, 1869, the transcontinental railroad from Omaha to San José was in working order. It would be an

---

[2] The indenture making this assignment, dated October 31, 1864, is printed in full in the appendix to the journals of the Senate and Assembly of the 20th Session of the Legislature of the State of California, Vol. 6 (1874), No. 2, pp. 27–29.   It covers not only the right to build and operate a railroad between Sacramento and San José, but also "all the rights, grants, donations, rights-of-way, loan of the credit of the Government of the United States, or the bonds thereof."

[3] United States Pacific Railway Commission, p. 2785, testimony Leland Stanford.

exaggeration to say that the line was in good shape. There was little or no ballast, and a good rain was said to make miles of the road-bed run like wet soap. Little had been done to eliminate grades and curves, sleeping-car accommodation at first was insufficient, the journey speed from Sacramento to Ogden was only 19 miles an hour, while schedules were not always adhered to. Cars were heated by stoves, and passengers disembarked for their meals. But in a measure these were conditions to be expected at the start, and interfered only in a minor degree with the interest and excitement of a transcontinental trip. The great fact was that a railroad existed which could be used, and over which relatively direct, rapid, and cheap communication with the East could be secured.

The greatest weakness of the Central Pacific Railroad in 1869 lay in its lack of terminal facilities on San Francisco Bay. When the company decided to begin work at Sacramento, its reasonable expectation had been that a railroad under one management would be built from that city around the southern end of San Francisco Bay to the city of San Francisco. The Central Pacific was willing to forego the advantage of this construction itself in order to gain friends, and did it the more willingly because this stretch of line was likely to be unprofitable by reason of steamship competition on the bay and on the Sacramento River. These conditions changed, however, when the Contract and Finance Company took over the construction of the railroad from Sacramento to San José. The Central Pacific interest then obtained a connection of its own with Niles near Oakland, and it was thus led to consider the question of terminals on the eastern side of San Francisco Bay.

The easiest part of San Francisco Bay for the Western Pacific Railroad to reach was undoubtedly the shore south of Oakland or Alameda. It would probably have been possible to build from Stockton to Richmond, as the Santa Fé did later, or to develop Benicia or Port Costa, or even to build a terminus

on an island in the bay. Yet as compared with these alternatives, the Oakland terminus had many advantages. It was
near to the Western Pacific main line; it was served by two
railroads which possessed valuable franchises that could be
bought at not too great expense; and, most important of all,
the conditions under which the water-front at Oakland was
held were favorable to the acquisition of the necessary terminal
facilities.

Oakland Water-Front

The situation at Oakland was briefly as follows: The first
army of settlers in the city had been squatters on a portion of
the Peralta grant. Among these had been Horace W.
Carpentier, Edson Adams, and A. J. Moon. In 1852 the state
legislature had incorporated the town of Oakland, had fixed
its boundary, and had granted to it the land lying between high
tide and ship channel along the whole of its water-front, with
a view to facilitating the construction of walls and other
improvements.[4] There were 75 to 100 inhabitants in Oakland
at this time, with half a dozen residences, two hotels, a wharf,
and two warehouses. There were no streets—only cattle trails.[5]

As soon as incorporated, the town held an election, and
chose Adams, Moon, Carpentier, and two others as trustees.
Mr. Carpentier did not qualify or serve. On May 17 and 18,
1852, the board of trustees made two important grants: In the
first place, it gave to Horace Carpentier for the period of
thirty-seven years, the exclusive right to construct wharves,
piers, and docks at any point within the corporate limits of
Oakland, with the right of collecting wharfage and dockage;
and in the second place, it sold, granted, and released to the
said Carpentier all the town title in the land lying within the

---

[4] Laws of California, 1852, Ch. 107.

[5] City of Oakland v. Oakland Water Front Company, transcript of testimony, p. 649,
deposition Horace W. Carpentier; p. 1755, testimony A. J. Moon.

limits of the town of Oakland between high tide and ship channel.

In return for this grant Carpentier agreed to build three wharves and a schoolhouse, and to pay to the town 2 per cent of his wharfage receipts—certainly a modest recompense. Mr. Marier, president of the board of trustees, later testified that Carpentier told him when the deed was signed that he would be willing at any time to reconvey the property to the town on being reimbursed for the moneys he had expended; and this was also the recollection of others.[6]   But the understanding, if any existed, never could be enforced,[7] so that Carpentier was firmly established in his control of the tide-lands of the city of Oakland, and in spite of petitions, riots, and litigation, sat unshaken in 1867 when the Central Pacific became interested in the matter.[8]

Oakland Water Front Company

Sometime prior to 1867 Carpentier had several talks with Leland Stanford, and endeavored to persuade him to build north from Niles across the Ravenswood cut-off.   In the fall of 1867, Carpentier and Stanford talked again, and Stanford came to entertain the idea as a matter of reasonable negotiation. John P. Felton was engaged by the city of Oakland to look into its rights.   Carpentier says that he offered the railroad one-half of his water-front if it would make his property its terminus.   He says that this mode of adjustment was acquiesced in by Mayor Merritt and Mr. Felton, and that about the end of the year (1867), it came to be understood between them and Governor Stanford and himself that something

---

6 City of Oakland v. Oakland Water Front Company, transcript of testimony, pp. 704–5, deposition Horace W. Carpentier; Wood, "History of Alameda County"; *San Francisco Examiner*, June 26, 1892, July 3, 1892.

7 Moon, one of the trustees who approved the grant, was afterwards taken into Carpentier's employ.   Adams, another trustee, secured the property now known as the "Adams Wharf" to the east of the narrow-gauge bridge.

8 City of Oakland v. Carpentier, 13 Cal. 540 (1859); 21 Cal. 642 (1863).   The Oakland ordinances were ratified and confirmed by act of the California legislature passed May 15, 1861.   (Laws of California, 1861, Ch. 377.)

should be done on approximately this basis.[9] Judge E. B. Crocker, however, attorney for the Central Pacific, asked that outstanding disputes regarding the water-front be first settled. The legislature was soon to be in session, and it was urged that all should act together in trying to get an authorization for the settlement of difficulties.

This was done.[10] On the 27th of March, 1868, as a part of a series of compromise arrangements, the Oakland Water Front Company was incorporated. The subscribers and original directors were H. W. Carpentier, president; Samuel Merritt, vice-president; Lloyd Tevis, secretary; Leland Stanford, treasurer; E. R. Carpentier and J. B. Felton. Mr. Tevis and H. W. Carpentier were in the same year directors of the Southern Pacific Railroad Company. The Oakland Water Front Company was capitalized for $5,000,000, and the stock was divided into 50,000 shares. Of these shares H. W. Carpentier subscribed for 23,000, or 46 per cent; Stanford for 17,500, or 35 per cent; and Felton for 4,999, or 10 per cent. Lloyd Tevis took 2,500 shares, E. R. Carpentier 2,000 shares, and Samuel Merritt 1 share.

On March 31, Mr. Carpentier deeded to the new corporation all the water-front of the city of Oakland, that is to say, all the lands, and the lands covered with water lying between high tide and ship channel, being the water-front lands described in and granted in the act of incorporation of May 4, 1852. He excepted from this deed only that water-front lying between the middle of Washington Street and the middle of Franklin Street and extending southerly to a line parallel with First Street. By Section 2 of an agreement made the following day, the Oakland Water Front Company agreed to deed this last-named area to the city of Oakland.[11]

---

[9] City of Oakland v. Oakland Water Front Company, transcript on appeal, pp. 652–54, deposition Horace W. Carpentier.

[10] Laws of California, 1868, Ch. 230.

[11] City of Oakland v. Oakland Water Front Company, transcript of testimony, *sup. cit.* pp. 976–80.

Cession of Land by Water Front Company

On April 1, 1868, two further agreements were signed. One, styled an indenture, was between the Oakland Water Front Company, the Western Pacific Railroad Company, Carpentier, Felton, and Stanford. Under this indenture, and in consideration of the deed of March 31, the Oakland Water Front Company declared that it held the property conveyed to it subject to covenants which were particularly set forth as follows:

The Western Pacific Railroad agreed to select within three months 500 acres from the property conveyed by the deed of March 31, including not more than one-half mile of frontage on ship channel, together with not to exceed two strips of land over the remainder of the premises from high-water mark to the parcels selected. The strips running from high-water mark were each to be not more than 100 feet wide at grade.

The Oakland Water Front Company agreed to convey to the Western Pacific Railroad the 500 acres selected, and to grant an exclusive right-of-way over the hundred-foot strips. It undertook, moreover, to sell no land west of the 500 acres, provided that these were located out to a westerly water-front of 24 feet depth of water at low tide, and to place no obstructions in front of them, or to do anything to obstruct the free approach of vessels to the parcels.

The Water Front Company further agreed to convey to the city of Oakland on demand "so much of the premises as [lay] between the middle of Franklin Street and the easterly line of Webster Street, and extending out to a line parallel with First Street, and two hundred feet southerly of the present wharf at the foot of Broadway," with the right of wharfage, dockage, and tolls thereon, and to designate and dedicate as a navigable water course for public use, the channel of San Antonio Creek, from ship channel to the town of San Antonio, to a width of not less than 200 feet over the shallow water at the bar, and 300 feet wide above that place.

The Water Front Company, in the third place, undertook to convey 25,000 shares of its stock to Carpentier, 5,000 shares to Felton, and 20,000 shares to Stanford.

Finally, the Water Front Company authorized the city of Oakland, or other parties, to construct a dam above the Oakland bridge, across the estuary, so as to keep the land above submerged to high-tide mark, for the use of the owners of the adjoining lands, and of the public.

The second paper, also signed on April 1, was an agreement between the Western Pacific Railroad Company, Leland Stanford, and the Water Front Company. By it the railroad agreed to construct or to purchase within eighteen months and to complete a railroad from its main line, then at Niles, to and connecting with the parcels of land described in the indenture of the same date, together with the necessary buildings and structures for a freight and passenger depot on the premises. The railroad agreed to expend in new work within three years $500,000. The railroad company agreed that in construction across the estuary between Oakland proper and Brooklyn it would leave a space for forty feet free for the passage of vessels.[12]

Attitude of City

Up to this point the city had not entered into any contracts. On April 1, however, the city council passed an ordinance ratifying and confirming the grants made under the early ordinances of 1852 and 1853, and the conveyance by Mr. Marier as president of the board of trustees, and granted, sold, and conveyed to the said Carpentier in fee simple forever, the city water-front, that is to say, the lands lying between high

---

[12] City of Oakland v. Oakland Water Front Company, transcript of testimony, pp. 657-64, deposition Horace W. Carpentier.

tide and ship channel. This ordinance further provided that Carpentier should convey to the Oakland Water Front Company the property and franchises conveyed at that time by the city to him, to be used in accordance with the terms and stipulations of the contract between the Oakland Water Front Company, the Western Pacific Railroad Company, and other parties. On the following day the council passed still another ordinance reciting that inasmuch as the terms and stipulations previously provided had been complied with by Carpentier, the grant was finally settled upon him.[13]

The result of these somewhat complicated negotiations was that the Central Pacific acquired 500 acres of water-front property in Oakland, with a frontage of one-half mile on ship channel, merely as a reward for coming to the city. In addition, Mr. Stanford, acting presumably on behalf of his associates, received 40 per cent of the capital stock of the Oakland Water Front Company, which on its part owned substantially all of the water-front remaining. The city attorney, who was supposed to represent the interests of the city, was rewarded with 10 per cent of the stock of the Oakland Water Front Company, and the position of director. The mayor of the city, Mr. Merritt, was made vice-president of the same corporation, although the extent of his personal interest in it is not known. He seems to have held only qualifying shares.[14]

---

[13] See the Ordinance of the City of Oakland, No. 302 (April 2, 1868). An excellent account of these transactions is given in an unpublished manuscript in the University of California Library, prepared by Stephen S. Barrows, one-time student in the University of California. It is of some interest to observe that among the direct beneficiaries of the agreements cited were Messrs. Carpentier, Felton, and Merritt, all three at one time or other mayors of Oakland. Mr. Merritt was mayor at the time ordinances Nos. 300, 301, and 302 were passed. The compromise described was effected under authority of an act of the California legislature dated March 21, 1868.

[14] By ordinance passed August 31, 1867, the Oakland City Council voted to pay Mr. Felton a fee equal to 15 per cent of all the property recovered by the city in the water-front litigation. (Transcript of testimony, *sup. cit.* p. 759.) Mr. Merritt was subsequently accused of having promoted the settlement between the city of Oakland and the Oakland Water Front Company in order to derive a pecuniary profit for himself. In 1869 the city council of Oakland authorized the appointment of a committee of three to ascertain by what title Mr. Merritt held certain water-front property near the foot of Broadway in Oakland. On report of the committee the council exonerated Mr. Merritt. (*Ibid.*, pp. 1406–7, 1410–21.)

In subsequent years the relations between the city of Oakland and the Oakland Water Front Company were repeatedly subjects of most bitter controversy. Extravagant as had been the consideration of the grant to the Central Pacific for coming to Oakland, this matter was less serious than the circumstance that the control of the remaining water-front by the Central Pacific through the Oakland Water Front Company appeared to make it impossible for any rival transportation company to gain a footing in the city. The city long endeavored to free itself from this monopoly. It contended at one time that Carpentier had secured the election of his own agents to the board of trustees which had made his grant, and that in any case Carpentier had agreed to reconvey the property to the city. Neither statement could be proved. On the contrary, in 1897 the Supreme Court of California definitely pronounced the compromise of 1868 binding upon the municipality, although it interpreted the words "ship channel" to mean the low-tide line and not a depth of three fathoms at low tide as had at first been supposed.[15]

Water-Front Monopoly Broken

Ten years later the title of the Oakland Water Front Company was again questioned in a case brought by the Western Pacific Railroad Company. By this time two jetties had been built by the United States government extending the lines of San Antonio Creek westward to deep water. As a result of the deposit of material taken out of the channel of the estuary and placed north of the northern training wall, and of additional deposits from dredging operations conducted by the Central Pacific and by private parties, the line of low tide had been moved appreciably out into the bay. Under the general rule that accretions belong to the proprietors of riparian lands, the Southern Pacific, as successor to the Oakland Water Front

---

[15] City of Oakland v. Oakland Water Front Company, 118 Cal. 160 (1897).

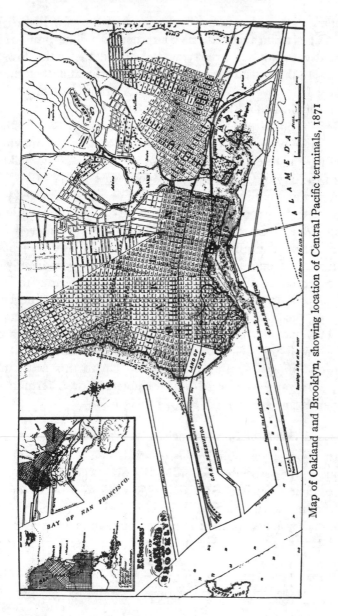

Map of Oakland and Brooklyn, showing location of Central Pacific terminals, 1871

Company, asserted title up to the limit of the new line of low tide. This claim the federal court denied. The limit of the railroad company's property was declared to be the low-tide line of 1852, extending first northwesterly and then northeasterly from the mouth of the San Antonio estuary at Sand Point as indicated in the map on page 93.[16]

This at one stroke transformed the Southern Pacific's holding from a water-front to an interior location, by making it clear that the title to the substantial area between the bulkhead line of the city of Oakland and the low-water mark of 1852 lay in the city and not in private hands. The city had indeed given away its water-front as it existed in 1852, but the creation of a new water-front during the following years relieved it of the effects of its negligence. It thus appears that the alienation of the water-front of Oakland in 1868 did not permanently vest in the Central Pacific interest control of the tide-lands to which the compromise of that year referred. For the time being, however, the company secured a well-nigh complete monopoly. Not only had it convenient access to tide-water for its own trains, but it was able for many years to keep other railroads from obtaining a similar advantage. Up to this point, however, no arrangement had been completed for a terminus on the San Francisco side of San Francisco Bay.

Proposed Grant of San Francisco Water-Front

In order to establish the Central Pacific with complete adequacy, the associates accordingly now turned to the western side of San Francisco Bay and took steps to provide terminal facilities in the city of San Francisco itself. Possibly this was because they had acquired or were about to acquire a controlling interest in the San Francisco and San José Railroad; pos-

---

[16] Western Pacific Railway Company v. Southern Pacific Company, 151 Fed. 376 (1907). The court also pointed out in the decision that although the low-tide line was projected across the mouth of the estuary for the purpose of determining the boundary of Oakland, this should not be done in ascertaining the limit of the railroad grant.

sibly it was due to Carpentier's influence, or perhaps it was merely a recognition of the advantages of a terminal location in San Francisco.

Unlike Oakland, the city of San Francisco had never received title to all its tide-lands from the state, and application had to be made to the legislature at Sacramento, direct. Early in 1868 the Senate Committee on Commerce and Navigation, of the state legislature, reported a bill granting to the Western Pacific Railroad Company and to the Southern Pacific Railroad Company, submerged and tide-lands in the Bay of San Francisco, from the foot of Channel Street to Point San Bruno, with the right to extend the railroads of said companies or construct branches thereof, and to purchase other railroads, and use the same for the purpose of reaching the place or places on said premises selected as termini for said railroads, and to maintain and operate the same by steam or other power from the present lines of said railroads to the said termini on said premises, and with all necessary and proper depots, side-tracks, etc.

The boundaries of this extraordinary grant are indicated on the map on page 96.[17]

The total length from the foot of Channel Street to Point San Bruno was a little over 8 miles. The maximum breadth was approximately 2½ miles, and the area was estimated by opponents of the scheme to be not less than 6,620 acres. The value of such a water-front on the principal city of the Pacific Coast was to be measured in millions of dollars, and its importance to the Huntington interests was not limited to a money value alone. The possession of the San Francisco water-front south of Channel Street meant the occupation of the only part of the city at which a first-class railroad could reach tide-water. The reason for this is that all railroads must come into the city

---

[17] The boundaries are set forth in the *San Francisco Times* of March 7, 1868. As later amended and confined to the area north of Point Avisadero, they are described in the *Daily Alta* of March 14, 1868.

of San Francisco from the south or the southwest on account of the shape of the peninsula, and no railroad can conceivably be allowed to cross the main thoroughfare, Market Street, or to penetrate the thinly settled residential districts in the north.

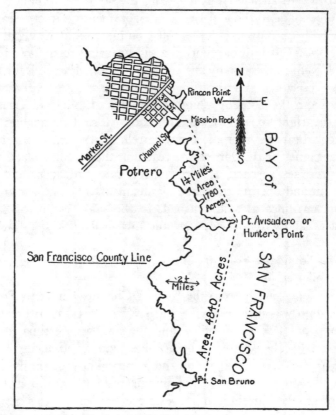

Boundaries of Railroad Tide-Land Grant, as proposed in 1868.

The bill provided that the Central Pacific, Western Pacific, Southern Pacific, and the San Francisco and San José railroads, which were the proposed grantees, should pay the fair market cash value of the submerged lands at the time of the passage of the act, being not less than $100 per acre for the lands lying north of Point Avisadero. But it was also provided that the surplus over $100 due for the land north of Point Avisadero might be spent in reclamation and improvement of the premises, and the companies were to receive patents if within five years not less than $1,000,000, in addition to such surplus, had been spent in this way. In plain English, the tide-lands were to be sold for $100 an acre, but in the case of some of them the beneficiaries might be required to spend additional amounts in improvements. The Senate committee defended its recommendation by saying that it was desirable to have the water-front improved, and that this was the way to have the thing done. It expected that the railroads would build a sea-wall; and observed that this wall, water-front, and docks would be subject to the control of the state harbor commissioners. How a rival railroad in the future would get access to the docks, it did not say.[18]

Scheme Opposed

Generally speaking, arrangements for the alienation of city water-front property into private hands are to be looked upon with suspicion unless extensive powers of control are reserved by state or city, and unless there is provision for the reversion of the property, including improvements, to the public at the end of a stipulated time not too far removed, on conditions and in a manner clearly stated. In the particular case in hand there were no such safe-guards to the public interest, except a general reservation of jurisdiction and control over the water-front by the State Board of Harbor Commissioners, and a provision that the grantees should charge no tolls or wharfage on the water-front sold to them. This was not enough. It was therefore fortunate under the circumstances that the improvident

---

[18] Appendix to journals of Senate and Assembly of the California Legislature, 17th Session, Vol. 3, 1868.

nature of the proposed contract was understood and its defects given full publicity by the San Francisco press. The *San Francisco Bulletin* commented as follows:

> The scheme is an outrageous one. A proposition to sell to the Railroad Companies at a reasonable price, so much of the southern water-front as would be actually necessary for depots, warehouses, workshops, etc., might be considered favorably, but a proposal to give to what is or will be virtually a single corporation two-thirds of the frontage of a city destined to be the second in America, is utterly indefensible . . . this immense property will be worth eventually as much as the Pacific Railroad itself.[19]

The *Alta* said:

> If the parties who have so modestly presented their humble petition for this concession had gone one step farther, and asked for a grant of the whole State of California—all its tide and marsh lands—the control of all its rivers, bays and inlets, we do not know that the public amazement would have been any greater.[20]

Even the conservative *San Francisco Times* suggested that it would be well for the railroad companies to submit detailed estimates of the land needed for terminals and the uses to which this land was to be put,[21] while it refrained from commenting on the *Bulletin's* assertions that it was the intent of the railroads to locate their terminus well south of the city of San Francisco to the great profit of parties from Sacramento who were buying lands around Hunter's Point.

Another Plan Substituted

Whether or not this last accusation was well founded, the opposition of the city grew so intense that the legislature did

[19] *San Francisco Bulletin,* March 7, 1868.
[20] *Daily Alta California,* March 10, 1868.
[21] *San Francisco Times,* March 13, 1868.

not dare to carry out its original plan.[22] Instead, the Southern Pacific and Western Pacific were offered each 150 acres, to be located by the companies within specified limits south of Channel Street, and still later the amount was reduced to 30 acres apiece, and a donation was substituted for a sale. So amended, the act became law on March 30, 1868. It granted and donated to the Southern Pacific Railroad Company and to the Western Pacific Railroad Company for a terminus in the city of San Francisco, to each of said companies, 30 acres, exclusive of streets, basements, public squares, and docks. The land was to be selected by the railroad companies within ninety days, but it was to lie south of Channel Street, and outside of the Red-Line water-front of Mission Bay, and was not to extend beyond 24 feet of water at low tide, nor to within 300 feet of the line which should be selected by the tide-land commissioners as the permanent water line of the front of the city. A 200-foot right-of-way was given to the companies to provide access to their tide-lands. The lands were to be located and $100,000 spent upon them by each of the grantees within thirty months, or the grant would revert to the state.[23]

Compared with their original projects, the Act of 1868 represented a considerable check to the plans of Mr. Stanford and his friends. Yet the grant in San Francisco was important, and, added to what had been secured in Oakland, provided satisfactorily for the Central Pacific's transportation needs.

In 1871 the San Francisco supervisors granted to the Southern Pacific and Central Pacific railroads rights on various streets in the city in order that they might reach and enjoy their lands and depot grounds in Mission Bay. Late in the same year Stanford indicated his willingness to make Mission Bay the main terminus of both the Central Pacific and Southern

---

[22] See resolutions of a meeting of San Francisco business men in March, 1868, recommending that the legislature grant 150 acres each to the Central Pacific and Southern Pacific; and the admission of the Southern Pacific that it could get along with 250 acres.

[23] Laws of California, 1867–68, Ch. 543.

Pacific, in consideration of a subsidy of $3,000,000 and of alterations in the terms of the Mission Bay grant so as to make it more acceptable. Nothing came of these last negotiations, nor of somewhat similar proposals made in 1872 by a citizens' committee engaged in fighting the Goat Island scheme (see below) and submitted to popular vote. In 1873-74, however, the city granted Stanford additional though minor franchises, enabling him to run trains on certain city streets.

Proposed Occupation of Goat Island

It will be readily understood that feeling ran high both in Oakland and San Francisco while the railroad negotiations for terminal facilities were going on. Nor was the public excitement allayed by the attempt of the Huntington group to occupy Goat Island, which occurred at the same time. Goat Island, formerly known as "Yerba Buena" Island, is a small body of land lying about midway between San Francisco and Oakland. Reference to the inset accompanying the map of Oakland will show its exact location. It is obvious enough why the Central Pacific wanted the use of this island and of the mud flats lying directly north. It is just as obvious why, in the absence of regulation, the public should have objected to its exclusive occupation by any single railroad company. Yet, in March, 1868, one day after the action granting to the Central Pacific and to the Southern Pacific 60 acres of tide-lands in San Francisco, the state legislature granted to the Terminal Central Pacific Railroad Company—a corporation controlled by the associates —a defined area not to exceed 150 acres of the submerged shoal lands north of the island, with the right to reclaim these lands for railroad depot and commercial purposes, and to connect them by a bridge with the Oakland, Alameda, and Contra Costa shores. The company agreed to pay the fair appraised value of the lands into the state treasury, and to put into operation within four years a first-class rail and ferry communication between the city of San Francisco, the premises conveyed to it, Oakland and Vallejo.[24]

Two years later the time for the completion of the promised road was extended, and a railway to the Straits of Carquinez, opposite Vallejo, was accepted as sufficient to fulfil the requirement of a line to the town of Vallejo itself,[25] and in 1871 a still further extension of time was given. The road which the Southern Pacific proposed to build was probably that indicated in the notice of new construction filed at Sacramento in March, 1867—that is to say, it was a line running from Sacramento east of the Sacramento River past Freeport, crossing the mouth of the San Joaquin River, and continuing west through Antioch and over the hills to San Francisco Bay. Such a road could easily have been brought to Carquinez Straits, but it could not have reached Vallejo. The associates did not at this time intend to enter the territory west of the Sacramento River.

Project Lapses

Following the vote of the California legislature, a bill was introduced in Congress, providing for the grant to the Central Pacific Company of the right to use Goat Island itself. This logical sequence to the state legislation was opposed by the United States military authorities and by the city of San Francisco. It appeared that residents of San Francisco anticipated the permanent loss of a large part of the transcontinental business if the Central Pacific should occupy Goat Island. The *San Francisco Bulletin* insisted that there was room enough on the island and on the adjacent flat to accommodate all the warehouses and large shipping, mercantile, and financial establishments of a seaport of 500,000 inhabitants. It was stated

---

[24] Laws of California, 1867–68, Ch. 386. A lively account of the circumstances attending the passage of the Goat Island bill through the legislature was published by an old newspaper man, Sam Leake by name, in the *San Francisco Bulletin*, March 17 and 19, 1917. There is, however, no way of verifying this story, and it cannot be accepted on Mr. Leake's authority alone.

[25] Laws of California, 1869–70, Ch. 381.

that the advantages of the location would draw the warehouses, that other firms would follow, and that men who had business on the island would not live in San Francisco, but would make their homes on the eastern side of the Bay where land was cheaper, more level, and more fertile. These statements were generally believed.

Nothing was done in 1869, 1870, or 1871 beyond the steps just mentioned. In March, 1872, however, the San Francisco chamber of commerce passed resolutions and prepared a memorial addressed to the President and to Congress opposing the proposed grant, and a mass meeting was held in San Francisco to make public protest. Following this, conferences were held between a committee of citizens and the president of the Central Pacific in the hope of arriving at some general understanding relative to terminal facilities, and eventually the whole Goat Island project lapsed.[26]

Purchase of Other Roads

By the middle of 1868 the Central Pacific had thus secured satisfactory water-front facilities in both Oakland and San Francisco, amounting in the case of the former city, through the Oakland Water Front Company, to monopoly control. Needless to say, it had also abundant accommodations at Sacramento. Through the Southern Pacific Railroad it had also franchises in San Francisco, including the right to maintain tracks in the vicinity of Third and Townsend Streets. Up to August, 1868, however, it does not seem to have made the connections between its main line and Oakland that were necessary to enable its trains to reach San Francisco Bay at all. In that month Stanford, Huntington, Hopkins, and Crocker

---

[26] Mr. Stanford has asserted that the whole trouble was caused by six gentlemen, three of whom had interests near Ravenswood, where it was thought that the Central Pacific might cross, and three of whom had interests in Sausalito. He says he was informed by a member of Congress that he could have had necessary legislation in Congress for $10,000. This refers to the campaign of 1875–76. (United States Pacific Railway Commission, pp. 3170–71, testimony Leland Stanford.)

bought a majority of the stock of the San Francisco and Oakland Railroad, and the following year they purchased likewise the San Francisco and Alameda Railroad. The first-named company had 2 or 3 miles of track eastward from Oakland's point. The Alameda company had about 16 to 18 miles. Both had valuable franchises, and both owned ferry-boats and piers extending some distance into the bay. In 1870 both of the companies were joined in the San Francisco, Oakland and Alameda Railroad, and in the same year this company was consolidated with the Central Pacific. By 1869 the gap between the end of the San Francisco and Alameda Railroad and Niles had been filled, and this in a real sense completed the transcontinental line.

CHAPTER VI

ACQUISITION OF THE CALIFORNIA PACIFIC

Tendency to Monopoly Control

The first intimation that the Central Pacific Railroad was on its way to something like a monopoly control in the state of California is to be found in the negotiations for terminals on San Francisco Bay. But it was not long before more evidence came to light. Looking back with the advantage of knowledge of the company's later history, it seems probable that the possibilities of monopoly control of the railway business of California were present to the owners of the Central Pacific as early as 1868. The task of securing such control was not, after all, so very great. California had few railroads in the sixties, and those which were in operation were small and unprosperous, and could be cheaply acquired.

Besides this, the topography of the state lent itself to schemes of conquest by a sharp separation of the interior valleys from each other and from the coast. It was not necessary to occupy the whole country, for an effective control over one valley could be maintained in spite of the fact that an adjacent valley was in hostile hands. Nor was there any public opinion in California at the time thoughtfully critical of monopoly, as such. The country was new. Theories covering the relations of large corporations to the consuming public had not been developed. People hated monopolies because monopolies meant high prices; but the very persons who were most likely to object to monopoly were also likely to seek positions of advantage for themselves when possible.

Under conditions like these, Stanford, Huntington, Hopkins, and Crocker were almost sure to attempt to dominate the railway system of the state as soon as they determined to make their connection with it more than temporary. This decision was made as the Central Pacific approached Ogden in 1868 and 1869. Had the associates been able to sell out before this time, it is likely that they would have done so. Indeed, it is credibly reported that 80 per cent of the stock of the Central Pacific was offered to D. O. Mills as late as 1873, for a price of $20,000,000,[1] and this was probably the last of several offers made to different parties.

The evidence seems to show, however, that by 1870 the Huntington group were inclined to remain in the railroad business. Strategically, the associates then occupied a very strong position. They possessed the only railroad line from California to the East. They dominated the Oakland water-front, and held important concessions in San Francisco. Branch lines, like long tentacles, stretched from Roseville north to Chico, on the way to the Oregon state line,[2] and from Lathrop south to Modesto, to be extended to Goshen by August 1, 1872.[3] By 1869 the Sacramento Valley Railroad, with its extension to Placerville, had been bought, and the California Central Railroad from Folsom to Marysville was under Central Pacific control. Even the budding project for a Southern Pacific Railroad had received the attention of Stanford and his associates. Indeed, the only really weak spots in the associates' position were their failure fully to occupy the San Joaquin Valley, and

---

[1] United States Pacific Railway Commission, pp. 3496-3500, testimony D. O. Mills.

[2] The California and Oregon Railroad Company was subsidized by Congress by Act of July 25, 1866, to build from a point on the Central Pacific Railroad to the Oregon boundary, where it was to meet a railroad coming south from Portland. Tracks reached Chico, July 2, 1870. In 1870, the California and Oregon was consolidated with the Central Pacific. In 1872 it reached Redding, and on October 5, 1887, the state line. The federal legislation relating to the California and Oregon Railroad is notable for the liberality of the land grant made.

[3] This branch was known as the San Joaquin Valley Railroad. The company bearing this name was incorporated in 1868. Stanford, Huntington, Hopkins, Charles, and E. B. Crocker were directors. In 1870 it was consolidated with the Central Pacific. Stanford declared in 1887 that the trunk lines up the San Joaquin and Sacramento valleys were the most important factors in the Central Pacific's local business.

the fact that they did not control the short line between Sacramento and San Francisco. We will, accordingly, consider the

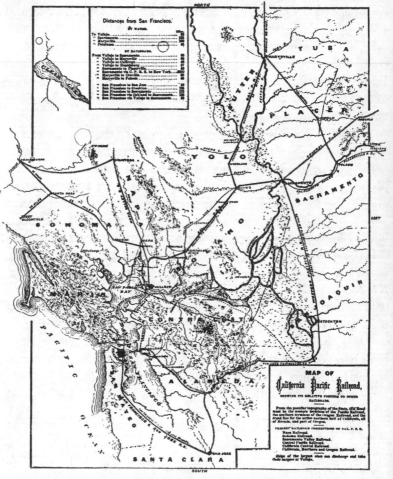

Map of California Railroad, about 1870.

situation and the policy of the Huntington group in these respects.

Competition of California Pacific

The most direct railroad route from Sacramento to San Francisco is by way of Vallejo or Benicia, across the Straits of Carquinez, and along the eastern shore of San Francisco Bay. In 1865, after the Central Pacific had begun work in earnest, the California Pacific Railroad Company was incorporated to occupy this route from Sacramento as far as Vallejo. Contracts were let, though no material progress was made for two years. In 1867 the work was taken up with fresh energy, and in 1869 the road was finished between Vallejo and Sacramento, with a branch from Davisville to Marysville. The newly built Napa Valley Railroad from Adalanta, California, to Calistoga, was acquired at the same time. In 1870 the system reported 163 miles of road, of which 22 miles consisted of a ferry connection from Vallejo to the city of San Francisco.

It seems more probable that the California Pacific was originally intended as a connection for the Central Pacific than that it was built as a competitor with the larger road. This was satisfactory enough to the Central Pacific so long as this company terminated at Sacramento. But there is no manner of doubt that the California Pacific became a formidable competitor to the Central Pacific when the latter acquired its circuitous line to Oakland via Stockton. This was especially true with respect to the passenger business. The distance from Sacramento to San Francisco via Vallejo was 87 miles, via Stockton 137½ miles; the time via Vallejo was 3½ hours, via Stockton 5 hours. It appears that transcontinental passengers on Central Pacific trains often changed cars at Sacramento, sacrificing the balance of their through ticket and paying extra fare in order to save time.[4] Of the local passenger business between Sacramento and San Francisco, the California Pacific claimed three-fourths. How large a share

---

[4] United States Pacific Railway Commission, pp. 3628–29, testimony J. P. Jackson; p. 3613, testimony Leland Stanford.

of the freight went by the shorter line does not appear, but it must have been considerable, for Mr. Stubbs later estimated that the cost of operating the Benicia route could not have been more than 50 per cent of the cost of operating the Western Pacific,[5] and it is in evidence that the Central Pacific sent most of its freight via Benicia as soon as it obtained control of both lines.

It should be remembered also that in addition to its competition for local business, the California Pacific had ambitious plans in other directions. We know, for example, that it proposed an extension eastward via Beckwourth's Pass to a connection with the Union Pacific, at or near Ogden. This line was to be built by the California Pacific Railroad Eastern Extension Company, incorporated at Sacramento in March, 1871, with a capital stock of $50,000,000.[6] Other reports credited it with an intention to enter the San Joaquin Valley;[7] while its influence in Sonoma, Marin and Napa counties was recognized. In short, by 1870 the California Pacific was not only important in respect to what it had actually accomplished, but it had in it the germ of a railroad system in no way inferior to that of the Central Pacific itself.

Rival's Weakness

Unfortunately for the California Pacific, the company's physical and financial position in 1871 did not measure up to the magnitude of its ambitions. Counsel for the Central Pacific in later years drew a vivid picture of the condition of the railroad in 1867 which probably contained more than a grain of truth. According to this account, the right-of-way of the California Pacific was unfenced, its sidings were few, and its stations were insufficient. The road-bed was almost wholly

---

5 United States Pacific Railway Commission, pp. 3366–67, testimony J. C. Stubbs.

6 *Ibid.*, pp. 3628–29, testimony J. C. Jackson.

7 *San Francisco Bulletin*, November 29, 1869.

unballasted, and inadequately supplied with ties. Embankments were so narrow that the ends of the ties projected on both sides. The slope of the cuts was insufficient and upon the Napa branch the rails were fastened to the ties with wrought nails without heads which were bent back over the flanges of the rails after being partly driven, in order to hold the rails in position.[8]

On the other hand, in spite of the imperfect character of its construction, the California Pacific had paid large prices to contractors in its bonds and stock. In December, 1870, the company was compelled to borrow money to meet the January interest of 1871. By the following spring it was indebted to the extent of $8,450,000, of which $1,200,000 was floating debt, and had to prepare to meet an annual interest charge of $667,500. This was more than the company's earnings could stand.

In 1871 the Central Pacific, taking advantage of the weakness of its rival, proceeded to the attack by arranging to construct a branch from Sacramento, by way of Davisville, to Vallejo. In pursuance of this arrangement it accumulated iron and ties, made surveys, and succeeded in effecting a contract with an organization known as the Bridge Company of the City of Sacramento, for the exclusive use of its bridge for their new enterprise.[9] The California Pacific was already suffering from the competition of river boats, and the construction of the new road would have ruined it. The pressing nature of the danger was appreciated by the managers of the road, and Milton S. Latham, director and treasurer of the California Pacific, and agent for the holders of three-fourths of the capital stock of that company, promptly opened negotiations with the Central Pacific, through Collis P. Huntington,

---

8 Main v. Central Pacific, argument of Harvey S. Brown, of counsel for the defendants, 1886.

9 *San Francisco Chronicle*, August 16, 1874, statement Milton S. Latham. This was the bridge over which the California Pacific was entering Sacramento.

for an adjustment of difficulties. This was precisely the situation which the Central Pacific desired to bring about.

Control of California Pacific Acquired

The agreement that resulted from the conditions described may probably be explained as an elaboration of the Central Pacific's statement to Mr. Latham that the company was willing to buy the California Pacific but did not have the money. It took the form of the following consecutive transactions:

By agreement dated July 13, 1871, between Latham, Leland Stanford, and Mark Hopkins, Mr. Latham agreed to deliver 76,101 shares of the California Pacific Railroad Company, to assign three-fourths of the capital stock of the California Pacific Eastern Railroad Extension Company to the other parties to the contract, and to stipulate that the total indebtedness of the two companies named should not exceed $8,421,000. In consideration of this delivery, Stanford and Hopkins agreed to pay to Latham $1,579,000 in bonds of the California Pacific Railroad Company.

On August 9, 1871, Mr. Latham presented, and the directors of the California Pacific at a formal meeting approved, resolutions to the effect that the sum of $1,600,000 was necessary for the purpose of constructing and completing an additional track, and for strengthening the California Pacific embankments across the tule lands. The directors further voted that the money be borrowed, and the necessary bonds be issued. President Jackson then stated to the board that a contract had been made, and the execution of this contract was approved.

Under date of August 9, 1871, the California Pacific covenanted with Stanford, Hopkins, and Huntington for the construction referred to in the previous paragraph. The associates agreed

> . . . to enlarge the embankment of the railroad of the said party of the second part, where embankment is required, and

erect and widen the trestle work, where trestle work is required,
from the bridge across the Sacramento River to Davisville,
in the county of Yolo, in the State of California, and place
thereon a good and sufficient superstructure, consisting of timber and ties and iron railroad thereon, so as to make an additional railroad track from said bridge to said Davisville, fully
equal to the present railroad on the present embankment and
to connect the same with proper switches with both the main
track to Vallejo, and the track to Marysville of the railroads
of the party of the second part. Said parties of the first part
to furnish all the material for the said additional railroad track,
and embankment, and trestle work, and to have the same completed and ready for use on or before the first day of January,
in the year one thousand eight hundred and seventy-three.

In consideration of this construction, the California Pacific
was to pay the associates 1,600 second mortgage California
Pacific bonds.

On August 19, 1871, the Huntington group, now controlling a majority of the board of directors of the California
Pacific, entered into an agreement with the California Pacific
under which the Central Pacific undertook to pay the California Pacific $5,000 per month, to furnish the equipment for
passenger business, and to guarantee the interest on 1,600
second mortgage bonds, while the California Pacific in return
agreed to transport to or from San Francisco, passengers beginning or ending their trips on the Central Pacific or connecting roads, and to maintain its fare for other passengers at $4 be-
tween San Francisco and Sacramento. On September 1, 1871,
the Central Pacific took full control of the California Pacific,
and moved its offices from San Francisco to Sacramento.[10]

Motives Behind Transactions

Two explanations of these transactions are possible. Counsel for the Central Pacific, in 1886, maintained that the con-

---

[10] Main v. Central Pacific. Statement of facts. The closing argument of L. E. Chittenden, of counsel for plaintiffs, 1886. See also *San Francisco Chronicle*, August 16, 1874,
statement of Milton S. Latham.

tracts fell into two distinct classes or groups. The California Pacific, according to this point of view, arranged for an additional track between Sacramento Bridge and Davisville, and for still more important enlargement in embankments and widening and erection of trestle work, by the transfer to defendants of second mortgage bonds. These bonds, it was alleged, though considerable in amount, had little value because of the desperate financial condition of the California Pacific. In the second place, the Central Pacific gave value to bonds which it held by a guaranty, and used them to buy a controlling interest in California Pacific stock. Of this, the minority stockholders of the corporation had no right to complain.

Counsel on the other side maintained that the essential feature of the whole transaction was the purchase of California Pacific stock, and that the various contracts merely supplied a method of buying this stock without paying for it. Starting, therefore, with the contract of July 13, they pointed out that the defendants agreed to purchase California Pacific stock from Latham with California Pacific bonds which were not yet in existence, stipulating for full control of the California Pacific before payment should be made, in order that they might obtain the purchase price from that company. When Latham anounced that he was ready to deliver the stock, it became necessary for the defendants to secure about $1,600,000 in California Pacific bonds. These bonds could be legally issued only for new construction, hence the contract for a second track from Sacramento to Davisville. When issued, and in the hands of the defendants, it was necessary to have the Central Pacific's guaranty. For this the Central Pacific required the California Pacific to enter into the traffic agreement of August 19, obtaining thus a full *quid pro quo*. The result was that the California Pacific furnished first the bonds and then a consideration for the Central Pacific's guaranty, which together served to purchase the California Pacific stock.

Plausible Explanation

There were several circumstances which made this second version plausible. It seems extraordinary, for one thing, that a company in the straits to which the California Pacific was reduced should have issued bonds for double-tracking 13 miles of road.[11] If it be answered that the strengthening of the road against the immediate danger of flood was the real reason for the issue, then it was still extraordinary that the time limit for construction of the work should be set as it was, eighteen months away, on January 1, 1873. As a matter of fact, the section of the California Pacific across the tule lands was washed away before the associates got around to strengthening it. This made it impossible for Stanford, Huntington, and Hopkins, or the Contract and Finance Company, to which they had assigned their contract, to carry out the original agreement. Instead, Mr. Montague, chief engineer of the California Pacific, reported to his board that the cost of restoring the washed-out line would be equal to the cost of carrying out the original contract, and the board, on November 15, 1872, authorized the substitution of this work for that agreed on in the contract of August 9, 1871.

Owing to the subsequent destruction of the books of the Contract and Finance Company, there is no way of telling accurately what the cost of restoration actually was. The Contract and Finance Company finished the job, however, in six weeks after the work was actually commenced, and what information is available leads one to doubt if the expense was very great. Another circumstance which raises a question as to the good faith of the consideration offered for the 1,600

---

[11] Opponents of the Central Pacific described the transaction in 1886 as follows: "Huntington, the incarnation of this hostility, whose name was an inspiration of personal aversion, entered the state on the 24th of June; and the suggestion is, that the Court shall believe that under these circumstances, the directors of the California Pacific loaded their staggering trust with a new debt of $1,600,000, on which interest should commence at once, to pay for a second track, not to be finished until about two years, at the small end of their railroad where there was no need of it, at a point where it was doubtful if one track would stand—and contracted with their hereditary enemies to do it—all without the remotest reference to any purchase of, or intended future control of the corporation!"

California Pacific bonds, is the coincidence that the par value of the bonds issued for construction was practically identical with the amount needed to pay for the 76,101 shares of stock sold by Latham to Stanford, Huntington, and Hopkins. Still another peculiar incident was that of the execution, contemporaneously with the main contract, of a supplementary agreement, under which the Stanford group agreed to pay Latham $250,000 in a six months' note, besides the other consideration for California Pacific stock, if he would visit New York at once, obtain the consent of the stockholders whom he represented, and personally assume all the obligations of the California Pacific above the sum of $8,421,000 specified in the bond.

Whatever the true motives for the transaction described, the coincidence of the stock sale with the other transactions relieved the representatives of the California Pacific of any intense interest in the matter, and must inevitably have made them pliable as to terms. The directors present at the meeting of August 9, when the contract for the construction of the second track was approved, were Jackson, Hammond, Latham, Sullivan, and Atherton. Of these gentlemen, Hammond, Sullivan, and Atherton each held five shares only, transferred to their names to qualify them as directors; while the shares of Latham and Jackson were ready for transfer to Stanford, Huntington, and Hopkins. Hammond, vice-president of the company, as well as a director, subsequently said, referring to the contract for a second track: "I don't recollect that I ever saw or knew what that contract was, until it was brought into the board . . . This contract was made with a party who was purchasing the majority of the stock of that company, and whose interest would be to do that work in a workmanlike manner." Certainly this was not a desirable point of view for a representative of the California Pacific to take.

Undisputed Control

The inevitable result of the various contracts and agreements which have been described was to place the Huntington group in undisputed control of the California Pacific. On August 10, 1871, Mr. Stanford was elected president *vice* Jackson, and on August 2, Mark Hopkins was elected treasurer *vice* Latham. The following year Hammond and Moses Hopkins took the positions of president and treasurer, respectively, while Stanford and Mark Hopkins and Collis P. Huntington were appointed general agents of the company, with large powers.

Once in control, Stanford and his associates proceeded to make the best use they could of the California Pacific in connection with other roads in their system. It does not appear that they felt any particular tenderness toward the enterprise. Most of the operating arrangements between the Central Pacific and the California Pacific were subsequently arranged by Mr. Towne for both parties, on terms favorable to the Central Pacific. It is on record that the California Pacific was allowed but $1 out of $16.75, the fare from Reno to San Francisco, for its haul from Sacramento to San Francisco, although the total distance was 240 miles, and the Sacramento–San Francisco haul amounted to 92 miles. Likewise, contracts were made with the Contract and Finance Company which were later complained of as extravagant. Special mention is made of lumber which was bought of the Contract and Finance Company at $30 a thousand when the market price was $18. Mr. Towne was asked in 1886:

> *Q.* You say that you have done all that you could to increase the earnings of the California Pacific, do you?
> *A.* Having a due regard for the other company; yes, sir.
> *Q.* Did you make that qualification?
> *A.* I do now.

Perhaps a policy of this sort was to be expected as the result of the conquest of a dangerous rival. Yet certain other arrangements between the Central Pacific and the California Pacific went beyond what one might have expected. It appears, for instance, that soon after the Stanford group obtained control of the last-named company, that portion of the contract of August 8, 1871, which provided for the payment of $5,000 monthly by the Central Pacific to the California Pacific, was eliminated. This elimination was said to have taken place by "mutual consent," a meaningless phrase when the same men had charge of the negotiations for both sides.

Independent Security Holders

It has been charged, also, that Stanford and Huntington deliberately endeavored at this time to depress the value of California Pacific mortgage securities in order to induce independent holders to reduce their claims. In support of this contention there is evidence that very strong pressure was brought to bear upon independent security holders in 1874, and that as a result of this pressure the fixed charges of the California Pacific were reduced from $763,500 in 1875, to $303,500 in 1886. No part of this burden was borne by the second mortgage bonds held by Stanford, Huntington, Hopkins, and Crocker, nor was any assessment levied upon the company's stock.

As a part of the campaign, during the period mentioned, wide publicity was given by the management of the California Pacific to financial difficulties, real or alleged, with which the company was confronted. Thus in June 1875, the board of directors confessed a judgment of $1,309,041.84 to one J. P. Haggin, assignee of certain claims of the Central Pacific, the Contract and Finance Company, and the associates, for advances previously made. Mr. Haggin had no interest in the matter, merely allowing the use of his name.[12] The following month, Vice-President Gray, of the California Pacific, made

---

[12] Colton case, pp. 3214-15.

an extremely pessimistic report to his directors, declaring that
the company's deficit to date was $1,370,061.71, and that a
large part of the outstanding bond issues of the company were
represented by no construction that he was able to discover.
On July 25, 1874, finally, a local capitalist named Michael
Reese, acting in all probability on behalf of the associates,
filed sensational charges against Mr. Latham, formerly general
manager of the California Pacific, which called forth as sensational a reply.[13] These various activities roused holders of
California Pacific Railroad Extension bonds to petition to have
the California Pacific declared bankrupt, and drew forth a
statement from the company, on the other hand, that it did not
regard these bonds as constituting a valid legal claim upon it.
The result was a compromise. The extension bondholders
surrendered their 7 per cent bonds for a reduced amount in
new 6 per cent securities, and the outstanding income bonds
likewise exchanged their holdings for 3 per cent bonds. Both
classes of bonds were guaranteed by the Central Pacific, and
in consideration of the guaranty the California Pacific was
leased to the Central Pacific on July 1, 1876, for 29 years, at a
rental of $550,000 per year, plus three-fourths of the net earn-
ings of the company above that amount. At a subsequent
period in December, 1879, when the Central Pacific was about
to turn a considerable volume of business over the short line
by way of Benicia, the California Pacific gave up its right to

---

[13] *San Francisco Chronicle*, August 16, 1874. According to A. A. Cohen, a San Francisco lawyer one time in the employ of the Central Pacific and intimately acquainted with
its policies, Stanford told Latham that he, Stanford, was extremely sorry that the Reese suit
had been commenced, and that it would not have been if he had known anything at all about
it. Cohen, however, made public the following letter, written by Stanford the day before
the suit was brought, which puts an altogether different face upon the matter. Stanford
wrote as follows:

"July 24th, 1874.

DEAR COHEN:
    Regret on your own account that you are so ill. Send Mr. Yost over particularly to re-
port, and carry this message. Michael Reese is willing to commence suit as stockholder.
Please transfer to him 150 shares of your stock in the California Pacific. Hoping to hear
a more favorable account of your health, I remain,

Yours truly,
STANFORD."

The inference from this letter is, of course, that the Reese suit was brought at Stanford's own instance.

payments over the $550,000 minimum in consideration of a fixed additional payment of $50,000 a year.[14]

By and large, the California Pacific proved a good investment for the larger company, especially after the Northern Railway had been built and a new route established between Oakland and Sacramento. The reason for its original acquisition was, nevertheless, in all probability, not the chance of a direct profit, but the advantage expected from a monopolistic control of the territory north of San Francisco Bay.

---

[14] United States Pacific Railway Commission, pp. 3936–42, testimony L. E. Chittenden.

CHAPTER VII

BUILDING OF THE SOUTHERN PACIFIC

San Francisco and San José Railroad

The Huntington interests had secured control of the California Pacific. The next logical step was to strengthen the position of the Central Pacific south of San Francisco Bay. A start in this direction had already been made through the construction of a branch from Lathrop on the Central Pacific to Goshen in the San Joaquin Valley, finished in August, 1872. But this was not enough. Not only did the Central Pacific fail to reach the city of San Francisco, but the company was threatened in 1869 with the possibility that an independent Southern Railroad system might be created, no less ambitious than the California Pacific, and penetrating a richer if less developed territory. This projected system was that of the Southern Pacific Railroad, and in respect to it Mr. Stanford frankly said some years afterwards:

> Well, the necessity of obtaining control of the Southern Pacific Railroad was based really upon the act of Congress providing for its construction. It became apparent that if that last was constructed entirely independent to those who were interested in the Central Pacific, it would become a dangerous rival not only for the through business from the Atlantic Ocean, but it would enter into active competition for the local business of California. It was of paramount importance that the road should be controlled by the friends of the Central Pacific; and all our anticipations consequent upon the control of that road have been realized.[1]

The small beginning of what later came to be known as the Southern Pacific Railroad system is to be found in the San

---

[1] United States Pacific Railway Commission, p. 3614, testimony Leland Stanford.

Francisco and San José Railroad, which ran from San Francisco down the peninsula in a southerly direction to the city of San José. Originally this company was a local project only, and for some years an unsuccessful one. Several parties tried their hands at building it, but failed because they could not raise the necessary funds. In 1860 the project was taken up by a group of local capitalists of more than ordinary energy and resources, contracts were let, and four years later a line to San José was actually in running order. It was to these capitalists that the Central Pacific transferred its rights in the Western Pacific, and it seems to have been expected that the San Francisco and San José and the Western Pacific together would form the western end of the transcontinental line.

This expectation was disappointed, as was the hope that the San Francisco and San José would participate in the federal subsidies and land grants provided in the Pacific Railway Acts of 1862 and 1864. The city of San Francisco did, however, subscribe $300,000 in city bonds to San Francisco and San José Railroad stock, and the counties of Santa Clara and San Mateo, $200,000 and $100,000, respectively. At this time the Huntington group had no interests south of Sacramento. In 1869 the San Francisco and San José was extended to Gilroy by a company known as the Santa Clara and Pajaro Valley Railroad Company.

Southern Pacific Railroad Company

Shortly after the completion of the San Francisco and San José, another company, the Southern Pacific Railroad Company, was incorporated [2] by local parties in San Francisco to build a line of railroad in as direct a route as feasible from San Francisco to the town of San Diego, through the counties

---

[2] On December 2, 1865. United States v. Southern Pacific, transcript of testimony, p. 1284. Hereafter referred to as "United States v. Southern Pacific." This company was organized under the general California statute relating to incorporations approved May 20, 1861.

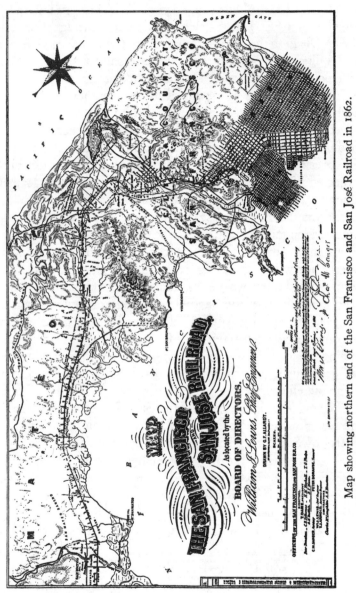

Map showing northern end of the San Francisco and San José Railroad in 1862.

of Santa Clara, Monterey, San Luis Obispo, Tulare, Los Angeles, and San Diego; thence eastward through the county of San Diego to the eastern boundary of the state of California. It is quite possible that this new company was organized in anticipation of further legislation at Washington. At any rate in July, 1866, Congress granted to the Southern Pacific Railroad, besides a right-of-way, ten alternate sections of unreserved and unappropriated public lands on either side of the road, in the state of California, on condition that it construct a line, presumably from San Francisco, to a connection with a projected railroad known as the Atlantic and Pacific Railroad, which was authorized to extend from the state of Missouri to the Pacific Ocean. In case any portion of the twenty sections indicated should be found to be occupied or reserved, the Southern Pacific was to be given the privilege of selecting other lands within 20 miles of its road. The company was to begin work within two years, and to complete not less than 50 miles annually after the second year. No money or bond subsidy was given.[3] By Act of July 25, 1868, Congress extended the time for the construction of the Southern Pacific line, requiring the completion of the first 30 miles by July 1, 1870, and subsequent construction of 20 miles annually.[4] This was plainly an enterprise of first-class magnitude.

The evidence suggests that the San Francisco and San José and the Southern Pacific Railroad companies fell under the control of Stanford, Huntington, Hopkins, and Crocker some time in 1868. Mr. Stanford published a statement on March 6, 1868, to the effect that any rumor that the Central Pacific or Western Pacific Railroad Company or any person connected with either of them had purchased the Southern Pacific or the San Francisco and San José or any property or franchises con-

---

[3] 14 United States Statutes 292 (1866). An act granting lands to aid in the construction of railroad and telegraph line from the states of Missouri and Arkansas to the Pacific Ocean. The provisions of this act were promptly accepted by the Southern Pacific. See United States v. Southern Pacific, pp. 1672–73.

[4] 15 United States Statutes 187 (1868).

nected therewith, or that any negotiations had been made tending to that result, was utterly without foundation.[5]   On the other hand, it was Collis P. Huntington who signed a letter dated September 25, 1868, addressed to the Secretary of the Interior, at Washington, transmitting the annual report of the Southern Pacific Railroad required by the act of Congress. If Stanford told the truth in March, these two circumstances would indicate with sufficient precision the time when the associates took charge.   In any case their influence was presently to appear.[6]

Consolidation

On October 12, 1870, the San Francisco and San José Railroad, the Southern Pacific, the Santa Clara and Pajaro Valley Railroad, and a new company, the California Southern, organized on paper only, were consolidated into a corporation known as the Southern Pacific Railroad of California.   The directors for the first year were Lloyd Tevis, Leland Stanford, Charles Crocker, C. P. Huntington, Mark Hopkins, Charles Mayne, and Peter Donahue.   Plainly, Central Pacific interests were in control.   The purpose of the new company was stated to be to construct and operate a railroad from San Francisco to the Colorado River, through the counties of San Mateo, Santa Clara, Monterey, Fresno, Tulare, Kern, San Bernardino, and San Diego, together with a line from Gilroy through the counties of Santa Clara, Santa Cruz, and Monterey, to a point at or near Salinas City.   This was not the line proposed in the articles of incorporation, as an examination of the accompanying map will show.   It was, however, in the main the route designated by the Southern Pacific in 1867, upon which land had been withdrawn from entry by the government at Wash-

---

5 *San Francisco Bulletin*, March 14, 1868.

6 United States v. Southern Pacific, Defendant's Exhibit No. 23.   Neither Huntington nor Stanford signed the articles of association of 1870 as holders of stock of the consolidating companies.   This may merely mean, however, that the stock of these companies was placed under other names for purposes of convenience.

Proposed route of the Southern Pacific Railroad, according to map filed with the Commissioner of the General Land Office on January 3, 1867.

ington, and it had the advantage of reaching the eastern boundary of California with less mileage and fewer grades than the line originally laid out.[7]

In 1871, an additional route from Los Angeles to Yuma was designated under the authority of the twenty-third section of the act to incorporate the Texas Pacific Railroad, which authorized the Southern Pacific Railroad Company to construct a line of railroad from a point at or near Techachapi Pass, by way of Los Angeles, to the Texas Pacific Railroad at or near the Colorado River, with the same rights and privileges, and subject to the same limitations and restrictions as were provided in the Atlantic and Pacific Act of 1866.[8]

Ambitious Construction Program

Because of the terms of the federal Act of 1866, it was necessary for the Southern Pacific to proceed steadily in its construction to the south. The first piece of road offered in satisfaction of the requirement for a minimum annual construction, was that from San José to Gilroy. Then came an extension to Tres Pinos, which ended, for the time being, building on the Northern Division. What happened was that the associates found the southern end of the San Benito Val-

---

[7] The change of route was authorized by Congressional resolution, dated June 28, 1870 (16 United States Statutes 382 [1870].) It should be observed that the so-called Mussel Slough "massacre" resulted from a dispute over the ownership of land south of Hanford, Tulare County, which lay along the line of railroad as designated in 1867, but not along that proposed in 1865. It appears that a number of persons settled upon and improved tracts near Hanford before the railroad applied for patent to land in this vicinity, but after the Southern Pacific had filed the map showing its intended route with the Commissioner of the General Land Office in 1867, and after lands along this route had been withdrawn.
When the railroad secured title it offered to sell this occupied land to the parties who had settled upon it, but at prices which were much above those current for unimproved farm land. That is to say, the railroad asked from $11 to $35 an acre, instead of the customary $2.50 to $5 an acre. The settlers understood from this that the company was trying to make them pay for improvements which they themselves had made, and resorted to active opposition. In 1876 the settlers petitioned Congress to restore a portion of the land grant in question to the public domain, on the ground that no railroad had ever been constructed along it.
In 1881 the railroad attempted to take forcible possession of two pieces of the disputed land. There was resistance, and in the shooting which followed, eight men were killed, including six settlers. This was the "massacre." There seems to be no question but that the railroad possessed legal title to the Tulare County property. The weakness of its position lay in the fact that it was attempting to build a railroad in one place and to secure a land grant in another—a procedure never contemplated by Congress, and one not unlikely to lead to hostile legislation. Eventually the railroad title was sustained, and the land sold by the company, though at reduced prices.

[8] 16 United States Statutes 573 (1871).

ley, in which Tres Pinos is located, relatively poor in traffic, and difficult to build in. Stanford visited the country personally, and found no business there, nor, in his opinion, any prospect of business. He accordingly shifted construction from the Tres Pinos line to the territory south of Goshen, and caused the Southern Pacific to build its next 20 miles in that section, expecting to connect with the San Joaquin Valley branch of the Central Pacific which ultimately came to Goshen in August, 1872. The Southern Pacific track reached Delano on July 14, 1873, Caliente on April 26, 1875, and Mojave on August 9, 1876. The stretch of 240 miles from Mojave to The Needles was not finished until June 22, 1883, but that to Fort Yuma was completed in 1877.

In later years there was discussion concerning the right of the Southern Pacific to refuse to build the stretch of road lying between Tres Pinos and Alcalde, connecting the San Benito and the San Joaquin valleys. It was insisted that the contract implied in the Congressional land grant of 1866 was an entire one, and that the amount of land given had been fixed in consideration of the difficulties of mountain construction between the valleys named. This contention is not, however, borne out by the terms of the Act of 1866, and there seems to be no good reason why Congress should have stipulated for the building of this particular bit of road, when satisfactory connection between the San Joaquin Valley and San Francisco could be secured in another way. On their part, the associates never intended to build across the Coast Range, at least not out of the San Benito Valley. In 1872 the articles of association of the Southern Pacific Branch Railroad Company contained provision for a line from a point at or near Salinas City in the county of Monterey southeasterly to a point in Kern County south of Tulare Lake, intersecting the San Joaquin Division of the Southern Pacific. Even this road never was built.[9]

9 See on this matter Colton case, p. 1621, Crocker to Colton, February 12, 1875.

At the time when the Southern Pacific Railroad entered upon its ambitious project for southern construction, the territory south and east of Goshen was very slightly developed. Los Angeles was a city of 5,728 persons in 1870, with an assessed valuation of $2,108,061, and an average of one saloon to every fifty-five inhabitants.[10]   San Diego had a population of 2,300, and Santa Ana 1,445.   These were the largest concentrations of people to be found, and they amounted to nothing more than little country towns.[11]   Nor were the statistics of industry much more striking.   Los Angeles and Kern counties produced respectable amounts of wool, and in the matter of wine the output from the former amounted to nearly one-third of that for the entire state and one-sixth of that reported for the United States as a whole.   The number of cattle was also considerable.   But in grain only a beginning had been made, the yield of the orchards was still small, and the volume of general agriculture, to say nothing of manufactures, was insignificant.

The railroad construction in the territory consisted of two local railroads connecting Los Angeles with the harbors of San Pedro and Santa Monica, to which should be added mention of the Texas Pacific project of Mr. Scott.   The Los Angeles and San Pedro Railroad was organized in 1868 and was finished on October 26, 1869.   The city of Los Angeles subscribed $75,000 in city bonds, and the county took an additional amount of $150,000, also paying in bonds.   City and county bonds both bore 10 per cent.   The construction of this railroad marked the fruition of efforts begun as early as 1861, but the credit for final accomplishment of the work was due to Phineas Banning, the principal business man of Wilmington.[12]   General Banning is said to have entered the California

---

[10] Guinn, "A History of California," pp. 254, 276.

[11] Ninth Census of the United States, 1870.

[12] Newmark, "Sixty Years in Southern California."   The Los Angeles and San Pedro was built to Wilmington only in 1869.   It was not extended to San Pedro until 1881.

legislature in order to advance his project and to have successfully overcome a great deal of opposition in his own district
in order to put it through.   The company was consolidated
with the Southern Pacific in 1874.[13]

In addition to the Los Angeles and San Pedro, reference
should be made to the Los Angeles and Independence, a railroad built in 1875 by Senator John P. Jones, of Nevada, partly
to afford an outlet to certain mines in Inyo County from which
the senator expected large results, and partly to develop property on Santa Monica Bay.   This road was also acquired by
the Southern Pacific interests, but at a later date, and at the
instance of Mr. Huntington against the judgment of at least
one of his associates.

Grant by Los Angeles

By the acquisition of the Los Angeles and San Pedro Railroad, the Southern Pacific provided itself with a southern
terminal, in advance even of the completion of its main line.
At the same time it used the advantage which the location of
its mileage in the San Joaquin Valley gave to it in order to
persuade the people of Los Angeles to grant it aid in the
measure they could afford.   Speaking after the event, it is
sufficiently obvious that sooner or later the Southern Pacific,
or some other transcontinental road, was bound to seek an outlet on the Pacific Ocean either at San Diego or at San Pedro,
and of these two San Pedro was the most likely to be chosen.
But this fact, clear at the present time, was not obvious to the
inhabitants of Los Angeles; on the contrary, the possibility
that Los Angeles might be passed by caused them the liveliest
concern.   This feeling was known to the officials of the Southern Pacific.   In May, 1872, two citizens of Los Angeles wrote
Mr. Stanford stating that they expected to call a meeting of

---

[13] Ranchers near Los Angeles feared lest the construction of the railroad would do away
with horses and the demand for barley

View south from over the San Fernando tunnel—Southern Pacific Railroad

tax-paying citizens of the county in a few days, for the purpose of selecting from among them an executive committee which should have full power to meet the representatives of any railroad company who might visit Los Angeles, in order to agree upon some plan whereby a railroad to Los Angeles might be constructed.[14]

The meeting was called, and the committee appointed. Harris Newmark, a prominent business man of Los Angeles, says that before the meeting he and ex-Governor Downey went to San Francisco and canvassed the whole situation with Mr. Huntington. A delegation from the citizens' committee made a second visit and returned with a man named Hyde, who represented the railroad company. Between Mr. Hyde and the new committee terms were presently agreed upon. The Southern Pacific demanded a donation of 5 per cent of the assessed valuation of the county, which was the maximum authorized by state law. Since the county valuation in 1872 was set by the State Board of Equalization at $10,554,592, this meant a gift of $527,730. To cover this the county proposed to issue $377,000 in new 7 per cent bonds, and to turn over besides $150,000 in stock of the Los Angeles and San Pedro Railroad, which it held by virtue of its subscription to that company in 1868. The city added $75,000 in Los Angeles and San Pedro Railroad stocks, and 60 acres of depot ground. This made a clear gift in the aggregate of $602,000, besides whatever the depot ground might be worth, or $100 per capita for a population of 6,000 souls. On its side the Southern Pacific agreed to build 50 miles of its main trunk line in the county of Los Angeles, 25 miles to be built northward and 25 miles eastward from Los Angeles city. Later the company promised to add a branch to Anaheim. The whole arrangement was submitted to popular vote on November 5, 1872, and was then approved.

---

[14] "Illustrated History of Los Angeles County" (Chicago, 1889), p. 136.

Inconveniences of Travel

Construction in accordance with the terms of the agreement of 1872 was promptly begun. San Fernando and San Pedro were reached in 1874, Anaheim in 1875, and the Southern Pacific main line in September, 1876. A vivid picture of the inconvenience of travel between Los Angeles and the East while the work was in progress, is given in the reminiscences of Harris Newmark, who has just been mentioned in connection with the negotiations between the railroad and the county of Los Angeles:

Before the completion of the San Fernando tunnel, a journey east from Los Angeles by way of Sacramento was beset with inconveniences. The traveler was lucky if he obtained passage to San Fernando on other than a construction train, and twenty to twenty-four hours, often at night, was required for a trip of the Telegraph Stage Lines' creaking, swaying coach over the rough roads leading to Caliente—the northern terminal—where the longer stretch of the railroad north was reached. The stage lines and the Southern Pacific Railroad were operated quite independently, and it was therefore not possible to buy a through ticket. For a time previously, passengers took the stage at San Fernando and bounced over the mountains to Bakersfield, the point farthest south on the railroad line. When the Southern Pacific was subsequently built to Land's Station, the stages stopped there; and for quite a while a stage started from each side of the mountain, the two conveyances meeting at the top and exchanging passengers. Once I made the journey north by stage to Tipton in Tulare County, and from Tipton by rail to San Francisco. The Coast line and the Telegraph line stage companies carried passengers part of the way. The Coast Line Stage Company coaches left Los Angeles every morning at five o'clock and proceeded via Pleasant Valley, San Buenaventura, Santa Barbara, Guadalupe, San Luis Obispo, and Paso de Robles Hot Springs, and connected at Soledad with the Southern Pacific Railroad bound for San Francisco by way of Salinas City, Gilroy, and San José, and his line made a specialty of daylight travel, thus

offering unusual inducements to tourists. There was no limit
as to time; and passengers were enabled to stop over at any
point and to reserve seats in the stage coaches by giving some
little notice in advance.

In 1876, I visited New York City for medical attention and
for the purpose of meeting my son Maurice, upon his return
from Paris. I left Los Angeles on the twenty-ninth of April
by the Telegraph Stage Line, traveling to San Francisco and
thence east by the Central Pacific railroad; and I arrived in
New York on the eighth of May.[15]

The San Fernando tunnel to which Mr. Newmark refers
is located 27 miles north of Los Angeles in the valley of the
same name. It lies along the most direct and convenient route
from Los Angeles into the San Joaquin Valley. Because of
its length, nearly one and a quarter miles, and the unfamiliarity
of the people of the coast with projects of this kind, there was
much interest in the work and many doubts as to whether it
could succeed. Governor Stevenson was credited with the
statement that a tunnel could not be constructed. Other critics
maintained that people could never be induced to travel through
so long a tunnel, and that in any case the winter rains would
cause it to cave in, to which Stanford replied that it was "too
damned dry in Southern California for any such catastrophe."
So far as the records now show, however, there was no unusual
obstacle encountered in the work, although the slowness with
which the bore advanced and the large expense connected with
construction caused considerable anxiety to the management of
the Southern Pacific.

Western Development Company

In carrying out their plans for the occupation of Southern
California, the Huntington group naturally followed the same
general policy that had proved profitable to them in the case

---

[15] Newmark, "Sixty Years in Southern California," pp. 496–97.

of the Central Pacific. That is to say, they organized construction companies, controlled by themselves, caused these companies to contract with the Southern Pacific for the construction of specified sections of line, and in their capacity as stockholders of the Southern Pacific required that company to issue and turn over large quantities of stocks and bonds in payment for work done. No further comment upon this method of procedure is necessary.

The first construction company which did work for the Southern Pacific, under the plan outlined in the preceding paragraph, was the Contract and Finance Company. This was the same organization that had completed the Central Pacific. It appears that the Contract and Finance Company simply shifted men, teams and equipment from the Central Pacific to the Southern Pacific line between San José and Tres Pinos. Later it built the road from Goshen to Sumner, and that from San Fernando via Los Angeles to Spadra. In all, it built for the Southern Pacific 143.65 miles, including the stretch from Gilroy to Tres Pinos. In 1874 the Contract and Finance Company was dissolved and the Western Development Company took its place.

The Western Development Company was incorporated December 15, 1874, for the announced purpose, among other things, of carrying on construction, manufacturing, mining, mercantile, mechanical, banking, and commercial business in all their branches, and also for the purpose of constructing, leasing, and operating all kinds of public and private improvements. That is to say, its powers were made as extensive as could well be imagined. Stanford, Hopkins, Huntington, and Crocker each held one-fourth of the stock.[16]

Under date of February 2, 1875, the Western Development

---

[16] Articles of incorporation are printed in Colton case, pp. 5475–77, testimony F. S. Douty. See also *ibid.*, pp. 2993–95, testimony Reynolds. The material and accounts for repairs possessed by the Contract and Finance Company were turned over to the Western Development Company at this time at a valuation of $431,530.53.

Company agreed to construct a railroad and a telegraph line on the routes selected by the Southern Pacific, between certain specified termini. The mileage actually built was that from Sumner to San Fernando, from Spadra to Fort Yuma, and from Goshen to Huron. Bills were rendered for this work on the basis of $72,000 per mile, or $29,153,520 for 404.91 miles, half in Southern Pacific first mortgage bonds and half in stock.[17]

In addition to its contract with the Southern Pacific, the Western Development Company undertook certain miscellaneous construction, including work on the Northern Railway, and the San Pablo and Tulare Railroad, the building of steamers for the Central Pacific, bridges and buildings for the Central Pacific and Southern Pacific, general repairs for the various companies controlled by the associates, and even finally private residences for Hopkins, Stanford, and Crocker. In short, during its existence the Western Development Company, besides completing the major part of the Southern Pacific, did incidental building of any sort which the associates desired to have done.

Pacific Improvement Company

The death of Mr. Hopkins in 1878, and the temporary unwillingness of Mrs. Hopkins to participate in the financing of new construction, together with the death of Mr. Colton in the same year, led Stanford, Huntington, and Crocker to close up the affairs of the Western Development Company, and to continue their more or less speculative building enterprises under a new organization. This new company, incorporated November 4, 1878, was known as the "Pacific Improvement Company." Its relations to the Southern Pacific and to the associates were the same as those of the Western Development

---

[17] Colton case, pp. 362–65, 7806–22, testimony F. S. Douty. The actual payments were, as the result of certain adjustments, slightly less.

Company, except that Mr. Colton, who had taken one-ninth of the Western Development Company stock in 1875, was not a stockholder, and that Mrs. Hopkins at the beginning took no part. Even the capital stock was placed at the same amount, $5,000,000.

The main accomplishment of the Pacific Improvement Company was the construction of the Southern Pacific between Mojave and The Needles. Besides this, however, it extended the Southern Pacific from Soledad to San Miguel, built the Southern Pacific in Arizona and the Southern Pacific in New Mexico, completed the California and Oregon, and Oregon and California railroads, and continued the Northern Railroad from Willows to Tehama. The contracts made were similar to those executed by the Western Development Company, although the consideration varied.[18]

The Pacific Improvement Company is still in existence. After the construction work for which it was incorporated was completed, Mr. Huntington sold his stock to the Hopkins estate. This gave to the Hopkins interest, then represented by Mr. Searles, possession of 50 per cent of the stock of the Pacific Improvement Company. The other 50 per cent remained in the hands of the Stanford and Crocker interests. At a later date the Searles stock passed to the University of California. The Pacific Improvement Company is now in process of liquidation. It owns some thirty town sites, a considerable amount of real estate, including much unimproved property in the Potrero district of San Francisco, land in the Monterey peninsula, and other property in Buffalo, New York. It has, besides, the stock and bonds of certain railroad companies, stock of the Carbondale Coal Company of Washington, and of the Oakland Water Front Company of Oakland, California, and what is still more important, it holds a large number of bills receivable covering property of all sorts which it

---

[18] United States Railway Commission, p. 2701, testimony F. S. Douty.

has sold in recent years but which has not been entirely paid for. The Pacific Improvement Company's construction outfit was sold to the Central Pacific in 1883.

The last of the construction companies, the Southern Development Company, became responsible for construction east of the Arizona state line when the Pacific Improvement Company left the field. It was of minor importance and may be dismissed with a word. In respect to ownership and operation it resembled the Contract and Finance Company, the Western Development Company, and the Pacific Improvement Company.

Identical Control of Companies

There is a great deal of history about the operation of the various construction companies mentioned, that has not been, and perhaps never will be, written. The men out on the road seem to have known little about any of them. The contact of these men was with Stanford, Huntington, Hopkins, and Crocker. They neither knew nor cared whether they received orders from the associates in their capacities as directors of the Central Pacific or of the Southern Pacific, or as stockholders in one of the construction companies. Nor was it easy for them to keep informed. The same construction force moved from place to place. The same man in the same pay-car paid off employees of the Central Pacific, the Southern Pacific, and the construction companies indiscriminately.[19] The same general shops furnished track materials.[20] The same equipment was found on all the different lines, except perhaps on the northern division. There was small wonder that even the higher engineering officials were unable to locate accurately the stretches built for each of the principal companies which they served, nor that men under them should have been altogether confused.

---

[19] United States v. Southern Pacific, pp. 553–55, testimony Redington.
[20] *Ibid.*, pp. 533–35, testimony Luckett.

As a matter of fact, the various corporations interested in the building of the Southern Pacific were, after 1870, only different manifestations of the activities of one group of men. It does not appear that any attempt was ever made to interest outside investors. On the contrary, Hopkins, Huntington, Colton, and perhaps the other partners as well, agreed that if anything happened to one of them, their stock in the Western Development Company should not go to outside parties until the existing stockholders had had a chance to take it.[21]

This was a distinct contrast to the attitude of the same men when the Contract and Finance Company was formed, and indicates that they anticipated no such difficulty in raising funds as they had experienced when they built the Central Pacific. Had this not been true, it is probable that they would have let the Southern Pacific alone, competition or no competition.

Construction Financing

Under the terms of their contracts with the Southern Pacific, the construction companies received substantially all of the stock and bonds which that company put out. The same parties were, therefore, directly or indirectly in control both of the railroad and of the companies which did work for the railroad. These securities had, however, no market for many years, at any price. County donations, of which there were a few, also yielded but little, and the federal land grant was not easily or early sold. The real source of financial supplies for the Contract and Finance Company and its successors, the Western Development and the Pacific Improvement companies, in their work upon the Southern Pacific, were the Central Pacific, as a corporation, and the associates as individuals.

As in the case of the Contract and Finance Company, the associates paid no money on their stock subscriptions, but de-

---

[21] Colton case, p. 7637, Colton to Huntington.

posited funds in varying amounts which were credited to them as loans. Interest was paid on these advances at rates varying from 6 to 10 per cent. It appears that the contributions by the associates to the Western Development Company began to be considerable in May, 1876. By January, 1877, they had reached the sum of $3,421,458.35. By March, 1878, the total advance was in the neighborhood of $11,000,000. It remained at this figure through 1878, and the major part of 1879. The largest contributions were made by the estate of Mark Hopkins and by Collis P. Huntington, though both Crocker and Stanford kept substantial balances. There is no record of the size of advances made to the Pacific Improvement Company, but we know that the same general practice was continued.

In addition to the advances made by the Huntington group, the construction companies benefited substantially by the assistance rendered them by the Central Pacific. This was a sort of help which the Central Pacific itself and the persons who built it had never known. It took a variety of forms. A very obvious service which the Central Pacific could and did offer was the operation of sections of the Southern Pacific as fast as completed in connection with the Central Pacific main line. Besides this, the Central Pacific acted as banker when the construction companies had spare funds. More important still, the Central Pacific on occasion lent considerable sums to the Western Development Company. This was later denied by representatives of the Central Pacific, but the evidence seems conclusive that the loans were made.[22]

Similar advances were probably made by the Central Pacific to the Pacific Improvement Company,[23] and to the Contract and Finance Company, sometimes without interest. Money in the Central Pacific sinking fund was invested in this way,

---

[22] Colton case, pp. 231–32, testimony F. S. Douty; United States Pacific Railway Commission, pp. 3626–27, testimony F. S. Douty.
[23] United States Pacific Railway Commission, p. 2832, testimony Leland Stanford.

at interest.[24]   Like use was made of surplus funds belonging
to the Occidental and Oriental Steamship Company, which the
Central Pacific was holding, until the Union Pacific discovered
the matter, and, being interested in the money, demanded that
its share be handed over.[25]   There is even evidence that the
associates borrowed money from the Central Pacific between
1874 and 1878, and that the treasurer of the company entered
the sums taken on so-called "cash-tags," carrying them as
cash in his accounts.[26]   How much all these transactions
amounted to, it is very difficult to say, but it is probable that
the aggregate was large.

Profits of Associates

There is no way of estimating the profits which Stanford,
Huntington, Hopkins, and Crocker drew out of the Western
Development, Pacific Improvement, and Southern Development companies. We know they were great, because the associates died very rich men. Mark Hopkins engaged in no
important enterprise outside of his hardware business, except in
railroad construction and operation, and yet in 1878 he left
an estate appraised at over $19,000,000. Eleven years later,
Charles Crocker's estate was appraised at $24,142,475.84.[27]
Stanford's estate was not appraised in 1893, or at least no
figures of value were made public, and Huntington did not
die until long afterwards. Inasmuch as the associates up to
1878 were all interested in the same business together, and
since the most important of their investments were in railroad
construction work, it is fair to assume that the profits of the
construction companies were considerable. Whatever they
were it must, however, be remembered that they consisted in
the main of Southern Pacific securities and of California real

---

[24] United States Pacific Railway Commission, p. 2994, testimony C. F. Crocker.
[25] Colton case, pp. 7646–54, 1586.
[26] *Ibid.*, pp. 9669–73, testimony Charles Crocker.
[27] *San Francisco Examiner*, October 8, 1889.

estate, neither of which were immediately salable. As a construction enterprise, the whole Southern Pacific affair was speculative. It was from the point of view of the owners of the Central Pacific alone that the construction of the Southern Pacific presented itself as a necessary policy, both for the protection of an existing investment, and for the full exploitation of the possibilities of monopoly in California.[28]

[28] Jay Gould once testified that Huntington had offered an interest in the Southern Pacific to himself and his Union Pacific associates, and that they had offered to take an interest, provided that Huntington would cut the Southern Pacific bonds outstanding from $40,000 to $25,000 per mile, and throw the stock in. Gould thought that $25,000 per mile was all that the road had cost. (Colton case, deposition Jay Gould, pp. 8, 23–24.)

It should be observed that a great deal of the mileage now owned by the Southern Pacific Railroad was not originally built by that company, but by or for small separate companies, most of them organized by the Huntington group, which were later consolidated with the parent corporation. The complete list of these consolidations is as follows:

October 12, 1870. Consolidation of the Southern Pacific Railroad Company, the San Francisco and San José Railroad Company, the Santa Clara and Pajaro Valley Railroad Company, and the California Southern Railroad Company.

August 19, 1873. Consolidation of the Southern Pacific Railroad Company and the Southern Pacific Branch Railroad Company.

December 18, 1874. Consolidation of the Southern Pacific Railroad Company and the Los Angeles and San Pedro Railroad Company.

May 14, 1888. Consolidation of the Southern Pacific Railroad Company, the San José and Almaden Railroad Company, the Pajaro and Santa Cruz Railroad Company, the Monterey Railroad Company, the Monterey Extension Railroad Company, the Southern Pacific Branch Railway Company, the San Pablo and Tulare Railroad Company, the San Pablo and Tulare Extension Railroad Company, the San Ramon Valley Railroad Company, the Stockton and Copperopolis Railroad Company, the Stockton and Tulare Railroad Company, the San Joaquin Valley and Yosemite Railroad Company, the Los Angeles and San Diego Railroad Company, the Los Angeles and Independence Railroad Company, the Long Beach, Whittier and Los Angeles County Railroad Company, the Long Beach Railroad Company, the Southern Pacific Railroad Extension Company, and the Ramona and San Bernardina Railroad Company.

April 13, 1898. Consolidation of the Southern Pacific Railroad Company, the Northern Railway Company, the Northern California Railway Company, and the California Pacific Railroad Company.

March 7, 1902. Consolidation of the Southern Pacific Railroad Company (of California), the Southern Pacific Railroad Company (of Arizona), and the Southern Pacific Railroad Company of New Mexico.

CHAPTER VIII

ORGANIZATION OF THE CENTRAL PACIFIC–SOUTHERN PACIFIC SYSTEM, FROM 1870 TO 1893

Extent of System

By 1877 the Central Pacific–Southern Pacific combination was in control of over 85 per cent of all the railroads in California, including all the lines of importance around San Francisco Bay, except the San Francisco and North Pacific Railroad, and in the Sacramento and San Joaquin valleys. Not only had the associates established the monopoly which they desired, but the operations of their system had reached an extent which they themselves would have thought inconceivable a few years before. The operated mileage of the Central Pacific–Southern Pacific line on June 30, 1877, was 2,337.66 miles, the capitalization $224,952,580, and the gross earnings $22,247,030. There was a continuous stretch of road from Ogden to Sacramento, San Francisco, and Oakland, and from these cities to Los Angeles and Yuma, by way of the San Joaquin Valley; while a line from Mojave to the Colorado River and The Needles was in course of construction.

Legally and technically, this comprehensive system was divided into five parts. The original Central Pacific Railroad ran from 5 miles west of Ogden to Sacramento. In 1870 this company consolidated with the Western Pacific Railroad, operating between Sacramento and San José via Stockton, the San Francisco, Oakland and Alameda Railroad, which connected the Western Pacific with the city of Oakland, the San Joaquin Valley Railroad branch from Lathrop to Goshen, and the California and Oregon Railroad, which left the main line of the Central Pacific near Roseville, and ran in a northwesterly direction to Redding toward the Oregon boundary. All these lines were directly under one operating control.

A second important part of the system was the California Pacific between Sacramento and Vallejo, with a branch from Davis north to Marysville, and another from Napa Junction to Calistoga. The ownership of the third portion was vested in the Northern Railway. This company had been chartered in 1871, and had projected a line from Woodland, on the California Pacific, to Tehama, of which 82.20 miles were completed in 1875. In 1878 the company built from Oakland to Martinez, and from Benicia to Suisun, and still later it constructed a line from Benicia to Fairfield. This last bit of road enabled Central Pacific trains to run from Sacramento to San Francisco via Benicia, instead of passing through Vallejo. The San Pablo and Tulare, completed about the same time as the road from Oakland to Martinez, connected the Northern Railway with Tracy on the main line of the Central Pacific.

The fourth part of the Huntington-Stanford system was the Northern Division of the Southern Pacific Railroad from San Francisco through San José to Soledad and Tres Pinos. The Tres Pinos line has been referred to in the previous chapter. The extension from Gilroy to Soledad up the Salinas Valley was in operation by 1877, and formed the first part of the route which later became the coast route to Los Angeles. The fifth and last part of the system was the Southern Division of the Southern Pacific Railroad from Goshen to Mojave, Los Angeles, and Yuma, with branches from Alcalde to Huron, and from Los Angeles to Wilmington. In addition to the main groups mentioned, there were certain minor extensions, such as the railroads from Sacramento to Shingle Springs (the Sacramento Valley and Placerville Railroad), from Stockton to Milton (the Stockton and Copperopolis Railroad), and from Peters to Oakdale (the Stockton and Visalia Railroad)

Lease and Stock Control

The various parts of the system were held together by a combination of leases and stock control. The associates in 1877 held all or a majority of the stock of each railroad company which has been mentioned. Usually this stock had come to them in their capacity as shareholders in the various construction companies which had built the roads. In some cases, however, as with the California Pacific and the Northern Division of the Southern Pacific, the greater part of it had been acquired by purchase. But the associates in most instances preferred to add to their control by stock ownership the further security of a lease—a procedure which had the additional advantage of simplifying the conditions under which the companies were operated, by concentrating operations under a single management. Only in the case of the Northern Division of the Southern Pacific do they seem to have temporarily departed from this procedure, and this exception can probably be explained by the special circumstances of the case.

So long as the same parties held all the securities of all the companies in the Central Pacific–Southern Pacific system, it made little difference how payments under the various leases were determined. Yet the possibility that the Central Pacific might sometime divest itself of some portion of its property, was kept in mind, and rentals were fixed so that in most cases they were materially less than the net earnings of the leased mileage. This was probably not true of the Southern Pacific in early years, but it had become so by 1880. In form, the leases showed surprising variety. The rental of the Northern Railway to the California Pacific in 1876 was at the rate of $1,500 per mile per year.[1] Mr. Stanford thought that this was based on an estimated cost of construction.[2] In 1879 the same property was leased to the Central Pacific for a payment

---

[1] Colton case, pp. 1522–24, 1529.

[2] United States Pacific Railway Commission, pp. 2791–92, testimony Leland Stanford.

of a given sum per mile for each piece of equipment passing over the road. That is to say, 25 cents per mile was paid for each passenger or freight locomotive, 20 cents for each passenger car, and 8 cents for each freight or caboose car.[3] This proved to be a very expensive rental, and was changed to a monthly payment of $47,500.[4]

The lease of the California Pacific to the Central Pacific in 1876 carried a rental of $550,000 per year, plus three-fourths of the net earnings of the California Pacific above that amount. The Central Pacific guaranteed principal and interest on $3,000,000 of bonds. This was changed to a flat payment of $600,000 per year in 1879.[5] The Central Pacific leased the Amador branch between Galt and Ione for $3,500 per month. In the case of the Stockton and Copperopolis, however, it undertook only to pay principal and interest on $500,000 of thirty-year bonds, at 5 per cent, with the provision, however, that the net earnings should apply on the Stockton and Copperopolis floating debt.[6] These variations, if they show nothing else, are persuasive that the associates had no standard method of procedure but suited their arrangements to the facts in each individual case.

Lease of Southern Pacific

Perhaps the most interesting relations between the different companies in the Huntington-Stanford system were those existing between the Central Pacific and the Southern Pacific— the Central Pacific's most important extension. It has already been noted that during the early period of construction the Southern Pacific lines south of Goshen were turned over to the Central Pacific operating department as fast as they were completed. At one time the authority of some Central Pacific

---

[3] Colton case, pp. 1524–29.

[4] *Ibid.*, pp. 1510–13.

[5] United States Pacific Railway Commission, p. 3445, testimony E. H. Miller, Jr.

[6] For terms of leases see especially United States Pacific Railway Commission, pp. 3443–53, testimony of E. H. Miller, Jr.

officials reached east to New Orleans, though the general superintendent, Mr. Towne, seems never to have had jurisdiction beyond Vermillionville, 144 miles from New Orleans.[7] The advantages of this arrangement were obvious. Under the lease, the Central Pacific paid the Southern Pacific $500 per mile per month rental, less $250 per mile per month to cover operating expenses, or a net sum of $250 per mile per month. As amended in 1879 and 1880, the leases made no mention of the $500 payment, but the Central Pacific engaged to keep the Southern Pacific in good repair, and to pay $250 per mile monthly.[8] In its first form the lease contained the implication that the operating ratio of the Southern Pacific was only 50 per cent, and it has been suspected that this was deliberately arranged in order to assist Mr. Huntington in disposing of Southern Pacific securities in New York. The lease was originally terminable on twelve months' notice, but in 1880, on demand of New York bankers who contemplated the purchase of Southern Pacific bonds, it was changed to run for at least five years.

The fact has already been mentioned that the lease of the Southern Pacific system to the Central Pacific never included what was known as the Northern Division, running from San Francisco through Gilroy to Tres Pinos and from Carnadero to Soledad. Its officers reported directly to the executive officials of the Southern Pacific Company, and not to Mr. Towne. The difference in treatment of this part of the line was striking. The Northern Division lay west of the Coast Range, and was separated to some extent from the lines of the San Joaquin Valley; yet it gave the main system entrance to the important city of San Francisco, and should

---

7 United States v. Southern Pacific, p. 708, testimony Julius Kruttschnitt. This was a case brought in 1915 before the District Court of the United States for the District of Utah in order to compel the separation of the Central Pacific from the Southern Pacific railroad. The suit was brought under the Anti-Trust Law of 1890, and in the course of the testimony the history of the Southern Pacific was very fully brought out.

8 Colton case, pp. 814–26.

have been operated in close harmony with its connections at San José.

One suspects that Mr. Huntington desired to separate the Central Pacific and the Southern Pacific in the public mind in order that he might more successfully oppose Mr. Scott's Texas and Pacific plans at Washington. "I think it unfortunate," he wrote in 1875, "that he [Stanford] should so closely connect the Central Pacific with the Southern Pacific, as that is the only weapon our enemies have to fight us with in Congress." [9] "I think it important," he said in another letter about the same time, "that the Southern Pacific should be disconnected from the Central as much as it well can be. And . . . I think it should have a superintendent that does not connect with the Central Pacific, although I think it would be difficult to get a man as good as Towne." [10] Opinions like these were likely to perpetuate distinctions between the Central Pacific and the Southern Pacific railroads which could not be explained on other grounds.

Arrangement Reversed

A second stage in the connection between the Central Pacific and the Southern Pacific companies began in 1885 when a lease of the Central Pacific to the Southern Pacific took the place of the earlier arrangement in which the Central Pacific was the lessee. It appears that Timothy Hopkins, treasurer of the Central Pacific and director of the Southern Pacific Railroad of California, received a telegram from Mr. Stanford in the summer of 1884, asking him to come to New York. When Hopkins arrived he found Stanford, Huntington, and Crocker, and it was explained to him that the meeting was desired in order to go over the affairs of the associates generally, and in particular to take up the question of the

---

9 Colton case, pp. 1643–44, Huntington to Colton, May 28, 1875.
10 *Ibid.*, pp. 1615–16, Huntington to Colton, December 10, 1874.

organization of a new company for the purpose of holding and
operating the railroad companies that were owned by the associates and controlled by them, both those under the management of the Central Pacific and those east of El Paso
in Texas and Louisiana.[11]   The meeting was recognized
as important and minutes were kept, which have been preserved.

There were several circumstances which made a reorganization at this time desirable. In the first place, the period of
exceptional profits for the Central Pacific was passing away
with the decline in the mining business in Nevada and the
opening of other transcontinental lines. In the second place,
the Southern Pacific was beginning to realize the earning
power which it was to have as a completed road. It had now
a through line to New Orleans; it reached San Francisco
while the Central Pacific did not; it was handling 45 per cent
of the transcontinental business in 1885; and while it could
hardly yet be called a profitable enterprise, its prospects were
bright. Southern Pacific bonds were first sold in New York
in considerable quantities in 1880, when they brought between
86 and 90. Except on the supposition that the ownership of
the Central Pacific and Southern Pacific was identical, there
was beginning to be reason for the owners of the latter to feel
dissatisfied with a lease like that of 1880, which compelled
them to be contented with a fixed return.

Stock Holdings

On this last point the evidence, though not entirely conclusive, offers some interesting suggestions. Up to 1880 the
number of stockholders in the Central Pacific remained small.
Mr. Huntington had stock of the four associates for sale, and
made efforts to place it in New York, but without success.
In 1878 the report of the Central Pacific Railroad to the Cali-

---

[11] United States v. Southern Pacific, p. 655, testimony Timothy Hopkins.

fornia Railroad Commission showed 82 stockholders, of whom 56, with a total holding of 432,563 shares, were residents of California. Mark Hopkins held 102,812 shares when he died in that same year, and Mr. Huntington, Mr. Stanford, and Mr. Crocker presumably possessed equal amounts. During the early eighties, however, while the Central Pacific was paying substantial dividends, large quantities of stock were sold in Europe. James Speyer has testified that when he came into the New York office of Speyer and Company, some time between 1883 and 1885, large blocks were held in England and Holland. The sales had been made before 1884, probably at a price above 50.

No record of the amount disposed of in these years is available,[12] but it is known that in 1884 the number of shares standing in the names of Huntington, Stanford, Crocker, and the Hopkins interests was considerably less than a majority of the stock outstanding.[13] Mr. Jackson, employee in the secretary's office of the Central Pacific in 1885, estimated the amount at from 30,000 to 35,000 shares apiece.[14] According to Mr. Brown, who inventoried the stock of the associates in 1884, the combined holdings of Stanford, Huntington, Crocker, and Mrs. Hopkins, including stock in the name of the Pacific Improvement Company, were 157,535 shares out of a total outstanding of 592,755 shares at this date.[15] Timothy Hopkins later suggested that Brown's figures might have included only stock free and available, and that the associates might have owned other stock pledged as collateral, but this was only a suggestion, without proof. As final bits of evidence, it is on record that Crocker possessed 34,049 shares of Central Pacific stock at his death in 1889,[16] while Stanford told the

---

[12] United States v. Southern Pacific, pp. 1191–96, testimony James Speyer.
[13] Ibid., pp. 613–18, testimony George T. Klink.
[14] Ibid., p. 645, testimony George R. Jackson.
[15] Ibid., p. 1695, Defendant's Exhibit No. 21.
[16] Ibid., p. 871, inventory of Charles Crocker estate, filed July 12, 1889.

United States Pacific Railway Commission in 1887 that he owned 32,000 shares.[17]

The conclusion to which this evidence leads is that Huntington and his friends did not own as much as 30 per cent of the Central Pacific shares outstanding when they met together in New York in 1884. Their control of the company depended on the proxies which were sent them, and in particular upon the fact that the individual liability imposed on corporation stockholders under California law led new purchasers of Central Pacific stock to delay recording their ownership, or even to place their stock under the name of third persons in New York. Dividends were collected by presentation of coupons clipped from stock certificates.[18] Mr. Klink testified that the majority of the stock was voted by proxy in 1885, and that the bulk of it was in the name of people in the New York office of the company. On the other hand, during the period in which the ownership of the Central Pacific became scattered, the stock of the Southern Pacific continued to be closely held by the original associates: Stanford, Huntington, Crocker, and the estate of Mark Hopkins.

It is not difficult to understand why the associates should have gradually shifted their main interest from the Central Pacific to the Southern Pacific if we remember that their interests were widely extended as the result of their building enterprises in Southern California, and that Central Pacific securities were the only parts of their holdings on which they could realize in cash. Southern Pacific stock and bonds had no market in New York; Central Pacific stock and bonds had such a market. Doubtless, the associates could not have afforded to dispose of their Central Pacific holdings if this would have imperiled their control of the Ogden route, but such a result did not necessarily follow, as we shall see. Hav-

---

[17] United States Pacific Railway Commission, p. 2657, testimony Leland Stanford.
[18] United States v. Southern Pacific, pp. 615, 645, testimony George T. Klink.

ing sold Central Pacific securities in large quantities, however, it was natural for the Stanford-Huntington group to wish to make the company in which their main interest now lay a dominant partner in the Central Pacific–Southern Pacific combination. And this is probably the explanation of the transaction which we are about to describe.

New York Meetings

Let us return to the meeting of Huntington and his associates at New York in the summer and fall of 1884, at which the details of the reorganization were worked out. The first business there considered was the purchase of the interest of one T. W. Pierce in the Galveston, Harrisburg and San Antonio Railway and the making of certain adjustments of interests of the associates in connection therewith. The next was the taking of an inventory of securities on hand in New York and those used as collateral for the payment of liabilities of Stanford, Huntington, Hopkins, and Crocker. On September 11 the question of the reorganization of the Southern Pacific system was taken up, and the following order of business was agreed upon: (1) consolidation of all the lines of the Southern Pacific system in one company; (2) separation of Central Pacific business from Southern Pacific business; (3) leasing of the Central Pacific system to the Southern Pacific system (new organization); (4) general consolidation of lines from San Francisco to Newport News.

The fourth item referred to a proposal that Stanford, Crocker, and the Hopkins estate enter with Huntington into the ownership of the Chesapeake and Ohio Railroad, opening the way for a transcontinental rail line from coast to coast. This offer was declined; no further reference need be made to it.[19]

On September 25, the associates came together again, and from that time until November 7, meetings were held almost

---

[19] *United States* v. Southern Pacific, p. 666, testimony Timothy Hopkins.

daily. From the meager reports of the proceedings kept by their secretary, we glean that more than one plan of adjustment was considered. It was agreed at one time that the Southern and Central Pacific companies might terminate their leases, and that the Central might lease from the Southern that portion of the railroad between Goshen and Mojave. Then a running arrangement was to be made between the Central Pacific and the Southern Pacific Company (new organization) to cover the line from Mojave to San Francisco and other California points.[20]

This plan was not finally adopted. On October 1, Leland Stanford was appointed a committee of one to formulate his proposed method of leasing the several roads which should form the through line of the Southern Pacific Company. It was agreed that the stock of the Southern Pacific Company, which had been organized the previous year, should be raised to $100,000,000. During the following three weeks the discussion turned largely about the details of the Southern Pacific organization and the best methods of liquidating the Southern Development Company. On November 5, the question of leasing the Central Pacific system to the Southern Pacific came up. It was agreed to lease the property, and temporarily to fix the rental at fixed charges and a guarantee of 2 per cent upon the capital stock, plus all the earnings of the Central Pacific system over and above that percentage until the amount should reach 6 per cent. All profits beyond 6 per cent were to go to the Southern Pacific Company. The last meeting was held on November 7.

Reorganization of System

The result of these exhaustive discussions was a threefold operation. In the first place, the Southern Pacific Company of Kentucky, organized in 1884 with a charter granting power

---

[20] United States v. Southern Pacific, pp. 1688–1702, Defendant's Exhibit No. 21.

to do most things in the world provided it did not operate in Kentucky, issued $100,000,000 in capital stock, and acquired in exchange for its certificates the stock of the Southern Pacific Railroad Company and that of the subsidiary companies completing the through line to New Orleans.[21]

Secondly, the Southern Pacific Company leased the Southern Pacific Railroad and these same subsidiaries for ninety-nine years from the 10th of February, 1885, undertaking to keep the properties in repair, and to pay over 93½ per cent of the net profits to the lessors in specified proportions.

In the third place, the Southern Pacific Company leased the Central Pacific Railroad for ninety-nine years from the first of April, 1885, for a rental which might vary from $1,200,000 to $3,600,000 a year, according as the earnings of the Central Pacific and leased lines north of Goshen might be small or large. This substantially corresponded to the 2 per cent and the 6 per cent on the capital stock mentioned in the minutes of the associates. The Southern Pacific assumed all Central Pacific obligations except the payment of the principal of indebtedness incurred or guaranteed by that company, and various minor adjustments and assignments were made which it is not necessary to describe.[22]

Mr. Stanford has testified that in fixing the rental of $1,200,000 the business of the previous years and the prospects of competition in the future were taken into account.[23]   The

---

[21] United States v. Southern Pacific, pp. 621–22, testimony George T. Klink. It has been suggested that Huntington had the charter of the Southern Pacific Company taken out in Kentucky, in order to enable the company to conduct its suits in California in the federal and not in the state courts.

[22] J. M. Bassett said of the action of Kentucky in granting a charter to the Southern Pacific Company, that it amounted to granting a letter of marque to that company on the condition that it make no reprisals in Kentucky. He argued that the lease of the Central Pacific was defective because its duration was to be greater than the life of the Central Pacific under its articles of incorporation, because the liability of Southern Pacific stockholders was not unlimited as in the case of California corporations, and because the rule of comity under which foreign corporations operated in California could not be expected to apply to a corporation which was forbidden to do business in the state of its nativity. None of these objections, however, proved to have any practical importance.

[23] United States Pacific Railway Commission, pp. 2812–13, testimony Leland Stanford.

United States Pacific Railway Commission approved the terms of the lease two years later.

In 1888 the minimum rental was changed to $1,360,000 and the maximum to $4,080,000, in consequence of the extension of the Central Pacific from Delta, California, to a connection with the Oregon and California Railroad at the Oregon boundary. In 1893 the Southern Pacific complained that it was suffering very considerable losses under the lease and the terms were once more revised. Instead of a rental with a fixed minimum, the Southern Pacific now agreed to pay $10,000 a year for the leased property, plus all net earnings up to 6 per cent on the capital stock of the Central Pacific Railroad and one-half the excess over 6 per cent.[24]

It was provided in the fourth article of the new lease that if the Southern Pacific should make any advances for payment on account of the Central Pacific, it should be entitled to receive interest on these advances at the rate of 6 per cent. On the 22d of March, 1894, this fourth article of the amended lease was again changed by inserting the words "lawful interest" instead of "interest at 6 per cent per annum" upon advances which might be made by the Southern Pacific Company. At the same time it was agreed between the Central Pacific and the Southern Pacific that if at any time it appeared that, by

---

[24] The following table shows the result of operation under the lease for each year from 1885 to 1893:

NET PROFITS AND RENTALS CENTRAL PACIFIC RAILROAD, 1885-93

Period	Net Profit Central Pacific Railroad Company	Rental Paid to Central Pacific Railroad Company	Excess of Rental over Net Profit
April to December, 1885	$ 1,482,033	$ 1,482,033	....
1886	1,324,998	1,324,998	....
1887	1,086,733	1,200,000	$ 113,267
1888	962,830	1,360,000	397,170
1889	1,035,418	1,360,000	324,582
1890	999,223	1,360,000	360,777
1891	2,144,425	2,144,425	....
1892	861,874	1,360,000	498,127
1893	784,717	1,360,000	575,283
Totals..........	$10,682,251	$12,951,456	$2,269,206

Brice Report, 53d Congress, 3d Session, January 28, 1895 (Senate Report, No. 830, Serial No. 3288).

the operation of the agreement, either party was being benefited at the expense of the other, the agreement should be
revised and changed. On the whole the earnings of the Central Pacific were less than were expected under the lease, particularly during the years 1888-93. Yet part of the difficulty
arose from preferential solicitation of freight over the Sunset
route, and for the rest the rental of the property was adjust-
able, as experience showed.

CHAPTER IX

THE CASE OF DAVID D. COLTON

Meeting the Associates

During the seventies the associates took a new partner. This was David D. Colton, one-time sheriff of Siskiyou County, brigadier-general of militia, second to Broderick in the famous Terry-Broderick duel, and still later colonel of United States Volunteers. In spite of these various military titles, Colton seems never to have seen service. But he had been active in California politics as a delegate of the Union Democratic party in 1861, and as chairman of the state central committee of that organization, and was widely known throughout the state. He was a man of fine physique, and endowed with a quick if not a profound intelligence.

Colton first made the acquaintance of Charles Crocker in 1867, when the latter was on his way to inspect the work of construction of the Central Pacific beyond Elko. Three years later Crocker invited Colton to accompany him to Evanston, California, where he intended to look over, and perhaps to purchase, certain coal mining properties. According to Crocker, Colton said that he also would like to have an interest in the mines in question. Crocker, who had in the meantime completed negotiations for the purchase, replied with an offer to make Colton president and manager of the coal company if he would buy a thousand shares of its stock, which Colton immediately did.[1]

---

[1] Colton case, pp. 8839-42, testimony Charles Crocker. A discussion of the relations between Colton and the Huntington group which differs from that given in the text is presented in Russell, "Stories of the Great Railroads," 1914.

The relations thus begun rapidly became more intimate. As early as 1868, Mr. and Mrs. Colton had invitations from Mr. Crocker and passes to travel on the Central Pacific. In 1869 or 1870 the two families visited the Yosemite together, and in 1871-72, when the Crockers went to Europe and the two Crocker boys were left behind at a military academy in Oakland, the Coltons looked after the children generally, and had them at the Colton house for week-ends:[2]

It was through his acquaintance with the Crockers that Mr. Colton met the other members of the Stanford group. Mr. Huntington was favorably impressed with him; Stanford and Hopkins less so. Huntington was becoming dissatisfied about this time with the amount of work done by his associates, and the suggestion soon made that Colton join the other members of the group and share the burden of managing the Central Pacific enterprise with them, met his approval. "I was worked," he said later, "up to my full capacity, whatever that might be. Mr. Crocker was in the habit of going to Europe and having a good time and the Governor owned ranches, and his horses took a great deal of his time; in fact, the Governor never could confine himself right to the office; that is, I don't consider that he could, to close, hard work, and we wanted somebody there to do that work; and Mr. Colton convinced me that he, of all men, was just the man that we wanted." And again, speaking of his partners and of Colton, Huntington said: "He knew I was not satisfied with some things that my associate co-directors were doing there. The way they used to go to Europe and go away from business, while I was working every day in the year almost, and about fourteen hours a day; he knew I was not quite satisfied with the hours they put in." [3] The fact that Mr. Hopkins' health was not strong was an additional reason for taking in a new partner.

---

[2] Colton case, pp. 2446–50, testimony Mrs. Colton.
[3] *Ibid.*, pp. 172–73, deposition C. P. Huntington.

Agreement Signed

The result of these preliminary discussions was the conclusion of an agreement, dated October 5, 1874, whereby Colton received 20,000 shares of Central Pacific Railroad stock and 20,000 shares of Southern Pacific stock in return for his promissory note for $1,000,000, maturing in five years.[4] At the same time it was mutually understood that Colton should share in all the responsibilities and liabilities of the associates for five years in proportion to his stockholdings, and should stand in their shoes, as it were, holding the same positions and relations which they had to the Central Pacific Railroad, and to the Contract and Finance Company. The contract called for no cash payment, for obvious reasons.

Mr. Huntington says he felt in 1874 that Colton was receiving something very handsome, and the opinion was not without some justification. Certainly, in the long run the opportunity to share in the profits of the associates was valuable. Colton was not a man of large means to begin with, yet after two years and three months with the Central Pacific, he inventoried his assets at $961,506.18,[5] and at the time of his death his rent roll alone amounted to $2,500 to $3,000 a month.[6]

This was a very substantial compensation, even for very valuable service. But on the other hand, it is evident that Mr. Colton put himself entirely in the hands of the associates when he signed the agreement and the promissory note which have been described. He not only pledged his services for five years, but he assumed an unconditional liability to pay $1,000,000 at the end of this period, in return for which he obtained only 40,000 shares of unsalable securities and a right to participate in the management of the associates' property which was re-

---

[4] Colton case, pp. 5872–74. See also Colton manuscript, pp. 36–40. It was stipulated that either party might cancel the agreement at any time within two years, upon which stock and promissory note were to be mutually returned, and the parties placed in the same position relative to each other as before the agreement was made.

[5] Colton case, pp. 7018–19.

[6] *Ibid.*, p. 6529, testimony H. K. White.

vocable at the pleasure of Huntington and his friends at any time within two years. This was a dangerously exposed position. It was not a wise thing even for the Huntington-Stanford group to put Colton in such a predicament, and much subsequent difficulty resulted therefrom.

In 1876 the associates served notice on Mr. Colton, dissevering his connection with them. Mr. Crocker relates that Colton was very much affected. He said, according to Crocker, "It is generally known that I am here with you, and there is no one knows these relations are only temporary, and it will be next to ruin to me to have them dissevered now." In fact, he wept. Crocker later testified that he liked the general very much, and was touched by his distress. Colton wished him to go and see the others, and Crocker did so. The result was that the notice was reconsidered and a second contract made.[7] After this, Colton bought one-ninth of the capital stock of the Western Development Company, and commenced to deposit money with that organization in the same manner as did the other members of the group.

"Financial Director"

During substantially the whole period from 1874 to 1878, Colton took active charge of the financial affairs of the Huntington group at the San Francisco end. His office and title beginning August 31, 1875, was that of "financial director." Formally he acted under the direction of the treasurer of the company, Mr. Hopkins. Practically he reported to Mr. Huntington and perhaps to Mr. Crocker, more than to Mr. Hopkins, but exercised a good deal of independent initiative.[8] With the operation of neither the Central Pacific nor the Southern Pacific had he anything to do. On the other hand, it was either Colton in San Francisco, or Huntington in New York,

---

[7] Colton case, p. 8869, testimony Charles Crocker.
[8] *Ibid.*, pp. 1058, 1064–66, testimony E. H. Miller, Jr.; p. 8957, testimony Charles Crocker.

as we shall presently see, who attended to the negotiation of short-time loans, often necessary to take care of interest on the railroad properties. It was also Colton who had particular charge of the many affairs of the Western Development Company;[9] it was Colton who was responsible head of the Rocky Mountain Coal and Iron Company's mine at Ione; and it was Colton who took particular interest in finding a market for the output of this corporation.[10]

From the tone of Mr. Huntington's letters to Colton, it seems as though the former was reasonably well satisfied with the way the business in the West was conducted after 1874. On his part, Colton cultivated the idea that the interests of the five associates, himself included, were inextricably bound together. "I have learned one thing," he wrote in 1878, "we have got *no true friends* outside of *us* five . . . . People will profess friendship to one of us, just to either try to find out something, or when the time comes, lie about the rest of us. We cannot depend on a human soul outside of ourselves, and hence we must all be good-natured, stick together, and keep our own counsels." [11]

Yet, in spite of his assumption of the permanency of his relations with the Huntington group, Mr. Colton certainly understood that his position had no legal security whatever. Of this the episode of 1876 must have been a disagreeable reminder. In particular, as has been observed, there was a reasonable likelihood that he would be called upon to pay his note for $1,000,000 in 1879, before the Central Pacific and Southern Pacific shares, which secured it, had become salable. It is evident that these matters were in Mr. Colton's mind constantly, and gave him great concern. No other reason can be

---

9 Colton case, pp. 2711–12, 478–81, testimony F. S. Douty.

10 Newell Beeman, superintendent of the Rocky Mountain Coal and Iron Company, says that Colton knew nothing about the practical working of the mine. (Colton case, pp. 3849–50, testimony Newell Beeman.)

11 Colton case, pp. 7612–13, Colton to Huntington, January 31, 1878.

offered for his efforts to secure title to property with such feverish rapidity. How should he protect himself against the automatic presentation of a note which might require the sacrifice of all his accumulations to pay? How should he put himself in a position where his income was not wholly dependent on the forbearance of four men, with only one of whom he had ties of personal friendship? If Mr. Colton's moral fiber weakened somewhat under the strain of the situation, the fact need occasion no great surprise.

Western Development Dividend

Some time after 1874 Colton suggested to Crocker that the salaries of the associates be raised. They were all drawing $10,000 a year, and were giving all their time for that salary. Colton said it was an insignificant sum. Men such as the associates ought to have $25,000 a year, at least. But Crocker replied prudently that a salary of $10,000 could always be justified, while one of $25,000 might not be. He preferred to let the matter stay as it was.[12]

Three years later, when the period of his contract was drawing to a close, Colton took more drastic action by causing the Western Development Company to distribute a substantial part of its assets in the form of a dividend. This provided him with property, upon which as security he might have borrowed considerable sums of money. A dividend was declared on September 4, 1877, which consisted of $13,500,-000 in Central Pacific stock, $6,300,000 in Southern Pacific Railroad bonds, and $1,562,500 in other securities, amounting to between one-half and one-third of the holdings of the Western Development Company. Colton's personal share was one-ninth.[13]

---

[12] Colton case, p. 8915, testimony Charles Crocker.
[13] United States Pacific Railway Commission, p. 3255, testimony F. S. Douty; Colton case, pp. 423–24, testimony F. S. Douty.

Ostensibly the Western Development Company's dividend was a distribution of surplus profits. In reality it was a division of capital. Nobody knew, in 1877, how great the profits of the Western Development Company had been, nor even whether the assets of the company equaled its liabilities, for the reason that the value of these assets was speculative and uncertain, and if realized on all at once, would have amounted to scarcely anything at all. It was known, of course, that the creditors of the company were also its stockholders, so that the distribution was not quite so reckless as it otherwise might have appeared; but yet the various stockholders were not holders of stock in the same proportions as they were creditors, and the heavier creditors, such as Huntington, might well have felt that their interests were not being sufficiently protected.

Nothing was said about the Western Development dividend to any of the associates at the time it was declared. Charles Crocker was in San Francisco, but knew nothing of it.[14] The fact came out, however, in August of the following year, when Huntington was in the West. Stanford, Huntington, and Crocker were all together in one of the Southern Pacific offices when Colton came in, accompanied by a couple of subordinates with their hands full of bonds, and said, "Gentlemen, here are your dividends." Both Huntington and Crocker became at once very angry, and hot words seem to have passed. Huntington said that there was no sense in the dividend—it was wrong, the company ought to pay its debts before it paid a dividend—the stocks and bonds were of no particular value, but their distribution would leave the Western Development Company shorn of its resources, and they must be returned. Crocker agreed with Huntington. Colton begged the others not to injure him in the eyes of the employees of the company by compelling a return of the securities, and pledged his honor that he would not part with his shares, and would return them

---

[14] Colton case, pp. 8883, 8887, testimony Charles Crocker.

David D Colton

if needed. Stanford thought the matter might be passed with this understanding, and it was so agreed, not, however, without a good deal of resentment on the part of Huntington and Crocker.[15]

Misappropriation of Funds

The Western Development dividend and Colton's request for a higher salary were, in a measure at least, open and above board. The same cannot be said of a number of other operations—in general, it is true, of minor importance—which took place between 1874 and 1878, and which became known only after Colton's death. How far Colton was guilty of positive dishonesty during these years has been a matter of bitter dispute. There is no question, however, that he drew or credited himself with considerable amounts of money without the knowledge of the other partners, and that no vouchers were ever made out which sufficiently explained these transactions. Charges of embezzlement were even later made and not disproved. Three of four illustrations of such incidents may be given.

1. Salary drawn from the Rocky Mountain Coal and Iron Company. Mr. Colton was made president of this company in 1871 at a salary of $100 a month. In 1874 the associates agreed that Colton should receive a salary of $10,000 a year, as partner. No separate mention was made of the Rocky Mountain Coal and Iron Company in 1874, but it is reasonable to suppose that the new salary of $10,000 covered Colton's work in supervising the coal property, as well as his share in the general administration of the railroad, especially as the coal business took comparatively little of his time. As a matter of fact, however, Colton restricted himself to $100 a month only during 1871. In 1872 he drew $400 a month, except during

---

[15] Colton case, pp. 8881-82, testimony Charles Crocker; pp. 36-37, deposition C. P. Huntington.

the month of March, when he took $366.50. In 1873 he took $23,500, of which a considerable amount was for back salary. In 1874 Colton drew $12,000, and in 1875, 1876, and 1877, $6,000 annually. According to the testimony of expert accountants who later went over the company's books, Colton took $54,966.50 in salary during the years 1871-77 in excess of what he should have taken according to his agreement with Mr. Crocker, and beyond the amounts which the other associates intended he should have.[16]

2. Interest on Rocky Mountain Company balances. It is admitted that Mr. Colton deposited the balances of the Rocky Mountain Coal and Iron Company, running all the way from $30,000 to $90,000, in his own private bank account, and used them in his own private transactions.

3. Receipts from sale of coal. It appears that the Rocky Mountain Coal and Iron Company sold coal to the Central Pacific. For some time this coal was paid for at the rate of $2 and $2.65 per ton. In July, 1874, the Central Pacific made an extra payment of $11,622 to Mr. Colton for the purpose of increasing the price paid during the months from January to May, 1874, to $2.85 per ton, and arranged to pay this increased amount thereafter. In his instructions to the superintendent of the mine, Mr. Colton made no mention of the retroactive payment, and apparently pocketed the $11,622.

4. Appropriation of interest coupons. In 1876 Mr. Tevis wished to exchange some Southern Pacific bonds which he held, for certain lands owned by the Railroad Company. Colton agreed to facilitate the transaction by taking the bonds and giving his individual check for $140,700. Tevis delivered the check and $10.13 in cash to the Southern Pacific land agent, and got his deed. Colton eventually redeemed his check by delivery of the bonds to the treasurer of the Southern Pacific,

---

[16] Colton case, pp. 2335-46, testimony Gunn; pp. 3127-29, 3227, testimony W. G Fullerton.

but when the bonds came in, two interest coupons were missing. A similar transaction between the same parties, but for a lesser amount, took place later the same year, and again interest coupons were clipped from the bonds before Colton turned them in.[17] In each case Mr. Smith, the treasurer of the Southern Pacific, was compelled to hold Colton's check for a considerable period before it was redeemed, and during this time Colton had, of course, the use of the money.

In addition to matters such as those here partially enumerated, there were a multitude of instances in which Colton charged relatively small sums to various accounts without supplying any evidence that the charges were legitimate. Doubtless the other associates did the same, but Colton's position in the group was peculiar, and he could not afford to allow himself equal freedom with Huntington and Stanford. It would serve no useful purpose to discuss these instances in detail.

The aggregate of all the sums which Colton thus gathered into his control was considerable . The Western Development dividend alone supplied him with 700 Southern Pacific bonds that might have been used as collateral security for a loan, as well as with other securities, mostly of still uncertain value. Items of excess salary, interest on balances, and miscellaneous unaccounted-for expenses totaled $130,831.13. Had Colton succeeded in increasing his salary as financial director to $25,-000, he would have added from $75,000 to $100,000 to his resources. Substantial progress was evidently being made toward meeting the million dollar note.

Colton's Death and Mrs. Colton

Upon all the activities which have been described, Colton's death in October, 1878, in the prime of life, fell with crushing force. In the first place, Colton's manipulations were such as to be unforgivable by his business friends. Devious as Hunt-

---

[17] Colton case, pp. 7187–92, testimony Madden; pp. 7217–24, testimony N. T. Smith.

ington's ethical code was at times, he had no hesitation in pronouncing Mr. Colton guilty of robbery; that he himself was partly responsible was not likely to occur to him. In the second place, Colton's assets at the time of his death were such as to render immediate liquidation impossible, and yet this was precisely the thing most likely to be demanded. Mrs. Colton, the sole heir, was a woman of unusual ability, clear-headed, definite in speech, and, although inexperienced in business, apparently quickly able to understand business problems. She had, moreover, a good adviser in the person of a San Francisco lawyer named S. M. Wilson. Her position was, nevertheless, one of disadvantage, which was intensified by her wish to shield her husband's reputation.

It does not appear that the associates were aware of the true state of affairs during the weeks immediately following Mr. Colton's death. Mr. Huntington wrote cordial though not altogether sincere letters to Mrs. Colton, expressing willingness to serve her in those matters in which General Colton was interested with the associates,[18] and Crocker called at Mrs. Colton's house and wept there while speaking of the death of Mr. Colton. This attitude soon changed, however, and Mr. Crocker became less friendly in his intercourse with Mrs. Colton, and at last ceased to visit her altogether.[19] In fact, all pretense of sympathy with Mrs. Colton was presently abandoned, and negotiations between her and the associates were continued upon a cold business basis.

The attitude of the Stanford-Huntington crowd was officially that they were willing to have Mrs. Colton pay her obligations and continue with them. This meant a settlement of claims arising out of the improper withdrawal of moneys by Mr. Colton, but also more particularly the payment of the

---

[18] Colton case, pp. 2436-39, Huntington to Mrs. Colton, November 15, 1878, and November 21, 1878.

[19] Ibid., pp. 2485-92, testimony Mrs. Colton; pp. 8892-99; testimony Charles Crocker.

$1,000,000 note.   It involved, also, for the future continued investment of funds in the Western Development Company, and the payment of assessments which might be levied upon Southern Pacific stock.   It was insisted, however, that the matter be settled quickly, partly because Mr. Huntington was about to leave the city, and partly because the period for filing claims against the Colton estate would soon expire.[20]

In the event that Mrs. Colton should not desire to continue with them, the associates demanded an accounting in which the liabilities of Mr. Colton on account of the $1,000,000 note, his share of the net indebtedness of the Western Development Company, and the sum of the alleged embezzlements, should be set against the estimated value of the stock and bonds of which Colton died possessed.   In estimating the value of Mr. Colton's securities, moreover, the associates declared that the question was not as to the amount which could be realized eventually and after the underlying property had had a chance to prove itself, but the market value at the time of negotiations.

Mr. Crocker's testimony on this point expresses very fully the attitude of the associates.   He said:

> Mr. Wilson and I had frequent conversations, and he some-times asserted we could do so and so with these bonds, that we could realize 80 or 90 cents on them.   I said in reply, "Possibly we can; I don't know; it is a matter of speculation; it depends on the future of the roads."   Sometimes he would claim they would bring 80 or 85 cents; and then I would say, "Very likely they may," but it would require time to do it, and a great deal of management necessarily to bring that out, and if Mrs. Colton desired to realize the full value of these securi-ties after this lengthy handling of them, all she had to do was to pay the amount of the note and continue in the company and we would manage them for her, as well as we would for our-selves, of course, and she should receive the full benefit of our knowledge and experience in handling these securities, and we

---

[20] Colton case, pp. 16–32, deposition S. N. Wilson.

would get every dollar out of them we could, and she should have her share to the last cent. Then he would reply: "Well, that can't be. We are determined to go out of this." "Well," I says, "then it is a matter of speculation." [21]

Unquestionably these were hard terms, for it was out of the question for Mrs. Colton to continue with the associates in 1879, a fact of which these gentlemen must have been well aware. She did not have the necessary money, she could not afford in any case to risk her livelihood in so speculative an undertaking as building railroads in southern California, and the relations between her and the Huntington group did not savor of trust and confidence. The expressions of willingness to continue to treat Mrs. Colton as one of themselves cost the associates nothing, and were worth as much. Nor was the standard of valuation of the Colton assets offered by the associates, easily to be defended on ethical grounds. Mr. Colton had not played fair, it is true, but on his part he had been led into an improvement agreement and caused to sign a $1,000,000 note, in at least partial reliance upon the value of the stock of railroads under the associates' control, which was given him in exchange. It was hardly appropriate for the Huntington group now to insist that the collateral security had no value.

Settlement with Mrs. Colton

Hard as the terms were, Mrs. Colton finally acceded to them. By agreement dated August 27, 1879, she turned over 408 shares of the capital stock of the Rocky Mountain Coal and Iron Company, all of the shares which she held of the Occidental and Oriental Steamship Company, all claims to the 40,000 shares of Central Pacific Railroad and Southern Pacific Railroad stock, pledged as collateral for the $1,000,000 note, all of the capital stock of the Western Development Com-

---

[21] Colton case, pp. 8931–32, testimony Charles Crocker.

pany standing to Colton's credit, and some $587,500 in par value of bonds of the Central Pacific–Southern Pacific system, of which $500,000 was in first mortgage bonds of the Southern Pacific Railroad itself. In return for all this, the associates agreed to cancel Colton's note for $1,000,000, and to release Mrs. Colton from any claims on the part of themselves, the Western Development Company, the Central Pacific, and its allied companies.[22]

This settlement left Mrs. Colton with property reasonably valued at half a million dollars, and with an income of perhaps $28,000 a year. That she withdrew with so much to her credit was due to the interposition of Mr. Tevis on her behalf at the last moment, in consideration of a contingent fee,[23] and to the fact that the associates were on the point of floating large amounts of Central and Southern Pacific securities in New York. Mrs. Colton felt, however, that she had been robbed, and in May, 1882, commenced suit to reopen the whole transaction, and to annul the compromise agreement. It has been estimated that this famous suit cost the parties $100,000 apiece. Mrs. Colton alleged fraud and the withholding of essential facts which the associates should have disclosed by reason of the trust relations which had existed between Colton and his partners. In particular she insisted that the statements given her in 1879 with reference to the affairs of the Western Development Company had been misleading and untrue. She now offered to pay Colton's $1,000,000 note, and other liabilities, and asked for the return of the securities which she had previously surrendered.

The more important facts developed in this litigation have been dwelt upon in the preceding discussion, and need not be repeated here. The case went to the Supreme Court of the

---

[22] In the case of the Central Pacific claims, the qualification "so far as known at the time" was introduced.

[23] Colton case, pp. 2815–16, testimony Mrs. Colton; pp. 8943–44, testimony Charles Crocker.

state, where Mrs. Colton was finally defeated. A careful reading of the evidence leads to the conviction that the court was right. Mrs. Colton had done the best she could under the circumstances and was properly held to an agreement she had made with her eyes open, some three years before. Yet the fault of the whole unsavory affair was not hers, nor altogether Mr. Colton's, and the reputation of the associates thereby properly suffered in the public mind.

CHAPTER X

FINANCIAL DIFFICULTIES FROM 1870 TO 1879

Excessive Construction

We may now return to the more general considerations affecting Central Pacific finance which characterized the years from 1870 to 1879. There is a good deal of evidence that the years during which Mr. Colton was connected with the Central Pacific enterprise were years of financial difficulty for the associates, due in part to general depression, in part to a disproportionate amount of new construction, and in part to the continued inability of the Huntington-Stanford group for many years to interest eastern capital in western railroads.

During the years from 1869, when the Central Pacific was first opened to Ogden, to 1874, the earnings of the Central Pacific main line, both gross and net, steadily increased. The following table sets forth the facts relating to this progress, as well as figures for the succeeding years from 1875 to 1881.

EARNINGS AND EXPENSES OF THE CENTRAL PACIFIC
RAILROAD, 1874-81 [1]

Period	Gross Earnings	Operating Expenses	Net Earnings
(Calendar years)			
November 6 to			
December 31, 1869	$ 1,024,680	$ 777,348	$ 247,332
1870	7,519,983	6,009,426	1,510,557
1871	8,862,054	5,937,890	2,924,164
1872	11,963,641	8,645,276	3,318,265
1873	12,867,600	7,822,638	5,044,962
1874	13,726,561	6,468,145	7,258,416
1875	15,665,082	9,937,465	5,727,617

[1] Report compiled by the Commissioner of Railroads, 47th Congress, 1st Session House, Executive Documents No. 123, 1882, Serial No. 2030.

EARNINGS AND EXPENSES OF THE CENTRAL PACIFIC
RAILROAD, 1874-81—*Continued*

Period	Gross Earnings	Operating Expenses	Net Earnings
(Calendar years)			
1876	$ 16,994,216	$ 10,970,599	$ 6,023,617
1877	16,471,144	12,761,639	3,709,505
1878	17,530,859	12,005,535	5,525,324
1879	17,153,163	11,126,298	6,026,865
1880	20,508,113	12,814,121	7,693,992
1881	24,094,001	14,546,899	9,547,102
	$184,381,097	$119,823,379	$ 64,557,718

The greatest continuous drain upon Mr. Huntington and
his friends during the decade from 1870 to 1880 came from
the necessity of raising funds to provide for construction in
southern California as described in earlier chapters. Had business considerations alone controlled, there is little doubt that
this construction would have ceased. It did not pay for
itself, and could not be expected to be profitable until the
country served had been developed. Indeed, Charles Crocker
once declared that when the Southern Pacific was built through
the southern San Joaquin Valley, the company could have
started with a railroad train at Sumner at the south of the
valley and come to Stockton, and with one engine and one
train of cars, hauled every living soul that lived in the valley
out at one haul. The settlers between Yuma and San
Bernardino could have been carried in one carload. This was
as late as 1876.[2]

Inability to Get Eastern Capital

It was largely owing to this construction, as well as to the
general hard times, that the gross earnings per mile of the
Central Pacific and leased lines fell from $12,068.63 in 1875,
to $7,677.84 in 1879. The Central Pacific did not dare stop

---

[2] Crocker manuscript, pp. 40–41.

work for fear that the federal government might be persuaded to subsidize another transcontinental road, and so deprive it of the monopoly which it was so anxious to retain; but it built as slowly as it could, and endeavored to make up by retrenching in other directions. Had the associates been able to sell securities in New York, the slowness with which the earning power of their system developed would not have been so serious a handicap. The territory was after all a rich one, and given time was sure to yield substantial profits. But a market for their stock and bonds was impossible to secure for many years. We have seen the opinion expressed by the associates in the Colton settlement, with respect to the salability of Southern Pacific–Central Pacific securities. There is no reason to doubt that this judgment was correct. Before 1880 it does not appear that there was a market for any of the Huntington-Stanford issues except the Central Pacific first mortgage bonds, and the sale of these was very slow.[3]

There is evidence that the associates not only recognized this situation, but that they took what steps they could to meet it. Central Pacific stock was listed on the New York Stock Exchange in 1874, and on the San Francisco Stock Exchange in 1878, not so much with the idea of selling any large number of shares, as in order to make a beginning which might ultimately lead to an established market. Arrangements were made to have the stock called at San Francisco every day, and the associates stood always ready to buy it back at a slight decline. The payment of dividends was begun in 1873 and continued until by the end of 1877 the sum of $18,453,670 had been distributed. Yet all this had little result for many reasons, among which doubtless should be again mentioned the personal liability attaching under California law to holders of stock in California corporations.

---

[3] Colton case, p. 248, testimony Douty; United States Pacific Railway Commission, p. 3494, testimony D. O. Mills.

Naturally Southern Pacific securities of any type were still more difficult to sell than Central Pacific stock. Mr. Huntington found that the Southern Pacific Railroad was not known in the East, even by parties who had spent some considerable time in California.[4] To overcome this he advertised Southern Pacific stock and bonds in a great variety of ways, sometimes by personal conference with eastern bankers, sometimes by the issue of pamphlets or by the insertion of items in the newspapers, sometimes by the manipulation of bond sales upon the Stock Exchange. Occasionally he bought a few outstanding Southern Pacific bonds in order to support the credit of the company.[5] But here again, in spite of his efforts practically no bonds were sold, and Southern Pacific stock could not be disposed of at any price.

Market for Securities

A good deal of specific testimony by New York brokers is available to show the estimation in which Central Pacific and Southern Pacific securities were held late as 1879. It is all cumulative, and to the effect that no market existed at that time for any of these issues except Central Pacific first mortgage bonds. Thus S. H. Thayer said of Central Pacific stock: "I don't think it would have found any market; I do not think it would have been possible to have sold it at any price; the stock had no friends, nobody knew of it, nobody traded in it; that is, in a general market; I do not know what might have been done by private negotiation; but in the public market nothing could have been done with 20,000 shares towards selling it." [6] Similar testimony was given by D. O. Mills, of San Francisco. Mr. Mills was asked what price could have been obtained in the San Francisco market in 1879 for

---

[4] Colton case, p. 1662, Huntington to Colton, May 1, 1875.

[5] Ibid., pp. 1729-31, Huntington to Colton, June 24, 1875; pp. 1743-45, Huntington to Colton, December 4, 1875.

[6] Ibid., miscellaneous depositions, p. 41, depositions S. H. Thayer.

$13,000,000 in Southern Pacific bonds, and replied that he did not think these bonds were salable then, that it would have been a matter of bargain and sale, and would not have depended upon any market value.[7] Mr. Thayer also testified that the Southern Pacific bonds were on the stock exchange list in New York, but were bonds no one dealt in, and about which few were informed.[8]

It would probably be a mistake, in spite of this testimony, to attribute the reluctance of eastern investors to buy Southern Pacific bonds solely to unfamiliarity with the security. Not only was the economic development of southern California slight and the probable earnings of the Southern Pacific for some years small, but the state as a whole was not in the seventies an attractive field for investment. During the decade from 1860 to 1870, California had grown rapidly in wealth and prosperity. Population had increased and manufactures had begun to develop. In agriculture, fruits, berries, and grapes had been added to the important quantities of grain and vegetables already produced. But the immediate effects of the completion of the transcontinental railroad had been harmful to California, rather than beneficial.

For this there were several reasons: (1) speculation in real estate around San Francisco Bay had so discounted the completion of the line that the actual opening of communication caused a reaction rather than an advance; (2) the combination of a stimulated immigration due to greater facilities for travel, with the sudden release of a considerable part of the labor used in railroad construction, had forced down wages, while, on their part, California merchants had become exposed to competition from eastern distributing houses; (3) droughts in the South, the decline in the production of the mines, and the collapse of speculation in Nevada silver properties, all had

---

[7] Colton case, p. 33, deposition D. O. Mills.
[8] *Ibid.*, p. 45, deposition S. H. Thayer.

given rise to acute suffering and discontent. These things in turn had reacted on political conditions, and had produced, first, the so-called sand-lot excitement, and then the agitation that led in 1879 to a revision of the state constitution. Meanwhile the passage of the Thurman Act, and the various disputes between the Pacific railroads and the federal government had provided special reasons for distrusting the securities of the Southern Pacific and Central Pacific companies, quite apart from conditions peculiar to the section in which their mileage lay.

Short-Term Borrowing

To repeat, it was this failure to dispose of the railroad stock and bonds which they had to sell that threw the associates back upon the necessity of raising money by short-time loans at extravagant rates of interest, and which, in the late seventies, peculiarly exposed them to the dangers of stringency in the New York money market. The partners at times paid as high as 12 per cent for loans.[9] Every element affecting their credit had to be closely watched, lest lenders refuse to discount their paper, and interest on the company's bonds go by default; for it was a customary practice for the associates to take care of interest, at least over short periods, by loans.

In December, 1876, Huntington wrote that the January interest would this time have to come out of earnings, as he had been away from New York so much that he had not been able to secure loans there.[10] The same month Huntington complained of certain pamphlets which one A. A. Cohen had been sending East. "If the parties that inaugurate such fights as we now have with Cohen," he wrote, "and have with the *Sacramento Union* and Senator Booth . . . had to raise money outside of California, where our property cannot be

---

9 Colton case, pp. 1684–85, Huntington to Colton, November 13, 1875.
10 *Ibid.*, pp. 1747–48, Huntington to Colton, December 20, 1876.

seen, I am disposed to think such fights would be few." [11]
In May, 1877, Huntington let his partners know that reports
from California to the effect that the railroad magnates there
were spending their money for personal expenses with
unexampled recklessness had hurt the Central Pacific credit.[12]
At another time he reported that the rumor was abroad that
the Central Pacific had no power under its charter to give
notes for money, and that this had been denied.[13]

All through 1877 the letters exchanged between Huntington and his partners in the West show the strain which the
Central Pacific was under. Huntington was continually wiring
for money in lots of $50,000 to $100,000. Colton was sending
it, sometimes by telegraphic transfer, sometimes in coin. As
early as in May, 1877, Colton was talking of dull business and
of reducing expenses. On August 23 he said that he did not
exactly like the present financial outlook. The following day
he spoke of the need of keeping credit good. "We cannot afford
to ever be called on for money," he wrote, "and not be able
instantly to respond. Our affairs are too extended and extensive for us to take any chances of suspicion. It would hurt us
in many ways, and take a long time to restore confidence . . . .
I will now commence to renew our loans for six or twelve
months, and take in sail everywhere." [14] In September he
repeated, "I am going to send you, for the next three months,
every dollar I can, and, for God's sake, keep all you can for the
January interest. That must be paid. We will not pay out
a dollar here, I am not obliged to. I read *every* department a
lecture on economy about once a week." [15] Earlier in the year
the accounts of the Huntington group with the London and San
Francisco Bank and with the Bank of California had been

[11] Colton case, pp. 1746–47, Huntington to Colton, December 8, 1870.
[12] *Ibid.*, pp. 1768–70, Huntington to Colton, May 6, 1877.
[13] *Ibid.*, pp. 1772–73, Huntington to Colton, May 9, 1877.
[14] *Ibid.*, pp. 7517-18, Colton to Huntington, August 24, 1877.
[15] *Ibid.*, p. 7523, Colton to Huntington, September 28, 1877.

overdrawn from $150,000 to $350,000 each, and Colton was picking up every dollar outside which he could secure without showing his hand.[16]

Indorsement of Notes

As a general practice the associates seem to have refused to put their personal indorsement on the notes which they discounted. Huntington was very insistent that no indorsements be given; yet in January, 1878, conditions had grown so bad that Huntington asked the associates to indorse 100 blank notes and send them to him, to be used as a last resort, and this was done in spite of the violent protest of Mark Hopkins. Colton wrote Huntington:

> I told him [Hopkins] I felt the wise thing for us *all* to do, was to stand in and protect all interests against the debts now owing, but to *all* agree *not to incur any more, not to build any* more road, or to buy *any* steamship, or property, either jointly or individually, until we got out of debt, and had the money in bank to pay for what we bought. That proposition just met his views, and he said that if I would agree that we would *all* live up to that, he would sign 20 of the blank notes, which he did, 10 of each.[17]

Conditions in California grew worse rather than better after the notes were sent, but those in the East improved, and

---

[16] Colton case, pp. 7625-26, Colton to Huntington, March 13, 1878.
It is extraordinary that a man in Colton's position with his intimate knowledge of the precarious condition of Central Pacific finance should have allowed that railroad to declare a 4 per cent dividend in October, 1877, great though his personal necessities may have been. This was, however, done. In reply to a letter from Huntington criticizing this action, Colton later wrote:
"I never had the least intimation of objecting to the dividend until some time after it was declared. Governor Stanford informed me that you had telegraphed him, advising relative to this October dividend. We discussed it some time afterward in the Board meeting and found the whole matter of dividend had been written up in the books, and had gone so far before it had been brought before the Board that it was considered best to let the matter stand as it was. . . . I did not give the matter any attention outside of the Board meeting, for I felt it was a matter that Governor Stanford was personally attending to.
"I do not, however, see the matter in just the light you do, and think so few will know of it that it cannot hurt us in Washington, for if you who are one of the largest stockholders, have not found it out, I do not see much show for outsiders. That there were ample surplus earnings to declare it there is no doubt. So it was a question of policy. . . . I would think in a business way the Government would be glad to see us doing well and prosperous, and evincing ability to pay dividends and *all* of our *debts*." (Colton case, pp. 7533-34, Colton to Huntington, November 24, 1877.)
[17] Colton case, pp. 7608-14, Colton to Huntington, January 31, 1878.

the indorsed notes do not seem to have been used. Yet, of course, the large accumulation of floating indebtedness of the Central Pacific could not be hidden altogether, and the credit of the company was correspondingly impaired.[18]

Sale of Securities

The first successful negotiations for the sale of Central Pacific and Southern Pacific securities were initiated in 1878 with the firm of Speyer and Company, of New York, and resulted in two agreements, dated the 27th and 28th of January, 1880, respectively. On the former date Huntington agreed to deliver, on or before January 31, 1880, as might be demanded, 50,000 shares of the capital stock of the Central Pacific Railroad at 72, ex-dividend, to Roswell P. Flower, John D. Prince, and Daniel Probst, representing a syndicate formed for the purpose. In case the parties took the stock just referred to, Huntington agreed further to deliver 50,000 more shares within six months from the date of the agreement, at 77. In any event, and provided that the syndicate took the first 50,000 shares mentioned in the agreement, Huntington undertook that no other Central Pacific stock beyond a stipulated amount of 40,000 shares should be sold to any other parties for a period of seven months from the date of the agreement.[19]

The syndicate which took Central Pacific stock at this time seems to have considered the enterprise a speculation justified by the resumption of dividends by the company, and by the improving stock market conditions of the time. Mr. Probst

---

[18] In 1885 the Central Pacific directors authorized the issue of $10,000,000 in bonds to pay off the floating debt. (United States Pacific Railway Commission, p. 3019, testimony C. P. Crocker.) There is some reason to suspect that Stanford was individually embarrassed in 1878, as a result of the financial stringency in California. Huntington telegraphed Colton in September of that year to let him know Stanford's financial condition as near as he could ascertain it, and proposed to have the Western Development Company assume Stanford's indebtedness, taking Southern Pacific bonds from Stanford in exchange, at 65. Colton replied that the Western Development Company would have to take about $3,000,000 in Southern Pacific bonds under such an arrangement to cover Stanford's obligations. The French bank in San Francisco had just closed its doors, and he, Colton, was anxious about Stanford's collaterals. He thought that Stanford had $800,000 of United States bonds in that institution. Michael Reese's executors were calling for money. It does not appear what conclusion was finally reached.

[19] Colton case, pp. 704-705.

said that the general market had become so strong in the latter part of 1879 that it was a good time to sell anything.[20] On conclusion of the agreement a regular stock market campaign was opened with the usual accompaniment of matched sales to give an appearance of activity.[21]   The stock nevertheless steadily declined, and the option held by the syndicate to take a second block of shares was not exercised.

The day after the arrangement for the purchase of the Central Pacific stock was concluded, and partly because of its conclusion, Speyer and Company entered into a written contract with the Western Development Company, containing a variety of provisions which together show the factors upon which the value of Southern Pacific securities then depended in the eyes of eastern bankers.   Under an agreement dated January 28, the Western Development Company agreed to sell to Speyer and Company $1,000,000 in Southern Pacific bonds, within ten days, at 86.   Within the year it undertook, in addition, to sell, if Speyer and Company should wish to buy, an additional $4,000,000 in bonds, at 87.51, and a still further amount of $5,000,000 at 90.   On their part, the Western Development and Southern Pacific companies agreed not to sell any of the said bonds within a year to others than Speyer and Company, and the Central Pacific agreed not to issue bonds under the mortgage in question, to exceed $40,000 per mile.

Terms of Contract with Bankers

The more important features of the agreement with Speyer and Company in 1878 were, however, the following, relating to the lease arrangements between the Central Pacific and the Southern Pacific.   Under these provisions the Southern Pacific agreed to secure a new lease from the Central Pacific within three months, containing (1) a provision that the lease should

---

[20] Colton case, p. 112, deposition J. D. Probst.
[21] *Ibid.*, pp. 146–47, deposition A. L. Thompson.

continue five years from the 1st of May, 1879; (2) a provision that the lease should be extended if the Southern Pacific was not connected with the eastern system of railroads, on the 32d parallel, within five years, until such connection should be made, provided that the extension of time should not exceed five years; and (3) a provision that the Central Pacific should pay a rental under the lease, sufficient to cover interest.

The Southern Pacific also agreed with Speyer and Company that if at any time before the expiration of nine years from the date of the lease contemplated, a railroad should be extended so as to connect the railroad of the party of the first part with the eastern system of roads, and the Central Pacific Railroad Company should refuse to prorate with the party of the first part, then the party of the first part would, before the expiration of one year from the date of such refusal, fill up or cause to be filled up one of the two gaps then unfinished between Tres Pinos and Huron, and between Soledad and near Lerdo, whichever it might choose to build.

The Southern Pacific finally undertook to furnish to the parties of the third part, within ninety days from the execution of the agreement, the written opinion and certificate of the chief engineer of the Southern Pacific, that the line of road either between Tres Pinos and Huron or between Soledad and near Lerdo could be completed and put in running order within twelve months of the commencement of work thereon, and could be constructed for the bonds reserved per mile.

The stipulation in the agreemeents relating to the lease of the Southern Pacific to the Central Pacific, and those anticipating further construction along the coast route, are of special interest. It is evident that the credit of the Central Pacific and not that of the Southern Pacific was the basis of the whole transaction. At the time the contract was signed, the option to take Southern Pacific bonds at 86 and 90, respectively, was considered valuable, but in fact this option was not exercised.

Later Improvement

After 1880 financial conditions generally improved. The earnings of the Central Pacific–Southern Pacific roads were still subject to fluctuations, but for several years substantial dividends were declared, and the sale of large quantities of Central Pacific stock in Europe enabled the associates to reduce their commitments. Moreover, by 1883 the long delayed extension to The Needles was completed and the necessary outlay for new construction was greatly lessened. The year 1883 may be taken as the close of the construction period of the Huntington system. Henceforth, in the absence of special disaster, and subject to successful settlement of its indebtedness to the government, the solvency of the Central Pacific and Southern Pacific railroads may be said to have been assured. We may therefore at this point turn away from the more personal and financial aspects of the enterprise, to the consideration of certain important political matters with which the associates were long concerned.

CHAPTER XI

THE RAILROAD COMMISSION OF 1880 TO 1883

Early Agitation Against Company

It is more difficult to describe the relations of the Central Pacific to the legislative bodies of California than it is to trace the history of the system in most other respects, because the details are less matters of public record. Some connection between the railroad and politics undoubtedly existed at an early date. Indeed, Stanford and Colton were politicians before they became railroad men, and the state and local aid which the railroad secured at the very beginning of its construction but confirmed an attitude favorable to continued relations between the corporation and the body politic which these gentlemen might have been expected to approve.

Before 1876, the only regulation which the associates had to encounter was that resulting from the general railroad law, which required a minimum subscription before a railroad corporation could commence business, established proportionate liability of stockholders, and reserved to the legislature the right to reduce rates when the net income of any company exceeded 20 per cent. These and other provisions of like tenor were little calculated to interfere with the profitable operations of a railroad business except perhaps that the proportionate liability established by the law to some extent discouraged participation in railroad enterprise. In 1874 and in 1876, maximum rates and fare enactments were discussed in the legislature but failed of passage. In 1876, nevertheless, the accumulated resentment of the California public over what it considered the grasping and monopolistic policy of a selfish corporation led to important additions to the law. This resentment had been growing for several years. The Sacramento reporter for the *San Francisco Bulletin* wrote, in March, 1868:

> There is a strong prejudice existing here and daily growing stronger, against the Central Pacific Railroad Company. The members from Placer, Nevada, and El Dorado counties are all of them, I suppose, pledged to endeavor to obtain a reduction of the rates of freight and fare on the line. Petitions, apparently signed by nearly all the residents of the districts which use the road for the transportation of freight and travel, have poured in upon the legislature, asking a reduction of prices. It is said that traders who complain of the rates are discriminated against. A general feeling exists that, considering how liberally it has been dealt with by Congress and the State, the management of the business and affairs of the company is extremely illiberal . . .

In like vein the *Stockton Independent* said of the owners of the Central Pacific in 1871:

> No set of men on the face of the globe were ever placed in a more enviable position, or in one where by the exercise of a reasonable foresight, they could have retained their popularity and the friendship of the people. It is now hardly two years since this work was completed, and how remarkable has been the change in public sentiment. Along the whole line of their main trunk road from San Francisco to Ogden, as well as along the various branch roads of this company, nothing is heard but one continuous murmur of complaint, and it is safe to assert that this shortsighted, illiberal, and suicidal policy of the company has so completely changed the sentiment of the people that there is not in a single town on any of their lines of road, either in this state or Nevada, one individual who approves of this course, nor one who will speak well of the company, unless it be one of their subsidized agents or strikers.

Beginnings of State Regulation

It is not necessary to dwell at this point on the reasons for the opinions voiced in these extracts from the press. The feeling of the general public, of which these extracts are the reflection, was doubtless due in part to anger at the methods employed by the Central Pacific in promoting subsidy legislation, in part to disappointment over the results of railroad construction, and in part to reaction against policies of the Central Pacific such as have been outlined in previous chapters. However this may be, the result was the passage of the so-called O'Connor bill in 1876, which erected a State Board of Transportation Commissioners, and defined and prohibited extortion and unjust discrimination. The commissioners were not only to enforce these prohibitions, but they were given extensive authority to secure information from the steam railroads of the state, and were charged with the duty of supervising all such railroads with reference to the security and accommodation of the public.[1]

It appears from the report of the commissioners appointed under the O'Connor Act that the railroads in California, and in particular the Central Pacific, refused to render the reports required by the legislature, and that the commission was unable to compel them to do so.[2] Two years later the commissioners were legislated out of office, and a single commissioner was appointed in their place, acting under a statute similar in most important respects to that administered by his predecessors.[3] Mr. Tuttle, the new commissioner, accumulated certain statistics during his two-year term of office, but otherwise did little to which the railroads could object.

---

[1] Laws of California, 1875–76, Ch. 515. For a readable account of the history of the California Railroad Commission up to 1895, see Moffet, "The Railroad Commission of California—A Study in Irresponsible Government," (Annals of the American Academy of Political and Social Science, March, 1895).

[2] Report of the Board of Commissioners of Transportation to the Legislature of the State of California, December, 1877.

[3] Laws of California, 1877–78, Ch. 641.

The development of railroad regulation was thus temporarily arrested. Yet for several reasons the check to the progress of public control was not lasting. Feeling in the state was running high. The times were hard, both for reasons affecting the whole country, and because of circumstances peculiar to the Pacific Coast. The rainfall of the winter of 1876-77 was slight and, as happens in such cases, great loss of cattle on the ranges occurred, and the grain crop was seriously deficient. At the same time the yield of the Nevada silver mines declined —in fact the dividends of the important Consolidated Virginia mine stopped altogether in January, 1877, to the great disturbance of the stock market at San Francisco. Under these conditions unemployment and suffering were the experience of the working classes, while riots and later, political agitation also resulted. Even the radical labor leader, Dennis Kearney, in spite of his lack of character and self-restraint, or even of unusual mental ability, served as the temporary expression at this time of a real distress, and had some influence on the course of legislation.

Railroad Question in Constitutional Convention

So far as the railroads were concerned, the effect of the unrest throughout California and the activity of the Workingman's party is seen in the railroad clauses of the Constitution of 1879, and of the Act of 1880, which carried them into effect. The call for a convention was issued by the same legislature which passed the railroad control bill of 1878.[4] Mr. Colton thought the call most unfortunate,[5] but there is no reason to suppose that the legislature had anything particularly radical in mind.

When the convention began its sessions, however, its membership was found to include a majority of persons determined

---

[4] Laws of California, 1877-78, Ch. 490.
[5] Colton case, p. 7646, Colton to Huntington, May 23, 1878.

to force thoroughgoing regulation upon the railroad system of the state, as well as a minority opposed to government control of any kind. Just how regulation should be made effective, it is true, few members of the first-named group knew. Some were opposed to corporations as a class, and thought that at least unlimited liability should be imposed on holders of corporate stock. Others were in favor of declaring railroads public highways, upon which all persons should be allowed to run cars and locomotives under such regulations as might be prescribed by law. Still others desired to set a maximum limit of 10 per cent to the return on investment in railroad property. The extreme position on the other side was taken by men like McFarland, of Sacramento, who maintained that the clamor about railroads and corporations was a mania evolved from the inner consciousness of members of the convention, as spiders spin their webs.

The discussion of railroad regulation by the Constitutional Convention of 1879 began on November 18 and ended on December 7. It was systematically conducted, participated in by men with a wide variety of views, and resulted in constructive conclusions of importance. More could scarcely be asked of a deliberative assembly. The main decisions reached were as given below.

New Regulative Commission

The first conclusion of the Constitutional Convention was that the regulation of railroads in California should be entrusted to an elective commission, holding office for four years, and vested with the power to establish and publish rates, to examine the books and records of transportation companies, and to prescribe a uniform system of accounts. Heavy penalties, including fine and imprisonment, were provided for failure to obey the orders the commissioners might make.

The principal objection made to the establishment of a

commission was that its power would be excessive. It was pointed out that the commission would combine legislative, judicial, and executive functions, and that its members could lower rates and increase railroad expenses at will. Mr. Wilson, of San Francisco, declared:

> Here, then, will stand in our government a constitutional triumvirate as great in many respects as that of Rome in the olden time. They may raise and lower the rates of freight and fare to suit their powers, and thus they can play with the value of the stock in the market, and determine the value of the bonds and mortgages on the road . . . They will be sole judges of what are abuses . . . They will determine complaints on their own notions of right and wrong, and however erroneous or malicious their acts, there will be no remedy or appeal.

Reference was made to the English Railway Commission of 1873 and to the Massachusetts Commission of 1869, and the Wisconsin experiment of 1874 was held up as something to avoid. The reply to this kind of objection was that the power to control rates must be lodged somewhere, and that the legislature was inexpert, slow to act, and subject to corrupt influences.

Other Constitutional Provisions

The second decision of the convention was that a general prohibition of discrimination should be placed in the fundamental law. The clauses finally adopted provided that no discrimination in charges or facilities for transportation should be made by any railroad or other transportation company between places or persons, or in the facilities for the transportation of the same classes of freight or passengers within the state, or coming from or going to any other state. In addition to this general prohibition, it was enacted that persons and property transported over any railroad, or by any other transportation company or individual, should be delivered at any station at charges not exceeding the charges for the transportation of persons and property of the same class, in the same direction, to any more distant station. This amounted to a stringent prohibition of greater charges for shorter than for longer hauls. Speakers opposed to the discriminative clauses insisted that only unjust discrimination, not all discrimination, should be prohibited, and pointed out that the proposed law was unconstitutional in that it applied to commerce between the states. Neither objection was sufficient to persuade the convention that the proposals should not be approved.

Besides the fundamental clauses relating to a commission and those prohibiting and defining discrimination, the Constitutional Convention of 1879 forbade railroads to grant passes to persons holding any office of honor, trust, or profit in the state; forbade them also to agree to divide earnings with owners of vessels entering or leaving the state, or, under certain conditions, with other common carriers; granted to all railroads the right to connect with, intersect, or cross other railroads; and provided that no officer or employee of any railroad or canal company should be interested in the furnishing of material or supplies to such company. One apparently important clause declared that a railroad which should lower its rates of fare or freight for the purpose of competing with any other common carrier, should not again raise these rates without the consent of the governmental authority in which should be vested the power to regulate fares and freights.

Act of 1880

Special emphasis should be placed upon the constitutional provisions adopted in 1879 because they created the framework upon which railroad regulation in California was to hang for thirty years. For a full understanding of the system the act of the legislature approved April 15, 1880, should also be consulted. This act defined certain terms used in the law. It also fixed the salary of the commissioners at $4,000 each, provided a mechanism for enforcement of the commissioners' orders through the courts, placed the office of the board in the city of San Francisco, and required rates established by the commission to be posted in all offices, station houses, warehouses, and landing offices to or from which the rates applied. Finally, it granted to the commission, in general terms, all the necessary means and the authority to adopt any suitable procedure to make effective the powers conferred by the Constitution.[6]

Harvey S. Brown, attorney for the Stanford interests, once said that the Constitution of the state of California was conceived in communistic malice, was framed by unpardonable ignorance, adopted in frenzied madness, and was valuable only as a beacon to other states and peoples to avoid its principles and results.[7]

The document certainly compelled the associates to consider the best method of defence against a political attack which threatened to sterilize the monopoly control which they were slowly establishing over the railroad system of the state. From their point of view the danger was like any other—one to be met by skilful strategy, displayed in a new field, but resembling in impelling motive and essential character their action in adjusting rates and in dominating the terminal situation on San Francisco Bay.

Personnel of First Commission

According to the Constitution, one railroad commissioner was to be elected from each of three districts into which the state was to be divided. Elections were held in 1880, and

---

6 Laws of California, 1880, Ch. 59. Under the view that a clause in the Constitution merely amounted to a mandate to the legislature, an enactment such as that of 1880 was obviously necessary. It should be said, however, that in later years this conception has somewhat changed, and constitutional provisions have been held to be self-executing. This was not the case in 1879. (McMurray, "Some Tendencies in Constitution Making," in *California Law Review*, March, 1914.)

7 City and County of San Francisco v. L. Stanford, Charles Crocker, *et al*, argument in the Circuit Court of the United States, 9th Circuit, District of California.

J. S. Cone, C. J. Beerstecher, and George B. Stoneman were returned. Cone was a ranch owner, business man, and capitalist at Red Bluff, with an income of $50,000 a year, and property worth perhaps $200,000. He had been on friendly terms with Stanford before he became commissioner, and had known most of the prominent railroad officials of the state for twenty-five years. By association and point of view he represented the interests of large business in the state. Stoneman was a politician of the better type, later governor of the state, a Democrat, and believed to be a defender of the public interest.[8]

The third member of the commission was C. J. Beerstecher, a San Francisco lawyer with a miscellaneous practice amounting to perhaps $50 a month. Judge Lawler, of the Superior Court of San Francisco, who knew Beerstecher well, says that he came to San Francisco, with nothing but a gripsack, and built up a small practice, mainly divorce suits, among the poorer classes in the city. For some time Beerstecher used Lawler's office, living in rooms in the same building, for which he paid $15 a month; Lawler befriended him, and a man named Steinman advanced him money for electioneering expenses. In return for this, apparently, Steinman was later made bailiff to the railroad commission. That is to say, Beerstecher was poor, with no reputation to lose, and in circumstances in which his good-will had value.

One would scarcely expect effective regulation of a commission composed of a wealthy farmer, a cheap lawyer, and a man who looked to a career in the public service. Nor was such regulation in fact secured. Stoneman once told Judge Reagan, of Texas, that when the California commissioners were elected, he, Stoneman, was elected because it was understood that he represented the popular interests; another gentle-

---

[8] The *Visalia Delta* said of Stoneman, with unconscious humor: "France has her Napoleon; Italy her Garibaldi; America her Washington; Ireland her O'Connell; and the state of California her Stoneman."

man (J. S. Cone) was elected because it was understood that he represented the feeling of the corporations, and a third (Beerstecher) was a sand-lot man. He added that, having the sandlot man with him to take care of the interests of the people, he thought he was all right, but in a short time the sand-lot man sold out and did not amount to anything.[9] Cone also considered Beerstecher a reliable pro-railroad man. There is no direct evidence that Beerstecher accepted railroad money, but the probabilities are strong. Before discussing this point, however, the activities of the new commission may be briefly described.

Indifference of Commissioners

The evidence shows that from the very first the three members of the California commission devoted but a small portion of their time to the work of regulation. Mr. Beerstecher was accustomed to visit his office twice a day, spending perhaps an hour there each time. This was while Beerstecher was a resident of San Francisco. In the latter part of his term he lived in the Napa Valley and probably spent even less time on his official duties. Nor did Beerstecher compare unfavorably with his fellow appointees in application to his work. Governor Stoneman devoted five or six days a month to affairs of the commission; Mr. Cone about the same. Of 127 meetings held by the board between May 3, 1880, and January 8, 1883, Cone was present at 99, Stoneham at 80, and Beerstecher at 109.[10]

It seems beyond belief that a new commission, established to initiate public control of a great industry, should have approached the problem in this indifferent way. The undertaking called for the fullest exercise of the powers of all the com-

---

[9] Arguments and statements before the Committee on Commerce, House of Representatives. 47th Congress, 1st Session, 1882, House Misc. Doc. 55, p. 262, Serial No. 2047.

[10] Report of the Committee on Corporations, 1883, testimony W. R. Andros, secretary to the commission (in appendix to journals of the Senate and Assembly of the Legislature of California, 25th Session, 1883).

mission's members; but it was approached as a casual task to be accomplished in the spare hours of busy men.

As a natural result of their attitude with respect to the importance and urgency of railroad regulation, the commissioners failed to make effective the most primary requirements of the law. Instead of preparing new rates except as hereinafter stated, the commission established the existing rates of the companies operating in the state. Instead of prescribing a system of keeping accounts, the existing system was adopted. Mr. Stoneman once tried to investigate the railroad books, but said they were all Greek to him, and he had no authority to employ an expert. Beerstecher testified that the commission asked certain questions, but that he did not, as an individual commissioner, consider that it was his business to go prying around into the business of the railroad companies.[11]

Some slight attention was paid to the posting of rates, but the only inspection seems to have been by the bailiff of the commission. Doubtless the original cause for the failure of the commission in the respects mentioned was lack of money; but it was for the members to formulate boldly their ideas of what should be done, and to educate public opinion as to its necessity, making use meanwhile of all the authority which they could wield. It was gross negligence and indifference to rest content while the law stood unenforced.

Adoption of First Rate Schedule

The largest task eventually undertaken by the commission was the formulation of rate schedules for passengers and freight. During the spring and summer of 1880, the commissioners traveled through the state taking testimony and hearing complaints. In the winter and spring of 1880-81, they attempted to formulate results. It appears that in May, 1880, Stoneman introduced a resolution to the effect that maximum

---

[11] Report of the Committee on Corporations, 1883, p. 48, testimony C. J. Beerstecher.

rates in California should not exceed five cents per ton per mile for distances 100 miles and over, and six cents per ton per mile for distances under 100 miles, and that maximum fares should not exceed four cents and five cents per mile within the same limitations. This was defeated by a vote of two to one. Nothing was done between this time and February, 1881, when the board unanimously adopted a schedule of passenger fares with maxima varying from five cents to three cents per mile.[12]

At the same time that the passenger schedule was introduced Mr. Cone submitted a freight tariff, which was also adopted. This schedule cut rates mainly on agricultural products originating in the northern part of the state. Stoneman objected to it—but later said that he did not prepare an alternative schedule because he knew it would not be adopted. He did, however, call the attention of the board to the fact that southern California was being discriminated against.[13] Beerstecher had no part in the preparation of the new rates, but made no opposition to them.

Delay in Enforcement

Armed with the new passenger and freight schedules, Mr. Cone went over to the Southern Pacific offices and left the figures with Mr. Towne, general manager, for comment. The railroad people at once objected. They said they were building the Southern Pacific and selling bonds to raise the money. The proposed reductions would injure their credit and could not be accepted. Cone was anxious to avoid litigation and to get quick action.[14] Moreover, Stanford wished to get away and go to Europe, and Cone did not like to keep him.

---

[12] This schedule was prepared under the direction of Stoneman and was approved by Beerstecher on the understanding that the railroad companies were to be asked to show cause why it should not be adopted. (Report of the Committee on Corporations, 1883, testimony C. J. Beerstecher.)

[13] *Ibid.*, p. 11, testimony G. B. Stoneman. Mr. Cone says that the freight schedule was not fully prepared till March, 1881.

[14] *Ibid.*, testimony J. S. Cone.

George Stoneman

As Cone said in another connection, Stanford was pretty winning in his ways. The result was that the railroad agreed not to contest the new freight rates and Cone consented not to press the reduction in passenger rates, at least not until October, 1881. There is no evidence that Cone possessed authority from the commission to negotiate with the Central Pacific, but he seems to have acted in confidence that Beerstecher would support him in action favorable to the railroad and Stoneman in action of contrary tenor.

As a matter of fact the board did not take further action in regulation of passenger fares until August, 1882, a year and a half after the question had first been raised. By this time Cone had become convinced, so he says, that Stanford would concede no further reduction in railroad charges. On the 15th of August, Stoneman accordingly reintroduced his original passenger schedule, but slightly changed. The matter was laid over for a month, and in September, at a meeting at which only Cone and Stoneman were present, a substitute resolution was adopted, setting a maximum fare of four cents per mile. Stoneman thought the maximum should be three cents, but Cone would not consent. The new maxima were suspended in October "until further order of the board" in order to give the railroad companies an opportunity to be heard. Before the commission came together again, however, Stoneman had resigned. This left Beerstecher and Cone—with two as a quorum. It is eloquent of Beerstecher's attitude that he attended no meeting of the board after November 22, 1882, and that on that day his action in respect to passenger rates was to move to postpone consideration.

In two years and seven months the only reductions in rates and fares secured by the Railroad Commission were certain cuts in the rates on products of agriculture conceded to the farmer member of the commission by his railroad friends. The commission formulated no principles and worked out no effective procedure. Even its reports to the legislature had little value. The first two were prepared by Mr. Beerstecher, the third by Mr. Tuttle, former railroad commissioner but no longer in any official way connected with regulation work. When the commission was not unanimous in its decisions, the division usually was that of Cone and Beerstecher against Stoneman —a fact which leads us back to the question of the nature of the influence which the Stanford group was able to exert.

Bribery Committed

The charge is made that the Central Pacific bought and paid for Beerstecher's services while a member of the Railroad Commission, and that Cone was so influenced by his personal and business relations with the managers of the Central Pacific as to be unable to view their activities in the critical and impartial way which his position demanded. The evidence in the case is purely circumstantial, but seems to be convincing. So far as the former is concerned we have the admitted fact that Beerstecher was richer at the end of his term of office than at the beginning by at least $12,000 and probably by a good deal more. As he put it, he thought he saved his entire salary of $4,000 a year as commissioner, during these years. Beerstecher asserted incidentally that his legal practice while a member of the Railroad Board amounted to from $1,200 to $1,500 a year —although the records of the Superior Court of San Francisco, before which Beerstecher practiced, show that this was highly unlikely,[15] and the testimony of the baliff to the commission is directly to the contrary. $12,000 may be regarded as adequate compensation for a man of Beerstecher's type.[16]

---

[15] Report of the Committee on Corporations, 1883, testimony C. J. Beerstecher.

[16] When Beerstecher came up for re-election in 1882, the opposition press asserted that a railroad official handed every employee of the railroad in Beerstecher's district a Republican ticket with Beerstecher's name printed on it, with orders to vote it. (*Mussel Slough Delta*, May 12, 1882.)

Gerke Transaction

Cone's case is not quite so simple. It seems unlikely that a man of his standing should have consciously accepted a bribe. There is, however, direct evidence of a reliable character that Cone was given unusual consideration by the railroad in connection with the purchase of certain lands in the northern part of the state, and Cone himself admitted that while he was commissioner he had bought some lands from a man named Gerke and had resold them within two or three months to the treasurer of the Southern Pacific at a profit of $100,000.[17]

What happened in the first of these two instances was this: It seems that there was a tract of about 34,000 acres of the Oregon grant of the Central Pacific lying east of Cone's ranch —rough, chapparal land, graded at from 50 cents to $2.50 an acre. Cone was running about 20,000 sheep at the time, and was using the land without paying for it, as certain other individuals were also doing. Among these other persons was a man named Wilson, who was not only a small sheep owner, but an actual settler as well. Wilson originally applied to purchase from 5,000 to 7,000 acres of the tract, and was quoted the first graded price, $1.25 to $2.50 an acre. At this quotation he took some land that had water on it, but in general could not afford to buy. Later the land was regraded, and Redding, the Central Pacific land agent, told Wilson that the regrade price was 50 cents. A few months after, in June, 1881, Wilson applied to purchase, although he believed that the application was unimportant, since as a settler he was entitled to second grade. He had the land fenced by this time.

Meanwhile, on the 21st of April, 1880, Cone had negotiated with the Central Pacific for a tract of 34,097.45 acres, including the land in which Wilson was interested. He did not offer to purchase, but asked to have the lands that were free

---

[17] Report of the Committee on Corporations, 1883, testimony J. S. Cone.

reserved for him, that he might ascertain the bounds of his range. In fact, when the statement of the cost of the lands was made out for him he refused to take them at the graded price, and abruptly left the Central Pacific land office, exhibiting considerable ill feeling. This was the situation when Wilson applied. Properly considered, Wilson seems to have been entitled to purchase at the new price. His application was subsequent to Cone's conference with the Central Pacific land commissioner, but Cone had then refused to pay the price asked, which left the lands open. The Central Pacific, however, through Mr. Redding, its agent, refused to sell. Mr. Redding later said:

> When Mr. Wilson demanded a right to purchase a portion of these lands because Mr. Cone had bargained for them and then refused to take them, I told Mr. Wilson the circumstances and said to him that Mr. Cone had refused under so great an exhibition of temper that it was my duty to wait until Mr. Cone became more calm. I also added that the new Constitution and the people had given Mr. Cone and his associates powers that were more extensive than those of the Czar of Russia; that he and his associates could virtually confiscate the property of the stockholders of the railroad company, and that I could not afford to add to a quarrel which by any possibility might be construed into an excuse for unjust action.

The result was that Wilson hunted up Cone and tried to get a relinquishment. Cone offered to let Wilson have the land at the graded price—the first graded price, as Wilson understood it. This offer was naturally refused, and Cone subsequently bought the whole tract for $29,199.67. Although the facts are somewhat complicated, it seems clear that Mr. Cone received special treatment, due to his position as railroad commissioner.

Of the Gerke transaction, Cone testified:

> I would say that the ranch was held under a deed of trust, and parties were foreclosing it, and at the time I bought it it

would have been sold under a deed of trust in fourteen days, and the party came to me and asked what I would pay for it and I didn't dream they intended to sell it because I didn't know the condition the land was in, and they insisted on my making an offer that day for it. I made an offer and it was accepted.

Mr. Storke: What was your profit on that transaction?

A. I think in the neighborhood of one hundred thousand dollars, and the worst trade I ever made when I sold it.

Finding of Legislative Committee

Dealings of this kind were improper, to say the least, and calculated to interfere with the impartial discharge of a commissioner's duties. On the whole subject a committee of the California legislature reported as follows:

As to the second subject of inquiry, whether the Commissioners, or either of them, during their term of office, may have made any extraordinary acquisition of property . . . your committee report that in their opinion Commissioner Stoneman did not make any extraordinary acquisition of property; that Commissioner Cone made a large acquisition to his wealth, which was already great when he was elected Railroad Commissioner, and your committee believe that such acquisition of wealth was largely due to extraordinary and unusual facilities afforded by the railroad officers; and that Commissioner Cone, in the purchase of thirty-four thousand acres of land for twenty-nine thousand dollars, was made a privileged purchaser, and received from the railroad company facilities in this regard denied to other applicants for portions of the tract; and further, that the transaction by which the Gerke farm was purchased by Commissioner Cone in April, 1881, and sold in September of the same year to Nicholas Smith, the Treasurer of the Southern Pacific Railroad Company, at a profit of one hundred thousand dollars, gives rise to the suspicion that more was contemplated in the purchase and sale than appears on the face of the transaction. As to Commissioner Beerstecher, your committee find that by general report, and in the opinion of his associates, he was without means at the time of his election, and his sudden acquisition of wealth while Commissioner was without adequate explanation. . . .

As to the fourth subject of inquiry, your committee report that Commissioners Cone and Beerstecher knew of and permitted both systematic and casual discrimination in charges and facilities for transportation between persons and places by railroad corporations in this State, and that through their conduct in permitting and upholding the same, Commissioner Stoneman was unable to accomplish a redress of such discriminations while Commissioner. Further, under this fourth subject of inquiry, your committee find that Commissioner Cone sacrificed the best interests of the State through personal friendship for Governor Stanford, and in return therefor received favors from him; and that Commissioner Beerstecher's conduct admits of no other explanation than that he was bribed, and that in the opinion of this committee Commissioners Cone and Beerstecher acted in the interests of the railroad corporations rather than of the people.

This finding of the legislative committee is justified by the facts elicited in their investigation.

CHAPTER XII

THE SOUTHERN PACIFIC AND POLITICS

Appeals to Public

We may now consider in a more general fashion the political methods of the Southern Pacific group during the first thirty years of their railroad history. We have seen that they not only relied upon the talents of their legal staff in taking advantage of defects in the law, but that in two cases—the case of the railroad commission of 1880, and that of the subsidy in San Francisco in 1863—they probably resorted to the direct use of money to accomplish their ends. Yet a whole state cannot be bought, though individuals may be, and it would do injustice to the breadth of view of the associates to suppose that they limited themselves to any such crude device. Indeed, the frequency with which money bribes were offered probably diminished as time went on.

Consideration of the general policies of Mr. Stanford and of Mr. Huntington seems to show that they met the public demand for regulation of rates and fares in no less than five distinct ways.

The first method consisted of appeals to the general public through testimony before legislative committees, communications to the newspapers, letters to private organizations which interested themselves in the government control of corporations, and other similar devices. By these various means Stanford, at least, spread his philosophy of industry widely abroad. He took the general position that agitation upon the subject of railroads was due to misapprehension of the facts. Most alleged abuses were imaginary, but the Central Pacific stood ready to correct any that were shown to exist.[1] Railroad fares and freights were cheaper in California than anywhere else in the world, all things considered.[2] In case further reduction were desired, the true policy was to place as few burdens upon the railroads as possible, to encourage in this way new construction, and to rely on competition for the desired result. The interests of the railroad and of the public were the same.[3] Monopolies in the United States were possible only to the extent that they were beneficent. There was properly no right of control in the state. The Granger decisions of the Supreme Court of the United States were a flagrant violation of the principles of free government. If the people wanted to exercise control over a railroad they must do as the state does when it exercises the right of eminent domain; that is to say, they must pay to the individual owners the full value of whatever was taken for public use. Anything else was confiscation. Moreover, at best, regulation could not be complete, because it could not ever compel the shipper to ship equally over all lines, and because, while commerce was world-wide, American governments could regulate but one link in the chain. In California, regulation was peculiarly inexpedient so long as the railway system of the state was incomplete.[4]

---

[1] Letter to Senate Committee on Corporations, California Legislature, January 22, 1874; San Francisco Chronicle, January 23, 1874.

[2] Testimony before Senate Committee on Corporations, February 16, 1874 (in appendix to journals of Senate and Assembly, 20th Session California Legislature, Vol. 4); San Francisco Chronicle, February 17, 1874.

[3] Letter to Committee of the New York Chamber of Commerce, January 20, 1881.

[4] The following interview with Charles Crocker, reported in the Placerville Democrat for March 3, 1883, suggests how the doctrine described in the text was concretely applied: "A gentleman of Placerville called upon Mr. Charles Crocker, of the railroad company, in San Francisco last Saturday, to ascertain just what we might calculate upon in reference to the extension of the railroad from Shingle Springs to Placerville. He reports that Mr. Crocker conversed freely on the subject, and with an appearance of perfect candor. He said emphatically that his company would not build or extend any branch roads under existing conditions as to uncertainty of action by the Railroad Commission, and the apparent state of public opinion as manifested in the Legislature and portions of the public press. He says that if the Commission intends to make sweeping reductions on the branch roads, such action would make these roads valueless, and he is not disposed to build roads to be thus destroyed. In answer to a direct question, with a full understanding that it was to be reported to our people, he said that if the Robinson suit were settled, and the position of the Commission ascertained as disposed to non-interference with the branch roads, his company was anxious to and would immediately extend the road to this place."

Huntington's Views

Mr. Huntington shared Mr. Stanford's views, or at least approved the conclusion to which they led, but does not seem to have courted the same publicity in respect to the matter. Interviews he distrusted. "I notice," he wrote in 1875, "that some correspondent of a San Diego paper has been interviewing Mr. Crocker. It is very difficult for any one to be interviewed by an infernal newspaper without getting hurt; and Mr. Crocker is not the most unlikely to get hurt of all the men I know."

Yet in spite of this attitude towards the newspaper reporter, Huntington had a keen appreciation of the importance of shaping public opinion, and was familiar with the ordinary devices used for the purpose, including the manipulation of the press. He was concerned over the attitude of the *Sacramento Record Union*. "If I owned the paper," he said, "I would control it or burn it." [5] "I wish you would have it sent over the wires as often as you can that the Southern Pacific is being rapidly built," he wrote Colton from New York in 1877. [6] Again, "Yours of November 28 with Northern Pacific clips is received. Many of the articles are very good. It is much better that all such articles with petitions be sent direct to members of the Senate and House, we keeping in the background as much as possible." [7]

In November, 1875, Huntington wrote Colton that:

Gwynn left for the South yesterday. I think he can do us considerable good if he sticks for his hard money and anti-subsidy schemes; but if it was understood by the public that he was here in our interest, it would no doubt hurt us. When he left I told him he must not write to me, but when he wanted I should know his whereabouts, etc., to write to R. T. Colburn of Elizabeth, New Jersey. [8]

---

5 Colton case, pp. 1717–19, Huntington to Colton, April 27, 1876.

6 *Ibid.*, p. 1754, Huntington to Colton, January 22, 1877.

7 *Ibid.*, p. 1814, Huntington to Colton, December 7, 1875.

8 *Ibid.*, pp. 1684–85, Huntington to Colton, November 13, 1875.

Influential Individuals Favored

A second method employed by the associates in their efforts to oppose public regulation of corporate affairs was that of paying personal attention to men who possessed or were believed to possess influence. In its simplest form this involved the employment at liberal salaries of the ablest legal talent which could be found. The policy was, however, pushed much further than the statement made would indicate. Huntington's letters to his associates in the West were full of suggestions as to what should be done and of commendations for, or criticism of, what had been accomplished.

In April, 1875, Huntington wrote Colton that he had given Dr. Linderman, director of the United States Mint, a letter of introduction to him, Colton, at San Francisco. This was because the location of a new building for the Mint might be of importance to the Central Pacific.[9] In October of the same year Huntington gave a pass to a certain congressman and ex-governor, but warned Colton that the man was a slippery fellow and should not be trusted too much.[10] Crocker wrote to Colton in February, 1875:

> I fully appreciate your position there and need of . . . a Senator of the United States. We tried to get him off sooner the best we knew. I think he did not want to go, and I fear when he gets there he will not be earnest in our interest as formerly. Stanford thinks I am mistaken and I hope I am.[11]

A letter dated July 26, 1876, shows that Huntington was trying to get up a party of twenty-five southern members of Congress to visit California over the Southern Pacific. He wanted none but the best men—that is, men who would "go for the right as they understand it, and not as Tom Scott [12] or

---

9 Colton case, pp. 1642–43, Huntington to Colton, April 26, 1875.
10 *Ibid.*, pp. 1676–77, Huntington to Colton, October 19, 1875.
11 *Ibid.*, pp. 1624–25, Crocker to Colton, February 8, 1875.
12 Tom Scott was president of the Pennsylvania Railroad at one time and an active opponent of Huntington before Congress.

somebody else understands it," but he was willing to pay the expenses of the trip for such men.[13]   In order to help persuade representative men to make this trip, Huntington telegraphed Colton to have some of the prominent men in San Francisco wire Senator Gordon, of Georgia, urging that the visit should be made.[14]   "I noticed you are looking after the State Railroad Commission," Huntington adds in another letter to the same address, "I think it is time." [15]   Again:

> I am scrry to learn that the receipts are so very poor south of San Francisco, but it is a good time to take the State Railroad Commissioners over the roads.   I am glad to notice that you are looking after the Commissioners.   I think it very important.[16]

Still again, in May, 1877, Huntington wrote:

> I am glad you are paying some attention to General Taylor and Mr. Kasson.   Taylor can do us much good in the South. I think, by the way, he would like to get some position with us in California.   Mr. Kasson has always been our friend in Congress, and as he is a very able man, has been able to do us much good, and he has never lost us one dollar.   I think I have written you before about Senator . . . .   He may want to borrow some money, but we are so short this summer, I do not see how we can let him have any in California.[17]

Letters like these cover only one period and refer to the activity of only three out of the five associates, but there is sufficient outside evidence of a general nature to indicate that this policy was systematically followed by the Stanford group.

Lobbying in Washington and Sacramento

In addition to the attempt in a general way to gain the good-will of the public or of influential members of it, the

---

[13] Colton case, p. 1735, Huntington to Colton, July 26, 1876.
[14] *Ibid.*, pp. 1736–37, Huntington to Colton, August 7, 1876.
[15] *Ibid.*, pp. 1756–58, Huntington to Colton, March 7, 1877.
[16] *Ibid.*, pp. 1763–65, Huntington to Colton, March 31, 1877.
[17] *Ibid.*, pp. 1776–77, Huntington to Colton, May 15, 1877.

Central Pacific was regularly represented at Washington and Sacramento when legislation was pending. Huntington, as has been said, took care of the company's affairs in Washington. He had offices in New York and Boston also, and divided his time between the three places while Congress was in session—four days in Washington, two in New York, and one in Boston.[18] Stanford attended to matters in Sacramento, either in person or through representatives such as William Carr or Stephen T. Gage. The latter was also for many years the company's agent in Nevada. Both Huntington and Stanford, of course, were assisted by a corps of lawyers and political aides-de-camp, some of whom were very highly paid. General Franchot, for instance, Huntington's chief assistant, received at one time a salary of $20,000 a year, besides a liberal expense account. Much criticism has been directed at the activity of Central Pacific agents in the lobbies at Washington and Sacramento, but a large portion of it was probably legitimate.

Correspondence from Washington

Certainly the watch which the associates kept on legislation was very close. Huntington's own activities in 1875, 1876, 1877, and 1878 are vividly described in the letters which he wrote Colton during these years, and some few of these deserve to be reproduced if only for the picture they suggest of the man who wrote them. In March, 1875, Huntington wrote:

> I notice a bill passed the House some few days since, called up by Williams of Michigan. I forget its title, but it called for reports, etc., etc., from the Pacific roads. Of course it was something ugly or it would not have passed.[19]

This was mere routine. By June, 1876, however, the legislative work had increased. Mr. Huntington told Colton:

---

[18] Huntington manuscript, p. 17.
[19] Colton case, pp. 1622–23, Huntington to Colton, March 3, 1875.

There is a terrible fight kept up on us in Washington. But
while they may bite us, they will not eat us up. Sherrell telegraphed me to come to Washington in great haste, as Lawrence
was to pass his bill at once; so I went over and got the committee to recall it from the House back to the committee, so the
demagogue from Ohio cannot trouble us before the 6th of July.
In the meantime we will be working on our land proposition
in the Senate. Just what we can do I cannot say, but I shall
surely keep trying.[20]

The following month he added:

I returned from Washington last night. Our matters look
better there, but we are not out of danger. It has been so very
hot here for the last few weeks that it has come near using
me up. You know I do not spare myself when I have anything
to do.[21]

In August, 1876, Huntington wrote Colton:

I have thought I could stand anything, but I am fearful this
damnation Congress will kill me. Senator Edmunds told another Senator yesterday that he would pass his Pacific Railroad Sinking Fund Bill before Congress adjourned, but I think
he will not, and I have some hope Congress will adjourn by
the time this reaches you.[22]

And in March, 1877, he was able to say:

Congress has adjourned, and we have not been hurt, except
by the paying out in Washington of some money for hotel bills,
etc.
I am quite sure that we stand better in Washington at this
time than we ever did before.
The Pacific Mail Steamship Co. got no aid. I will tell you
some things about that some time. The Sinking Fund Bill did
not pass, but is in a much better shape to pass than it has ever
been before. I stayed in Washington two days to fix up the
Railroad Committee in the Senate. Scott was there, working

---

[20] Colton case, p. 1728, Huntington to Colton, June 21, 1876.
[21] Ibid., pp. 1731-32, Huntington to Colton, July 16, 1876.
[22] Ibid., p. 7669, Huntington to Colton, August 1, 1876.

for the same thing, but I beat him for once certain, as the committee is just what we want it, which is a very important thing for us. You will no doubt notice before you get this that we were not able to pass the Texas-Pacific bill.[23]

The committee with which Huntington was so content was changed somewhat later, much to his disgust.[24]

It was not until the first part of 1878, however, that his letters show him again hard at work. In January, 1878, Huntington wrote to Colton:

I notice what you write of the communists in the California Legislature, and am very sorry to know it, but the feeling in Congress is not much better, and yet, somehow, I do not think we shall be much hurt, although Scott is working hard and developing more strength than I supposed he had. He had the Railroad Committee of the House. I think we have it now.[25]

The following month he said:

I returned from Washington last night, and I am as near used up as I ever was in my life before. I am spending my last winter at Washington. As I feel today, I would not agree to spend another there for all the property we all have. Our matters are looking fair in Washington, Scott is very bitter in the discussion. He used some business compliments and all such stuff, and I am compelled to play him; but it is very distasteful to me.[26]

This letter is followed in the record by a series of others of the same tenor, which will be presented without comment.

. . . I have done all I can to prevent certain bills from being reached, and do not think any bills can be that will hurt us, but if there are, they will pass, as this Congress is, I think, the worst set of men that have ever been collected together since man was created.[27]

[23]Colton case, p. 1756,Huntington to Colton, March, 7, 1877.
[24] Ibid., p. 1758, Huntington to Colton, March 14, 1877; pp. 1812–13, Huntington to Colton, December 5, 1877.
[25] Ibid., pp. 7776–77, Huntington to Colton, January 11, 1878.
[26] Ibid., pp. 1847–48, Huntington to Colton, February 9, 1878
[27] Ibid., p. 1833, Huntington to Colton, New York, June 15, 1878.

I returned from Washington last night. I am almost happy to think I shall not be called there again this session, as Congress has adjourned its first session, and may the likes of it never meet again. I think in all the world's history never before was such a wild set of demagogues honored by the name of Congress. We have been hurt some, but some of the worst bills have been defeated, but we cannot stand many such congresses.[28]

Friend Colton: I returned from Washington this morning and found on my desk yours of the 10th inst., No. 74. Thurman's funding bill has not passed the House yet, but it will, I think, although I am endeavoring to get it to the Judiciary Committee. If I can I think we can get it amended, but even that is doubtful. There were some mistakes made by us when the bill was in the Senate; the greatest was in Gould going to Washington; but it is too long a story to write now. I will tell you when we meet, if we have nothing better to talk of. This Congress is nothing but an agrarian camp, the worst body of men that ever before got together in this country. Scott is making a hard fight on his Texas and Pacific bill. He has made a combination with the Northern Pacific, which will give him some strength, how much I cannot tell. The Northern Pacific are to ask for guarantee of their bonds by the United States. I shall come to California soon after Congress adjourns. Find some one to buy me out of everything there. I am tired and want to quit.[29]

. . . I notice what you say of Thurman's Sinking Fund Bill—of course it is bad, but if we could have amended it so as to make it a finality, and give us 6 per cent on the fund, it would not have been so bad. It may not pass, but I think it will for this is the worst Congress we have ever had; if it should, we must beat it in the courts, if we can.

I go to Washington tonight; I should have gone last night, but for the reason that Clara has been quite sick for some days.

Mr. Sherrell telegraphed me yesterday that I must not fail of being there this morning. I cannot attend to this Washington business much longer.[30]

---

[28] Colton case, pp. 833–34, Huntington to Colton, New York, June 20, 1878.
[29] Ibid., p. 1822, Huntington to Colton, New York, April 19, 1878.
[30] Ibid., pp., 1823–24, Huntington to Colton, New York, April 23, 1878.

I returned from Washington last night. I hope to get through there without being hurt any more; but it seems as though every committee in both Houses had something before them that we had an interest in.[31]

Skilled Wire-Pulling

There is no need to comment in any detail upon these letters. Their occasional indication of discouragement doubtless meant nothing more than that Huntington sometimes grew tired and hot and angry with the opposition which he encountered. A characteristic of the man was that he never really gave up. The Thurman bill referred to will be described in another connection.

Scott was a railroad man, at one time president of the Pennsylvania Railroad, who was seeking to persuade Congress to subsidize a transcontinental railway by the southern route. The land proposition was a scheme of the associates to induce the federal legislature to buy back a portion of the Central Pacific land grant at the government price. As a whole, the letters so far quoted show that Huntington was a persistent and energetic lobbyist, although the record of Congressional legislation shows that he was far from uniformly successful.

On the whole, the railroad managers pulled wires with a skill which rapidly increased with experience. Sometimes the company was made to appear prominently, and sometimes it was kept in the background when legislation was desired. Huntington found that some members of Congress were disinclined to talk to him concerning Southern Pacific matters. In such cases he had recourse to third parties—perhaps a constituent of the member in question, perhaps a friend. The same methods were employed in dealing with state legislation. In 1875 the Southern Pacific desired a franchise permitting it to build through Arizona. Huntington wrote Colton that he thought this would cost less if other interests than the asso-

---

[31] Colton case, pp. 1828–29, Huntington to Colton, New York, May 24, 1878.

ciates stood at the front while the franchises were being obtained, but that after the charters were obtained it should be known that they were controlled by the Southern Pacific.[32] He said:

> I am inclined to believe that if you could get the right man on that line in Arizona to work with the few papers they have there, to agitate the question in the territory, asking that some arrangement be made with the S. P., at the same time offer the S. P. a charter in the territory that would free the road from taxation, and one that would not allow for any interference with rates until ten per cent interest was declared on the common stock, I believe the Legislature could be called together by *the people* for $5,000 and such a charter granted. Then we would take the chances of having such a charter made good by Congress or the State when it became one.[33]

At one time Huntington even suggested that the Southern Pacific might bear the expense of an extra session of the Arizona legislature in order to hasten consideration of legislation favorable to the company.[34] The desired legislation was eventually obtained, but not until February, 1887.

Unethical Dealings

Did or did not the Huntington group, including Stanford at Sacramento and Reno, and Huntington at Washington, employ improper means in their endeavor to influence votes? This is another question upon the answer to which much depends. That passes were issued to members of the legislature, members of Congress, and judges of courts, and that gentlemen of these types were entertained at dinner in Sacramento was generally known. We have Mr. Gage's statement, at least, that no more than this took place in Nevada. He told the United States Pacific Railway Commission of

---

[32] Colton case, pp. 1673–74. Huntington to Colton, October 9, 1875.
[33] *Ibid.*, pp. 1679–81, Huntington to Colton, October 29, 1875.
[34] *Ibid.*, pp. 1669–70, Huntington to Colton, September 27, 1875.

1887, that his expenditures in that state over a period of eight years had amounted to $2,000, and added:

> . . . and I would like to produce to you the files of the newspapers in order to show the existence of the misapprehensions that existed among the good people of Nevada, as indicated by their press, concerning my relations with the legislature of Nevada, session after session for the sixteen years. I remarked yesterday that it was one of the greatest sources of regret that I had, the imputations which were cast on my character, and which I feel I have not deserved, and which I feel I may not live long enough to outgrow. One of these is that I have spent money in the Nevada legislature for the Central Pacific like water; and those things were constantly asserted, and I believe frequently believed by a good many good people in the State, but they were not true. As I asserted to you yesterday, I have kept an accurate account of the expenses for the first eight years that I was attending the sessions of the Nevada legislature, which included my personal expenses during that time, and they figure up $2,000, or a fraction under it, as it was. Now, if any one thinks that $2,000, or less, could corrupt a legislature for eight years, including the personal expenses of myself, he must invoice members of the Nevada legislature at a very low price, and "buy them by the string."[35]

Mr. Gage would not say, however, when asked pointblank, whether or not he had paid any money or made any provisions of advantage or reward to any member of the legislature of California or Nevada.[36] Nor would Mr. Stanford say more in reply to the inquiries of the United States Pacific Railway Commission than that the company would not include in any settlement with the United States, vouchers to which objections were made.[37]

On the whole, there is a good deal of evidence that the owners of the Central Pacific went further in influencing

---

[35] United States Pacific Railway Commission, p. 3276, testimony S. T. Gage.

[36] Ibid., pp. 3287–88, testimony S. T. Gage.

[37] Ibid., pp. 4174–75, testimony Leland Stanford.

legislation than any strict system of ethics would allow. Huntington once stated his own position as follows:

> If you have to pay money to have the right thing done, it is only just and fair to do it. . . . If a man has the power to do great evil and won't do right unless he is bribed to do it, I think the time spent will be gained when it is a man's duty to go up and bribe the judge. A man that will cry out against them himself will also do these things himself. If there was none for it, I would not hesitate.[38]

Further Evidence

More important than the record of such general expressions of opinion are the affidavits filed in the San Francisco subsidy litigation described in an earlier chapter. Nor is anyone likely to read the letters of Mr. Huntington to Mr. Colton in the late seventies without becoming convinced that the possibility of purchasing votes was constantly before Huntington's mind. Huntington wrote Colton at one time that the (Southern Pacific) company could not get legislation unless it paid more than it was worth.[39] In another communication he said: "If we pass the Sinking Fund Bill and beat Scott and the Union Pacific, it will hurt us not less than half flora"; [40] and in still another we find the cheery comment: "Matters do not look well in Washington, but I think we shall not be much hurt, although the boys are very hungry and it will cost considerably to be saved." [41]

In November, 1877, Huntington wrote Colton:

> You have no idea how I am annoyed by this Washington business, and I must and will give it up after this session. If we are not hurt this session it will be because we pay much

---

[38] Huntington manuscript, p. 80.

[39] Colton Case, pp. 1802-3, Huntington to Colton. November 9, 1877.

[40] *Ibid.*, pp. 1843-45, Huntington to Colton, January 28, 1878. J. M. Bassett declared that Huntington paid out $1,700,000 to prevent Scott from securing a subsidy for the Atlantic and Pacific Railroad.

[41] *Ibid.*, p. 1840, Huntington to Colton, January 12, 1878.

money to prevent it, and you know how hard it is to get it to pay for such purposes; and I do not see my way clear to get through here and pay the January interest with other bills payable to January 1st, with less than $2,000,000, and possibly not for that. . . . I think Congress will try very hard to pass some kind of a bill to make us commence paying on what we owe the Government. I am striving very hard to get a bill in such a shape that we can accept it, as this Washington business will kill me yet if I have to continue the fight from year to year, and then every year the fight grows more and more expensive; and rather than let it continue as it is from year to year, as it is, I would rather they take the road and be done with it.[42]

In one case where the salary to be paid a certain individual was under consideration, Huntington wrote Colton frankly that it was important that the man's friends in Washington should be on the railroad's side, and that if this could be brought about a salary of $10,000 to $20,000 a year would be worth while. Huntington wanted the man to make a proposition in writing, however, that he would control his friends for a fixed sum.[43] When asked about the meaning of his correspondence, Huntington denied that these expressions had any vicious significance. He said he kept on high ground,[44] and even objected to the free use of liquor and cigars.[45] Specifically, he gave instructions to his people never to use money in any immoral or illegal sense. "Buying votes in a legislature was bad policy," said he, and his position in these matters received the formal support of Stanford. But such assertions are entitled to less weight than Huntington's less guarded phrases.

Heavy General and Legal Expenses

There is no question that the control exercised by the Central Pacific management over the legal and miscellaneous

---

[42] Colton case, p. 1803, Huntington to Colton, November 15, 1877.

[43] *Ibid.*, pp. 1700–1, Huntington to Colton, January 14, 1876.

[44] *Ibid.*, pp. 1712–13, Huntington to Colton, March 23, 1876.

[45] United States Pacific Railway Commission, p. 3738, testimony C. P. Huntington.

expenses of the company was informal to the last degree. Huntington had a great deal of money to spend and he turned it over to trusted agents without too many questions. He would pay $5,000 or $10,000 at a time to General Franchot, for instance, without inquiring where it went or how it was paid.[46]   Checks were made out in all cases to I. E. Gates, Mr. Huntington's assistant in New York, and were indorsed by him either to payee or in blank.[47]   Vouchers covering such items were made out simply to "Expense," or to "Legal expense." [48]   In many cases expenditures authorized by Stanford, Crocker, or Huntington were represented by no vouchers at all,[49] the filing of vouchers being subsequently waived at stockholders' meetings.

All in all, the general and legal expenses of the Central Pacific between the years 1875 and 1885 averaged over $500,-000 annually. The only reply to the government inquiry as to what this money had been paid out for was Stanford's statement already quoted that vouchers to which there were objections would not be included in any settlement with the United States, but that the moneys would be treated as still in the treasury.[50]   This was plainly an evasion of the point at issue.

Company in Politics

Still another question is how far the headquarters of the Central Pacific in the various capitals were used as agencies for the election of legislators and other persons who owed their position to railroad influence.   It is the unhesitating popular judgment that the railroad at an early date "entered politics."   In a long letter dated August 26, 1873, Eugene Casserly asserted that the Central Pacific aimed to be and was

---

46 United States Pacific Railway Commission, pp. 35–36, testimony C. P. Huntington.
47 *Ibid.*, p. 3869, testimony I. E. Gates.
48 *Ibid.*, p. 3697, testimony C. P. Huntington.
49 *Ibid.*, pp. 2995–99, testimony C. F. Crocker; p. 3200, testimony Leland Stanford.
50 *Ibid.*, pp. 4174–75, testimony Leland Stanford.

a third party in the politics of the state, holding the balance of power between the Democratic and the Republican parties, and controlling or seeking to control at will each or both of them. "This third party," continued Mr. Casserly, "has the usual attributes of a political party, the same apparatus and appliances. It has its leaders, its managers, its editors, its orators, its adherents. It selects these from both parties, but mostly from the party in the majority. Whether they call themselves Republicans or Democrats, and however they divide or contend on party issues, they move as one man in the cause of the railroad against the people. To that cause they give their first allegiance."

Bassett Polemic

This statement of Mr. Casserly calls to mind another charge or series of charges made by a man named J. M. Bassett in the years following 1892. Mr. Bassett was one of the early pioneers. He came to California in 1851, and was at various times miner, printer, newspaper man, railroad employee, and member of the Oakland city council. At one time he was Leland Stanford's secretary. After Mr. Stanford had been forced out of the presidency of the Southern Pacific, Bassett began to publish a series of open letters to Collis P. Huntington, and continued them weekly, with occasional intervals, for several years. The sustained vivacity and pungency of this polemic, and the systematic virulence with which Bassett reviewed and criticized the Huntington policies make the series a noteworthy journalistic achievement. Mr. Bassett denounced Mr. Huntington for the overcapitalization of the Southern Pacific system, for its failure to pay taxes, for its carelessness of the lives of its employees and of the public, for its attempt to evade repayment of the debt which it owed to the United States government, and for the general mismanagement which, he asserted, had taken place under Huntington's control. With respect to the interference of the Southern Pacific in politics, Bassett wrote to Huntington in 1895:

> What chief executive of the State, before the present incumbent, has there been who did not owe his nomination and election to the Southern Pacific Company and in acknowledgment of his debt hasten to obey its slightest command? Has there ever been a Board of Railroad Commissioners before last November in which you did not own at least two members? Have you not named every Harbor Commissioner appointed during the past twelve years?
>
> Have you not hitherto chosen San Francisco's Police Commissions and do you not now exercise a dictatorial power over the city's police, especially the Harbor Police? Were not the Judges of the two United States Courts in San Francisco appointed at the instance of Leland Stanford? How many Superior Courts are there in the State in which a citizen may bring an action against you in full confidence that he will be fairly and impartially dealt with? Doubtless there are such but the difficulty is to find them. Before the recent elections how long did you control the government of San Francisco? Have you not dictated the government of Oakland for the past twenty-five years? Until last election had you not continuous control of Alameda County's government? . . .[51]

When one desires to test the accuracy of accusations like those of Casserly and of Bassett, one has first to remember that they are in accord with the substantially uncontradicted declarations of men of all degrees of prominence in California over a period of fifty years. Political campaigns have been waged on the question of the railroad versus the people. Not only newspapers like the *Sacramento Union* and the *San*

---

[51] Most of the so-called "Dear Pard letters" from which the above is taken, appeared in the *San Francisco Daily Report* after November, 1892. In the majority of cases the letters were printed in the Saturday edition. The correspondence continued with varying frequency until Bassett's death in 1903. It was credited with a considerable share in preventing the refunding of the Central Pacific indebtedness to the United States government on terms favorable to the corporation, and Bassett himself believed that his "exposures" had seriously injured Southern Pacific credit in the financial markets.

Francisco Examiner, but men like John T. Doyle, at one time state railroad commissioner, General Howard, a leading member of the Constitutional Convention of 1879, and H. H. Haight, at one time governor of the state of California, have asserted that railroad influence was a real and important factor in the politics of California. While neither a corporation nor an individual can properly be convicted on the strength of current report, the presence of so much smoke, over so long a period, is fair evidence of some fire.

Documentary Evidence

Direct testimony relating to the political activity of the Huntington group comes from Mr. Huntington himself in two ways. In the first place there have been published certain letters which passed between Huntington and his associate, Mr. Colton, in the years 1875 to 1878. These documents have been referred to in other connections. They came out in the course of court proceedings, and have the weight of confidential communications, not intended for publication. Extracts from these letters will presently be given. Besides this, certain statements were given by Huntington to the press in 1890 which bear directly upon the point at issue. These statements were intended to discredit Stanford, but in the course of the heated controversy to which they gave rise they were not denied by Stanford nor withdrawn by their author.

On May 1, 1875, Huntington wrote Colton:

> I noticed what you say of Piper; he is a wild hog; don't let him come back to Washington, but as the house is to be largely Democratic, and if he was to be defeated, likely it would be charged to us, hence, I should think it would be well to beat him with a Democrat; but I would defeat him anyway, and if he got the nomination put up another Democrat and run against him, and in that way elect a Republican. Beat him.[52]

---

[52] Colton case, p. 1661, Huntington to Colton, May 1, 1875.

Asked to whom the letter referred, Huntington later said that if he remembered the person, and he thought he did, he was a man whose views ran contrary to all human interests.[53]

A letter in June, 1876, reads as follows:

> I hope . . . will be sent back to Congress. I think it would be a misfortune if he was not. . . . has not always been right, but he is a good fellow and is growing every day. . . . is always right, and it would be a misfortune to Cal. not to have him in Congress. Piper is a damned hog, and should not come back. It is shame enough for a great commercial city like San Francisco to send a scavenger like him to Congress once. . . .[54]

Again, in November, 1876, Huntington wrote Colton:

> I hope . . . is elected and . . . defeated, as it was generally understood here that our hand was over one and under the other. . . .[55]

A still later letter relates to the pending election of a senator from California. Huntington said:

> We should be very careful to get a U. S. Senator from Cal. that will be disposed to use us fairly, and then have the power to help us . . ., I think, will be friendly, and there is no man in the Senate that can push a measure further than he can.[56]

Controversy between Associates

The correspondence which has just been cited is not offered in order to discredit Mr. Huntington, or for any reason except to show that it was Huntington's belief in the years 1875, 1876, and 1877 that the influence of the Central Pacific should

---

53 United States Pacific Railway Commission, p. 3721, testimony C. P. Huntington.
54 Colton case, pp. 1726–27, Huntington to Colton, June 7, 1876.
55 *Ibid.*, pp. 1740–41, Huntington to Colton, November 11, 1876.
56 *Ibid.*, pp. 1765–66, Huntington to Colton, April 3, 1877.

be used to advance the political interests of persons favorably inclined toward his railroad system and to discourage those in opposition. The personal controversy which took place between Stanford and Huntington in 1890 brought out some additional evidence of the same sort. This dispute arose ostensibly because of the election of Stanford in 1883-84 as senator from California in place of A. A. Sargent, one of Huntington's friends. In reality it was probably only the final outcome of a growing tension between the two men, due to dissatisfaction on Huntington's part with the small amount of time which Stanford devoted to railroad affairs, and perhaps to jealousy of the prominence which Stanford enjoyed in public estimation.[57]

However this may be, Stanford resigned the presidency of the Southern Pacific Company at the annual meeting of the stockholders on April 9, 1890, and Huntington was elected in his place. In his address to the board of directors of the company, Huntington used the following words:

> Gentlemen, for the honor that you have done me in electing me President of the Southern Pacific Company . . . I promise you that I will be as true to the interest of the company in the future as I have been in the past. I can promise you nothing more, for at all times my personal interest has been second to that of the company. It shall be so in the future, and in no case will I use this great corporation to advance my personal ambition at the expense of its owners, or put my hands into the treasury to defeat the people's choice, and thereby put myself into positions that should be filled by others; but to the best of my ability will I work for the interest of the shareholders of the company and the people, whom it should serve.[58]

---

57 It has also been asserted that the failure of Mr. and Mrs. Stanford to attend one of the Huntington weddings was sharply resented by Mr. Huntington. J. M. Bassett, at one time secretary to Mr. Stanford, says that the latter came to regard Huntington as an individual of shady characteristics, and was not inclined to trust him further than he could throw Trinity Church up the side of Mt. Shasta. For his part, Huntington spoke of Stanford as a "blanked old fool." (*San Francisco Daily Report*, July 21, 1894.)

58 *San Francisco Examiner*, April 10, 1890.

This statement attracted attention, and Huntington was asked to explain. In an interview with a reporter of the *San Francisco Examiner* he said further :

> From this time on we are going to follow one business. We are railroad men and intend to conduct a legitimate railroad business. To do that successfully politics must be let alone . . . If a man wants to make a business of politics, all well and good; if he wants to manage a railroad, all well and good; but he can't do both at the same time.
>
> I have seen the ante-rooms down here in this building full of men trying to learn or get something out of politics. Why should they come here? This is no place for them. But then they were not to blame. The tip went forth that political work was being done at Fourth and Townsend streets, and they merely followed the tip. Well, there won't be any more tips sent out of these railroad offices. Politics have worked enough demoralization in our company already, and they have gone out of the door never to return. . . .
>
> Things have got to such a state, that if a man wants to be a constable he thinks he has first got to come down to Fourth and Townsend streets to get permission. Hereafter people who come to Fourth and Townsend streets must have railroad business to transact. The Southern Pacific Company is out of politics, and will attend to its business like any other private company or individual should do.[59]

Such statements naturally led to an open breach between Huntington and Stanford.[60]

The point at issue was not, however, whether it was proper for the Southern Pacific to defend itself against political attack. On this there is every reason to suppose that all parties were agreed. It was rather whether the company should be used as an instrument to advance the personal interests of individuals. In the same connection the question arose whether railroad men should act together in political matters not connected with railroad affairs. Huntington, who

---

[59] *San Francisco Examiner*, April 10, 1890.   [60] *Ibid.*, April 13, 1890; April 18, 1890.

had little interest in general politics, thought they should not. It is probable enough that Stanford or some of his subordinates had, on the other hand, used their influence as railroad men for personal and party ends

Unscrupulousness of Associates

One rises from the study of the political activities of the owners of the Central Pacific with a feeling of indignation at the selfishness of these men, their indifference to all save considerations of private gain, and their readiness to use any and all methods which would advance their financial interests. The associates met the proposal of government regulation as a threat to rob them of their property and resisted it as they would have opposed any other attack. They never conceded that any question of public interest was involved which it was necessary for them to respect. They frankly defended the use of money as a method of persuading men to do what was right—which inevitably meant, of course, what in their judgment was right. They fell out among themselves, not because any one of them questioned the philosophy which inspired their opposition to public control, but because one of them was suspected of using power, developed in the course of the defense of railroad interests, to advance personal ambitions which ran counter to the views of his associates. These things should be plainly stated and their force clearly understood.

It is the writer's opinion, however, that the amount of money spent by the Central Pacific in the purchase of legislative or other votes has probably been overestimated in the public mind. Direct bribery is a clumsy weapon and one difficult to conceal if practiced on any considerable scale. It was probably also unnecessary to a corporation such as the Central Pacific with other favors to bestow. Members of Congress might, indeed, be employed by the railroad when legislation was pending. Huntington maintained that this was legitimate,[61] and Gage once admitted that the company had to employ everybody who could pull a pound. The practice was more easily defensible than bribery, and could be applied to a better class of men. Other men might be reached through patronage, still others through discrimination in rates or through preferences. The suggestion that unfavorable legislation would hinder construction was potent with legislators from districts which still lacked rail connection. Yet Huntington once said of a man who was opposing him and whom he thought he could bribe, that his better judgment told him the associates could not afford to take the scamp into camp,[62] and this probably represented the situation at most times. Whether this worked for the eventual salvation of the Huntington group, is for the moralist to say.

---

[61] United States Pacific Railway Commission, pp. 3697–98, testimony C. P. Huntington.
[62] Colton case, p. 1729, Huntington to Colton, June 24, 1876.

CHAPTER XIII

WATER COMPETITION

Rate Policy

We may now pass from the question of the relation of the Central Pacific-Southern Pacific system to legislative bodies in California and in Washington, to another matter of general importance in respect to which Southern Pacific policies profoundly affected the development of the West—the matter of railroad rates. Just as the associates were compelled to face the possibility of government regulation soon after they were fairly launched in their careers as railroad men, so they had to consider and determine the rate policies which they should adopt, independent of regulation, with respect to the shipping and traveling interests of the territory which they served. Their decisions in rate matters were certainly of no less significance than their attitude toward political control, and deserve the same broad consideration.

We shall attempt in the following chapters to describe the conditions which affected the ability of the associates to set rates in California and on business to and from that state, and to consider the attitude of the Southern Pacific with regard to the more important questions of rates and of competition which arose. For reasons which will become apparent as the discussion proceeds, the scope and importance of water competition in the West will first be set forth.

Water Transportation

One of the most important conditions affecting railroad business in California is the ease with which freight and passengers may take advantage of the water routes. The long

coast line of California affords relatively few good harbors, but
it is broken in the center by the splendid bay of San Francisco,
and in the south by the less commodious but still adequate
ports of San Pedro and San Diego.   Between these termini a
considerable commerce has long been carried on.

Still more important than the coastwise trade, however,
has always been the deep sea commerce of San Francisco, and
to a less extent that of the other ports.   San Francisco is a
focus for ocean lines connecting the Pacific Coast of the United
States with the Atlantic seaboard, with Europe, with South
America, and with the Orient.   Likewise from San Francisco
steamers ply up the Sacramento and San Joaquin rivers, carrying traffic well into the interior of the state.   A mere mention
of these facilities is sufficient to suggest the part which water
transportation has played in the commercial and industrial life
of the Far West.

River Traffic

The local river traffic which helps to distribute the cargoes
brought by ocean boats to San Francisco attained some importance as early as 1847.   In that year a small side-wheel
steamer seems to have plied between San Francisco and Sacramento.   In 1849 and 1850 larger boats were put on, the Sacramento was navigated to Colusa, and steamers ascended the
San Joaquin to 150 miles above Stockton.   In 1856 two
steamers usually left San Francisco for Sacramento each
afternoon at 4 P.M., arriving between 12 and 3 A.M. of the
following morning.   Corresponding boats left Sacramento at
2 P.M., arriving between 9 and 11 P.M.   Often as many as four
boats left San Francisco loaded in one day.[1]

The total tonnage of steam vessels plying on California
rivers and bays was estimated by the State Transportation

---

[1] Report of the chief engineer upon the preliminary survey, revenue, and cost of construction of the San Francisco and Sacramento Railroad, 1856.

Commission in 1878 at 30,704. The bay vessels were all ferry-boats and tugs, but river vessels with a total tonnage of 10,990 tons made trips of considerable length. Most of these were small craft, but the larger river steamers ranged between 400 and 520 tons each, while the ferry-boats sometimes reached a size of 1,600 or 1,700 tons. Vallejo, Benicia, Napa, Knight's Landing, Colusa, Chico, Red Bluff, Antioch, and Pacheco were among those able to take advantage of the water service.[2]

Generally speaking, the importance of the river traffic was diminished by the fact that after 1853 most of it fell under the control of one company, the California Steam Navigation Company,[3] and that in 1869 this company sold its steamships to the Central Pacific. The volume of river traffic also fell off because of railroad competition. In spite of these drawbacks competition on the river was lively at times and rates were low, to the disgust of some merchants in the interior cities. The California Steam Navigation Company charged $8 and $6 per ton for freight, and $10 and $8 for cabin fares from San Francisco to Sacramento and Stockton. Meals were a dollar apiece. These were, however, the rates in the absence of competition. When the steamer "Willamette" was brought from Oregon to Stockton, rates were fixed at $3 for freight, $3 for cabin fare, and $1 for deck passage. In December, 1860, the fare from Sacramento was $1 in a cabin and 25 cents for deck accommodation. People traveled because it was as cheap to go as to remain at home.[4]

Ocean Commerce

The first regular water connection between the eastern and western coasts of the United States was provided by the clipper

---

[2] Biennial Report of the Commissioner of Transportation of the State of California for the years ending December 31, 1877 and 1878.

[3] Hittell, "The Commerce and Industries of the Pacific Coast of North America,' 1882, Ch. XI; Sheppard, "F. F. Low, Ninth Governor of California" (in *University of California Chronicle*, April, 1917); *San Francisco Argonaut*, June 22, 1878.

[4] *Sacramento Union*, December 19, 1860.

ships on the route around Cape Horn. These swift sailing vessels supplied the gold miners with the tools and manufactured goods necessary for their enterprises, and took back such commodities as California was able to export. Oil, soap, cement, coal, iron, nails, paper, glass, tobacco, liquors, dry goods, and the like moved west—hides, wool, canned fruits, salmon, sugar, wine, and grain went east. The business was for the most part handled by ships chartered for single voyages, not by lines of ships operating on regular schedules.[5]

As early as October, 1848, however, at least one regular line, the Pacific Mail Steamship Company, entered the field. The establishment of the Pacific Mail service was made possible by the grant of a government contract for the carriage of mails—its profits during the early years were largely derived from business arising out of the gold discoveries in California. The business of the Pacific Mail grew rapidly. In 1851 it operated eleven steamers varying in size from 600 to 1,300 tons, and had a capital stock of $2,000,000. Thirty years later it operated fourteen ships, large and small,[6] reported gross earnings of $3,762,083 (1882) and had $20,000,000 in stock outstanding. At first the Pacific Mail operated steamships between Panama and San Francisco. Later it extended its service to Astoria; and still later it established a line across

---

[5] In 1869 a committee of the California legislature estimated the volume of California products annually arriving at and exported from the port of San Francisco as follows (in appendix to journal of Senate and Assembly, 18th session, California Legislature, Vol 2):

Products	Annual Receipts	Annual Exports
Wheat	225,000 tons	200,000 tons
Barley	30,000 "	10,000 "
Oats	15,000 "	2,500 "
Corn	5,000 "	1,000 "
Hay	40,000 "	1,000 "
Potatoes	37,500 "	10,000 "
Beans	3,600 "	1,000 "
Hops and broom corn	3,600 "	1,000 "
Beets, carrots, tomatoes, parsnips, peas, cabbages, melons, squashes, etc.	40,000 "	500 "
Butter and cheese	10,000 "	500 "
Brandy and wine	6,000,000 gals.	4,000,000 gals.
Fruits, dried and fresh	20,000 tons	500 tons
Beef, mutton, and pork	6,000 "	....
Poultry and eggs	12,000 "	....
Wool	7,500 "	4,000 "
Hides	168,000	one-half

[6] Hittell, "Commerce and Industries on the Pacific Coast," Ch. 11.

the Pacific to China and Australia. Among its competitors
by sea at one time or another, besides the clipper ships, were
Mr. Vanderbilt's Atlantic and Pacific Company, the Mexican
Coast Steamship Company, and Messrs. Goodall and Perkins.
At one time Jay Gould, at another Trenor W. Park, of the
Panama Railroad, were dominant in its affairs.

Problem of Water Competition

There is much of romance in the history of ocean transportation into and out of San Francisco, and in its proper
place the story should be told at length. Some aspects of the
water service, indeed, will be touched on later in this book.
Attention is directed to the matter at present, however, not for
its own sake, but because the fact of water competition raised
one of the problems with which the Southern Pacific had to
deal. It seems clear that the associates were compelled to
define their attitude toward water competition as soon as their
through line was completed in 1869.

Broadly speaking, the alternatives were competition or
agreement. In respect to the Pacific Mail, however, the situation was complicated by the fact that the relations between the
railroads and the shipping lines were of two sorts: In the first
place, the Pacific Mail served as a valuable connection for the
transcontinental railroads on business originating in or destined to China and Japan. Tea and silk eastbound were usually
delivered by the steamships to the rail lines at San Francisco.
Westbound the higher classes of manufactured goods likewise
moved part way by rail and part way by water haul. During
the ten years ending in February, 1881, the Pacific roads
carried 177,278,505 pounds of tea and other Asiatic goods,
secured to them by the co-operation of the Pacific Mail Steamship Company, resulting in earnings of $3,264,456.44.[7] On

---

[7] United States Pacific Railway Commission, p. 3576, testimony Richard Gray, general
freight agent, Central Pacific Railroad.

the other hand, the rail and water lines were competitors in important respects.

Steamship Company Organized

In 1874 the Huntington interests organized the Occidental and Oriental Steamship Company and chartered three steamships to ply between San Francisco and the Far East. This was said to be the result of a decision of the Pacific Mail to make Panama the terminus of its transpacific route, relegating San Francisco to the secondary position of a port of call.[8]

Huntington wrote to Colton, on November 9, 1874:

> I am surprised to learn that anyone should think it was for our interest to put on the China line seven steamers to start with. I think three is plenty, and we shall, no doubt, have such an opposition on the start that we shall have to run them at a loss, but with those three we can make the prices for the old line, and I think there is enough to break them with, unless the managers of that company are changed, and then we most likely can get their steamers.[9]

Huntington intended to develop the Occidental and Oriental Steamship Company as a permanent connection of the Central Pacific for Oriental business in competition with the Pacific Mail. At the time his decision was made he discussed with his associates the advisability of asking enough eastern lines to join with the Central Pacific to form a single transcontinental route from the Pacific to the Atlantic coasts for export and import traffic, but decided against this project because it would make enemies of the railroads which were not included, and because also the admission of partners would make it impossible for the Central Pacific to control by itself a majority of the shares of the Occidental and Oriental Company. Huntington's letter to Colton on this matter is a model of sound reasoning on a large question of policy:

---

8 United States Pacific Railway Commission, p. 2924, testimony Leland Stanford.
9 Colton case, pp. 981–83.

I think very likely we could make out a through line. Very likely the Baltimore and Ohio would come in, and make up a line that would run to Omaha or Fort Kearney, passing through St. Louis and Chicago. But if this was done, very likely it would be difficult for us to control the steamship Company, and if we make up this line, leaving out the roads above mentioned, of course they would not expect any of the China business coming over our road, and then would they not be likely to work against us by allowing the Pacific Mail Steamship Company and any other companies to give bills of lading from China and Japan to Chicago, St. Louis, etc., over their roads, and to bring freight from those points to the sea coast here, to go by steamer and sail to California? . . . We cannot be too careful in starting this steamship line, for it is one of the things that if we go into, I have little doubt we shall hold it for years, and therefore the more reason why we should hold a majority of the stock of the company, as almost every road here is controlled by those that are always short or long of stock and endeavor to render everything bend to their particular wants. If short, they want to put the stock down, and if long they work for the reverse and we cannot afford to be in their power.[10]

Ownership of Shares

Doubtless for financial reasons the policy here laid down was departed from sufficiently to allow the Union Pacific a half-interest in the new company. For their part, Stanford, Huntington, Hopkins, Crocker and Colton subscribed each to 10,000 shares of the stock of the Occidental and Oriental Steamship Company. The account was charged to the Western Development Company and was held by that company as an asset. The remaining 50,000 shares were owned by the Union Pacific, and Mr. Gould shared with the associates the management of the enterprise.[11] It may be added that the Occidental and Oriental owned no steamers, but chartered the "Oceanic," the "Belgic," and the "Gaelic." The "Oceanic" was a boat of

---

[10] Colton case, pp. 981–83, Huntington to Colton, November 9, 1874.
[11] Ibid., pp. 466, 495–96, testimony F. S. Douty.

3,800 tons; the other ships were of 2,600 tons each.[12] The first dividend was declared in July, 1878, and by 1881 the rate had been raised to 4 per cent. Mr. Stanford has testified that the company expected to lose $100,000 a year, but that its owners were pleasantly disappointed.[13]

Agreement with Pacific Mail

There is evidence that as early as 1870 some agreement was entered into between the Huntington interests and the Pacific Mail Steamship Company, and that in 1871 a formal contract was concluded by these companies, defining their relation to each other. The terms of the contract of 1871 are not available, but a subsequent agreement, dated October 1, 1872, contained the following principal provisions:

The Pacific Mail Steamship Company agreed to provide every month three first-class steamers to sail from the port of New York for the Isthmus of Panama, with connecting steamers on the Pacific Ocean for the port of San Francisco. The company undertook to supply space in these steamers for an amount of freight not exceeding 14,700 tons annually.

The steamship company accorded to the railroad company the exclusive right to fix the rates on freight of every description, moving from New York to San Francisco during the period of the agreement, provided that the rates should not exceed the rates then in force, nor in any event $160 first-class, $140 second-class, $90 third-class, and $60 fourth-class and special.

Out of the gross receipts on the freight westbound the steamship company was first to draw $735,000, or at the rate of $50 per ton on 14,700 tons. If the amount of the freight handled should not equal 14,700 tons, or if that quantity of freight should be handled but the receipts therefrom should

---

[12] Hittell, "Commerce and Industries of the Pacific Coast," Ch. 11.
[13] United States Pacific Railway Commission, p. 2924, testimony Leland Stanford.

not amount to $50 per ton, the railroad agreed to make up the difference, so that the receipts on the first 14,700 tons should always amount to $735,000. If, on the other hand, the steamship should collect thereon an average rate exceeding $50, the railroad was to be entitled to the surplus.

In the event that through westbound freight exceeded in volume 14,700 tons, the gross earnings on the excess quantity were to be divided between steamship company and railroad company as follows: first, $30 per ton was to be taken by the steamship company; additional receipts up to $50 a ton were to be divided equally between steamship and railroad; and earnings over $50 were to go to the railroad.[14]

The essential facts in this agreement were that the steamship company surrendered the power of fixing the westbound rates in return for a guarantee of $735,000 a year.

Later Contracts

This feature was also characteristic of later agreements between the same parties, different as the details of the subsequent arrangements sometimes were. In 1879 the Union Pacific, Central Pacific, and Pacific Mail companies agreed that the last-named should set aside space for 600 tons of railroad freight in each of its steamers moving monthly between New York and San Francisco. The railroads were to exercise full authority over the through rates of the steamship company, and for their part were to guarantee that the earnings on the railroad freight shipped were not to be less than $48,000 monthly westbound, and $35,000 monthly eastbound. In case the earnings on the 600 tons or less of railroad freight which might be sent in each vessel exceeded the guaranteed minimum, the balance of freight money was to be paid over to the railroad, while the moneys received on all freight between New York and San Francisco and between San Francisco and New York

---

[14] United States v. Union Pacific Railroad, pp. 3316–20.

in excess of 600 tons for each vessel were to be equally divided between the railroad and the steamship company.[15] An additional clause in this agreement bound the railroads to pay to the steamship company $5 for each passenger carried whose ticket was purchased at a point east of Ogdensburg, Suspension Bridge, Buffalo, Pittsburgh, and Wheeling, to a point west of Sacramento, and vice versa.

An agreement dated June 1, 1885, between the Transcontinental Association and the Pacific Mail does not differ strikingly from that of 1879 just summarized, except that the payments per month were to be $85,000 for a two-way service, instead of $83,000, and that there was no passenger subsidy. Moreover, the right of the steamship company to fix rates for the use of its capacity above the 600 tons mentioned in the agreement was specifically reserved. The $85,000 payment in this year represented a reduction from the figure of $110,000 contained in a contract dated March 4, 1880, and from one of $95,000 concluded in 1882. In 1887 the subsidy was set at $65,000, and in 1889, when still another arrangement between the Transcontinental Association and the Pacific Mail was signed, it was put at $75,000.[16]

From a statement made to the United States Pacific Railway Commission, it appears that the aggregate earnings guaranteed by the railroads to the Pacific Mail Steamship Company from September 30, 1871, to March 21, 1886, were $11,227,939.27. This did not include Central or South American business. Of the guaranteed sum the steamship company earned $5,854,-113.06, leaving $5,373,826.21 to be made up by the guarantors. The distribution of the burden among the railroads interested may be suggested by the fact that out of $146,170.29 which had to be paid during the three months from January to March,

---

[15] Message from the President of the United States to the House of Representatives transmitting copies of contracts and leases entered into by the Southern Pacific Company, etc., February 4, 1886. 49th Congress, 1st Session, House Exec. Doc. No. 60, Serial No. 2398.

[16] United States v. Union Pacific, pp. 3321-25.

1886, the Union Pacific paid $34,652.94, the Central Pacific $31,927.57, the Southern Pacific $30,172.79, the Santa Fé $15,086.11, the Galveston, Harrisburg and San Antonio $11,536.82, and seven other companies smaller sums.[17]

Change in Ocean Traffic

The change which took place in the volume of water-borne commerce in and out of San Francisco coincident with the arrangements between the railroads and the Pacific Mail which have been described, is clearly indicated in the following table: [18]

VALUE OF COMMODITIES SHIPPED FROM NEW YORK TO SAN FRANCISCO AND FROM SAN FRANCISCO TO NEW YORK VIA PANAMA EACH YEAR FROM 1869 TO 1884

Year ended June 30	Shipped from New York to San Francisco	Shipped from San Francisco to New York	Total
1869	$50,015,994	$20,186,035	$70,202,029
1870	15,334,945	3,259,310	18,594,255
1871	9,391,607	2,161,106	11,552,713
1872	6,739,563	3,086,874	9,826,437
1873	3,042,617	3,667,107	6,709,724
1874	7,049,821	1,752,653	8,802,474
1875	6,057,202	2,382,928	8,440,130
1876	4,470,594	1,983,261	6,453,855
1877	3,398,864	2,205,979	5,604,843
1878	3,976,358	3,211,245	7,187,603
1879	2,781,065	2,166,690	4,947,755
1880	2,963,065	2,865,237	5,828,302
1881	815,893	2,598,868	3,414,761
1882	1,270,900	3,153,902	4,424,802
1883	1,192,912	2,394,430	3,587,342
1884	1,040,495	1,264,682	2,305,177

If we compare the year 1869—probably the last in which the Pacific Mail and the Huntington interests were in active

[17] United States Pacific Railway Commission, pp. 4276–77.

[18] Report on the internal commerce of the United States, by Joseph Nimmo, Jr., Chief of the Bureau of Statistics, Treasury Department, 1884, Serial No. 2295.

competition—with the year 1884, it appears that the value of commodities shipped in and out of San Francisco via Panama during these years declined from about seventy to about two million dollars. Doubtless this falling off was not all due to agreements between rail and water carriers. For instance the sudden decline between 1869 and 1870 was occasioned in large part by the sudden diversion of bullion shipments from the water routes when the rail lines were opened, while passengers also rapidly deserted the water for the more speedy and comfortable rail service. Moreover, at a slightly later date the special contract system played its part in limiting shipments by sea. Yet it is not unfair to credit the arrangements between the Huntington group and the Pacific Mail with a considerable share of the reduction in water tonnage so desirable from the point of view of the land carriers.

Pacific Mail and Panama Railroad

The difficulty in bringing about a substantial lessening of competition by agreement with a water carrier is found in the fact that the sea is free, so that new ships and new shipping companies can readily take the place of those that are withdrawn. The peculiar strength of the Pacific Mail in negotiating with the railroad company lay in the fact that it enjoyed for many years the exclusive privilege of through-billing freight between San Francisco and New York, including the privilege of quoting a through rate. From all other steamship companies the Panama Railroad exacted a local rate for hauling freight across the Isthmus.[19] Inasmuch as this local rate was very high, it was impossible for a competing steamship company to handle through business at a profit. It was thus the railroad which determined whether competition by way of the Isthmus of Panama should succeed or fail. It may be

---

[19] Exception should be made of the period between December 16, 1900, and June 11, 1902, when there was no agreement between the Pacific Mail and the Panama Railroad. (United States v. Union Pacific, p. 2911, testimony Conner.)

added that after the year 1893 the Panama Railroad assumed the responsibility not only of the rail haul across the Isthmus, but of the water connection between Colon and New York as well, thus becoming the preponderant partner in respect to length of route, as well as in respect to strategic position.

In return for the exclusive right of through-billing, and of quoting through rates, as well as for its agreements not to operate vessels in the Pacific, the Panama Railroad was promised a certain division of the through rate, which was not to be less monthly than a stipulated minimum. The minimum varied, but always was a substantial part of the payment which the transcontinental railroads were making to the Pacific Mail. In 1878 the railroads guaranteed the Pacific Mail $90,000 a month, out of which the Panama Railroad received $75,000. When the Pacific Mail subsidy was lowered from $90,000 to $75,000, the amount guaranteed to the Panama Railroad fell off from $75,000 to $55,000.

It is a matter of history also that during the years 1876 to 1878, the Panama Railroad not only was a party to the elaborate traffic agreement with the Pacific Mail which has been described, but that it exercised for a time direct control of the steamship company by domination of its president and board of directors. This control was the outcome of a conflict between Jay Gould, then president of the Pacific Mail, and Trenor W. Park, of the Panama Railroad, which in 1875 resulted in the election of a board of directors satisfactory to the latter and in the choice of a new president.

The lever which the railroad used at this time was the cancellation of its contract with the Pacific Mail, the organization of a company known as the Pacific Transit Company, the purchase of three old refitted warships, and the threat to engage in active competition. Mr. Park was asked if he would desist from his attack on the Pacific Mail if a neutral board of directors were elected. He consented to this, and was satisfied by a board composed for the most part of Panama Railroad men. This was followed by the consolidation of the Pacific Mail and the Panama Transit Company, by the renewal of contracts between railroad and steamship, and finally in 1878, by the execution of a bill of sale by the steamship to the railroad company for twenty-two steamers to secure a loan of $1,000,000 in Panama Railroad bonds for four years.[20]

Railroads' Main Reliance

It thus appears that during the first ten years after the completion of the Central Pacific, the interests of the Panama Railroad and those of the Pacific Mail were closely bound together, so that during this period an agreement with the former was sufficient to control the route over which both were operating. It was upon this fact that the transcontinental railroads chiefly relied. Nor was there any important change in the relations between the Panama Railroad and the Pacific Mail, or in those between the Pacific Mail and the transcontinental railroads during the following twelve years. Mr. Park's control of the Pacific Mail proved only temporary, it is true, and the terms of the contracts between the parties changed from time to time; yet the principle of a guaranty of earnings to the Pacific Mail in return for the maintenance of rates was always adhered to, and the Panama Railroad always received the lion's share of this guaranty for a division. The amount of the subsidy paid by the railroad has already been given. When in 1885 the Pacific Mail received $85,000 per month from the transcontinental lines, it paid over $70,000 to the Panama Railroad. When the Pacific Mail subsidy was reduced to $65,000 in 1887, the payment to the Isthmian railroad likewise fell to $55,000. In 1881 the Panama Canal Company, a French cor-

---

[20] Bancroft, "Chronicles of the Builders," Vol. 5, Ch. 6; *San Francisco Chronicle*, November 10, 1878.

poration under the direction of De Lesseps, purchased the Panama Railroad for $20,000,000; but this does not seem to have affected the relations between the last-named railroad and the Pacific Mail.

CHAPTER XIV

THE RATE SYSTEM OF THE CENTRAL PACIFIC

City and Country in California

For more than forty years the Southern Pacific interests sought with varying success to modify the intensity of water competition by agreement with or by purchase of competing lines. During all this period the existence of alternative water routes was probably the principal influence determining the relative adjustment of rates between different towns upon the Pacific Coast. In deciding upon the rates which they should charge, the Southern Pacific interests had other factors to consider, however, besides the presence of water competition— factors which can be understood only after a careful study of local conditions in the Far West.

The state of California is characteristically a country of great distances, occupied by a relatively sparse and unequally distributed population. Its industry is primarily agricultural and mining. Although some manufactures have developed since 1870, such as foundries, woolen and sugar mills, glass, paper, cordage, powder, tobacco, tin, and hardware manufacturing concerns, yet even today the absence of adequate supplies of good coal, the smallness of the local market, and the distance from the great centers of population in the East hold manufactures within narrow limits. As explained in the previous chapter, the state is best fitted to produce and export products of the soil, and raw materials such as grain, fruit, wool, hides, and later wines, lumber, and oil. To this list should also be added salmon.

In such an economy, the cities of California play the part of distributing agencies rather than that of centers of industry.

Such was the first function of Stockton, Sacramento, Los Angeles, and indeed of San Francisco itself, and the work of distribution still remains these cities' principal means of support. Originally the chief profit of the northern towns came from supplying the mining population of the Sierras with supplies brought by sea from Europe or from the Atlantic Coast of the United States. The nature of California imports has somewhat changed since the early days; a larger commerce with the Orient and with the west coast of South America has developed, and a large part of the freight handled on the Pacific Coast now comes in by rail. This has multiplied the number of distributing points, and has to some degree built up the interior of the state. The character of the cities has not, however, changed and they remain as before—trading and consuming rather than producing centers.

Conflict of Interest

It follows from this division of labor between town and country on the Pacific Coast, and from the rivalry of different cities in the distribution of finished goods, that striking divergencies in point of view have arisen, both between individual cities, and also between the city communities as a whole and the farming and manufacturing interests of the state. These differences have received free expression in the discussion of railroad rates. Inasmuch as the articles distributed by the towns are in large part imported goods, the cities as a group have demanded low westbound carload rates from eastern sources of supply. The larger centers of population, however, have opposed low rates on small consignments, because that tends to deprive them of a rehandling profit by promoting direct relations between the consumer and the eastern wholesale house. As compared with the cities, on the other hand, the farming interests have been relatively indifferent to the level of westbound rates, so long as they have enjoyed low eastbound rates on the product of the farm and field; while the struggling manufacturers have resisted low rates westbound, because these have exposed them to the competition of eastern factories. The interests of the consumer have not until quite recent years been represented.

No Settled Rate Policy

Owing to these persistent conflicts between various classes of shippers, public opinion in California has not been easily enlisted as a whole in support of any concrete proposals for the readjustment of railroad rates, although complaints from all sections have been numerous. There has been, on the contrary, a persistent series of appeals to the railroad, now to favor one set of interests, now to favor another—appeals which, when granted, often have resulted in gross discrimination, and which, when refused, have swelled the tide of protest against the transportation lines. The serious side of this situation in California is that the conflict of interest between buyers of transportation has exposed the railroad to temptations which it has had neither will nor ability to withstand. Where there is constant demand for favors there is likely to be discrimination unless the person or institution to which demand is made is fortified by a clear view of public policy and a sense of morality more than ordinarily acute.

It is no secret that the Southern Pacific has had neither the one nor the other of these qualifications. For its part, it has acknowledged no duties other than those generally incumbent upon private business. It has insisted upon complete freedom to follow its own advantage. In a speech to the men in the railroad shops at Sacramento in September, 1873, Stanford explained his position by asking: "Does Governor Booth sell at the same per cent of profit his sugar, pork, beans, bacon, lard, candles, soap, spice, coffee, whiskey, brandy, and other articles? So with the mechanic, the manufacturer, the farmer, and others. The market price governs. A farmer takes two and one-half cents for his grain as justly and as cheerfully as one and one-half cents, the cost of producing being the same." [1] "The Southern Pacific," said Mr. William B. Curtis, of that company, in 1894, in the same strain, "sells transportation precisely as a merchant disposes of his wares, adjusting its tariff to conform to the situation with the object in view of inducing the largest amount of transportation at fair rates." [2]

This announced willingness to differentiate led in the course of time to the greatest variety of railroad rates in California, some rates being low, some high, some public, some secret. Generally speaking, indeed, rates were low where competition was present, and high where it was absent. The big man was favored over the little man, the shipper with an alternative route over the shipper confined to one railroad line. Some of the details of this interesting system will now be presented.

Separate Rate Classifications

In discussing the adjustment of local charges in California, attention will be first directed to the absolute level of local railroad rates. Separate mention must be made of the local classifications and of the local rates.

As late as 1877, each of the principal railroads in California had its own classification. These were far from being the same. Baled hops moved at one and one-half times first-class on the Central Pacific. On the Southern Pacific compressed hops took third-class. On the California Pacific pressed hops took double first-class. Liquors took one and one-half times first-class on the Central Pacific (in jars, owner's risk); second-class on the Southern Pacific (in glass, packed, owner's risk); double first-class on the California Pacific (in jars or glass);

---

[1] *California Mail Bag*, August, 1874.

[2] *San Francisco Examiner*, May 1, 1894. Discrimination was easy because rates were not published. Freight schedules were considered to be for the information of employees and not for general publication.

first-class on the North Pacific Coast (in glass, packed, owner's risk) ; and double first-class on the San Francisco and North Pacific (in glass or demijohns, owner's risk). Window glass took first-class on the Central Pacific, one and one-half times first-class on the California Pacific, and fourth-class on the Southern Pacific if not over three feet long. Boiler flues moved first-class on the Central Pacific, third-class on the North Pacific Coast, and fourth- or fifth-class according as made of copper or brass, or of iron, on the Southern Pacific.[3]

Generally speaking, however, the classifications were much less elaborate than they later became. A committee of the California Senate observed in 1893 that the theory of the local classification of the Southern Pacific was to simplify so far as possible. Hence that classification started out with the announcement, in effect, that all articles not named specifically therein would be charged for at merchandise rates. It then continued to indicate the exceptions, enumerating articles that were light, bulky, of excessive value, liable to damage, etc., proceeding in this way along the same lines as the Western classification.[4]

When the Santa Fé later built into southern California it brought in the Western classification, tariffs, rules, and conditions that governed its lines elsewhere, and applied the Southern Pacific schedules of merchandise rates to this classification. Since, however, the Southern Pacific had only one merchandise class, the Santa Fé applied the same rates to each of the first four classes of the Western classification in California. The result of this adjustment of tariff to the Western classification was to produce practically the same revenue as would have resulted from the local classification and merchandise rates of the Southern Pacific Company. In 1893 the Southern

---

[3] Report of California Commissioners of Transportation, 1877, table 1, pp. 34–38.

[4] Report of the Senate Committee on Constitutional Amendments, relative to constitutional amendment No. 8, abrogating provisions of constitution as to railroad commission (in appendix to journals of the Senate and Assembly of the Legislature of the State of California, 30th Session, Vol. 8, 1893.)

Pacific itself substituted the Western classification for the one which it had been using.[5]

Local Rates

Under the law the maximum rate which any California railroad could charge for the transportation of freight, was 15 cents per ton per mile. In spite of the statement of Mr. Stanford to the contrary,[6] the evidence is to the effect that this maximum was generally applied on short-haul local business as late as 1877 and perhaps afterwards. In some cases, the published rate was even greater than the maximum, though a note to the schedule provided that when the calculated rate exceeded the legal maximum, the latter would apply. The rates on the Central Pacific main line in 1866 were almost exactly 15 cents per ton per mile.

The report of the California Board of Transportation Commissioners in 1877 showed that generally throughout the state first-class rates for short hauls ranged from 14 to 30 cents per ton per mile. For the 10 miles from Lathrop to Stockton the tariff charge was $1.60 per ton, and for the 6 miles from Pleasanton to Livermore, the rate was $1. The charge from Roseville Junction to Truckee, 102 miles, was $15.20. When river competition entered in, rates were markedly reduced. The charge from San Francisco to Stockton, 92 miles, was $3.20 per ton, or 3½ cents per ton per mile; that from San Francisco to Sacramento, 140 miles, was $3.60, or 2⅗ cents per ton per mile. On the other hand, the rates of the California Pacific were somewhat higher than those of the other lines, except at competitive points.[7]

---

5 *San Francisco Examiner*, October 27, 1893. Even in the case of through rates more than one classification was used. It appeared in a case brought before the Interstate Commerce Commission in 1887 that while the Western classification governed shipments from San Francisco to Denver, another classification, known as the Pacific Coast eastbound classification, was used in connection with freight moving from San Francisco to the Missouri River. (Martin v. Southern Pacific Company, 2 I. C. R. 1 [1888].)

6 United States Pacific Railway Commission, pp. 2536–37, testimony Leland Stanford.

7 Report of California Commissioners of Transportation, 1877.

In later years the charges of the Southern Pacific naturally declined. Yet the rate on brick from San Francisco to Soledad in 1892 was 5½ cents per ton per mile on a haul of 143 miles, and that to San Miguel, 64 miles farther on, was almost 5 cents per ton per mile.[8] The average receipts per ton per mile upon the Southern Pacific system were 2.04 cents per ton per mile for all freight as late as 1885, in spite of the large quantity of long distance through traffic. Plainly the average receipts on local business were much greater. There seems little doubt but that the local rates in California were always distinctly higher than in the eastern states, although they have been lowered in recent years. The reason was in the main the relatively slight density of traffic upon all except the trunk routes, as well as the higher cost of coal, and the successful control of competition to which the Southern Pacific attained.

Rate Discrimination

Turning now from the absolute level of local rates to the question of the relations which those rates bore to each other, we come to the question of discrimination in California. Railroad discrimination may be personal, in which case it involves the quoting of different rates to different persons for the same or a similar service, or it may be local, as in instances where the interests of competing localities are concerned. Either kind of discrimination is of profound social importance, for, after all, it must be remembered that the significant question for the producing and distributing interests of a state is not how much they pay for transportation, but whether this amount, be it much or little, is less than is paid by their competitors. The remainder of the present chapter will be devoted to the discussion of personal discrimination; in the next chapter the topic of local discrimination will be considered.

---

[8] Statement of J. S. Leeds, submitted to the State Railroad Commission (*San Francisco Bulletin*, April 4, 1892).

The policy of granting special concessions in rates to special shippers was one which the Southern Pacific followed freely whenever it seemed likely to increase the profits of the company. There was never any disposition to apologize for this—it was known to be the practice of other roads as well, and the Southern Pacific accepted the system as a matter of course. The methods employed were various. One method was that of granting passes. Mr. Stubbs explained that passes were commonly issued in cases where shippers came to the Central Pacific and represented that they were offered transportation by the company's competitors over such competitors' lines. "They were our patrons," said Mr. Stubbs, "shipping our way, and I may say that wherever we were satisfied that the statement was true, we generally met the case by giving a pass!" [9]

Sudden Tariff Changes

In addition to granting passes, the Southern Pacific discriminated by changing open rates suddenly for the benefit of persons fortunate enough to be advised in advance. Mr. Stanford once explained that individual items in the company's tariff were changed whenever by so doing the company could encourage business in any direction.[10] Indeed, a tariff would scarcely be in force ten days before the necessity for changes would be apparent.[11]

How this might work was shown in 1892, when complaint was made of discrimination in favor of the Standard Oil Company. It was then alleged that the Central Pacific was lowering oil rates from $1.25 per hundred pounds to 82½ or 90 cents, when the Standard Oil desired to make shipments from eastern refining points to the Pacific Coast, the rates being subsequently raised when the shipments had been completed.

---

9 United States Pacific Railway Commission, p. 3344, testimony J. C. Stubbs.
10 Letter of Stanford to Committee of San Francisco Chamber of Commerce, December 1, 1873.
11 United States Pacific Railway Commission, pp. 3292–93, testimony J. C. Stubbs.

A letter to the vice-president of the Standard Oil Company, bearing upon an episode of this sort, written under date of December 4, 1888, got into the public press, and seems to establish the fact that transactions of this nature were going on. The letter follows and is self-explanatory.[12]

SAN FRANCISCO, December 4, 1888

W. H. TILFORD, Vice-President, Standard Oil Company,
    26 Broadway, New York

DEAR SIR:

. . . .

I herewith hand you copy of a letter I have just received from Mr. Sproule, Assistant General Freight Agent of the Southern Pacific Company, this city. This letter I interpret to mean the 90-cent rate is for us to stock up from time to time, and that the $1.25 rate will be in effect whenever we may desire. This $1.25 rate is what Mr. Sproule refers to in the latter portion of his letter, as my offer of 90 cents to Mr. Stubbs was on condition that he has the rate of $1.25 put into effect when we might ask him. This letter also reads as if the 90-cent rate and the $1 rate was to be put in effect January 1st. No doubt Mr. Stubbs was unaware that we were stocked up at the present rate of 82½.

The Transcontinental Association adjourned at Chicago yesterday, and I understand that Mr. Stubbs is now on his way home. I will see him on his arrival here, and if Chairman Leeds of the Transcontinental Association has been notified to put the 90-cent rate in effect January 1st I will have the same corrected by wire and the $1.25 rate put in. As soon as Mr. Stubbs reaches home I will telegraph you whether it is intended that the 90-cent rate should be put in effect January 1st or the $1.25.

Yours truly,

E. A. TILFORD

Relations with Standard Oil

The fact that relations between the Southern Pacific and the Standard Oil Company were very close during the late

[12] *San Francisco Examiner*, December 30, 1892, October 29, 1894; *San Francisco Bulletin*, January 31, 1893.

eighties and early nineties is well established, not only by the correspondence just referred to, but also by other available evidence. In June, 1892, to cite a small but interesting episode, the Union Pacific issued a circular applying a rate of 78½ cents per hundred pounds on oil from Colorado points to the Pacific Coast. This rate had been in effect some years before, previous to the organization of the Western Traffic Association, under a rule which made Missouri River commodity rates a maximum on business originating west of the 97th meridian. The rule in question had never been withdrawn, although it developed that the Southern Pacific had forgotten it, and believed that a rate of $1.60 applied.

At this time the independent firm of Whittier, Fuller and Company was endeavoring to find a market for the products of its Colorado plant upon the Pacific Coast. In order to head off this anticipated competition, the Standard Oil representative in San Francisco took the matter up with the general traffic manager of the Southern Pacific, Mr. Gray. The latter at once wired to Mr. Munroe of the Union Pacific as follows:

SAN FRANCISCO, June 10, 1892

J. A. MUNROE,
  Omaha, Nebraska

It is reported you are antagonizing Standard Oil Company in Colorado. I hope you will do nothing to affect our joint relation with that company with regard to Pacific Coast business. Have you observed the large tonnage you have lately been handling for them? I think it is so great you should be careful how you jeopardize your own interest in this direction.

R. GRAY

Under pressure from the Standard Oil, the Southern Pacific followed up this telegram by refusing to prorate on any basis lower than $1.60. As a result the objectionable circular was withdrawn.[13]

---

[13] *San Francisco Examiner*, October 30, 1894.

Rate Rebates

A third method of granting concessions to shippers whom the Central Pacific desired to favor, was that of the rebate. Rebates were usually granted in exchange for an undertaking by the shipper to send all his freight over the lines of the railroads by which the rebate was paid. Mr. Stubbs once explained to the United States Pacific Railway Commission that the granting of rebates was a regular practice, not only of the Central Pacific, but of all its connecting lines. He explained the mechanism of the operation as follows:

> Suppose that you were a merchant, and I should go to you to make a contract for the rail lines—because all the lines were parties to it between New York and San Francisco. It was not a Central Pacific affair. You understand that all the lines between San Francisco and New York, probably embracing all the roads in the East, shared in this reduced rate that was given to the merchant in consideration of his exclusive patronage— I should go to you and make a contract, and should say that it is impossible for us, in billing, to bill this to you at the net rates. We will bill it at the full rates, and when you receive your goods at the depot you pay the full rates, and we will refund to you the difference between the agreed rate under the contract and the rates which you have paid. Of course that is an overcharge. We overcharged those goods above the price that you had previously agreed to pay for the transportation of them.[14]

In the single year of 1884 the Central Pacific paid out $1,060,275.92 as refunds in behalf of itself and its connections.

Extent of Practice

Evidence showing how radically published rates were reduced by the practice of rebating is to be found in the following testimony by G. W. Luce, now freight traffic manager of the Southern Pacific, and long connected with the traffic depart-

---

[14] United States Pacific Railway Commission, pp. 3299, 3300, testimony J. C. Stubbs.

ment of that company. Speaking before the Interstate Commerce Commission of the period about 1887, Mr. Luce said:

> Just prior to that time I had in mind, there had been a very severe war in rates. I do not know whether that was the reason for the creation of this Commission or not, but the struggle had been very disastrous; two or three lines, I think, were very much crippled, going into the hands of receivers; and just before the act was passed, effective in April, 1887, I think, the lines got together and said, "Here, let us stop this foolishness; let us have some standard of rates and see what we can do on that basis. I believe the rates were made 50 per cent of the old tariff rate that had been used for two or three years. I presume the carriers thought that it would not be judicious to put their rates right up to standard 100 per cent, so they decided on a 50 per cent tariff.
>
> THE CHAIRMAN. You mean 50 per cent more than the published rate, or 50 per cent of the published rate?
>
> MR. LUCE. Of the published rate . . .
>
> THE CHAIRMAN. That means your published rates, which your line had published up to that time in the eighties, were probably about twice that much?
>
> MR. LUCE. Yes, sir.
>
> THE CHAIRMAN. And yet that was an effort to bring together a stability of rates, and to get more out of the traffic than you had been getting during this war, I suppose?
>
> MR. LUCE. Yes, sir.
>
> THE CHAIRMAN. So that, as a matter of fact, prior to that, you had not been getting even as much as . . . the 50 per cent basis?
>
> MR. LUCE. No, sir.
>
> THE CHAIRMAN. It was a general departure from the so-called published rates of more than 50 per cent?
>
> MR. LUCE. Oh, yes.[15]

Concrete Instances

The practice of quoting a lower rate to one person than to another in order to secure a specific shipment, or in considera-

---

[15] Railroad Commission of Nevada v. Southern Pacific Company, 21, I. C. C. R. 329. 349 (1911).

tion of an agreement for exclusive patronage of the railroad which granted the rebate, was clearly a case of personal discrimination. A concrete case which is illustrative of the general policy with which we are concerned was brought to public notice in California in the year 1886, when the Central Pacific was charged with rebating large sums to two favored shippers named Friedlander and Reed. It appeared in fact that the railroad had paid $6,000 at one time to Friedlander for rent of a wharf at Vallejo, and 25 cents a ton on a shipment to a certain Mr. Reed at Knight's, on business destined to Vallejo. These payments were explained by the company as follows:

The Friedlander wharf vouchers were explained by showing that, in consideration of the rental of said wharf, Friedlander agreed to, and did, send the whole of his immense grain purchases on the Sacramento River, and at other competing points on the California Pacific, by rail instead of by steamer and sail; and when one remembers the enormous quantities of wheat and barley purchased by him, the "grain king of California," there is no doubt that the contract was a source of much profit to the company. The Reed voucher for 25 cents per ton for loading wheat from his warehouse at Knight's Landing, was fully explained by Reed himself. He had a warehouse at that point on the bank of the river, and water craft would take his grain at the same rate charged by the railroad company, loading and unloading the same at their own expense, while the railroad company required the shipper to do the loading. When asked to patronize the railroad, Reed told Mr. Towne, general manager, that he could have the grain carried by water at the same price that the Southern Pacific demanded, and that the steamers and schooners would do the loading without charge. In order to secure the business, Mr. Towne told Reed that if he would ship by rail, the company would allow him 25 cents per ton for loading, thus securing business for the road that would have been otherwise lost.

"Special" Contract System

In all probability the Reed and Friedlander cases were but two of a great many instances of similar favors granted to large shippers, and to shippers strategically placed on water lines in California. This is certainly implied in the testimony of Mr. Stubbs before the United States Pacific Railway Commission. Moreover, there is good independent evidence to the same effect in the available data concerning the "seasonal" or "special" contract system which became notorious in California in the late seventies and early eighties. The outlines of this last-named arrangement were as follows:

As early as May, 1878, the Central Pacific Railroad offered to guarantee a maximum rate of $2 per hundred pounds upon all grease wool, eastbound, moving over its lines from San Francisco to New York. In consideration of this guaranty it required shippers to undertake to ship all wool which they sent to destinations east of the meridian of Omaha by way of the Central Pacific and such connecting lines as the Central Pacific Railroad Company might elect. In case of failure to live up to the agreement, the shipper bound himself to pay an additional rate of .75 cents per hundred pounds upon all shipments made or which might have been made by rail during the time of the contract. Before this arrangement was insisted on, shippers were accustomed to forward their finer wools by rail at the $2 rate, but to send their low-grade wool by sea at a rate of 50 cents per hundred pounds.[16]

The system of special rates and exclusive contracts was not at first applied to westbound freight, nor to general merchandise, whether moving east or west. Late in July, 1878, however, notice was given of advances in westbound merchandise rates which in many instances amounted to as much as 100 per cent, and at the same time a tender was made of rates below the published tariff to shippers who entered into special

---

[16] A copy of this contract is printed in the *San Francisco Chronicle* of May 7, 1879.

contracts with the railroad for exclusive handling of their freight. The Central Pacific management placed the responsibility for the rate advance upon the Union Pacific, and gave publicity to a telegram of protest signed by Mr. Stanford.[17] There is reason to believe, nevertheless, that the Central Pacific management was cognizant of the matter from the first, and it is certain that Mr. Stubbs, general traffic manager of the Central Pacific, warmly defended the system.

Terms of Contract

Under the special contract plan, the railroad company agreed to charge not more than certain specified rates on articles named in the agreement shipped from New York, Pittsburgh, Cincinnati, and Chicago, and other points taking the same rates to the Pacific Coast. Rates on freight not specifically provided for were not to exceed those published in the general tariff. In case rival railroads cut rates, or in case competition by the Pacific Mail should become active, the shipper was to be protected. That is to say, it was declared to be the intent and purpose of the agreement to guarantee to the contracting merchant rates which should be as low as those charged and collected upon the same articles, between the same points, by any other all-rail route which might compete for the traffic of California at any time during the term of the contract.

The carrier also agreed that in the event of active competition with the Pacific Mail for the traffic between New York and San Francisco, the rates charged by rail during the period of competition should not exceed those current on Pacific Mail vessels by more than certain named amounts, ranging from 50 cents on goods taken at rates not exceeding $3.50, to $3 on goods taken at rates exceeding $6. This guaranty was not to be enforced at times when the rates of the Pacific Mail were subject to the control of the railroads.

---

[17] *San Francisco Call*, August 1, 1878.

In consideration of these assurances the shipper agreed to forward "by way of the railroads owned or operated by the contracting carriers and such other connecting railroads as might be designated from time to time, all goods, wares, and merchandise handled by the merchants entering into the agreement which might or should be purchased in or obtained from any point in the United States or Canada east of the meridian of Omaha, during the term of this contract, for sale or use on the Pacific Coast." [18]

Rates under System

It appears that at the beginning the same rates were quoted to all shippers signing the contract. That is to say, two rate sheets were published, one known as the "white list," and the other as the "pink list." The white list contained the open, or public rate; the pink list contained the contract rate. Contracts were made with individual shippers that if they would give to the railroad line all of their traffic for a year to the exclusion of ocean carriers, they would have a rebate down to the figure fixed in the pink list. Somewhat later, however, jobbers on the Pacific Coast were individually dealt with, and the rates began to vary.

Mr. Stubbs says in describing this phase of the matter:

> We tramped the streets here for a couple of months, explaining our ideas to the principal importers. By some we were met with cordiality and approval. Others were a little indifferent. Where a merchant liked the scheme, we would sit down with him, and, by examining his bills of lading by Cape Horn and his insurance policies, we would get an idea of the quantity he would ship by the several routes and the cost to him by the use of the several routes. We would then aim to make the rate so that upon the whole it would average about the

---

[18] Report of the Committee on Corporations of the Assembly of California, 1883, *sup. cit.* See also testimony taken before the Senate Judiciary Committee of the legislature of California in considering Assembly Bill No. 10 concerning the Regulation of Railroads, 1884 (in Appendix to the journals of the Senate and Assembly of the Legislature of the State of California, 25th Session, Extra).

same. We would average the rate while he was using the three routes.

Still later the railroads returned to the one-rate policy. To arrive at this rate they adopted a plan of "harmonization"; they averaged the rates upon various commodities which had been charged to various shippers and made a new schedule of rates, from which they varied as emergency might require or expediency advise, by the current method of rebating.[19]

Administration of Contracts

The railroad company reserved from the beginning the option of way-billing the goods and collecting freights according to the printed rates, agreeing to return the difference on presentation of vouchers to the general freight agent of the Central Pacific at San Francisco after the lapse of a reasonable time for auditing and adjusting the bills. The carrier also always insisted on the privilege of examining the shipper's books in case it suspected a violation of the agreement. In some respects, the wording and administration of the contracts became more stringent in the later years. J. T. Doyle, a well-informed San Francisco attorney, asserts that at the beginning merchants were merely forbidden to import goods otherwise than by rail. Following this the prohibition was extended to the handling or buying of goods imported by sea by other parties. Finally the boycott reached to the offending importers themselves, and firms signing the contracts were bound not to sell or deliver goods to anyone who was in the habit of importing otherwise than by rail.[20]

Probably there was some difference in the treatment of different shippers in these matters. Mr. Hawley, a large importer of hardware, told a committee of the California legisla-

---

[19] Railroad Commission of Nevada v. Southern Pacific Company, 21 I. C. C. R. 329, 346 (1911).

[20] Letter written by John T. Doyle and printed in the *Nation*, December 8, 1881.

ture in 1884 that he was at liberty to buy a great many things "to sort up with," even goods sent via the Horn. On the other hand, there were a good many cancellations of contracts for alleged violations, and shippers lived in continual apprehension.

Taken as a whole, the special contract system was an exchange of a rebate by the railroad for an agreement for exclusive patronage on the part of the shipper. Prior to 1878, bulky, low-grade articles moving between the Atlantic and the Pacific coasts usually went by sea. Rates were lower and saving in time not important. High-grade goods and freight requiring quick transportation went by rail. It was the idea of the railroad that if compelled to choose, Pacific Coast business men would prefer to import all their freight by rail rather than to bring it all in by water, and that this would substantially increase railroad revenues even though incidental concessions in rates had to be made.

Objections to Contract Plan

This special contract plan was objectionable to shippers for three reasons. In the first place, it seemed likely to increase the rates which they would have to pay. Although the railroad undertook at the inception of the scheme to meet existing rates by water, at least to such an extent that the total expense to shippers who made special contracts with the railroads would not be increased, it needed no great prescience to foresee that the exclusion of water carriers from the business of the Pacific Coast would sooner or later bring about an increase in transcontinental rates. When special contracts were offered to merchants in Stockton, Los Angeles, Marysville, and Sacramento, San Francisco importers made the additional complaint that their natural advantages as residents in a seaport town were neutralized.

In the second place, the administration of the plan required a supervision over the business of individual dealers which was

extremely distasteful. It was asserted that the railroads placed
men on the wharves to take the marks of goods brought in by
sea, that they followed up the drays to see where the goods
went, and that they inspected the books of merchants to make
sure that importers who had signed contracts had no dealings
with firms who still patronized the shipping lines. Nor was
this a casual abuse, but a necessary feature in the plan.

Again, the system lent itself to discrimination. Mr. Stubbs
insisted that contract rates were open to all shippers, large or
small, who would sign the necessary papers, but it was not
denied that the first arrangements were made with large
dealers only,[21] nor that during at least one period the whole
scheme involved the abandonment of a published and open
tariff in favor of a system of bargains in which each shipper's
rate was individually and secretly determined. Under such a
plan it was inconceivable that discrimination should not develop.

Ostensibly the offer of a special contract was one which
shippers were free to accept or to reject as they saw fit. Practically, this was not so. If A took a contract and B did not,
the latter's ability to compete was seriously impaired. For B
had to import some things by rail in any case, while the fact
that less business in the aggregate reached the Pacific Coast
by sea reduced the shipping facilities which B otherwise would
have had at his command.[22]

---

[21] United States Pacific Railway Commission, pp. 3333–34, 3358–59, testimony J. C.
Stubbs.

[22] The special contract system had the bad effect of repressing complaints from shippers.
Mr. Overheiser, member of the State Grange, farmer, and resident of California since 1849,
testified in 1884 before a committee of the California Senate as follows:
"Q. Are you sufficiently acquainted with the commercial community of Stockton to
know whether they have any reluctance in making complaint . . . before any Court of
justice, or in going before the Railroad Commissioners, or an investigating committee? A.
All I know about it is the impressions I have drawn from what I have heard.
"Q. To what effect? A. I would be very reluctant to come before this body and
state what firm I belong to, or represent, for fear that the railroad might chastise me for it,
or my firm.
"Q. Is that opinion generally shared among the merchants? A. As I understand it,
that is the general opinion.
"Q. What do you mean by the word 'chastise'? A. They might take our contracts
away from us."
This testimony was corroborated by at least one well-established merchant in San Francisco, who declared before the same Senate committee that business men in San Francisco were
afraid to testify against the railroad for fear that their contracts might be broken. (Testimony
before the Senate Judiciary Committee of the Legislature on Assembly Bill No. 10, 1884.)

Transcontinental Traffic Stimulated

Special contracts seem to have been a distinct success from the point of view of the western carriers. When they were introduced the percentage of transcontinental freight carried by the rail lines was small, probably not over 25 per cent of the whole. At the end of six years under the new system this percentage had risen to between 60 and 75 per cent.[23] The change was certainly not entirely due to the policy of special contracts, but part of the change may be attributed to the plan.

The policy was nevertheless given up in 1884 owing to the refusal of the eastern trunk lines to take any further part in it. According to Mr. Stubbs, the eastern companies believed that the advantage of the system hardly paid them for the confusion in their accounts incident to this method of conducting business. Moreover, there was legitimate apprehension lest the contracts provoke antagonistic legislation at Washington. Mr. Stubbs tried to argue the question, but without success.[24]

---

[23] Business Men's League of St. Louis v. Atchison, Topeka and Santa Fé Railroad, 9 I. C. C. R. 318 (1902). The number of vessels with their tonnage which entered the port of San Francisco in the trade with the Atlantic ports of the United States by way of Cape Horn from 1867 to 1884 was as follows:

Year ended June 30	Number	Tonnage
1867	103	110,721
1868	119	124,504
1869	139	153,784
1870	111	126,726
1871	53	66,289
1872	63	70,956
1873	87	104,586
1874	62	83,248
1875	75	110,071
1876	88	124,793
1877	86	124,746
1878	68	104,544
1879	57	92,683
1880	53	86,332
1881	55	89,097
1882	67	104,157
1883	71	118,494
1884	48	84,196

[24] Proceedings of the Transcontinental Association, 1885. The special contract system was strikingly similar to the system of "deferred rebates," until recently in good repute among ocean steamship companies. The argument in defense of this last-named system shows how slowly an understanding of the advantages of equality in matters of transportation rates spreads in a community. It is the view of the writer that both the special contract and the deferred rebate systems were and are contrary to sound public policy, whether applied on land or sea.

CHAPTER XV

LOCAL RATES IN CALIFORNIA

Charging What the Traffic Will Bear

The general policy of the associates in dealing with problems of rate-making in which rival towns were interested, was the same as that which they adopted to meet differences in competitive power between different individuals. The tests applied were simple. What was the market to be reached? Had the community concerned an alternative route? Was there an alternative source of supply which limited the willingness of the community to pay freight? If so, was this second source of supply one served by the Central Pacific, or one which had the benefit of water communication, or possibly one which possessed a rival rail connection? To what extent should concession be made from the highest rate which could be charged, in order to promote the growth of business?[1]

The standard of rate-making just described, which may be summed up as a policy of charging what the traffic would bear, was not peculiar to the Southern Pacific at the time

---

[1] A miner in Shasta County wrote to the *San Francisco Examiner* in 1893:
"I will state some facts about the attempt that was made to ship ores from here. Up to 1887 little or no assorted gold ores had been shipped. It was so new an enterprise that it was not classified in freight rates of the railroad company. The company was asked to establish rates, which it did— at $50 per car from Redding to San Francisco. This was satisfactory to the miners. We commenced to ship, and in a few months were sending down over 100 tons per month and had hopes of building up a permanent business. All at once, without notice, the freight was increased to $73 per car, and in a short time it was again raised, this time to $95 per car, and lots of less than one car were raised from 48 cents to 76 cents per 100 pounds. I went to San Francisco to see why this was done, and after considerable trouble gained an audience with an official at Fourth and Townsend streets. I spoke to the official about the advance on ore freight rates. His reply was: 'Why, you are sending down ore that would make a prince rich. We can't pull high-grade ore on low-grade rates.' I reminded him that it was billed at a valuation of $100 per ton and that the railroad company's responsibility ended there, and that we wished rates on all grades of ore, as there were so many values we could not classify them.
"Then he made me the proposition that there be no regular rates established, but to ship to the smelter for one month and then bring my returns and he would take out what he might think a recompense for pulling these values over the road. For cheek as a business proposition I think this stands pre-eminent. Of course it was rejected, and I was given rates as follows: Anderson, $71; Redding, $73 per car." (*San Francisco Examiner*, May 8, 1893.)

257

it was adopted, nor was it particularly repugnant to public opinion in California, taken as a whole. The error must not be made of ascribing to the western communities of the seventies and eighties a clear conception of the reasons of public policy which are properly urged today against the unlimited recognition in railway rate schedules of the competitive forces which still have free play in private business. Such ideas have slowly developed only during the last forty years.

Limited Encouragement of Business

Nor was the policy of adapting rates to the ability of shippers to pay inconsistent with the rendering of important service to business men in California and elsewhere who were seeking to expand their sales. Only a few illustrations need be given of the promotion of business by rate adjustments, but they will serve as examples of many more about which information is on record.

One case of this sort, which shows the willingness of the Southern Pacific management to respond to what they considered a reasonable request, had to do with the shipment of beer from a place known as Boca, in the state of Nevada, to San Francisco. It appears that a gentleman named Hess once conceived the idea of establishing a brewery at Boca. This town was 220 miles from San Francisco, and yet all of Mr. Hess's beer had to find a market in the latter place, in competition with beer from Milwaukee and St. Louis. Mr. Stubbs, general traffic manager of the Central Pacific, welcomed the proposal to build a brewery in the West, and put in special rates to help shut out the eastern product. Every pound of brewery supplies, he reasoned, would have to go over the Central Pacific. It was all clear gain, like so much money picked up out of the ditch. In another case the Southern Pacific quoted special rates on sugar from San Francisco to the Missouri River, to enable the California Sugar Refining Company and the American Sugar Refining Company to sell their sugar at the Missouri River in competition with sugar reaching New York by water and thence moving westward.[2]

Still again, in 1884 an attempt was made to persuade the St. Louis–Kansas City lines to participate in a rate of 75 cents per hundred pounds on cast iron pipe from St. Louis to the Pacific Coast in order to encourage production in the Middle West in competition with that on the Atlantic seaboard. The matter of the 75-cent rate was taken up with J. W. Midgley, Trunk Line commissioner, who declined temporarily on December 24, 1884, on the ground that the rate would be a special one, and that there was an understanding that no special rates should be made prior to January 31 next ensuing, pending an anticipated agreement between the Transcontinental Association and its eastern connections.[3]

In the instances which have been given, the impelling motive of the Southern Pacific was frankly to increase its profit by increasing the movement of freight over its line. Yet the shipper was also benefited because his interests were substantially identical with those of the railroad company, and he warmly welcomed the powerful support of the railroad lines. These cases are not unimportant. The enumeration of such isolated instances, however interesting as they may be, affords no very clear picture of the aggregate of local rate adjustments with which the Southern Pacific interests were concerned. For this purpose a more systematic survey of the rate system administered by the Southern Pacific is necessary, and to this attention is now directed.

Distance the Governing Factor

The foundation of any system of railroad rates is the distance which commodities are carried. Generally speaking,

---

[2] United States Pacific Railway Commission, pp. 3319–20, testimony J. C. Stubbs.
[3] Proceedings of the Transcontinental Railway Association, 1885, pp. 17–18.

the Southern and Central Pacific railroads, like other companies in the United States and Europe, varied their local charges with the distance between point of origin and point of

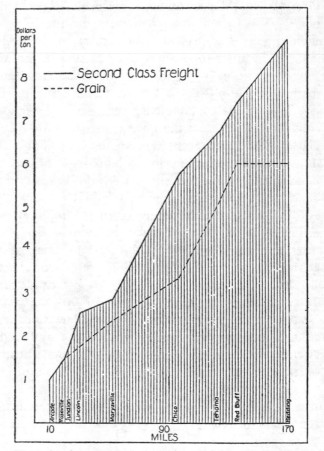

Chart showing rates on second-class freight and on grain in the Sacramento Valley, 1876.

destination. To illustrate this point briefly, two charts are here presented.

The first chart depicts the rates on second-class freight

and those on grain in January, 1876, between Sacramento and points in the Sacramento Valley north of that city. Second-class freight at this time on the Southern Pacific included

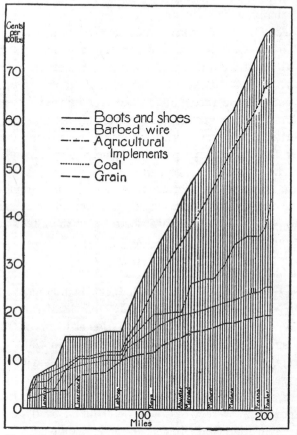

Chart showing rates on miscellaneous commodities in the San Joaquin Valley, 1892.

articles such as coal oil, agricultural implements, machinery, furniture, crated glassware, and wines and liquors. Freight of the description mentioned ordinarily moved north from the city of Sacramento. Grain, on the contrary, moved south. It will be observed that rates on the lines of the Southern Pacific increased with considerable regularity as point of origin or destination proceeded north into the non-competitive territory around Tehama and Redding.

The second chart displays rates between San Francisco and stations in the San Joaquin Valley as far south as Fowler, 205 miles distant from point of origin. These rates are for the year 1892.

Non-competitive rates in the San Joaquin Valley in 1892 increased as distance grew greater, much as they had increased in the northern territory sixteen years before. The rates given are for a few commodities only, namely, agricultural implements, barbed wire, boots and shoes, coal, and grain; but these are typical of the construction of schedules on a much larger number of articles. The extent of the increase was relatively greater to points beyond Lathrop because of the effect of water competition on San Francisco Bay.

Grades and Traffic Density

These two schedules illustrate a fact which could be readily proved by repeated examples, namely, that local rates in California were and are first based on the element of distance. Possibly such a fact might be assumed; yet in California, as elsewhere, the statement that railroad rates have varied with the distance traversed needs promptly to be qualified in order to be true. For, first of all, it was evident at the beginning that costs of transportation were not solely determined by distance, and that other considerations had to enter in. One of these other considerations was the matter of grades. Because of the conditions under which the Central Pacific was constructed, to say nothing of the extremely mountainous character of certain portions of the Central Pacific lines, differences in the rates per ton per mile between the valley and the mountain sections were introduced by the company at the commencement of its history.

A second characteristic of railway traffic which had a profound effect upon early railroad tariffs was the relative density of business. Mr. Stanford advanced the theory that the railroad should strive to secure a certain average earning per car; and in sections where business was light, as well as upon commodities which were bulky in proportion to their weight, a high average rate per hundred pounds was accordingly charged.

Relative grades and relative density of traffic were not the only conditions relating to cost which influenced the varying level of transportation rates in California, but, apart from distance, they were perhaps the most important, and in any case they may be taken as illustrative of the group of circumstances to which they belong. In addition to the whole class of facts relating to cost, however, the Southern Pacific gave heed to matters of value of service in the fixing of its rates. Nothing will be said here of the principles of classification of freight, principles which have to do in part with the value of the service rendered; nor of individual differences between shippers, which have been alluded to in the preceding chapter in the discussion of personal discrimination. The effect of competition in distorting distance schedules in California will, however, be dealt with at some length.

Water Competition

It has already been pointed out that the presence or absence of water competition has always been a most important factor in determining the relative adjustment of local rates in the state of California. This competition has been extremely pervasive. Although the scarcity of good harbors and the location of the Coast Range of mountains hinders access from the sea into the interior of California, yet, on the other hand, the ports of San

Diego, San Pedro, and San Francisco, and the long stretches of navigable water on the Sacramento and San Joaquin rivers have opened the possibilities of water shipment to a multitude of inland towns. Indeed, in 1883 General Manager Towne, of the Central Pacific, submitted to the State Railroad Commission a list of fifty-two points in California at which the Central Pacific and its leased lines met direct water competition. The water routes included San Francisco Bay and the Sacramento River and sloughs, Suisun Bay, Napa River, San Joaquin River, Feather River, the Pacific Ocean, Wilmington Bay, and the Colorado River. In addition, Mr. Towne enumerated eighty-two points where rates were affected by proximity to the competitive points previously mentioned.[4] On the face of things, the extent of the water competition thus indicated was sufficient to warp almost beyond recognition the simple distance scale of tariffs which a railroad completely protected from competition would naturally apply.

Low Rates to Competitive Points

An illustration of the effect of the water routes on local rates is found in the fact that the round trip fare from San Francisco to Sacramento by rail in 1878 was $3, while that to Woodland was $4.25.[5] The *San Francisco Chronicle* declared in 1879 that, according to a recently published schedule, the movement charge for grain, potatoes, vegetables, and wool from Lathrop to Mojave was exactly the same as to Ravenna, Newhall, or Los Angeles. The first-named distance was 288 miles, making the movement mileage rate 7.2 cents; the second-named distance was 337 miles and the rate per mile was 6.2 cents; the third distance was 356 miles, the rate being only

---

4 Letter to the State Railroad Commission, February 20, 1883.

5 *San Francisco Chronicle*, August 25, 1879. It appears that the fare from San Francisco to Sacramento by steamer had been $5 in pre-railroad days. When the California Pacific commenced operations in 1869, the fare fell to $4, and when the Western Pacific was opened, a $3 rate was put in. As far back as the fifties, rates were still higher. (A. A. Cohen, Letter to the State Railroad Commission, 1883.)

5.8 cents; and the distance to Los Angeles was 388 miles, or a mileage rate of 5.4 cents. The truth of the statement of the *Chronicle* is established by data published by the State Commissioners of Transportation in 1877, which show the striking contrast that existed in 1877 between non-competitive rates in the interior valleys and rates to points which enjoyed the advantage of nearness to the water routes.

Low water-compelled rates to Sacramento and to Los Angeles were in force as early as 1877. Yet this was only a beginning, and as time went on and the number of towns in California increased, the practice of recognizing the force of water competition was extended. Moreover, the Southern Pacific began to quote *lower* instead of merely equal rates to more distant points which enjoyed the advantage of nearness to a water location. Since the ability to make use of a competing railway afforded opportunities similar to those afforded by ability to use a water route, low rates were also extended to towns served by more than one railroad line. All this greatly complicated the rate situation in the state, gave rise to numerous complaints, and renders difficult the task of concise description.

Rates to Intermediate Points

Official confirmation of the general correctness of the complaint of discrimination which reached the public press from time to time is found in a comprehensive investigation of railroad rates in California which the Railroad Commission of that state undertook as late as the year 1916. This inquiry was provoked by an application by the Southern Pacific, Santa Fé, and other railroads in California for relief from the clauses of the amended state constitution and of the California Public Utilities Act prohibiting greater charges to intermediate points than were collected on shipments to more distant points over the same line. Although the legal aspects of the case were

therefore the result of modern legislation, the facts brought out
were typical of conditions of long standing.[6]

Exhibit No. 1 in the case in question referred to class rates
in the San Joaquin Valley. It appeared that class rates between
San Francisco, San José, Port Costa, Stockton, Sacramento,
Marysville, and intermediate points to Los Angeles, were 60
cents per hundred pounds first-class, and corresponding sums
less for the lower classes. These rates were shown to be con-

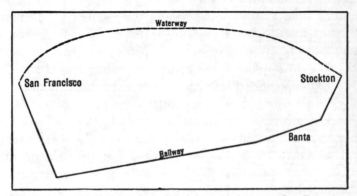

Diagram showing adjustment of freight rates between San Francisco
and Stockton, 1916.

trolled by the class rate of the Pacific Coast Steamship Company, which quoted a through first-class rate of 52 cents,
including wharfage and handling, between San Francisco and
Los Angeles via San Pedro. On all-rail shipments down the
valley, as well as on shipments over the coast rail route, however, water competition was not effective. The rate from San
Francisco to Simi, 429 miles from San Francisco, was therefore 80 cents, and that to Acton, 415 miles from San Francisco,
was 83 cents, although shipments from San Francisco to Los
Angeles passed through Simi and Acton on their way to Los

---

[6] Opinions and Orders of the Railroad Commission of California, 1916, Vol. 10,
p. 354 ff.

Angeles over the coast and San Joaquin Valley routes, respectively.

A condition similar to that at Los Angeles and at points in the San Joaquin Valley was developed in connection with shipments from San Francisco to Stockton. The diagram on page 266 will show the relative position of these two towns as well as that of an intermediate place named Banta.

The distance between San Francisco and Stockton was 91 miles, and the first-class rate was 10 cents per hundred pounds. This rate was identical with the rate charged by boat lines operating on San Francisco Bay, and on the Sacramento and San Joaquin rivers. But although these boats touched at some intermediate points, their competition was not everywhere effective; so that the first-class rate from San Francisco to Banta, 74 miles, could be and was 17 cents, although freight from San Francisco passed through Banta on its way to Stockton.

Other Instances

Still another illustration of the influence of water competition upon local rates in California may be drawn from the territory immediately north of San Francisco Bay. The towns involved in this adjustment were San Francisco, Sebastopol, and Santa Rosa, as shown in the diagram on page 268. The first-class rate from San Francisco to Sebastopol on the Northwestern Pacific was 23 cents. This rate was shown to be limited by the competition of a rail and water line, including a steamship haul from San Francisco to Petaluma and a haul over an electric railway from Petaluma to Sebastopol. The distance from San Francisco to Sebastopol over the Northwestern Pacific was 58.5 miles. The distances from San Francisco to the towns of Kenilworth and Santa Rosa, on the same railroad, were 45.7 and 52.5 miles, respectively. Shipments to Sebastopol passed through these places, but because neither enjoyed the advantage of an alternative route, the first-class rate to Santa Rosa was 25 cents and that to Kenilworth 28 cents—materially more than was charged for the longer haul to Sebastopol.

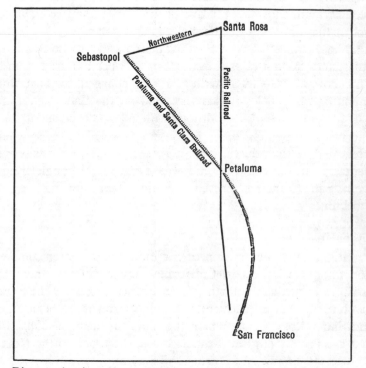

Diagram showing adjustment of freight rates between San Francisco, Santa Rosa, and Sebastopol, 1916.

While instances of the extreme discrimination of a greater charge for a shorter than for a longer haul were shown in 1916 to be usually the result of water competition, it has already been suggested that not all cases of discrimination were of this sort. A particularly striking case of unequal rates due to rail competition alone was brought out in the same proceedings from which the preceding illustrations have been drawn, by the application of the Atchison, Topeka and Santa Fé Railway to continue lower rates from Los Angeles to Mojave, Cali-

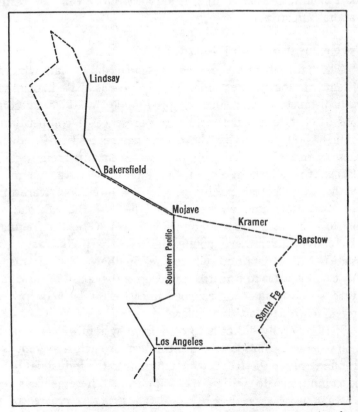

Diagram showing adjustment of freight rates between Los Angeles and points north and east of Los Angeles, 1916.

fornia, a distance of 212 miles, and to Lindsay, a distance of 411 miles, than were charged to Kramer, an intermediate point 174 miles from Los Angeles. The relative position of the points is shown in the diagram given above.

In this case the rate to Mojave at the time application was

filed was 52 cents first-class, and that to Lindsay 70 cents, while the rate to Kramer was 78 cents. But at both Mojave and Lindsay, the Santa Fé had to meet the competition of the short Southern Pacific line, while at Kramer this competition was not effective.

Development of State Retarded

The data which have been presented show that, while the system of local rates in California was based originally upon distance, it soon became profoundly modified by conditions of cost, and still more by the presence of competition at strategic points, and by the occasional necessity of reducing rates in order to stimulate the movement of freight. The charges for short hauls in the interior valleys where the Southern or Central Pacific possessed a monopoly were made high, because traffic was scant and because the railroad was able to exact a monopoly return. Rates were also regularly progressive under these conditions. In sharp contrast to the practice which obtained where the Southern Pacific was the only carrier, rates to points located upon the coast, on navigable rivers, or on competing railroad lines were relatively low and were often extremely irregular.

It is generally difficult to criticize a system of rate-making upon *a priori* grounds because the test of such a system is to be found only in the form which it gives to the industrial life of the community to which it is applied. There is reason to believe, nevertheless, that the local rate structure created by the Southern Pacific gave an advantage to a few shippers and to a few towns which affected unfavorably the development of the state. This is the fundamental objection to any system of rates in which competitive influences are recognized to an unlimited extent.

Without going further into the matter at this point, we will content ourselves with adding to our description of local rates in California some observations upon the attitude of California shippers with respect to railroad charges

Conflicting Claims of Cities

The rates of the Southern Pacific and of the Central Pacific railroads were unpopular in California because they were believed to be too high. Beyond this, and when it came to questions of relative adjustments, each community looked at the relations of rates which interested it from the narrow viewpoint of its individual advantage. Indeed, when one reviews the course of the controversy between railroad and shipper in the state, it seems very clear that, apart from questions of excessive profit, the objections which California cities entertained toward the irregular and unequal rates charged by the Southern Pacific Company were only slightly based on considerations of general policy, but were, on the contrary, due to the feeling of various towns that their distributing areas were unfairly circumscribed by the manner in which railroad rates were arranged.

One small piece of evidence to show that competition between rival towns or producing districts was the reason for some of the most bitter attacks upon the railroad, may be found in the complaint of the anti-monopolists of Tulare County in 1885 that their fruits, which ought to have found a market in the southern parts of the state and in Arizona, were subjected to higher freight rates than were the fruits of Sacramento and of San José, points more than 200 miles to the north.[7]

A few years earlier the merchants of Stockton insisted that the rates out of Stockton were extortionate as compared with the rates out of San Francisco. The distance from Lathrop to Stockton was said to be 10 miles, and the railroad rate per ton on wheat was $1.20, or 12 cents per mile. The distance from

---

[7] Declaration of Principles of the Anti-Monopoly Party of Tulare County (*Mussell Slough Delta*, February 24, 1882).

Lathrop to San Francisco was 82 miles, or more than eight times the distance to Stockton, but the price per ton for wheat was only $2.50, or about one quarter the price per ton per mile in the first instance. The price per ton from Lodi to Stockton was $1.40, and to San Francisco $2.50; but whereas the last-named sum was less than twice the former, the distance from Lodi to San Francisco was eight times as great as the distance to Stockton.[8]

In addition to their contention that mileage rates on shipments into Stockton compared unfavorably with rates on shipments into San Francisco, Stockton residents made the general charge that rates up the San Joaquin Valley were generally less than the rates down the valley. The rate from Stockton to Merced was said to be $6.80 per ton, but the rate from Merced to Stockton was $3.40. Stockton objected to forcing of the San Joaquin Valley to make San Francisco its market.[9]

Interstate Commerce Decision

Complaints similar to those voiced by Stockton were registered by the people of Los Angeles. In the eyes of inhabitants of that city, the rates on northbound freight from Los Angeles consigned to the San Joaquin Valley were relatively higher than the rates from San Francisco south into that same valley. Yet, dissatisfied as Los Angeles was with the relation which her rates bore to those out of San Francisco, it seemed to other cities in the south that her position was on the whole more favorable than was that of her neighbors. In 1889 a dealer in the city of San Bernardino protested against being forced to pay a higher rate from eastern points than was charged the city of Los Angeles. He showed that the rate on agricultural implements from the Missouri River to San Ber-

---

8 *San Francisco Chronicle*, August 27, 1879.
9 *Stockton Independent*, March 10, 1876.

nardino was $1.27 per hundred pounds while to Los Angeles it was $1.07. On stoves the rates were $1.19 and 99 cents, respectively, and on school furniture $1.55 and $1.35. This preference was alleged to be discriminative and illegal.[10]

In a decision approving the discrimination against San Bernardino, the Interstate Commerce Commission in 1890 remarked that originally southern California had been served from San Francisco direct; and that San Francisco jobbers had covered its territory. When the railroads reached Los Angeles they found it to their advantage to grant it low rates, not so much because it lay near the Pacific Ocean as because the interests of the Southern Pacific and especially of the Santa Fé demanded that some point in southern California should be given such a rate that merchandise from the East could be brought there all-rail and from that point be distributed. The fact that water competition was not the only influence which determined the Los Angeles rate from the eastern states was indeed shown later by the fact that the port of Los Angeles, San Pedro, did not receive a terminal rate until 1910, although Los Angeles itself had been given terminal privileges at least twenty years before.[11]

Stockton, Los Angeles, and San Bernardino thus illustrate in their conflicting claims the constant effort of cities in California to extend the area over which they might distribute goods. Among other instances of dispute between California cities may be mentioned the demand of Santa Barbara in 1907 to be made a Pacific Coast terminal,[12] and the angry contentions of Santa Clara, San José, Marysville, Santa Rosa, and Fresno

---

[10] San Bernardino Board of Trade v. Atchison, Topeka and Santa Fé Railroad Company, 3 I. C. C. R. 138 (1890). The Circuit Court for the Southern District of California refused to enforce the decree of the Interstate Commerce Commission in this case. (Interstate Commerce Commission v. Atchison, Topeka, and Santa Fé Railroad Company, 50 Fed. 295 [1892].)

[11] Harbor City Wholesale Company of San Pedro, California, v. Southern Pacific Company, 19 I. C. C. R. 323 (1910).

[12] Commercial Club of Santa Barbara, California, v. Southern Pacific Company, 12 I. C. C. R. 495 (1907).

in 1914 over the question of relative railroad rates from eastern points.[13]   The characteristics of the system of transcontinental rates which were involved in these complaints will be discussed in the following chapter.

---

[13] Santa Rosa Traffic Association v. Southern Pacific Company, 24 I. C. C. R. 46 (1912); 29 I. C. C. R. 65 (1914); Transcontinental Commodity Rate to San José, Santa Clara and Marysville, California, 32 I. C. C. R. 449 (1914).

CHAPTER XVI

THE TRANSCONTINENTAL TARIFF

Market and Railroad Competition

The chief difference between the local situation in California and the condition of affairs which prevailed in the case of through shipments to eastern points, lay in the fact that the competition of markets and the rivalry of competing carriers played a more important part in the through shipments than they did in local shipments. By market competition we mean the attempt of geographically distinct producing centers, each aided by a separate group of railroad lines, to sell in a common area of consumption. Such competition occurred, for instance, when California oranges sold in the Mississippi Valley in competition with oranges from Florida, or when California lemons sold in the same territory in competition with Sicilian lemons imported at New Orleans or at New York. We have already seen that cities competed with each other within California itself, but this competition was less important within the state than it was in the case of hauls across the continent.

It should be recalled that the Huntington interests possessed a virtual monopoly of local business, while the extent of the competition between carriers on through traffic may be briefly indicated by observing that the Central and Southern Pacific companies had direct relations with no less than six other transcontinental railroads, namely, the Union Pacific, completed in 1869; the Santa Fé, which reached the town of Deming and effected a connection with the Southern Pacific in 1881; the Texas Pacific, built to El Paso in 1882; the Northern Pacific, opened from St. Paul to Portland in 1883;

the Canadian Pacific, completed in 1887; and the Great Northern, which was finished in 1893. None of these railroads reached San Francisco except the Santa Fé, which obtained an independent California connection in the late nineties. The Santa Fé entered Los Angeles, however, in 1885, and the Union Pacific enjoyed a connection with Portland through the Oregon Short Line and the Oregon Railway and Navigation Company as early as 1884. From Portland, Los Angeles, and Vancouver, freight could be distributed by water all up and down the Pacific Coast.[1] Moreover, the competitive relations which Pacific Coast cities bore to each other made it necessary to keep their rates from the East on an approximate parity, and caused the Central Pacific to be affected by charges which were not on their face applicable to any point in which that company had an interest. There were combinations in respect to transcontinental railroad business from time to time, but none sufficient to control rates except for short periods.

Transcontinental Rate Adjustment

These differences in conditions between state and interstate traffic doubtless influenced Mr. Huntington and his advisors when they came to establish what is known as the transcontinental rate adjustment. Yet any examination of the through rates charged by the Central Pacific will show that in their relation to each other, at least, these rates were built upon much the same principles as the local rates discussed in the previous chapter. There is no essential difference between a rate schedule which applies a lower rate between New York and San Francisco than it applies between New York and Denver, and one which provides a lower charge between San

---

[1] In 1887 a steamer of the Pacific Coast Steamship Company left San Francisco weekly for Vancouver, where its freight was loaded upon cars of the Canadian Pacific Company and taken east across the mountains. The Canadian Pacific demanded, and in 1888 was conceded, the privilege of accepting freight from San Francisco to Chicago and points east at rates less than those charged by the other transcontinental lines. (Martin v. Southern Pacific Company, I. C. C. R. 1 [1888].)

Francisco and Los Angeles than between San Francisco and Bakersfield.

The tendency in public discussion is to regard the transcontinental rate structure as different from all other structures. It is not different, either from the rate systems in force in some other parts of the country, such as the Southern classification territory, or from the general arrangement of rates in business local to California. The reason why transcontinental rates to Pacific terminals are low is that there is competition at terminal points. The reason why rates to intermediate stations are high is that competition is lacking at such places. The reason why local rates between San Francisco and Los Angeles are low is that shipments must be diverted from the water lines; while the rates from San Francisco to points in the upper San Joaquin Valley are high either because competition is absent or because it is less severe. Similar general causes in both cases produce similar results.

Rate Structure

It is necessary to describe the transcontinental system at this point in order that the reader may have before him the outlines of the rate scheme for which the Huntington–Stanford group were in part responsible; but in view of the very general understanding which the public has of the system, the description will be brief. A summary account is as follows:

The primary fact in transcontinental rate-making is that railroad rates between the Atlantic and the Pacific coasts of the United States were originally made, and have remained relatively low. The lowest rates quoted, however, have never until recently been available at all points in California, Oregon, and Washington, but only at certain selected cities. The towns to which low rates have been quoted under the transcontinental adjustment are called Pacific Coast terminals. Terminals, being mostly located on the seaboard, or within easy reach of it, enjoy rates low enough to induce their residents to patronize the rail lines rather than the water lines around the Horn or the combined rail and water routes across the Isthmus of Panama and the Isthmus of Tehuantepec. This does not mean, of course, that rail rates to terminals have been as low as water rates, but it does mean that, all conditions of shipment, including speed, safety, and regularity, being taken into account, the advantages of shipment have been equalized. The rates to and from all terminals have been uniformly the same.

A characteristic feature of the transcontinental rate system is that the rates to towns and cities in the vicinity of terminals are determined by the absence of water competition. Inasmuch as a shipper located at an inland point is obliged to send his goods to the seaboard before he can avail himself of the advantage of a water haul, it becomes possible to charge him a rate equal to the sum of the terminal rate and the local rate which he will have to pay without causing a diversion of his freight from the rail to the water lines. It is true that there is a certain limit to the total charge which can be demanded from such a shipper, due to the circumstance that at some figure the expense of a direct haul from the local point in question to the final destination of the goods upon a non-competitive mileage basis will be less than the combination upon the terminal, but this limit is effective only in the case of communities located a considerable distance to the east of the seaboard shipping point. One result of the application of this system to local points is that towns situated upon the direct line between eastern cities and Pacific terminals often pay higher rates than are charged upon freight passing through these places and carried possibly several hundred miles beyond to the coast terminals. Local communities so situated are known as "intermediate" towns.

These three features of the transcontinental rate structure, namely, that rates between the Atlantic and the Pacific seaboards are low, that the lowest rates are charged only to selected towns, and that rates to places other than terminals are made by combination upon the terminals, are the elements which have given character to this adjustment, and are therefore the points in it which are best known. To make a statement of the broad outlines of the plan complete, however, two other statements must be added.

Group System in the East

The first additional characteristic of transcontinental rates is that on eastbound business, particularly in the case of the products of California agriculture, the same rates are applied from intermediate as from terminal points. This is to place the shipping communities of the state all upon an equal footing. The second feature has reference to conditions upon the eastern end of the transcontinental haul, rather than upon the western. In the eastern part of the country the system of terminal and intermediate rates is not applied upon transcontinental business. Instead, it has been customary to divide the area east of the Rocky Mountains into a series of great groups, now ten in number, and to quote to each of these groups rates which are either the same in all cases, or which increase as the distance grows greater.

This failure to apply in the East the same principles which govern in the West has been doubtless due to the insistence of cities like Chicago that her rates be at least as low on shipments to and from the Pacific Coast as the rates which New York enjoys, as well as to the desire of railroads which begin at Chicago or the Mississippi–Missouri River to encourage the growth of business in the Middle West. Mr. Huntington was credited with the desire to establish rates from the Missouri River which should be lower than rates from New York, and the reasons which were in his mind may easily be imagined. Such rates were actually in effect between 1887 and 1894, but the principle of graded charges was abandoned as a result of a rate war which broke out in 1894.[2]

Terminal Points

This brief description of a complicated rate adjustment will show that in through as well as in local rate-making the Central Pacific management yielded to the unequal pressure of competition, and particularly of water competition, at different points. Generally speaking, the most important of all the forms of competition which the company had to meet was water competition. Common alike to local and to through transportation, this was important because it was difficult to control, because it operated on a low cost basis, because it offered transportation facilities to a very wide variety of classes of goods, and because its possibilities for expansion were indefinite.

It is a mistake to believe that only low-grade commodities have been shipped by the water routes. While it is true that the principal movements by water are of the coarser freights, such as hardware, rails, pipe, sugar, hardwood lumber, and asphaltum, yet there has always been also a considerable transportation of higher grade articles, including cotton ducks and denims, beans, canned goods, and a large number of kinds of

---

[2] Business Men's League of St. Louis v. Atchison, Topeka and Santa Fé Railway Company, 9 I. C. C. R. 318 (1902).

When the Interstate Commerce Act was passed in 1887 the transcontinental carriers agreed to grade eastbound rates back to the Pacific Coast. Under tariffs issued April 5, 1887, Missouri River rates were applied for about 350 miles west of the river, from which point they gradually decreased to Denver. The Denver rates were applied from Denver to a point near Green River, over 300 miles west from Cheyenne. From Green River the rates again decreased gradually to the Pacific Coast. The tariff of April 5 was published in order to comply with Section 4 of the Interstate Commerce Law, and it was superseded by other tariffs in April and May, 1887, by permission of the Interstate Commerce Commission. (Martin v. Southern Pacific Company, 2 I. C. C. R. 1 [1888].)

In later years transcontinental rates to interior points were not uniformly built by combination upon the terminals. In many cases, even in westbound rates, the terminal rates served as maxima beyond which intermediate rates were higher than to terminal points, but not by the full extent of the local back. Thus on the Central Pacific in 1902 the company named class rates to intermediate points which acted as maxima to all points, which meant that when the specified intermediate rate was less than the terminal plus the local back, the lower rate prevailed. Nor must the influence of the Interstate Commerce Commission in reducing intermediate rates be left out of account. Yet it was the conclusion of this same commission as late as 1902, that the point where the direct rate from the East was at least as high as the sum of the terminal rate and the local rate from terminal to intermediate destination, was on the average 300 miles east of the Pacific Coast, and in some instances several times that distance, a fact which is sufficient to characterize the system as a whole.

general merchandise. Indeed, all the canned salmon and a very large percentage of the canned goods, together with two-thirds of the beans produced in California, originate near enough to the coast to reach tide-water at an expense not exceeding 20 cents per hundred pounds. The Interstate Commerce Commission has remarked that almost every article which moves from the East to the Pacific Coast has been at times carried by the ocean,[3] and the truth of this statement is generally conceded in discussions on the water business.

It was the pervasive character of water competition, and the fact that such competition was felt upon the Pacific Coast and not at interior points, which originally established the position of the Pacific terminal.[4] A terminal point, be it recalled, was, and is, under the transcontinental system, a place which enjoys rates low enough to attract traffic from the water to the railroad lines—a point also upon whose rates the rates to other points are based after the manner of the "basing point" system. San Francisco was a terminal. So was Stockton, Sacramento, Port Costa, Richmond, Oleum, Antioch, San José, Santa Clara, Los Angeles, and a considerable list of other towns. At the beginning the city of San Francisco received a lower rate than any other town because the competition of the water route between New York and San Francisco was most evident. Mr. Stanford, however, disclaimed responsibility for this limitation. His eastern connections, he said, were to blame. The Central Pacific was willing to be more liberal from the start, but the other lines would not join with it in establishing through rates, and insisted on their locals. For this reason goods originating at interior points were often hauled to San Francisco, and then back east, in part over the same line by which they had come.[5]

---

[3] Business Men's League of St. Louis v. Atchison, Topeka and Santa Fé Railway Company, 9 I. C. C. R. 318 (1902). See also Rates on Asphaltum, etc., 33 I. C. C. R. 480 (1915).

[4] In so far as there is rail competition between transcontinental carriers, this rivalry also is keenest upon the Pacific Coast, and weakest in the intermediate territory.

[5] Report of Senate Judiciary Committee on Assembly Bill No. 10, 1884, testimony C. S. Stevens.

Such a condition was highly unsatisfactory to California towns other than San Francisco, yet by 1873 Sacramento, Marysville, and San José had been given terminal rates,[6] and still later the list of terminal points was very greatly extended. In 1910 there were 152 terminal cities on the Pacific Coast, of which 97 were in California.[7]

Dissatisfaction with Rate System

Owing to the peculiar intensity of competition at their doors, Pacific terminals therefore enjoyed exceptional advantages in rates as compared with their less favored neighbors. On the other hand, even the terminal cities expressed some dissatisfaction with the transcontinental adjustment. It appears, for instance, that the growth of great distributing centers was difficult under the scheme of rates which was applied. So long as terminals were few in number, a considerable concentration in business was possible. But when the terminals multiplied, the territory controlled by any single city became limited by the low rates accorded to the near-by terminal cities, and expansion in any one spot became difficult. This rendered the volume of business of the Pacific Coast jobbers comparatively small. In the case of the Business Men's League of St. Louis v. the Atchison, Topeka and Santa Fé, already cited, the two eastern firms of most prominence in the proceedings were the Simmons Hardware Company, of St. Louis, and Hibbard, Spencer, Bartlett and Company, of Chicago. The former of these firms then did business in every part of the United States except New England, while the representatives of the latter testified that the operations of his house were limited only by the confines of the earth. Competition by concerns of this magnitude was difficult for California houses to meet, especially at times when the eastern

---

[6] Letter of Stanford to a committee of the San Francisco Chamber of Commerce, 1873.
[7] Railroad Commission of Nevada v. Southern Pacific Company, 19 I. C. C. R. 238 (1910).

firms used the Pacific Coast as surplus territory in which they could afford to operate at a low margin of profit.

Another ground for dissatisfaction on the part of the coast cities arose out of their belief that the system as applied, in spite of its recognition of the advantages of the Pacific Coast, still fell short of the real equities of the situation. It was insisted that San Francisco was improperly shut out from Denver, Cheyenne, Salt Lake City, and Ogden. The Southern Pacific was charged with carrying hats from New York by way of the Union and Central Pacific routes and then down the San Joaquin Valley to Yuma at a lower rate of freight than the San Francisco dealer could send the same goods from his city to the Colorado River.[8] This same complaint was repeated by Mr. Leeds, of the San Francisco Traffic Association, in October, 1892, with the observation that if the same rate per mile were applied on eastbound traffic from San Francisco that was charged on westbound business from Chicago to Utah common points, then San Francisco would do the lion's share of the Utah business instead of a mere 16 per cent.[9]

There is no doubt that a good deal of dissatisfaction with the transcontinental system was felt first and last by shippers to and from the terminal cities. Yet, after all, the situation of these cities as a group was excellent. The communities which were really handicapped were the towns intermediate between the Pacific terminals and the East, towns which paid higher rates for less service than did the terminal cities, and which found that this condition not only increased the cost of living to their consumers, but prevented their merchants from enjoying a profitable distributing trade.

It seems probable that the associates intended from the beginning to charge the mountain towns more on through hauls than was exacted from towns on the coast. Huntington relates a conversation which took place at Carson, Nevada, in

8 *San Francisco Bulletin*, March 26, 1892.　　9 *Ibid.*, October 12, 1892.

1861, between Stanford, Dr. Strong, Mr. Crocker, and himself, representing the railroad, and some twenty representative men of Nevada. The Nevada people observed that Huntington kept a pretty good hardware store, but that he was likely to leave it in the mountains if he started to build a railroad in Nevada. Huntington replied that he would look out for that, but, he continued, when the road was built he proposed to charge through rates which, while less than the Nevada people were paying for goods which then came to San Francisco by boat and were subsequently teamed across the mountains, would be materially greater than the rates to San Francisco. "We shall charge you for bringing back," said he, "almost as much as we shall charge from New York." After the road was built Huntington says he met one of these same men with whom he had talked in 1861. "Said I, 'You recollect that talk we had in the Curry House in 1861?' 'Yes, oh yes.' Well, we talked about that. He said, 'You've got me there, Huntington.' 'Well,' said I, 'I said you would grumble. Now,' said I, 'you shut up.'" [10]

Objections

It is to be presumed that Mr. Huntington's rejoinder was effective in the particular discussion which he relates. Yet the grievances of the interior towns found full and repeated expression after 1869, and indeed are still emphatically presented at the present day. The more fundamental criticisms of the transcontinental rate system are the following: The principal objection directed against the whole adjustment is that it leads to charges to intermediate points which are prima facie unreasonable. Speaking of the rates on iron and steel, a representative of the Traffic Bureau of Utah called the attention of the House Committee on Interstate and Foreign Commerce in 1918 to the fact that the rate on iron and steel articles

---

[10] Huntington manuscript, pp. 27–28.

for export from Chicago territory to Pacific Coast terminals was 40 cents per hundred weight or 3.54 mills per ton per mile. He continued:

> They take an identical carload of the same commodity, and when it is going to the Pacific Coast for domestic consumption the rate is 65 cents a hundred, or 5.76 mills per ton-mile. If they were to apply that rate at the Utah common points— the same 65-cent rate—it would pay 8.65 mills per ton-mile. But they say, "We cannot afford that; you must pay 10.84. We haul it for a man in Russia for 3.54, but that is only the out-of-pocket cost. We will make you a rate of 10.84, which is a lower rate than you are entitled to.
>
> I think any article, whether it is transportation or anything else, that could be produced at some profit at a price of 3.54, when you pay 5.76 for it you are paying a handsome profit; and if you pay 8.65 for it you are paying an abnormal profit; and if you pay 10.84 for the same thing you are being outrageously imposed upon, which is what we are doing.[11]

The second objection of the interior cities is that the system of transcontinental rates limits the territory in which intermediate wholesale firms can do a distributing business; and the third ground of complaint, resulting from the other two, is that the policy of permitting low rail rates to the coast cities has the effect of building up large cities on the seaboard at the expense of the whole interior country.

Reply of Railroads

In replying to these objections the coast towns take the position that they are not especially concerned with the rates to intermountain places, nor indeed with the rates which the railroads make from coast to coast, except in the sense that the greater the number of carriers which participate in transconti-

---

[11] Hearings before the Committee on Interstate and Foreign Commerce of the House of Representatives on H. R. 9928 (55th Congress, 2d Session, March 26 to April 2, 1918, pp. 84–85, testimony W. S. McCarthy).

nental business, the better the service is likely to be.   Secure in the possession of adequate water connection, they do not expect to pay higher rates than they have paid in the past, whatever policy the railroads may adopt.   They have no controversy with the intermediate territory, and only support the present adjustment because they conceive it to be for the best interests of the country as a whole.

The burden of the defense therefore falls upon the railroads, and the railroads assert that the policy of quoting low rates to meet the force of water competition is necessary if the comparatively moderate rates to intermountain territory are to be continued.   Unless—said Mr. Spence of the Southern Pacific, in his recent testimony before the House Committee on Interstate Commerce—the rail lines are permitted to make rates which will hold the through business, the terminal roads will lose all of the net revenue derived from the port rate upon what is a very large volume of traffic.   The millions of dollars involved cannot be withdrawn from the net revenues of the railroads without impairing their efficiency and usefulness, while to compel the carriers to apply sea-compelled rates to all traffic would yield an inadequate revenue, because it would mean that the traffic as a whole would be carried at rates which were not sufficient to cover all the elements of cost, including fixed charges and other similar expenses.[12]

Further Comments

The most casual description of any basing system such as the one which the railroads apply to transcontinental freight, suggests at once several matters in respect to which special defense and justification are required.   One just cause of complaint arises out of the fact that the through rate to any point

---

[12] Hearings before House Committee on Interstate and Foreign Commerce, *sup. cit.*, pp. 170-71, testimony, L. J. Spence.

except to a basing point is made up by the addition of two rates, each of which includes an allowance for the cost to the carrier of providing terminal facilities, or four terminals in all, whereas no actual shipment makes use of terminal facilities at more than two points, namely, the place of origin and the place of destination.

A second cause for criticism of a basing system is due to the striking disregard of distance which is inherent in it. Shippers are not only apt to feel that for reasons of natural right rates for transportation should vary with the distance moved, but, as we have seen, they are usually quite incapable of being convinced that the costs of shorter hauls are not less than the costs of longer ones, so that for this reason also the nearer places should enjoy the lower rates. Again, and this also has been suggested in the preceding discussion, a basing system is attacked because it is said to centralize business unduly by forcing the distributing business into the control of a few localities such as the Pacific Coast terminals, to the exclusion of outlying cities which could handle it more cheaply and more conveniently under a proper adjustment of rates, by reason of their greater nearness both to centers of supply and of consumption.

There is no question that the rate system upon the Pacific Coast made it difficult for intermediate and local towns to import supplies directly from the East and to distribute them through their own organization. This was not the result of the difference between terminal and local rates alone, but was the combined result of the practice of the transcontinental carriers with respect to rates and their practice with regard to carload shipments. That is to say, the carriers not only quoted generally lower rates, carload against carload, and small consignment against small consignment, to terminal cities than to intermediate or to interior towns, but they also granted many carload ratings to terminals which were altogether denied to their interior competitors. In some cases this occasioned an extraordinary difference in the total charge.

On the other hand, it should not be forgotten that to encourage distribution through Pacific Coast terminals was not necessarily to concentrate the whole business of distribution. The competition between the Pacific terminal and the eastern jobber was just as real as that between the Pacific terminal and the intermediate point. It is sometimes forgotten how active this eastern competition was. That it continually threatened the western distributor is shown by the fact that in spite of the advantages enjoyed by western terminals, 50 per cent of the jobbing business in the hardware trade in southern California was done in 1902 by houses east of the Missouri River, so that the Interstate Commerce Commission expressed the opinion that in the absence of some distinct advantage in the rate it would be very difficult for Pacific Coast dealers to hold their own.[13] In central California the proportion of the jobbing business done by eastern firms ranged from 25 to 40 per cent. Certainly no decentralization in business would have taken place had the California distributors been compelled to withdraw in favor of men in Chicago and St. Louis, nor would the aggregate cost of getting goods from producer to final consumer have been decreased.

Inconsistency

It has been made clear in the discussion of transcontinental rates, that the transcontinental carriers as a group have not been consistent in applying the principles upon which they rely in justification of their charges. Not only have towns like Los Angeles been given terminal rates for reasons of general policy, but cities in the Mississippi Valley, upon the other end of the transcontinental haul, have been granted the same rates as New York on business to and from the Pacific Coast, in

---

[13] Business Men's League of St. Louis v. Atchison, Topeka and Santa Fé, *sup. cit.*

order to place them on an equality with points on the Atlantic seaboard. As the Interstate Commerce Commission remarked when the matter was brought to its attention, there is no logical ground for recognizing the desire of Chicago to compete with New York, and for refusing to accord the same privilege to Denver.[14] If market competition is to be recognized in one instance, it should be in another.

It is a striking fact that when the commission was considering the question of transcontinental rates in 1910, it appeared that the great bulk of traffic destined to intermountain cities originated at Chicago or at points west. Thus out of 21,000,-000 pounds of carload freight moved from eastern territory to Reno, Nevada, during the year 1908, only 4,500,000 pounds originated east of Chicago, and of approximately 1,000,000 pounds of less than carload freight concerning which data were available, only 10 per cent originated at the Atlantic Coast cities of New York, Boston, and Philadelphia. The commission found in the case in which these facts were brought out that taking traffic to Reno as a whole, 75 per cent of it had its source between Chicago and Denver.[15] On this traffic, at least, the effect of water competition was slight, and yet it is upon the assumed presence of water competition that the transcontinental system primarily rests.

Not Responsive to Changed Conditions

Nor have the transcontinental carriers been quick to recognize changes in conditions which, temporarily at least, have eliminated water competition from coast to coast. When the Panama Canal was opened, considerable apprehension was felt

[14] Kindel v. Atchison, Topeka and Santa Fé Railway, 8 I. C. C. R. 608 (1900). In its first exercise of authority under the amended long- and short-haul clause, the Interstate Commerce Commission of 1911 prescribed the extent to which rates from eastern points of origin at and west of the Atlantic seaboard to Reno and other points upon the main line of the Central Pacific might exceed the rates to Pacific Coast terminals. (Railroad Commission of Nevada v. Southern Pacific, 21 I. C. C. R. 329 [1911].) Cf. Commodity Rates to Pacific Coast Terminals, 32 I. C. C. R. 611 (1915).

[15] Railroad Commission of Nevada v. Southern Pacific Company, 19 I.C.C.R. 238 (1910).

by the carriers lest the new all-water route between the Pacific
and the Atlantic seaboards should divert a substantial portion of
the transcontinental traffic formerly handled by the railroads.
On this ground the railroads applied to the Interstate Commerce Commission, and received permission not only to continue the practice of quoting higher rates to interior towns
than were charged between eastern points and the Pacific
Coast,[16] but actually to increase the difference upon a selected
list of eastbound articles.[17]   So much was directly in line with
previous action and was to be expected.

The carriers were not, however, so ready to recognize the
interruption of canal traffic as they had been prepared to take
notice of its beginning, and in spite of slides and war conditions
which suspended water competition, it took an order of the
Interstate Commerce Commission to secure an equality in the
treatment of intermountain and seaboard cities to which the
former in accordance with the fundamental theory of transcontinental rates were entitled under the new conditions.[18]

In forming an opinion upon the rate system of the Central
Pacific, however, too much weight must not be attached to
inconsistencies in application so long as these are not altogether
arbitrary, any more than to the demand of competing cities for
their "fair share" of the business that is to be done.   City
ambitions are limitless, and impossible to reconcile.   The question is not how to determine the territory within which a given
city may be said to have a right to distribute its goods, but
whether or not the rate system introduced by the Huntington
group, all things considered, promotes the interests of the
territory which is served better than some system that may be
suggested.

        [16] Commodity Rates to Pacific Coast Terminals, 32 I. C. C. R. 611; 34 I. C. C. R. 13
(1915).
        [17] Daggett, "The Panama Canal and Transcontinental Rates," (in *Journal of Political
Economy*, December, 1915); Rates on Asphaltum, etc., *sup. cit.*
        [18] Reopening Fourth Section Applications, 40 I.C.C.R. 35 (1916); Transcontinental
Rates, 46 I.C.C.R. 236 (1917).   See also Skinner and Eddy Corporation v. United States,
39 Supreme Court Report 375 (1919).

Basing Rate System Necessary

It is the writer's opinion that the transcontinental rate system has always had evident defects. In the first place, it has generally provided low rates to towns and it has quoted low rates on commodities which have no access to the water routes. In the absence of competition the distance principle should prevail. Second, it has often failed in the past to make concessions to the cost basis of rate-making, which would have removed complaint without altering the plan in principle, such concessions, for example, as the reduction of rates to interior points to something less than the sum of through and local rates to allow for the relatively small amount of terminal service rendered. And, finally, it has increased the amount of transportation incident to the distribution of a given amount of freight. While the assertion of cities without terminal privileges that they have the right to do a specified amount of business is to be received usually with skepticism, it does seem probable that the transcontinental railroads would have reduced the aggregate cost of distributing transcontinental freight had they encouraged more than they did the growth of the interior towns, provided that they had supported these towns both against Chicago and St. Louis and against the Pacific Coast.

This same policy would have had the important advantage, from the railroad's point of view, of developing industry at points which were not affected by every change in the rates of its competitors. The Central Pacific was not the first railroad in the country confronted with the problem of how to treat the non-competitive points upon its lines. Nor, unfortunately, was it the only railroad which adopted the drifting policy of quoting rates to hold the business, thus favoring the towns served also by its rivals in preference to towns more peculiarly its own, and through the stimulus given to such places, in the end creating a distribution of production which, of all possible alternative distributions, was the one which rendered its hold upon the business of its territory the least secure.

In spite of these defects, it is the writer's judgment that some basing rate system, in its broad outlines similar to the transcontinental system actually applied, was necessary and desirable for the development of the West. The principal advantages of such an arrangement were that it gave to the Pacific Coast the benefits of competing rail and water routes as no distance system could have done, and that it enabled the railroads to fill their trains with traffic which paid them something over the out-of-pocket costs. It is clear that the interior cities were mistaken in supposing that this practice increased the rates which they had to pay. On the contrary, it reduced them. There is also reason to believe that the transcontinental rate system decentralized the distribution of goods, while it certainly afforded western buyers and producers in most instances the important advantage of access on equal terms to the markets of Chicago and of New York.

There is little evidence that either Huntington, Stanford, Crocker, or Hopkins had an active part in moulding the local or the through rate structures of the Central and the Southern Pacific railroads. The work was probably done by the traffic experts whom they hired, of whom the chief was that very able individual, J. C. Stubbs. The contribution of the associates may be taken to have been a clear appreciation of the advantage of monopoly to railroad revenues, and the consistent support which they gave to the efforts of men who knew more about the subject of railroad rates than they did themselves.

CHAPTER XVII

THE TRAFFIC ASSOCIATION OF CALIFORNIA

Discontent

The discussion of the transcontinental rate structure leads naturally to a consideration of a very serious controversy in which the Southern Pacific became engaged in 1891. This controversy arose as the result of an attempt by certain merchants of San Francisco to secure lower distributive rates in the interior California valleys. The official statement of the shippers' side of the case in this lively conflict of the nineties has been compiled and published.[1] No similar statement of the position of the railroad has come out, but the important facts are pretty well on record.

There is no question that the political and commercial policies of the Southern Pacific had by 1890 engendered restlessness and discontent among the commercial classes on the Pacific Coast. It was believed that railroad rates from the East were high. It was thought that use of the water lines had been limited by the special contract system while that was in force, and that water competition had been affected subsequently by arrangements between the transcontinental lines and the Pacific Mail Steamship Company. The work of the State Railroad Commission had proved disappointing. In short, the situation was such that it needed only the pressure of the business depression of 1890 to 1897 to stir men to vigorous action.

---

[1] Wheeler, "The Valley Road—A History of the Traffic Association of California, the League of Progress, the North American Navigation Company, the Merchants' Shipping Association, and the San Francisco and San Joaquin Valley Railway" (San Francisco, 1896). See also Walker, "Pioneers of Prosperity" (San Francisco, 1895).

Coastwise Trade via Foreign Port

The episode which is to be described began with an attempt on the part of certain San Francisco merchants to use British clippers for the importation of freight from New York, in spite of the fact that the right to engage in coastwise traffic was limited by statute to ships flying the American flag. It appears that in 1891 a consignment of nails was shipped from New York in a Belgian vessel to Antwerp, consigned to a commercial house there. At Antwerp the merchandise was discharged and landed, and from that city it was then shipped on a British vessel to Redondo, California, where it was entered at the customs house as a manufacture of the United States, entitled as an American product to free entry under American law. Nor was this the only case of the sort. In all sixteen shipments were sent to California via European ports between October 16, 1891, and May 28, 1892.

The obvious intent of the whole transaction was to evade the statute governing the movements of merchandise by water between United States ports, in order to effect a saving in freight estimated to amount to $4 a ton. In spite of the somewhat transparent nature of the business, the District Court of the United States for the Southern District of California and the Circuit Court of Appeals both held that the operation had been legally accomplished. According to these courts the law forbade a method, not a result, and unless goods were transported from one port of the United States to another port in a vessel belonging in whole or in part to foreign subjects, no penalty was incurred.[2]

It may be doubted if the roundabout route followed by the nails, here the subject of litigation, would ever have afforded noticeable relief to importers on the Pacific Coast. Whatever chance existed was removed, however, by an amendment to

---

[2] United States v. 250 Kegs of Nails, 52 Fed. 231 (1892); 61 Fed. 410 (1894). See also *San Francisco Bulletin*, November 19, 1891.

ιe statutes in 1893, specifically forbidding transportation from
ιe port of the United States to another port of the United
tates via any foreign port except in an American vessel.[3] This
ιded the first phase of the revived competition of 1891.

ᵗrganization of Association

The same month which saw the entrance of the 250 kegs
ᵗ nails into the port of Redondo, saw also the establishment of
ιe so-called Traffic Association in San Francisco. The Traffic
ssociation was originally conceived as an organization of
ᵗerchants of San Francisco for mutual protection, and for
ᵥercoming by united effort an alleged unjust discrimination
ᵧainst the business interests of the city. In fact the name
ᵗst proposed for the new body was "Merchants' Traffic
ssociation," and it was intended that the executive committee
ᵗould be composed of eighteen members of the mercantile
ᵣmmunity. These details were, however, changed,[4] the words
ᵗerchant" and "mercantile community" were left out, and
hen the association was finally organized on October 30,
391, the constitution and by-laws provided merely for the ad-
ittance of merchants, manufacturers, producers, and others
ιterested in and favorable to its objects. Railroad employees
ᵗ persons holding free passes over railroads were the only
asses debarred. Subsequently an attempt was made to interest
ιrties outside of San Francisco, but without large success.
ᵗharacteristically the Traffic Association began and remained
ι association of San Francisco shippers for their own protec-
ᵣn, particularly in the matter of transportation rates. Fifteen
ιt of nineteen members of the first executive committee were
ᵗpresentatives of San Francisco firms, and 97 per cent of the
embership did business in that town. The first president was
ᵗr. Stetson, of Holbrook, Merrill, and Stetson, and from

---

[3] 27 United States Statutes 455 (1893). This bill was introduced by Senator Frye.
[4] Proceedings of the Merchants' Convention (*San Francisco Bulletin*, October 19, 1891).

first to last the overwhelming proportion of the association funds came from San Francisco.

The government of the Traffic Association was placed in the hands of an executive committee from which were to be selected the usual executive officers.   All power was to be vested in the committee; that is to say, the executive committee was to have, in general, entire control and management of the affairs of the association, and in particular was to appoint a manager and other employees, who were to be relied on for the active work.   By a special section the committee reserved the right to route all freight of members, should emergency require it and provided that the action was approved by at least ten members of the committee.   Membership fees ranged from $60 to $150 per annum, payable quarterly in advance.   Moreover, the constitution provided that any unusual work undertaken for the benefit of any particular line of trade, which entailed any unusual expenditure, should be charged pro rata to the firms or corporations most directly affected, and in accordance with the benefits derived.   No membership was to be for a shorter period than two years.[5]

Functions

Inasmuch as some controversy later occurred with respect to the proper purposes of the Traffic Association of California, it is necessary to be explicit regarding the functions which, at the beginning, it was expected that the association would perform.   According to the statements of its promoters, the association was not formed to fight the Southern Pacific or any other individual railroad company.   The assertion was repeatedly made, on the contrary, that the intent was, by organization, merely to enable the shippers of California to deal collectively with the railroads, instead of one by one as hereto-

---

[5] The constitution of the Traffic Association is printed in full in the *San Francisco Bulletin*, November 4, 1891.

fore, and so to secure a presentation of the shippers' point of view which would carry weight by reason of the united sentiment behind it. In this way the shippers' bargaining power would be improved without giving legitimate cause for offense to parties upon the other side, and without exposing individual complainants to retaliation.

In the invitation to the mass meeting which took up the question of organization on the 17th of October in San Francisco, it was explained that merchants, producers, and shippers could accomplish nothing at that time because they were disorganized. By opposing a solid front to the railroad combine, it was said, a good deal could be accomplished. Further, it was declared that the railroad would not resist such a movement. J. B. Stetson, chairman of the mass meeting, stated:

> Our object . . . is to organize a Freight Bureau or Traffic Association or whatever it may be termed, whose purpose shall be for mutual protection and extension of the interests of San Francisco; for overcoming, by united effort, discriminations and inequalities against the interests of San Francisco; for representation in conferences upon matters of importance to the shipping public to and with railroad or transportation companies. Associations similar to the one we propose forming here are in existence in all the eastern cities, and great benefits have accrued from them, and will not fail to prove successful here. We do not meet here for the purpose of waging warfare or encouraging antagonisms between the shipping public and the railroads, or any transportation lines. We believe that the same theory would govern them as would govern ourselves as business men in the redress of any grievance of our customers. We believe that by united action we can present to the railroad and transportation companies views in reference to freights, classifications, etc., that will cause them to make changes that will be beneficial both to ourselves and to them . . . I cannot too earnestly advise prudence and caution in the outset, for if this association is started properly, great

good will come from it and [it will] prove of lasting benefit to the commercial community.[6]

First Meeting

The first public announcement that a traffic association w⟨⟩ in process of organization was made late in September, 189⟨⟩ at which time merchants were asked to pledge themselves ⟨⟩ send representatives to a mass meeting of merchants, producer⟨⟩ and manufacturers to be held on October 17 in San Francisc⟨⟩ This mass meeting occurred as planned. There were speech⟨⟩ discussion, and amendment of proposed resolutions, and t⟨⟩ final indorsement of a plan for joint action. That is to sa⟨⟩ it was declared to be the sense of those present that an orga⟨⟩ zation be formed, that the management of it be entrusted to ⟨⟩ executive committee and to the usual officers, and that reven⟨⟩ be derived from dues. Most of the program was cut a⟨⟩ dried. Among the incidental but interesting features of t⟨⟩ meeting, however, was an address by a gentleman from Fres⟨⟩ calling for the construction of another competing railroad, a⟨⟩ the presentation of a communication from San Diego, sugge⟨⟩ ing that the Santa Fé be induced to extend its line to San Die⟨⟩ and that provision be then made for connection by sea betwe⟨⟩ that city and San Francisco.[8]

The net result of the meeting of October 17 was to rev⟨⟩ an interest in the plan for a shippers' organization wh⟨⟩ encouraged the promoters to go ahead, while at the same ti⟨⟩ the meeting provided the machinery which made further p⟨⟩ gress possible. From now on, matters moved rapidly. T⟨⟩ executive committee was appointed, and its membership w⟨⟩ made public on October 23;[9] on October 30 a complete c⟨⟩

[6] San Francisco Bulletin, October 17, 1891.

[7] San Francisco Examiner, October 8, 1891.

[8] San Francisco Bulletin, October 17, 19, 1891; San Francisco Chronicle, October⟨⟩ 1891.

[9] San Francisco Chronicle, October 24, 1891.

stitution and set of by-laws was adopted by the association, and on November 2 a general call for members was issued.[10]

Interior Towns

It was in securing members that the Traffic Association met with its first check—a check which consisted in the general refusal of residents of the country districts and of the interior towns to join with San Francisco in its fight against the railroads. It has already been pointed out that 97 per cent of the members of the association did business in San Francisco, and the check came in spite of a deliberate and persistent attempt by the Traffic Association to conciliate the interior. It was partly with the idea of gaining support from outside of San Francisco, for instance, that the mass meeting of October 17 changed the name of the association from that of "Merchants' Traffic Association of San Francisco and the State of California" to the simpler "Traffic Association of California." Another concession was the appointment of four outside members to the controlling executive committee—a proportion far exceeding either the relative outside membership or the funds contributed from that source. Still other attempts to gain support were made through meetings held in Fresno and San José at which the advantages of the Traffic Association idea were presented.[11]

Dissension

There appears, however, to have been some difference of opinion within the Traffic Association itself with regard to

[10] *San Francisco Bulletin*, November 4, 1891.

[11] It was the position of the executive committee of the Traffic Association, and in this they were supported by the traffic expert whom they employed, that it would be exceedingly bad policy for San Francisco to antagonize the interior by endeavoring to secure special advantages for itself. (*San Francisco Chronicle*, December 10, 1892.)

The Traffic Association was said to be, under its constitution and by-laws, a state institution, organized to promote the welfare of the whole state. The executive committee did not believe that San Francisco should be made the sole terminal even were this possible. The city would assume its proper and legitimate place not as the oppressor, but as the protector of every industry in the state, provided free competition and equally adjusted local rates could be secured. (*Ibid.*, December 18, 1892.)

the best policy to be pursued toward the interior. The fundamental complaint of San Francisco was that her distributing territory was being curtailed. Isidor Jacobs said quite frankly that San Francisco jobbers believed at the time when the Traffic Association was formed that the jobbing interests of the city were in a bad way. It was claimed, and with reason, he said, that San Francisco had natural advantages, and that in recognition of these advantages railroad rates from eastern points to San Francisco should be sufficiently less than to interior points, to enable San Francisco jobbers to control the distribution even of eastern goods as far as many Nevada points on the east, and as far as Tucson, Arizona, on the south.[12]

Ideas the same as those expressed by Mr. Jacobs appeared in a petition made public in December, 1892, and signed by over 150 firms in San Francisco, and in an address published at the same time which purported to be signed by 75 per cent of the membership of the Traffic Association.[13]

Nor were there lacking specific complaints to the same general effect. A San Francisco merchant explained that he had a carload rate of $1.75 per hundredweight on goods which he imported from Chicago to San Francisco. The rate on a hundredweight of the same commodity from Chicago to Fresno was $2. The local rate from San Francisco to Fresno was nearly half the rate per hundredweight from Chicago to Fresno, being in fact 90 cents per hundredweight. The addition of the 90 cents to the carload rate of $1.75 made it evident how small a chance he had to do a jobbing trade with the interior in these goods.[14] Another San Francisco dealer, a grocer by trade, was reported as saying that he had been compelled to give up his grocery business because his customers could buy directly from

[12] *San Francisco Chronicle*, November 3, 1892.

[13] *Ibid.*, December 7, 1892. The reply of the executive committee of the Traffic Association to this address is printed in the *San Francisco Examiner*, December 18, 1892.

[14] *Sacramento Union*, April 4, 1892.

the East more cheaply than he could supply them. The same man asserted that his customers could save a cent and a half per pound on tobacco by dealing direct with Chicago.[15]

It was unfortunate that dissension arose within the Traffic Association on so fundamental a point of policy as the proper attitude that should be taken toward interior towns, for the effect was, in spite of the best efforts of the men in control of association affairs, to deprive that body of the support of the interior. Moreover, opportunity was given to newspapers friendly to the railroads to attack the whole project as a selfish attempt on the part of San Francisco to improve her distributing position. The leading paper which took advantage of this opportunity was the *Sacramento Union*. This journal for a number of months denounced San Francisco as a city of hucksters, seeking a monopoly of the jobbing and wholesale trade of the Pacific Coast, not in the interest of the consumer, but in order to widen the margin between the cost of goods in which they dealt and the price at which these goods could be sold on the market. The charge was not fair, but the attitude of Mr. Jacobs and his friends embarrassed the Traffic Association in denying it.

Traffic Manager

In spite of the unwillingness of the state as a whole to join in a campaign which appeared to be designed primarily in the interests of San Francisco, the promoters of the new movement proceeded systematically with their plans. On November 18, 1891, the executive committee appointed a subcommittee to select a traffic manager for the association. Much depended on the choice, and the committee was fortunate in the man whom it secured, Joseph S. Leeds, of Ohio. Mr. Leeds was an individual of marked ability, with a valuable railroad ex-

---

[15] *Ibid.*, May 13, 1892.   San Francisco merchants declared that it was cheaper to send nails from San Francisco to Bakersfield via Los Angeles, water and rail, than to move them direct by rail over the floor of the San Joaquin Valley.

perience behind him. He had been telegraph operator, station agent, assistant general freight agent, general freight agent, and traffic manager on various eastern railroad systems, and at one time had held the position of chairman of the Transcontinental Association. He had been removed from his post of traffic manager of the Missouri Pacific some time before on a charge of rate-cutting, and might reasonably be believed to cherish some animosity toward the railroads which had once employed him. It may be added, as a fact of some importance to the future of the Traffic Association, that Mr. Leeds possessed qualities of energy and aggressiveness which unfitted him for a temporizing or conciliatory rôle. Under his leadership the association promptly became a fighting organization, and remained such until its demise. Mr. Leeds arrived in San Francisco on November 21, 1891, and at once entered upon his duties.[16]

Policy

For some weeks after Mr. Leeds' arrival, the policy which the Traffic Association should pursue remained unsettled. It will be recalled that the promoters of the association had originally contemplated a policy of harmonious co-operation with the railroad. This implied negotiation and exchange of views between shippers and railroad. Mr. Leeds, however, seems soon to have lost faith in such a method of procedure, if indeed he ever possessed faith to lose. He once remarked that no one ever got anything from a railroad just by asking for it. Moreover, the refusal of the executive committee of the association to push demands for preferential treatment of San Francisco as compared with other cities, removed from the field of negotiation a matter which called for readjustment of rates only, without reduction of railroad revenues, upon which

---

[16] *San Francisco Bulletin,* November 23, 1891. Mr. Leeds was given a two-year appointment, at a salary of $12,000 per annum.

San Francisco and the Southern Pacific might possibly have agreed, and left only demands which the railroad was likely to fight with all its strength Whatever the reason, no friendly approach to the Southern Pacific seems to have been made.

The apparent methods of bringing pressure to bear upon the rail carriers, on the assumption that the plan of friendly negotiation was to be abandoned, were three : the first was that of appeal to the Railroad Commission of the state and ultimately to the state legislature; the second was the encouragement of water competition; and the third was the construction, or assistance in the construction, of a competing railroad, if not across the continent, yet at least to a junction with one of the existing roads, such as the Santa Fé or the Union Pacific. It must be admitted that no one of these resources looked particularly promising in 1891, but together they exhausted the field. To appeal to the Interstate Commerce Commission was not thought of, and in view of the limited authority and brief experience of that body it is not probable that an appeal would have produced important results.

"Merchants' Shipping Association"

In December, 1891, the report of the Nicaragua Canal Commission to the federal legislature gave the Traffic Association opportunity to collect signatures to a petition, and generally to indorse the project for the construction of an Isthmian canal. The first circular emanating from Mr. Leeds' office, however, was dated January 6, 1892, and called the attention of shippers to a reduction in rates from San Francisco to Puget Sound points. This was followed later in the same month by a circular which attracted some attention, and which pointed out that shippers of freight had the legal right to designate the route over which their property should move from point of shipment to destination. It was recommended that all members of the Traffic Association route their freight in every case where they were the owners of the property at point of shipment. Meanwhile, a force of clerks was set to work, and elaborate data relating to railroad expenses and railroad rates in California and elsewhere were compiled.

The first aggressive step of the new association was taken early in 1892, when the executive committee directed the attention of members to the possibilities of water competition. This was done after a meeting of the executive committee in March, at which the committee voted that a line of clipper ships should be established between New York and San Francisco, and referred the preparation of plans for such a line to the president and manager of the association.[17]

In response to the proposal of the Traffic Association, nine of the larger jobbing firms in San Francisco formed in May, 1892, a so-called "Merchants' Shipping Association." It was the purpose of the new body to finance a line of clipper ships as proposed, and to cause it to be operated in free competition with the existing lines of William Dimond and Company, and Sutton and Beebe, concerns which, it was believed, were conducted in the interests of the Southern Pacific. This was too ambitious an undertaking for the Traffic Association to underwrite with its slender revenues of about $25,000 a year.

Three months later, in August, the membership of the Shipping Association was largely increased, and a guaranty fund of from $85,000 to $100,000 was subscribed. At this time most of the leading wholesale firms of San Francisco joined. The Traffic Association lent its full moral support to the enterprise, and was reported to have contributed $10,-000 to the guaranty fund just mentioned. Actual operation of the ships was entrusted to J. W. Grace and Company as agents. While the exact arrangements between the Shipping Association and these agents have never been made public, the merchants appear to have undertaken to meet all deficits, and

17 Walker, " Pioneers of Prosperity," *sup. cit.*, p. 46.

to supply at least two-thirds of the freight. According to statements made at the time, Grace and Company were expected to find freight in the open market up to one-third of the capacity of their boats. Practical details of operation were left entirely in the agents' hands.[18]

Effect of Competition

Some hint of the attitude of the older transportation companies toward this new rivalry may be found in a circular issued by the Traffic Association under date of June 22, 1892. This circular, after referring to the new Grace line, and after speaking also of the Atlantic and Pacific Steamship Company, and of a new clipper line established by Balfour, Guthrie and Company, continues as follows:

> It has already been given out by the old lines that these new competitors in the field will be short-lived, and that shippers who desert the old lines at this time will be remembered when the competitors are out of the way.
>
> For your information we desire to state that the new lines have been thoroughly investigated by the Committee and we are satisfied as to the reliability and stability of the enterprise, and that with our support they are here to stay and deserving of our patronage.[19]

In spite of the attempts of the older companies to crush the new adventure at its inception, the clipper ships thus established in 1892 with the support of the Traffic Association maintained an active competition with the railroad and older sailing lines over a period of more than a year. Short as this period was, there is no question that the effect upon water rates between San Francisco and New York was tremendous. The

---

[18] The Merchants' Shipping Association continued in active operation until January 1, 1894, when Grace and Company agreed to carry on the business on their own account. The first boat to arrive in San Francisco was the "Charles E. Moody," of 1,915 tons. The next two were the "T. F. Oakes," of 1,897 tons, and the "Emily Reed," of 1,488 tons. Subsequently, still other vessels were added.

[19] *San Francisco Bulletin*, June 24, 1892.

former rates of the Sutton and Beebe and of the William
Dimond and Company lines had been about $15 a ton. The
rates charged by all lines during the summer of 1892 were from
$3.50 to $6 a ton, a figure certainly below the cost of
operation.[20]

This reduction in rates, and the facility which merchants
in San Francisco enjoyed in securing through bills of lading
by sea and rail from San Francisco to points on the Missouri
River by way of Cape Horn and New York, enabled shippers to
reach the interior Mississippi Valley at a rate and with a
convenience superior to that obtainable by rail. According to
the *San Francisco Bulletin,* indeed, it was $2.15 a ton cheaper
to send California canned goods from San Francisco to Kansas
City by sea and rail than to ship them by rail direct. On west
bound freight the results were the same. The rate on canned
meats from Kansas City to New York was $9.40 per ton.
The rate from New York to San Francisco by sea, after adding
interest and insurance, did not exceed $15 per ton, making
total of about $25, which was $10 less per ton than the direct
rail rate from Kansas City to San Francisco.[21]

On heavy iron products the figures were quite as striking.
The all-rail rate on a number of such products was $24 from
Pittsburgh to San Francisco. From Pittsburgh to New York
the rail rate on the same articles was $3 a ton. Adding to the
$6 per ton for the clipper rate from New York to San Fran-
cisco, $1.25 per ton for insurance, and $2.50 per ton for interest, the total became $12.75, or $10.25 per ton less than the
all-rail rate.[22]

No wonder that the business of the water lines increased
and that railroad rates materially declined. Thus the rail rate
on canned goods out of San Francisco, which had been $1 per

[20] *San Francisco Chronicle,* August 6, 1892.
[21] *San Francisco Bulletin,* August 4, 1892.
[22] *San Francisco Examiner,* August 18, 1892.

hundred pounds, was reduced to 75 cents to Chicago and to 50 cents to New York. The rate on beans fell from $1.10 to 75 and 50 cents to the same destinations. On wine, brandy, borax, and wool, rail rates declined from 25 to 35 per cent.[23]

So far as the quantity of freight moving by water was concerned, it was estimated in August, 1892, that 42,000 tons of freight were on the way by sea to San Francisco from New York, and that 15,300 tons more were on the way via Cape Horn from Philadelphia. Twenty-four vessels were at sea or loading, bound from the Atlantic to the Pacific coast.[24]

Discontinuance of Pacific Mail Subsidy

The work which fell to Mr. Leeds and to his associates upon the Traffic Association clipper ship committee in this struggle between the rail and the water lines, was largely that of propaganda. This meant interviews with shippers to impress upon them the importance of the contest which was being waged against the railroads and against the Southern Pacific in particular. It meant also the soliciting of subscriptions to the clipper ship guaranty fund. Mr. Leeds threw himself vigorously into the fight, and as the movement progressed he allowed his satisfaction to appear. He wrote the Merchants' Shipping Association in August, 1892:

> I venture the prediction that if this movement is placed upon a permanent footing the Pacific Mail subsidy which has been assessed against the commerce of the coast for many years will be discontinued ... I predict that this will, if properly supported, prove the beginning of the end of commercial oppression for this city and this State. The doctrine of helping yourselves by every means you can command, holding fast to that which you have and reaching out for more, will prove the deliverance of San Francisco.[25]

[23] *San Francisco Bulletin*, January 5, 1893.
[24] Walker, "Pioneers of Prosperity," *sup. cit.*, p. 173.
[25] *San Francisco Bulletin*, August 31, 1892.

It was doubtless a considerable satisfaction to Mr. Leeds and to members of the Traffic Association that the water competition so vigorously inaugurated by the Merchants' Shipping Association was increased late in 1892 by the formation of an independent steamship line known as the North American Navigation Company. The foundation of this new company was not directly due to the Traffic Association, although the Association gave it what support it could. It was rather the result of the discontinuance of the railroad subsidy to the Pacific Mail, which actually took place in 1892, as Mr. Leeds anticipated, and to the consequent separation of the Pacific Mail and the Panama Railroad Company—a separation which assured to an independent steamship line upon the Pacific Ocean equal or even preferential treatment at the Isthmus of Panama. This meant that San Francisco shippers were no longer restricted to clipper ships and to the Cape Horn route, but could promote a shorter and speedier line with reasonable hope of success.

In the year 1892 the transcontinental railroads determined to dissolve the transcontinental railroad association. The reasons alleged were the withdrawal of the Northern Pacific Railroad from the association, and the announcement by the Canadian Pacific of reduced rates to take effect September 10. The dissolution of the association meant the termination of the subsidy which the railroads had been paying to the Pacific Mail, and notice of cancellation was promptly given. The Pacific Mail was then paying to the Panama Railroad $55,000 per month, an amount that was more than 70 per cent of the sum which it received from the association. In spite of the termination of its own relations with the transcontinental railroads, the Pacific Mail offered to continue the payment of a subsidy to the Panama Railroad, but the two companies proved unable to agree on terms. Mr. Stubbs later explained the break as follows:

When the contract between the Panama Railroad Company and the Pacific Mail Company expired, they found it impossible to agree on terms for continuing the business. The transcontinental railroad companies had quarreled, and freight rates were demoralized. The Panama Railroad insisted on the former basis of traffic, and the Pacific Mail refused to go ahead on that understanding. Then there was some bad management, and the two companies began to throw mud. The trouble got into the courts, and finally it was called to the attention of Congress. The Panama road and the Pacific Mail consequently found themselves to be bitter enemies, and it didn't seem that they could agree.[26]

Independent Steamship Line

Now it appears that a San Francisco shipping firm, the Johnson-Locke Mercantile Company, which was participating in the anti-railroad fight in 1891 and 1892 to the extent of operating a line of steamships around the Horn, noticed telegraphic advices in the San Francisco newspapers announcing the termination of relations between the Pacific Mail and the Panama Railroad. Describing the episode, Mr. Johnson later said:

I felt this was our opportunity, and immediately wired General Newton, of the Panama Railroad, suggesting that, in view of their determination to throw open the Isthmus and put on a line of their own steamers from New York to Colon, I thought we could secure the co-operation of the merchants of San Francisco, in this movement; that we had some steamers we were running between San Francisco and New York via Cape Horn, and asking, in the event of our organizing a company here, if they would join this company in maintaining a through line from San Francisco to New York.[27]

At this time the Panama Railroad was under the control of the official liquidator of the French Panama Canal Com-

---

[26] *San Francisco Examiner*, January 9, 1894. *Cf.* statement by General John Newton, president Panama Railroad Company, *ibid.*, November 29, 1892.
[27] Wheeler, "The Valley Road," *sup. cit.*

pany. The railroad had already decided to operate a line of steamships between New York and Colon, and it accepted readily Mr. Johnson's offer from the West. Yet Johnson himself lacked capital—as his own statement admits. To raise the necessary capital a new company—the North American Navigation Company—was at once organized, and subscriptions were solicited from San Francisco business men. Not all those approached were enthusiastic. Some merchants were afraid of antagonizing the Southern Pacific, some had an interest in it. James G. Fair said: "I am holding some millions of dollars in Southern Pacific bonds. Do you want me to put my eggs in a basket, get on a fence and chuck stones at it?" [28]

On the other hand, the promoters of the new company were able to make a strong plea based on the unsatisfactory conditions of water transportation in previous years. For the first time in fifteen years San Francisco shippers had a remedy in their own hands.

> With the successful operation of this company, San Francisco need fear no excessive prohibitory rates from the Transcontinental or similar associations; the relief in transportation will be immediate and ample, which, together with sailing ships via Cape Horn, solves the immediate question of cheap transportation, freedom from excessive freights, and makes our city again the distributing point, instead of an isolated terminus of a long haul by rail.[29]

The Raising of Funds

The original intention was to raise a fund of $100,000, and it appears that the Panama Railroad agreed to enter into a contract with the North American Navigation Company providing that sum were subscribed. When $80,000 had been promised, however, the promoters solicited the aid of the re-

---

[28] Wheeler, "The Valley Road," *sup. cit.*
[29] *San Francisco Examiner*, January 21, 1893.

cently formed Traffic Association, and upon its advice increased their capital to the sum of $200,000. As is frequently the case, in such campaigns no subscriptions were binding until the whole amount should have been subscribed. Before this point was reached the promoters nevertheless concluded their contract with the Panama Railroad. Perhaps they were over-optimistic, perhaps they felt that the chance of making such a contract should not be allowed to pass—at any rate they signed the contract and thereby agreed to dispatch steamers from San Francisco on fixed dates to connect with the rail line at the Isthmus. The text of the contract was not divulged, but the public was informed that it was to go into effect March 8, 1893, and that it gave to the North American Navigation Company the exclusive right of through billing between New York and San Francisco by way of the Isthmus of Panama.[30]

When the time came to dispatch the first vessel called for under this contract, the Navigation Company found itself in the uncomfortable position of a concern with important responsibilities and no money with which to meet them. Not a dollar of the capital stock had been paid in, and only $160,000 had been subscribed. Under these circumstances certain of the individuals most interested personally guaranteed the charter hire of the first boat, and the same was done for the second, and for the third, at intervals of twenty days. Before the time arrived for the departure of the fourth vessel, the entire $200,-000 asked for had been pledged. By December, 1893, this fund was exhausted, and $100,000 more was raised—not without difficulty, and with some feeling of discouragement on the part of the promoters.[31] The additional subscription made possible the continuance of the service approximately till the 1st of May, 1894, or for a total period of a little over a year. There

[30] *San Francisco Examiner*, February 28, March 5, 1893.
[31] *Ibid.*, December 20, 28, 30, 31, 1893, and January 3, 1894.

is some evidence that the managers of the company desired a still further extension, but if an attempt of this sort was made, it met with no success.

During the life of the North American Navigation Company five steamships were chartered: the St. Paul, Mexico, Keweenaw, Progreso, and Saturn. The "St. Paul" and the "Mexico" were small boats, with a net tonnage, respectively, of about 700 and 1,350 tons dead weight. The net tonnage of the "Keweenaw" was reported to be 2,004 tons, that of the "Progreso" and "Saturn" somewhat less.[32] Some passengers were carried by the line, but not many. The Pacific Mail also operated five vessels with capacity carrying from 2,000 to 2,500 tons. These were all small craft as compared with steamers of the present day. The original program, as has been said, called for a twenty-day interval between sailings, and the total estimated time consumed in shipment from San Francisco to New York was put at thirty-two days. It could scarcely have been expected that these ships could accommodate any large portion of the business of the Pacific Coast, nor indeed was there much chance for them to earn any considerable profit on the business which they did carry. The fact that so large a guaranty fund was insisted upon by the Panama Railroad before any exclusive through billing arrangement would be made, is evidence that a deficit was expected. As a matter of fact the total fund of $300,000 was used up before the fifteen months contemplated in the original agreement had entirely expired.

Drop in Railroad Rates

The principal purpose of the North American Navigation Company was, beyond question, to compel a reduction in transcontinental rates by rail and water by demonstrating that the business men of San Francisco could establish an independent

---

[32] *San Francisco Examiner*, April 1, 1893.

connection of their own.   This accounts for the enthusiasm
with which the project was greeted in the community at large.
The Navigation Company was looked upon as a kind of St.
George tilting against the dragon of monopoly.   The newspapers printed colums of description with pictures of the boats
chartered by the new line, the promoters gave out interviews,
and crowds gathered at the wharves to see the vessels leave.
And it was by pointing to the rate reductions accomplished that
the company subsequently justified itself.

Mr. Leeds, manager of the Traffic Association, estimated
that the 84,000 tons which he thought the new steamship line
would handle, added to what the clipper ships were carrying,
would leave about 250,000 tons for the railroads to transport
from coast to coast.   On this he expected to see a decline in
rates of not less than 20 per cent.   More exactly, he calculated
that the saving to shippers due directly to the operation of the
North American Navigation Company would amount to $660,-
000; that due to clipper ship competition would total $1,110,-
000; and that secured through a decline in railroad rates would
be $1,248,000; or a total of $3,018,000.[33] Captain Merry,
president of the Navigation Company, declared when all was
over that a saving of $3,500,000 had been made on Pacific
Coast products shipped east during the life of the company,
in addition to the saving of perhaps $1,500,000 on westbound
freight.[34]

Undoubtedly the operations of the Navigation Company
intensified the rate war started by the clipper ships, and the
reductions in transcontinental charges were considerable.   According to Mr. Leeds the cuts on eastbound transcontinental
freight, all-rail, on representative articles, by January, 1894,
were as follows:[35]

---

[33] San Francisco Examiner, March 19, 1893.
[34] Wheeler, "The Valley Road," sup. cit., pp. 32–33.
[35] San Francisco Examiner, January 10, 1894.

Reductions in Transcontinental Rail Rates to January, 1894

Article	Old Rate per 100 pounds	New Rate per 100 pounds	Reduction per cent
Beans	$1.10	$ .50	55
Canned goods	1.00	.50	50
Barley	.90	.30	66⅔
Dried fruits, raisins, and prunes (in boxes)	1.40	1.00	28
Wine	1.50	.37½	80
Mustard seed	1.10	.30	73
Wool, in grease	1.50	.75	50
Wool, scoured	2.50	.75	70

Uncertain Benefit

On westbound freight it was estimated that the reductions amounted to at least 50 per cent.   These estimates, however, do not distinguish between the results produced by the Navigation Company and those which were the consequence of the operation of the clipper ships—perhaps no separate estimate is possible or important.   On the basis of the rates charged, the railroad admitted that it was losing money, at least so far as eastbound freight was concerned.   It maintained, however, that it continued to make a profit on its westbound freight and on its local traffic.[36]   There was no question that the steamships and the Panama Railroad lost money, although they declared stoutly that they would meet any cuts which the railroads might make.[37]

Whether the shippers benefited by the general demoralization in rates which occurred during the war is uncertain, as it always is under such circumstances.   They certainly lost the $300,000 which they put into the North American Navigation Company, besides the guaranty fund subscribed by the Mer-

---

[36] *San Francisco Examiner*, September 21, 1893, statement by H. E. Huntington.
[37] *Ibid.*, April 25, 1893, statement by Agent Hinton of the Panama Railroad.

chants' Shipping Association. Moreover, they suffered from the competition of eastern jobbers during the hostilities, a competition which the railroads encouraged by reducing the differences between carload and less than carload rates, by the extension of the privilege of shipping in mixed carloads, and by reduction in westbound rates. On the other hand, they gained directly through lower rates, and indirectly by the demonstration that, to some extent at least, their access to eastern markets was not subject to railroad control.

New Transcontinental Tariff

The North American Navigation Company operated only a little over a year, as has been said. Its vessels, however, were taken over by the Panama Railroad, and competition continued until the end of the year 1895. Not long after that, it seems, negotiations between the shippers and the railroads began. Representatives of the transcontinental lines upon the coast were instructed to mollify Pacific Coast shippers so far as possible, and the shippers in their turn seem to have been anxious to meet this advance. In 1897 a communication was addressed to the railways by the jobbing interests upon the Pacific Coast, stating in substance that rates ought to be readjusted in the interests of the coast jobbers; that more rigid inspection rules should be enforced preventing their competitors in the Middle West from obtaining fraudulent rates; and intimating that if this was done they would not object to an advance in rates and would find it to their interest to place shipments largely with the railroads.

For the purpose of effecting some arrangement, a meeting of representatives of the transcontinental lines was held at Del Monte in the fall of that year. Representatives of the Pacific Coast jobbers and also of the jobbers of the Middle West were present. Both parties were heard separately and much discussion was had but no definite conclusion reached. The conference adjourned to meet at Milwaukee the following spring. The final result was a new transcontinental tariff effective June 25, 1898, which seems to have given reasonable satisfaction until attacked by representatives of the intermountain towns.[38]

[38] Business Men's League of St. Louis v. Atchison, Topeka and Santa Fé Railroad Company, 9 I.C.C.R. 318 (1902).

CHAPTER XVIII

THE SAN FRANCISCO AND SAN JOAQUIN VALLEY RAILWAY

Attempt to Fix Maximum Rates

Properly considered, the construction of the San Francisco and San Joaquin Valley Railway was the complement of the campaign for the encouragement of water competition which the Traffic Association waged between 1891 and 1897. The plans for the subsidizing of clipper ships and for the support of steamship service to and from Panama had from first to last one grave defect—they afforded no means of distributing from San Francisco the products which dealers might succeed in having brought in by sea. That is to say, while the consuming populations of San Francisco, Sacramento, and Stockton might benefit by securing their goods at lower cost because of the activity of water competition, these cities could not extend their markets unless the sum of the through rate from points of origin to terminal city and from terminal city to local point should be made lower than the direct rate from the Mississippi Valley or the Atlantic Coast to the smaller towns in California, Nevada, and New Mexico.

Now the question of local rates differed from that of through rates, in that it dealt with a matter over which the state legislature and the State Railroad Commission appeared to have complete control. In 1892 the Traffic Association accordingly made a serious attempt to persuade the state legislature to undertake direct regulation of railroad rates in California, and to insert a provision for certain maximum rates in the constitution of the state which should affect a considerable reduction in the rates then charged. This attempt failed, for reasons into which it is not necessary to go. There remained another method of influencing local rates, namely, the construction of a competing railroad which should lead from San Francisco Bay to the interior counties of the state, and to this alternative the San Francisco merchants turned in the year 1893. The movement was important, and will be discussed at some length.

First Proposal for Competing Railroad

The proposal that a competing railroad should be built from San Francisco Bay to the interior was not a new one in California in 1893. On the contrary, in February, 1892, President Stetson, of the Traffic Association, told a reporter that no less than nine propositions had been submitted to him as president of the organization, looking to give San Francisco a competing line of railroad. These were successors to still other plans prepared in earlier years. Most of the schemes proposed to Mr. Stetson involved the construction of lines out of San Francisco to a connection with the Santa Fé, but two or three of them contemplated construction from San Francisco across the Sierra Nevada Mountains to the termini of the Union Pacific or the Rio Grande Western. At the time, President Stetson replied that he was a merchant and had neither the time nor the money to build roads, although he added that San Francisco merchants desired more railroads and would under reasonable conditions and at the proper time furnish substantial encouragement to one or more feasible railway projects.[1]

Soon after this, possibly at the suggestion of Mr. Leeds, steps were taken to investigate the possibilities of a line from San Francisco or Oakland to Stockton and thence eastward through Nevada and Utah to Salt Lake City. In May, 1892, a company was formed under the name of the San Francisco and Great Salt Lake Railroad Company, to build from San

---

[1] *San Francisco Examiner*, February 4, 1892.

Francisco to Stockton, with an initial capital of $2,000,000. This was the moment when the Traffic Association was vigorously pushing its plans for the encouragement of water competition, and when it was beginning the legislative campaign mentioned in a preceding paragraph. Little active support could therefore be expected from the San Francisco shippers, although the executive committee of the Traffic Association authorized Mr. Leeds to give the projectors of the San Francisco and Great Salt Lake the benefit of his advice, and the California League of Progress formally indorsed the enterprise.[2]

The San Francisco and Great Salt Lake conducted extensive surveys and was said to have purchased a tract of land at Martinez for a terminal. The company was overtaken by the panic of 1893, however, before it had secured the financial support which was essential to its success. It suffered also from differences of opinion among its friends with respect to the policies to be pursued. Mr. Leeds insisted that to be a success the new road must have a through connection. Shippers, he said, would not patronize a purely local line when a through line was available, because a competitor with through facilities could afford them service which a local line could not.[3] On the other hand, there were capitalists who expressed willingness to subscribe to the stock of a local system, but who would not put a cent into an overland line,[4] and between the two parties the necessary subscriptions were not obtained. The project was finally withdrawn when the promoters failed to secure certain legislation which they thought necessary to make their plans a success.[5]

---

[2] *San Francisco Bulletin*, August 20, 23, 1892. The League of Progress was an organization composed of the younger business men in San Francisco in sympathy with the policies of the Traffic Association.

[3] *San Francisco Bulletin*, October 12, 1892.

[4] *San Francisco Examiner*, December 23, 1892.

[5] *Ibid.*, March 8, 1893. See also *ibid.*, March 4, 1893. With respect to the whole project Mr. Huntington said to a reporter:
"As to building a railroad to Salt Lake, I certainly have no objection to other people

Another Project

Following the failure of the San Francisco and Great Salt
Lake enterprise, plans for railroad construction in California
made no progress for several months. It had now become evident, however, that the state legislature was not disposed to
pass a maximum rate enactment, and that any reduction in the
level of local rates in California must come either from the
good-will of the Southern Pacific or from the construction of
competing lines. Under these circumstances, plans for railroad
construction were revived, this time under the direct leadership
of the Traffic Association of California.

Exactly when the Traffic Association took up the idea of
promoting a competing railroad in the San Joaquin Valley
cannot be stated with confidence. Newspaper reports indicate
that the project was discussed at least as early as April, 1893.
Whether or not a beginning was made in this month, it appears
that by June, 1893, plans had progressed sufficiently to permit
the publication of a prospectus, sent out with the approval of
San Francisco shippers. This prospectus invited the citizens
of San Francisco and of the state of California to subscribe to
the capital stock of a railroad which should run from the city
of Stockton to the head of the San Joaquin Valley, in Kern
County, a distance of about 230 miles. The plan was said
to be to secure as much money as possible in the city of San
Francisco, and then to ask the people of the valley, from Stockton up, to add thereto a fair quota. Construction was to begin

---

doing it. I should very much dislike to do it myself. I do not believe it would be for the
interest of San Francisco merchants to build it; hence I do not think it will be built. A good
railroad from San Francisco to Salt Lake, with good terminals, as good a road as the Central
Pacific, would cost at least $50,000,000. Of course, a road can be built for a much less sum,
but such a road would not compete with the present line, for certainly the present rates are
not as much as it would cost to haul the tonnage over a cheap line that could be built for
much, if any, less than the figure named. When the Central Pacific Railroad was built I
urged the moneyed men of San Francisco to take an interest with us on exactly the same
basis as I and my associates hold our interests. But no one here would take an interest.
If they would not take an interest then when every man, woman, and child in the State
wanted a road so that they could go East and see the old folks at home, they would hardly
be likely to take it now, with at least seven lines across the continent, charging rates of fare
and freight very, very much less than they were when the first road was built, or than they
expected these rates would be when the first road was inaugurated." (*Ibid.*, September 20,
1892.)

at Stockton instead of at San Francisco, in order to save expense and in reliance upon the effect of water competition on San Francisco Bay—a competition which was expected to maintain a low level of rates between Stockton and its larger neighbor. The cost of a good road from Stockton to Bakersfield was estimated at something less than $20,000 per mile.

Appealing particularly to San Francisco, the promoters of the new enterprise declared that a competing railroad was essential to that city's prosperity. San Francisco amounted to no more than any other collection of people unless it used its facilities as a seaport. Facilities unused might just as well not exist. It had been a part of the policy of all the transcontinental roads for many years to neutralize this seaport by all the means at their command, including the practice of maintaining excessively high local rates between the sea and the interior. This condition must be remedied. The prospectus also explained that the new line would benefit the producer and the consumer in the interior as well as in the city of San Francisco.[6]

Lack of Financial Support

Once the prospectus was out, the project for a local competing railroad was pushed with all the energy characteristic of Mr. Leeds and the Traffic Association. It received substantial support also from a portion of the San Francisco press. In order to test sentiment, a subcommittee of the executive committee of the Traffic Association started a canvass of the wealthy men of San Francisco, not to secure subscriptions, but to seek general assurances of co-operation. With one exception the citizens interviewed were reported to have promised to take stock in the road, and to have invited the committee to call again. Such an indication of unanimity was considered important.[7] Not only did the moneyed men of San Francisco

---

[6] *San Francisco Bulletin*, June 22, 1893.   [7] *Ibid.*, July 17, 1893.

encourage the enterprise at this time, but the newspapers printed accounts of the interest taken by men of small means. Mechanics and laborers were said to be coming to the offices of the Traffic Association, and offers to subscribe for small amounts of stock, payable in labor, were received.[8] Yet there is some question about the warmth with which the original proposal for a competing line was received. Certainly the minimum amount necessary to be raised in order to make all subscriptions binding was small—$350,000—and the slowness with which this sum was approximated did not indicate enthusiasm.[9] In the valley generally there were indications of interest, such as favorable newspaper notices, offers of rights-of-way for the new company, and resolutions of indorsement by boards of trade, and by meetings of citizens. But here, too, there were few subscriptions, and after the panic of 1893 the Traffic Association recognized that their initial attempt had failed.

Failure of Second Attempt

The second campaign for subscriptions to the stock of the Valley road began about August, 1894, when the executive committee of the Traffic Association decided to renew its search for funds. It was now decided to call the new enterprise the San Francisco, Stockton and San Joaquin Valley Railway Company, and to define its route generally as between San Francisco, or some convenient point on the Bay of San Francisco, via Stockton and Fresno by a convenient and practicable route thereafter to be determined, to some point in Kern County. The minimum subscription was again set at $350,000,

---

[8] *San Francisco Bulletin,* July 18, 1893.

[9] *Ibid.,* July 10, 1893. The stock was to be issued in the name of nine trustees, and was to be voted by these gentlemen. The trustees were to have the right to cause the consolidation of the proposed corporation with another company. Possibly the railroad project suffered somewhat from the fact that a plan existed for the construction of a ship canal up the San Joaquin Valley to Bakersfield. Fresno people were particularly interested in this scheme, which contemplated the connection of Fresno with the navigable part of the San Joaquin River at Crowe's Landing, or some other convenient point. (*San Francisco Examiner,* June 3, June 5, 1894.)

and, as in the earlier project, a trust was devised to hold the stock of the company and to preserve its status as an independent carrier.[10]

In October stock subscription books were thrown open to the public and some thousands of dollars of subscriptions received. Mr. Leeds went to Stockton to see what could be done there. In San Francisco, Mr. Van Sicklen, a member of the executive committee, endeavored to reach the business men of the town in a somewhat systematic fashion. Large subscriptions and small were invited, but once more small success was obtained. The members of the executive committee of the Traffic Association were busy men and disinclined to devote much time to personal campaigning, while, even had they done so, the chances of success were not good. The primary defect in the Traffic Association's campaign lay in the fact that no man in the group of promoters interested in the new enterprise had sufficient prestige so to impress the public imagination as to lead investors to have confidence from the beginning that the projected railroad would be built. The composition of the Traffic Association was admirable for the purpose of encouraging water competition. It was as inadequate to the financing of a large railroad to be conducted without government support as it had been shown to be to the management of a political campaign.

Nor was it unimportant that the organization was asking for a sum which on the face of it was insufficient to accomplish the purposes which were in mind. Nobody pretended that $350,000 would do more than permit of the organization of the San Francisco and San Joaquin Valley Railway. To build the line would cost ten times that sum or more. Indeed, the company was actually capitalized at $6,000,000, a not unreasonable figure under the circumstances. Thus a subscription to a fund of $350,000 merely committed the subscriber to an en-

---

[10] *San Francisco Bulletin*, September 27, 1894.

terprise which might involve him, if it was to be successful, in an additional large and undetermined expense, on the penalty of losing his original subscription if the additional sums were not forthcoming.

Final Success

We have now seen that two attempts to secure support for a new independent railroad in the San Joaquin Valley failed between June, 1893, and the end of 1894. The third stage in the progress of the Valley road began with a meeting called by the Traffic Association on January 22, 1895, for the purpose of interesting the realty owners of San Francisco in the construction of a railroad. By this time the Traffic Association's second campaign for subscriptions had failed as definitely as had its first. Only about one-half of the desired sum of $350,-000 was on hand. No more could be secured from the merchants of the city. There was little enthusiasm in San Francisco, and in the interior, cities like Fresno were becoming impatient and were turning to the south instead of to San Francisco for relief from the burden of high rates.[11]

It was at this point and under these conditions that the management of the enterprise passed to new men and that a complete reorganization of its affairs occurred. In the main this change in control and in the policies of the projected Valley railroad was due to the energy of one man. Claus Spreckels, of San Francisco, the leading sugar refiner of the Pacific Coast, was not a member of the Traffic Association, and was not pledged to the support of the San Francisco and San Joaquin Valley Railway. He was, however, one of the speakers at the January meeting, and when the formal proceedings were over he came forward with an offer to subscribe $50,000 provided that the minimum amount to be raised were increased from $350,000 to $3,000,000 or to $5,000,000. On

---

[11] *San Francisco Examiner*, January 18, 1895.

Spreckel's motion, moreover, the chairman was authorized to appoint a committee of twelve from among the property owners of the city to solicit subscriptions from holders of real estate. After the adoption of this motion the meeting adjourned.

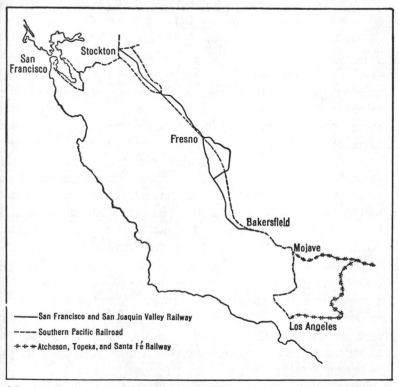

Map showing the line of the San Francisco and San Joaquin Valley Railway, together with portions of the systems of the Southern Pacific and of the Atchison, Topeka and Santa Fé, 1898.

The subscriptions in definite amounts received on Tuesday, January 22, 1895, did not much exceed $20,000. The committee of twelve met, however, on January 24 and Claus Spreckels was elected chairman. Soon after this, larger pledges began to appear. Spreckels himself now subscribed $500,000, or ten times his initial offer, and at his instance, John D. and Adolph Spreckels, his sons, subscribed $100,000 apiece. From this one family, therefore, came twice the sum which the Traffic Association had tried in vain to raise from all of San Francisco. The whole complexion of the business changed as a result of this beginning. By January 30 over $1,200,000 was pledged. Subscriptions through February 2 amounted to $1,536,500, and on February 8 the $2,000,000 mark was reached. This so encouraged the committee that it immediately resolved that the sum of $4,000,000 should and must be obtained from the city of San Francisco, and that with the aid of the interior the competing line could be constructed on a cash basis. To this end every effort was to be turned.[12]

It is very evident that the substantial wealth of the Spreckels group and the reputation for success which Claus Spreckels enjoyed, made a powerful impression both in San Francisco and in the San Joaquin Valley. The proposed railroad enterprise was the same as before, but the leadership was different. At the same time the amount of money necessary to be raised in the first instance was increased from $350,000 to $2,000,-000.[13] Large sums are sometimes easier to secure than small, for reasons both sentimental and practical, and it proved so in this case. Claus Spreckels said himself that he had never made a failure in his life, while with $2,000,000 in hand it seemed so unnecessary for anyone to fail that people hastened to share in the anticipated success.

Campaign for Stock Subscriptions

As we look back upon the circumstances attending the construction of the San Francisco and San Joaquin Valley Railway, it is evident that after January, 1895, its managers played their cards with considerable shrewdness. Regarded as a direct profit-

---

[12] *San Francisco Examiner,* February 9, 1895.
[13] *Ibid.,* January 30, 1895.

making enterprise, the ability of the new company to earn dividends was questionable. It was all very well to dwell upon the fertility of the San Joaquin Valley, and to point out the large proportion of the revenues of the Southern Pacific derived from this source.[14] Doubtless these conditions would count in the long run. Yet the fact remained that the new road was entering a not too highly developed territory already served by a through line of large capacity. It was expected to reduce rates, and was likely to be compelled to reduce them; and it was to do this while it was in the course of developing its own organization and establishing business relations with a new clientèle. Huntington said that he thought there was room in California for both the Southern Pacific and the new line. It required, he said, only a space of thirteen feet from the center of one track to the center of another, and there was lots of room in California. The projectors of the new road would have no trouble in finding room.[15] But this remark was not meant to convey comfort to subscribers to the stock of the San Francisco and San Joaquin Valley Railway, and probably did not do so.

What, then, were the conditions of success for the new road? They were: first, such a popular support as would minimize the cost of construction and maximize its business; and second, such an alliance with some other large railroad system as would give stability and permanency to its traffic relations. If the new company possessed these advantages it would probably be able to live and to render a useful service in distributing products brought to California and to San Francisco by sea; without them it was not likely to survive.

It was in order to increase their popular support, and not alone for the sake of the money involved, that the promoters of the San Francisco and San Joaquin Valley Railway early

[14] Statement of J. S. Leeds in the *San Francisco Bulletin*, October 1, 1894, and in the *San Francisco Examiner*, January 27, 1895.
[15] *San Francisco Examiner*, March 6, 1895.

began a campaign for small subscriptions. Claus Spreckels took pains to say that while large subscriptions were all right and desirable, it would be the $20,000, $10,000, and $5,000 stockholders who would control the property and its policy.[16] In February, after the first arrangements had been made for reaching the larger business interests of the city, attention was paid to the offering of facilities for subscription to all classes of investors in San Francisco. Districts were mapped out and assigned to canvassers.[17] The following month the *San Francisco Examiner,* which had taken a prominent part in the fight from the first, began to print subscription blanks in its daily issues. Arrangements were made by which persons might subscribe for fractions of shares by joining with their neighbors in share clubs. The *Examiner* offered a gold watch to the first person forming such a club, and when there was doubt as to priority, compromised by giving two watches. The formation of the first colored club was given special mention, as was the decision of a colored club in San Francisco to make one paid-up share in the San Francisco and San Joaquin Valley Railway a tug-of-war prize to be competed for at its annual games. The winning team was to constitute a share club, and was to choose a trustee from among its members.[18]

Appeal to Local Patriotism

While devices such as these were perfectly ineffective as a means for raising large sums of money, they did give the new road valuable advertising, and helped to predispose the whole community in its favor. For the same reasons that actuated the promoters in their attempt to gain the support of investors of small means, the San Francisco committee also made appeals to the public which rested upon moral and patri-

---

[16] *San Francisco Examiner,* January 31, 1895. As a matter of fact, the bulk of the subscriptions came from a very few sources.
[17] *San Francisco Bulletin,* March 1, 1895.
[18] *San Francisco Examiner,* April 27, 1895.

otic as well as upon financial grounds. Without going into this aspect of the matter at length, it may be said that there has probably never been a commercial enterprise launched on the Pacific Coast so advertised, and praised, and predicted about as was the project of the San Joaquin Valley Railway. Participation in the movement became a test of local patriotism. The railroad took the aspect not merely of a business expedient, to be considered solely from the point of view of monetary gain, but it also became an expression of the hopes of expansion entertained by a generation of business men, strengthened by the accumulated antagonism of years between the Southern Pacific Railroad and the shipping public.

Nor was this feature of the campaign confined to San Francisco alone. The main interest from first to last was of course in San Francisco. Yet the valley towns also showed sympathy with the new development, rising at times to excitement as construction became imminent, and questions of route had to be determined. Here, it is true, there was more business and less sentiment. "What is the new road going to do for Oakland?" a man asked John D. Spreckels one day in the Palace Hotel. "It is too early to put that question," replied Mr. Spreckels, "as it could only be answered by some theorist. The question is, What will Oakland do for the new road?" [19]

[19] The question as to what the valley towns would do for the new enterprise was repeatedly asked, and received a reasonably satisfactory reply. Depot sites and rights-of-way were freely offered, and subscriptions to stock were talked about, if not often pledged in any binding way. The Spreckels group tried to encourage donations of all kinds, and to play one town against another where this was possible. It refused to say, for example, whether the new road would begin at Stockton, as once proposed, or even whether the new route would not run through San José. Stockton organized a committee to present her claims. San José did the same. Mass meetings were held in both places, that in San José being marked by a procession, with transparencies and a band. Stockton merchants agreed to give to the San Francisco and San Joaquin Valley Railway rights-of-way 100 feet wide along the adopted survey for the railroad from the city of Stockton through San Joaquin County to the boundary line between San Joaquin and Stanislaus counties. They further agreed to convey to the railway company certain specified parcels of land in the city of Stockton, to aid the company in obtaining franchises and rights-of-way in Stockton, and to obtain subscriptions to the capital stock of the company to the amount of $100,000. (*San Francisco Examiner*, May 3, 1895.)

The San José delegation which came to San Francisco in March said that $148,000 had already been secured for the new road in their district, that $200,000 was in sight, and that $300,000 in subscriptions could be obtained with a guaranty of shipments by the new route from the large fruit packers, business men, farmers, and horticulturists. They added that

In spite of occasional skepticism, and here and there active opposition, the San Joaquin Valley received the new enterprise cordially. Among the Valley towns from which assurances of support were received may be mentioned Stockton, San José, Fresno, Madera, Modesto, Hanford, Merced, Visalia, Selma, and Bakersfield. Oakland also, though not properly in the Valley, manifested considerable interest in the work. Generally speaking, the directors of the San Francisco and San Joaquin Valley Railway asked local committees to select what in their judgment was the best route over which the railroad could pass. They then asked them to give rights-of-way, depot grounds, and terminal facilities, and to subscribe to all the stock that they could afford. It was announced that the railroad was being built on a business basis, and that it would go through the best country and where the greatest inducements were offered.[20]

This did not seem unreasonable to the local communities, and the company's requests were generally complied with. The principal reason for raising money under such an arrangement was to pay local property owners whose lands were taken for railroad purposes. There were no money subsidies, and no land grants except to the extent sufficient for the company's actual needs. Yet, of course, even so relatively moderate a provision of local aid materially reduced the cost of construction which the railroad company had to meet.

Purchase of Road by Santa Fé

Articles of association of the San Francisco and San Joaquin Valley Railway Company were filed at Sacramento in February, 1895, and construction was begun at Stockton

---

rights-of-way, 75 per cent of which would be free of cost to the company, and also terminal facilities in San José would be provided. (*Ibid.*, March 27, 1895.)

It is of some interest to recall that when the decision was made in favor of Stockton, her representatives had difficulty in making their promises good.   It was remarked at one time that apparently one of the things most needed to help on the era of progress in California was a number of judiciously selected funerals—presumably of opponents to the new developments.

[20] See address of Robert Watt at Bakersfield, *San Francisco Examiner*, April 29, 1895.

late in the same year. By the end of December, 26.1 miles had been built, carrying the railroad to the Stanislaus River. During 1896 the track reached Fresno, and in 1897 Bakersfield was attained. On June 30, 1898, the company reported a total mileage of 278.91 miles, including a branch to Visalia. It had at that time an authorized capital stock of $6,000,000, of which $2,464,480 was issued and paid in, a funded debt of $2,671,000, and current liabilities of $110,928. The bonds outstanding were mortgage securities bearing 5 per cent interest and maturing in 1940. In 1897 the company reported gross earnings of $209,133 (of which $178,494 were from freight), and operating expenses of $153,102, on an average operated mileage of 123.44 miles. For the year ending June 30, 1898, the earnings were $411,179 and the operating expenses $282,326, on a mileage, however, which was considerably greater. These were the only years for which statistics are available, for the company was purchased by the Santa Fé in December, 1898.

The circumstance that the San Francisco and San Joaquin Valley Railway was purchased by the Atchison, Topeka and Santa Fé only a few months after the company had completed its road to Bakersfield, served as a dramatic illustration of the fact that alliance with some larger railroad system was considered by its promoters to be essential to the road's success. There is no question but that this sale of the system came as a shock and a disappointment to many persons whose enthusiasm had been aroused by the proposal to build an independent railroad for the service of shippers in San Francisco and in the San Joaquin Valley. The high hopes of San Francisco merchants could scarcely be satisfied by anything short of a system permanently under the control of the commercial interests of that city. When the San Francisco press declared that San Francisco was preparing to reach out for the trade of all the western part of the American continent, and when the Spreckels committee declared that the new road was to be a people's road, owned by the people, and operated in the interests of the people,[21] the implication clearly was that the ownership of the property was to remain in the hands of the original subscribers to the stock or in the hands of other persons of like character. Nor was the argument that the construction of the San Francisco and San Joaquin Valley Railway would prevent the diversion of eastern freight from San Francisco to distributing centers of the South,[22] easily to be reconciled with the sale of the railroad to a company which, like the Santa Fé, had a terminus in Los Angeles.

Spreckels Interests

There were, on the other hand, indications from the beginning that the Spreckels group did not intend to commit itself to the permanent management of a railroad system, but that they regarded connection with, and perhaps amalgamation between, the San Francisco and San Joaquin Valley and the Atchison, Topeka and Santa Fé as the natural culmination of the former road's career. Like Stanford, Mark Hopkins, Huntington, and Crocker, Claus Spreckels, his sons, and the persons most intimately associated with them were not originally railroad men, and were not, when they began railroad construction, particularly interested in the railroad business as a business. They were therefore to be tempted to continue railroad management only by a chance for extraordinary profits —a chance which the San Francisco and San Joaquin Valley Railway did not offer. Looking at the matter from a business standpoint, it is not unreasonable to suppose that they saw that the best opportunity for withdrawing their capital from the valley speculation lay in negotiations with the Santa Fé. Of course this is surmise, and perhaps is mainly plausible as a

---

[21] *San Francisco Examiner,* January 30, 1895.
[22] Letter from the Spreckels' Committee to San Francisco Bankers, *San Francisco Examiner,* February 3, 1895.

late interpretation of happenings which we know took place, but it has a certain reasonableness in view of all the facts.

The concrete evidence that combination between the San Francisco and San Joaquin Valley and the Atchison, Topeka and Santa Fé was looked upon as a possibility from the first, is to be found in the provisions of the trust agreement entered into by subscribers to the San Francisco and San Joaquin Valley Railway stock, and in the negotiations between that railroad and the city of San Francisco and the state government of California, over what was known as the China Basin lease.

Trust Agreement

Soon after the promoters of the San Francisco and San Joaquin Valley Railway had successfully organized their corporation, subscribers to the stock of the company were asked to enter into a certain trust agreement or pooling plan designed primarily to prevent the railroad from falling into the hands of the Southern Pacific. Briefly summarized, this plan contemplated the transfer of the stock of the company to seven (later nine) trustees. Individual stockholders so transferring their holdings were to receive trust certificates clothing them with the powers and privileges usual in such cases. The trustees on their part were to administer the railway for a period of ten years unless three-quarters of the certificate holders should request an earlier termination of the trust, or unless all of the subscribers should die.

This administration was, however, subject to restrictions, of which two deserve special notice. In the first place, the trustees undertook to operate the railroad, when completed, on such a basis that the rates and fares charged should be the lowest rates and fares which would yield enough earnings to meet costs of operation, interest, and sinking fund requirements, and to pay a dividend not exceeding 6 per cent upon capital stock paid in. This clause was evidently intended to reassure shippers who had been or might become interested in the new railroad. But besides this, the trustees agreed that they would not knowingly vote said stock "for the benefit or in the interest of any person or corporation or interest hostile to the interest of, or in business competition with the San Francisco and San Joaquin Valley Railway Company, or of or to or in favor of any party or parties or company or companies owning or controlling any parallel line of road to the detriment and injury of the corporation hereinbefore mentioned." [23]

To this clause there was later added another of the same import, to the effect that the San Francisco and San Joaquin Valley Railway should not be leased to, or consolidated with, any company which might own, control, manage, or operate any of the roads then existing in the San Joaquin Valley, and that neither the trustees nor their successors should have any power as stockholders to assent to any such consolidation or lease, or in any way to put the San Francisco and San Joaquin Valley Railway under the same management as that of any other railroad then existing in the San Joaquin Valley.[24]

In so carefully worded a document as the trust agreement here under consideration, the prohibition of combination with competing railroads or with railroads then existing in the San Joaquin Valley had the force of an affirmative permission to the trustees to consolidate their property with that belonging to any company not in the prohibited class. As a practical matter this meant consolidation with the Santa Fé and with that railroad only, for the reason that there was no other system with which combination would have been significant. The trust agreement was approved at a meeting of stockholders held on April 5, 1895,[25] and by the middle of the following

---

[23] *San Francisco Examiner*, March 26, 1895.   [24] *Ibid.*, April 6, 1895
[25] *San Francisco Bulletin*, April 6, 1895.

month holders of more than three-fourths of the stock had given written assent to the trust conditions.

The fair inference from the terms of the trust agreement is that the promoters looked upon the union of the San Francisco and San Joaquin Railway and the Atchison, Topeka and Santa Fé as a proper and likely outcome of the construction of the former road. This same conclusion is strengthened by consideration of the China Basin lease, concerning which a few words may be said.

The China Basin Lease

The China Basin lease related to a tract of land on the water-front between the foot of Third Street and the foot of Fourth Street in San Francisco. The San Francisco and San Joaquin Valley Railway needed a terminus in San Francisco even before it entered upon construction west of Stockton, because it wished to encourage the shipment of freight from San Francisco up the Sacramento River to the head of its rail line at Stockton. It also looked forward to the day when it should have a railroad of its own to Oakland or to some other point on San Francisco Bay, possibly to the city of San Francisco itself.

According to the precedent set in the southern counties, the San Francisco and San Joaquin Valley should have applied to the city and county of San Francisco for terminal privileges. The piece of property which it desired, however, consisted of certain mud flats at China Basin, control over which had been specifically vested in the State Board of Harbor Commissioners by a law passed in 1878.[26] Not only were the flats in question thus removed from the control of the city, but the State Board of Harbor Commissioners itself had apparently no authority to conclude binding leases of this area covering a substantial period of time, although it did have power to

[26] Laws of California, 1878, Ch. 219.

grant temporary permits for the use of water-front property. Before any progress could be made, therefore, it was necessary to apply to the state legislature in order that the powers of the harbor commissioners might be enlarged, after which negotiations could be continued with the commissioners direct.

As a first step toward obtaining a lease of the China Basin tract, Claus Spreckels went to Sacramento in March, 1895, accompanied by other directors of the San Francisco and San Joaquin Valley Railway. With characteristic emphasis he declared to members of the legislature that if the promoters of the new enterprise did not get the mud flats they might as well give up the road.[27] No senator, he said, who voted against his bill could dare to face his constituents again. Senators who voted against the proposed amendment to the law voted to take the bread out of the mouth of the workingman's child. They voted to keep the unemployed out of work, and they voted for their own damnation.[28]

Necessary Legislation Enacted

There was little opposition in the assembly to giving the Spreckels group what it wanted. Principally the discussion was as to whether it was better to clothe the harbor commissioners in general terms with the power to lease water-front property,[29] or whether the board should be authorized only to lease a described parcel to a specified group of persons.[30] The fear was expressed in the course of the debate lest the tract desired by the San Francisco and San Joaquin Valley Railway might be leased to a corporation controlled by the Southern Pacific, and that other parcels might go the same way. On the other hand, it was pointed out that a provision for a lease

---

[27] *San Francisco Examiner*, March 9, 1895.
[28] *Ibid.*, March 11, 1895.
[29] This was the proposal of Mr. Powers, of San Francisco. See Journal of the Assembly, 31st Session, March 8, 1895, p. 904.
[30] Reid amendment, Journal of the Assembly, 31st Session, March 11, pp. 961–62.

to specified parties might prove unconstitutional as an example of special legislation.

In the end the "Gleaves" bill with the so-called "Powers" amendment passed the assembly by a vote of 60 to 9, and the senate by a narrower margin of 21 to 17. In its final form it authorized the State Board of Harbor Commissioners to lease any land belonging to the state which was required for terminal purposes, at a maximum rental of $1,000 a year. No land was to be leased for a longer period than fifty years, not more than 50 acres was to be leased to any one railroad, and no lease was to be assignable without the written consent of the commissioners. As a still further protection, it was provided that the beneficiary of the lease must be a railroad company. Such a company, moreover, must be incorporated within the state of California, and it might not be a corporation which, at the date of the passage of the act, had any terminal facilities in the city and county of San Francisco.[31]

Terms of Lease

Armed with the legislative sanction, Mr. Spreckels undertook negotiations with the Board of Harbor Commissioners and with Mayor Sutro, of San Francisco, and Governor Budd, which lasted from the middle of March, 1895, to the second week in July. In its main outlines the lease finally agreed upon offered to the San Francisco and San Joaquin Valley Railway Company the use of a defined area of 24¼ acres more or less located near the foot of Fourth Street, San Francisco, and bounded upon the water side by the sea-wall and thoroughfare established by the legislature of 1878. In return for this considerable grant, the lessee agreed to reclaim the lands granted from the tide, to place tracks, warehouses, and freight sheds upon them; to pay a nominal rental of $1,000 a year; and in addition, to commence within six months, and to construct and

[31] Laws of California, 1895, Ch. 171.

have in operation within ten years, not less than 50 miles in continuous railroad in addition to the mileage already constructed in 1895, one end of which was to be at some point on the Bay of San Francisco south of an east and west line drawn through Point Pinole.

The improvement of the leased property and the undertaking of new construction were obviously the real considerations for the lease. For the rest the terms of the lease carried out the spirit of the Gleaves Act by providing that the lease should terminate and all rights under it should cease if the demised premises, or the lessee corporation, should ever, by or through any corporate act of the latter, become, during the period of the lease, subject directly or indirectly to the control or dominion of any person, company, or corporation having railway terminal facilities on the Bay of San Francisco. Likewise the lease was to terminate if the party of the second part (the railway) should enter into any combination, arrangement, pool, trust, or agreement with any railroad corporation, or individual, having railroad terminal facilities upon, or adjacent to, the water-front of the city of San Francisco, for the purpose of preventing or limiting competition in the business of carrying freight or passengers. This wording permitted merger or agreement between the San Francisco and San Joaquin Valley Railway and the Atchison, Topeka and Sant Fé Railway Company, but not between the former company and the Southern Pacific, and was quite evidently intended to have this effect. In accordance with the terms of the Gleaves Act, the lease was made non-assignable.[32]

---

[32] Indenture dated July 8, 1895. The lease was to expire May 1, 1945. Five years after the lease was signed, however, the State Harbor Commission declared it terminated because of the failure of the railway company to make agreed improvements. A new indenture was then signed by the parties under date of November 21, 1900. By this document the state slightly increased the area leased to the railway company, and extended the term to December 1, 1950. For its part, the railway agreed to construct a definite length of sea-wall along the front of the leased property, and to spend $50,000 annually for six years on improvements. It is interesting to observe that while the new lease, like the old, was non-assignable, the restriction in the indenture of 1900 did not apply to any assignment or transfer that might occur at the expiration of the Valley company's corporate life through foreclosure of its bonded indebtedness, nor to any sale, transfer, or assignment to the Atchi-

Reasons for Consolidation

A very interesting statement issued in October, 1898, by a vice-president of the Valley road, Robert Watts, explains the development of the relations between the Santa Fé and the San Francisco and San Joaquin Valley Railway with what appears to have been considerable frankness. This statement is valuable enough to be quoted at length:

I have said that the Santa Fé Railroad was not consulted upon the organization of the Valley Road. This is strictly true. But it is also true that shortly after we began work that discussions arose among ourselves and the public as to a probable connection with that road, but we were not organized with that object in view. Wherever we have gone in the San Joaquin Valley the people have asked us when we would connect with the Santa Fé road . . .

For a little time we clung to the belief that we could make a traffic arrangement with the Santa Fé road, and from the day that we saw that connection with that road was inevitable we worked toward that end. We worked to keep the Valley Road in its original form, and give original stockholders a personal interest in the terminus of an overland line. But we found that our stockholders were not all actuated by the same sentiment that actuated the directors and trustees.

When we began to negotiate with the Santa Fé people we found that some of our richest stockholders had sold their stock at 50 cents on the dollar; and when we talked traffic arrangement with the Santa Fé people they showed us that in that way the Southern Pacific people could quietly buy in a control of the stock and could then abrogate their traffic agreement at the conclusion of the trusteeship in less than seven years and leave them no better off than they were.

It was only when we saw that there was absolutely no hope of making the overland connection without a sale of the stock and there was a possibility, if not a danger, that the Southern

son, Topeka and Santa Fé Railway Company. The Santa Fé road, successor to the San Francisco and San Joaquin Valley Railway, purchased additional property adjacent to and south of China Basin, but its terminals are still on the land leased from the state. This includes the company's freight ferry lands, its freight houses, and most of its yard tracks in San Francisco. See on this matter the annual reports of the Atchison, Topeka and Santa Fé Railroad, and also the *San Francisco Examiner*, November 15, 1898.

Pacific Company might obtain control of the stock of the road that we decided to talk with our stockholders and we laid the whole matter before them and told them not to sell their stock at less than par and then the option was taken upon the stock and it will undoubtedly be closed.[33]

This statement of Mr. Watts bears out the conclusion at which we had already arrived, namely, that the promoters of the Valley road appreciated from the first that they must connect their enterprise with some larger system in order to be permanently successful. At the same time the prominent mention of the Santa Fé Railroad in the statement, a railroad system which had neither rails in the San Joaquin Valley nor termini on San Francisco Bay, suggests why the promoters were willing to accept the restrictions imposed by the trust agreement of 1895 and by the China Basin lease.

Transfer of Control

In the fall of 1898, the directors of the San Francisco and San Joaquin Valley Railway requested the holders of trust

---

[33] *San Francisco Examiner*, October 27. 1898. Another point of view with respect to the consolidation of the San Francisco and San Joaquin Valley Railway with the Santa Fé is presented by W. B. Storey, chief engineer and general superintendent of the Valley line from 1895 to 1900 and now president of the Santa Fé. Mr. Storey writes:
"My views do not coincide with yours in regard to the reasons actuating the promoters of the railroad. Popular opinion in California believed that the domination of one railroad greatly retarded the progress of the state and it was the feeling that the prosperity of the state would be very greatly increased if competition could be provided. As a possible means of obtaining such competition resort was made to water competition and a steamship line was organized to handle freight via the Isthmus. This line was maintained until the money raised had been absorbed and it had been practically demonstrated that such a line could not pay. The public was, therefore, eager for any other competition that might present itself. It was the thought of the projectors that a local line should be built which might ultimately, if opportunity offered, become part of a transcontinental line. The Santa Fé, however, was not in a position to do anything, as it was at that time in a Receiver's hands. It was, however, the nearest railroad and it, therefore, seemed wise in projecting a new road branching from San Francisco to so locate it that it could later become part of the Santa Fé if that road desired an entrance to San Francisco. Most of the people who subscribed did so with the idea of providing competition and not with the idea of making money out of the investment. . . . By the time the road reached Bakersfield it became evident to the Directors that the road could not successfully compete with the Southern Pacific, because while for the time the people in the valley were giving the road all the freight that came from San Francisco, they were not able to turn the freight coming from the east over the Valley Road, the Southern Pacific refusing to make joint rates. The consequence was that the Valley Road had to depend exclusively on local business, and it was felt that in time even this would drop off materially by reason of the competitive methods of the Southern Pacific. Mr. Spreckels expressed the case in the following manner: It was not possible for the Valley Road to exist unless it became a transcontinental road and California could not raise money enough to make it such. The Santa Fé, by an extension to Bakersfield, could make it a transcontinental road and offered to buy a controlling interest."

certificates to deposit these certificates with the Union Trust Company of San Francisco, and to give an option for the purchase of them at par, valid for a period of three months. The prospective purchaser was not named, but the Santa Fé was understood to be the party interested. Certificate holders responded very generally to the request. Apprehensions were expressed by a number of shippers at this time, and also by some of the San Francisco newspapers, that the deposit of certificates under the conditions required meant an end of railroad competition in the San Joaquin Valley.[34] The plan was nevertheless considered by the trustees of the San Francisco and San Joaquin Valley Railway and was approved by them, Mr. Ripley giving written and verbal assurances in behalf of the Santa Fé that the Valley road would be continued as a competing line.[35] In due course the option was taken up and the expected transfer of control to the Santa Fé occurred.

It may be observed, to conclude this part of the story, that when the Santa Fé began negotiations with the managers of the Valley road in April, 1898, its operated mileage ran from Chicago west to Mojave, Los Angeles, and San Diego (National City). It had no route over the Tehachapi Pass between Mojave and Bakersfield, and thus no way of reaching the San Joaquin Valley save by traffic arrangement with the Southern Pacific. The purchase of the San Francisco and San Joaquin Railway gave to the Santa Fé control over a system of 279 miles, stretching from Stockton to Bakersfield, with a branch from Fresno through Visalia and Tulare, and an extension from Stockton to Point Richmond which, while not completed, was under way, and funds for the construction of which were in hand. Actual construction of the Stockton-Point Richmond line had begun in April, 1898. The work was con-

---

[34] See especially a letter written by John T. Doyle under date of September 29, 1898, and published in the *San Francisco Bulletin*, October 5, 1898. The whole matter was extensively discussed in the columns of the San Francisco press in October, 1898.

[35] *San Francisco Examiner*, October 27, 1898.

tinued by the Santa Fé, and the road was opened for freight and passengers, respectively, in May and July, 1900. There was talk also of building across the 68-mile gap between Mojave and Bakersfield. Eventually, however, an amicable arrangement with the Southern Pacific was concluded in this territory under which the use of the Southern Pacific line across the mountains was thrown open to both companies. This finally admitted the Santa Fé to northern California.

Reduction of Grain Shipment Rates

Did the building of the San Francisco and San Joaquin Valley Railway justify itself? From the financial point of view the answer is clearly in the negative. To say nothing of the energy spent in its development, investors in the stock of the railroad received no dividends. They therefore lost the use of the capital which they contributed for a period of three years. The principal of their investment they did, indeed, recover, but the interest upon it was gone. On the other hand, the enterprise was never regarded as likely to be a money-making affair in the narrow sense, and the financial point of view was not the chief one to be regarded. The real benefit expected from the construction of the Valley road was that which would come from a reduction in transportation charges between San Francisco and points in the San Joaquin Valley, and the success of the project was therefore to be measured primarily by the cuts in railroad rates for which it might be held responsible. We may consider the problem a moment from this point of view.

The first reduction in rates which may be attributed to the Valley road occurred in June, 1896, when the new railroad published a schedule of charges on wheat and on burlap bags to Stockton from stations upon its line south of the last-named city. This schedule showed substantial reductions. On September 15, 1895, the Southern Pacific rate from Ripon, a town

20 miles distant from Stockton, to Stockton was 95 cents per ton of 2,000 pounds. The Valley road in 1896 filed a rate of 80 cents a ton from Escalon, 21 miles distant from Stockton upon its own line. The Southern Pacific rate for the 29 miles from Modesto to Stockton was $1.35 a ton. From Empire, the nearest station to Modesto upon the San Francisco and San Joaquin Valley, the new railroad put in a rate of $1.10. The rate from Merced was $1.85 over the Southern Pacific; it was now made $1.70 by the Valley road. In addition to these reductions in the rates to Stockton, the new company afforded shippers a sensible relief by abolishing the switching charge of 15 cents per ton which the Southern Pacific had been accustomed to demand on grain handled at that point.[36]

As the Valley road extended itself to the south and added new stations at which it was prepared to receive business, the policy of rate-cutting was continued. In September, 1896, a wheat rate of $2.15 per ton was established from Fresno to Stockton, 20 cents less than the Southern Pacific charge.[37] By 1898 the line had reached Bakersfield, and grain rates were put in from towns between Hanford and that city which were from 10 to 15 cents per ton less than the rates which the Southern Pacific was accustomed to exact.[38] All the rates quoted were met by the Southern Pacific; moreover, word was sent to Mr. Moss, traffic manager of the San Francisco and San Joaquin Valley, that the Southern Pacific would continue to meet reductions as fast as they were made.

Merchandise Tariff

The first merchandise tariff to be established by the new line was somewhat slower in appearing than the tariff on grain, because the formulation of it was a more complicated matter. Nevertheless, such a tariff was filed with the State Railroad

---

[36] Biennial Report of the Board of Railroad Commissioners of the State of California for the years 1895 and 1896.

[37] *San Francisco Examiner*, September 19, 1896.   [38] *Ibid.*, June 28, 1898.

Commission on August 22, 1896. The new merchandise rates were based upon the Western classification, and were believed to represent reductions of from 10 to 50 per cent as compared with Southern Pacific rates before the competition of the Valley road had become effective. In the new schedule the first-class rate from Stockton to Merced was 31 cents per hundred pounds, or approximately .9 cents per ton per mile. On class five, the highest carload class, the rate was $4 per ton, or .6 cents per ton per mile.[39] As in the case of the grain rates, the publication of new merchandise schedules continued as the Valley road proceeded south. Thus when the company reached Bakersfield it put in a first-class rate of 83 cents per hundred pounds, a cut of 19 cents under the Southern Pacific tariff, with rates on other classes reduced to correspond.[40]

In addition to grain and merchandise rates, the Valley road also quoted commodity rates. The rate on flour from Merced to San Francisco was set at $2.75 per ton, and that on potatoes and on lime at $1.85 per ton, as compared with rates of $4.20 and $3.10 over Southern Pacific lines.[41] Likewise passengers were carried from Stockton to Fresno and to intermediate points at a flat rate of 3 cents per mile. Later, the fare from San Francisco to Hanford was reduced from $7.30 to $4.65, that to Visalia from $7.40 to $5,[42] and that to Bakersfield from $9.10 to $6.90.[43]

Relative Position of San Francisco Improved

It should be added that the adjustment both of grain and of merchandise rates was such as to improve the relative position of San Francisco as compared with other cities, as well as to reduce directly the freight bills which she had to pay. Generally speaking, the grain rates between points in the San Joaquin Valley and San Francisco were made 50 cents per ton

---

[39] San Francisco Examiner, August 23, 1896.   [40] Ibid., June 4, 1898.
[41] Ibid., July 18, 1896.   [42] Ibid., September 15, 1897.   [43] Ibid., June 4, 1898.

higher than the rates to Stockton. This in itself represented a reduction of 50 cents under the Southern Pacific rates, inasmuch as the Southern Pacific had been accustomed to quote a rate to San Francisco which was $1 per ton higher than the rate to Stockton, in order to encourage shipments to Port Costa. The Southern Pacific rate to Port Costa, exceeded its rate to Stockton by only 50 cents, and was less than the Southern Pacific grain rate to San Francisco by the same amount.[44]

The differentials in the case of merchandise southbound varied. On first-class the rate from San Francisco to valley points was 5 cents per hundred pounds higher than the rate from Stockton. On second-class the differential was 3 cents, and on third and fourth classes it was 2 cents per hundred pounds. Groceries and supplies for country stores generally fell in classes two, three, and four. These figures compared with Southern Pacific differentials of 5 cents on classes one and two, and 4 cents on classes three and four.[45] Here again the relative position of San Francisco was improved, not unnaturally to the satisfaction of dealers in that city.

It is clear from the facts set forth in the last few pages that the San Francisco and San Joaquin Valley Railway accomplished a considerable reduction in rates, at least for a time, in the San Joaquin Valley. When we bear in mind that this was the principal purpose for which the road was built, and when we recall that after all its promoters escaped without considerable financial sacrifice, it is hard to avoid the conclusion that the enterprise was justified, and may be considered to have been worth what it cost. The company did not fulfil the hopes of its projectors; it failed to maintain its inde-

---

[44] In order to make possible its low San Francisco rate, the San Francisco and San Joaquin Valley Railway concluded an arrangement with the California Navigation and Improvement Company by which the latter agreed to run two steamers a day each way between Stockton and San Francisco, and to handle all wheat shipments to Port Costa, Benicia, Vallejo, and San Francisco which were delivered to it by the Valley road. The same rate was to be charged from Stockton to all the points named. (*San Francisco Examiner*, July 9, 1896.)

[45] *Ibid.*, August 23, 1896.

pendence, and only for a few years served as an aggressive competitor of the system which San Francisco business men so cordially disliked. But it did do something to relieve the mercantile community, at no great expense to the persons who invested in it, or to the city which promoted it, and so, in a modest way the railroad may be considered a success.

CHAPTER XIX

OPERATING CHARACTERISTICS OF THE SOUTHERN PACIFIC LINES

Proprietary and Leased Properties

Let us now leave the general questions of rates and competition in California, and return again to the more intimate history of Southern Pacific development, and particularly to the story of the later years. The present chapter describes the organization and operating characteristics of the Southern Pacific system after 1885; the chapters next following take up that all-important financial problem which faced the Central Pacific in the later nineties—the repayment of the government debt.

A glance at the annual report of the Huntington lines shows that from the point of view of ownership the system, as early as 1885, was divided into two parts. The first of these was known as the "proprietary companies," and included the Southern Pacific Railroad of California, the Southern Pacific Railroad of New Mexico, the Southern Pacific Railroad of Arizona, Morgan's Louisiana and Texas Railroad and Steamship Company, the Louisiana and Western Railroad, the Texas and New Orleans Railroad, the Galveston, Harrisburg and San Antonio Railway, and the Northern Railway. The second was known as the "leased companies," and its principal components were the Central Pacific Railroad, the California Pacific Railroad, and the Oregon and California Railroad.

The difference between leased and proprietary lines was not in the operating relations between the two groups and the Southern Pacific Company, for as a matter of fact all were "leased lines" in this regard, but in the circumstance that the

Southern Pacific Company held substantially all the stock of the proprietary companies in its treasury as the result of the issue of its own stock in exchange; this was not true of the so-called leased companies. In December, 1896, the Southern Pacific reported 5,250 miles of proprietary lines, and 2,128 miles of leased properties.[1]

From the standpoint of operation the distinction between proprietary and leased lines was completely disregarded, and naturally so because, as has been said, both kinds of properties were operated after the same general fashion. Instead of being classed as proprietary or leased companies, the Southern Pacific lines were divided for operating purposes between the Pacific system including the mileage south of and including Portland, Oregon, and west of Ogden and El Paso, and the Atlantic system, including the railroads east of El Paso. In 1889 local legislation compelled the separate operation of the lines in Texas. In 1896 there were 4,966 miles of main line in the Pacific system, 1,967 miles in Texas, and 445 miles in Louisiana. Mention should also be made of over 3,500 miles of water routes, chiefly those connecting New Orleans and Morgan City with the West Indies and with New York.

Bigness of System

The fact concerning Southern Pacific properties that seems to have most impressed observers was their sheer size. A company controlling 7,300 miles of railroad and 3,500 miles of water lines, and operating between Portland, New Orleans, and New York, was unusually large even to men accustomed

---

[1] The relations between the Southern Pacific Company and the proprietary companies were governed by what was known as the "omnibus" lease, under which the Southern Pacific agreed to operate and to maintain the properties of the proprietary companies, to pay all fixed and other charges, including interest on bonds and floating debt, and to divide the surplus net profits between the parties to the agreement in stipulated proportions. In 1896 the percentages for division of profits were as follows: Southern Pacific Railroad of California, 44 per cent; Southern Pacific Railroad of Arizona, 10 per cent; Southern Pacific Railroad of New Mexico, 6 per cent; Louisiana Western Railroad Company, 7 per cent; Morgan's Louisiana and Texas Railroad Company, 23 per cent; Southern Pacific Company, 10 per cent.

to the great eastern corporations which operated in the nineties. The railroad mileage of the Southern Pacific in 1896 exceeded that of the Union Pacific by 2,600 miles, that of the Santa Fé by 940 miles, and that of the Northern Pacific by 2,800 miles. Even the Pennsylvania Railroad operated only 6,700 miles in 1896, including lines both east and west of Pittsburgh, while the reported mileage of the New York Central and Hudson River Railroad was but 2,395 miles in the same year.

In respect to earnings also, the Southern Pacific bulked large among its contemporaries. In the single year 1892, with its affiliated railroads and ferries, it took in nearly $49,000,000 on 6,486 miles of line, or more than half the earnings of the Santa Fé, Union Pacific, and Northern Pacific combined. In 1896 the earnings of the Southern Pacific were about the same as in 1892 upon a substantially greater mileage, but the earnings of its competitors had also greatly declined. Naturally enough, the great extent of the Southern Pacific system made its problems those of extensive rather than of intensive operation. Locomotive runs were longer on the Southern Pacific than elsewhere, and more attention was paid to questions of organization, particularly in later years.

There were other features about the Southern Pacific lines, however, besides their length, which deserve at least a passing mention. The system enjoyed, for example, the advantage of a highly diversified traffic. The year 1900 was not exceptional in this regard, yet in 1900, 22 per cent of the freight carried by the Southern Pacific fell in the class of products of agriculture, 17 per cent was manufactures, 15 per cent was products of the forest, 10 per cent products of mines, 8 per cent merchandise, and 4 per cent animal products. When we recall that in the same year 47 per cent of all the freight carried by the Pennsylvania Railroad Company consisted of anthracite and bituminous coal, and that nearly half of the freight transported over the Chicago, Milwaukee and St. Paul Railroad consisted of products of agriculture and of the forest, we can understand the unusual position in which the Southern Pacific was placed.[2]

High Average Earnings

Generally speaking, on a railroad system which handles a large traffic in manufactured goods, the average return per ton per mile will be large. This is particularly true when the company's coal tonnage is of small proportions. In the case of the Southern Pacific, the effect of such a distribution of business was increased by the fact that the company possessed the well-nigh exclusive control of a large local business on the Pacific Coast, on which high rates could be charged. This was where the efforts of the associates to maintain a monopoly of rail transportation in California bore fruit. Eighty-two per cent in weight of the commercial freight handled in 1883 by the Central Pacific Railroad was classified as local, and almost two-thirds of this company's earnings were derived from local business. Indeed, the local freight during the early years of operation exceeded expectations as much as the through freight fell behind what was thought would be its probable development. Prior to the construction of the Union and Central Pacific railroads, it was supposed that for many years the through business of the new lines would constitute by far their principal source of revenue. It was also supposed that the traffic of the companies would consist very largely in the transportation across the continent of the products of Asia in transit to the states situated east of the Mississippi River and to Europe. Both of these anticipations proved entirely mistaken.

Partly, then, because of the character of the freight which it handled, and partly because of the fact that a large propor-

---

[2] In later years the lumber business of the Southern Pacific developed, but the coal business has always remained small.

tion of its business was local, the average rate upon the Southern Pacific was very high. The average freight receipts of the Central Pacific in 1872 were 3.66 cents per ton per mile. While they declined in subsequent years, the figure was still 2.75 cents in 1878, and 2.14 cents in 1881. In 1878, while the Central Pacific was earning 2.75 cents per ton per mile, the Santa Fé received only 2.12 cents, the Union Pacific 2.27 cents, the Chicago and Northwestern 1.72 cents, the Pennsylvania .92 cents, and the Lake Shore and Michigan Southern .73 cents.[3] Fourteen years later, the average receipts on the entire Southern Pacific system were exactly twice the average receipts per ton per mile on the Illinois Central, and materially greater than those of most roads in other parts of the country.

It is evident that the average earnings of the Southern Pacific system were superior to those of the other transcontinental railroads, to say nothing of such eastern properties as the Illinois Central and the Chicago and Northwestern. To break the force of the comparison, Mr. Huntington was wont to compare Southern Pacific figures with the averages reported by the Interstate Commerce Commission for the so-called Group X, which included the Pacific Coast. These statistics showed, for example, in 1894, that the average receipts per ton per mile of railroads in Group X were 1.343 cents, while those of the Southern Pacific (Pacific system) were 1.316 cents. Territorial averages, however, made up of returns from small companies and from large, from local and from through concerns, may reasonably be expected to be higher than averages which apply only to large systems. The Southern Pacific received more on the average than its competitors, and almost as much as the group in which it lay, in spite of the fact that it enjoyed a through business in which a great many of the small western lines had no share.

---

[3] *Cf.* Annual Report of United States Commissioner of Railroads, 1883–84.

Long Average Haul

The influence of through business on the Southern Pacific lines was, on the whole, opposed to that of the local business. Not only was the through business highly competitive, but, as might be anticipated, it was characterized by an extremely long haul. Indeed, in the year 1895 the average length of haul on the through freight transported over the Pacific system of the Southern Pacific was 844 miles. The average haul of freight on the entire business of the company was 279 miles. During the same year the New York Central Railroad reported an average haul of 169 miles, and the Erie one of 156 miles.

The reason for the extraordinary length of haul on the Southern Pacific lay in the fact that the company served a rich community far removed from eastern centers of population, yet relying to a considerable extent upon these centers both as a market for its produce and as a source for its supplies. Moreover, the commodities of California, such as fruit and lumber, wool, fish, and wine, and the imports through the port of San Francisco, such as tea, sugar, and silk, were sufficiently distinct in character from the typical products of the East to give something of the stability of international division of labor to the movements between the Pacific Coast and the eastern states. Much the same can be said of the transportation of manufactured goods westbound in view of the high price of labor in the West and the scarcity of coal.

These matters have been considered in a preceding chapter. Their effect was to make it easy to secure a great many full cars, or even trainloads, and to reduce terminal expenses to a minimum. Inasmuch, however, as the raw products of California were heavier and took up more space than the manufactured goods received in exchange for them, a very considerable excess of eastbound tonnage often existed. In 1888, to take a year at random for purposes of illustration, the tons of through freight carried one mile eastward on the Pacific system were reported as amounting to 335,330,035, while the through westbound freight amounted to only 232,682,578. This meant light loads and empty mileage on the westbound traffic. The difference would doubtless have been greater had it not been for the large westward moving company freight. Such a tendency called for constant effort on the part of the officials of the Southern Pacific to secure eastern manufactures for westbound transportation, and this effort in turn gave rise to friction between the railroad and the manufacturing interests upon the Pacific Coast.

On the other hand, the tendency of the passenger traffic was in the direction of an excess of westbound business, because of the migration of permanent settlers to California. During the three years from 1888 to 1890, 328,892 through passengers were reported as moving westward on the Pacific system alone, and only 241,643 as moving eastward, or an excess of 36 per cent in favor of the West. The excess of westbound passenger traffic during these three years reached the large total of 76,580,470 passengers, or more than the total eastbound movement in any one year of the period.

Earnings Density

The greatest density of earnings on the Southern Pacific system was on properties such as the Central Pacific and the California Pacific, which together with the Northern Railway formed the main trunk line from San Francisco to the East. In 1895 the Central Pacific earned $9,537 per mile and the California Pacific $9,266, amounts which were far inferior to the results of the operation of railroads in thickly settled districts east of the Mississippi River, but which yet exceeded the returns on the Santa Fé, the Illinois Central, and even those reported on the western portions of such a railroad as the Baltimore and Ohio.

Next to the California Pacific in the Southern Pacific sys-

tem, in respect to earnings, came, in 1895, the South Pacific
Coast Railroad, with gross earnings of $8,000 per mile; the
Southern Pacific railroads of New Mexico, California, and Arizona, with earnings ranging from $6,500 to $5,800; the Northern Railway with $5,177; and finally the Northern California
and the Oregon and California Railroad companies, with earnings per mile of $2,600 and $2,400, respectively. The figures so
far given all relate to the Pacific system. In general it may be
said that the earnings of Atlantic system lines were slightly
greater per mile than those of the western properties. This
statement does not, however, hold good of all the Atlantic
companies, nor, on the average, for the Texas roads, statistics
for which are given separately.

Diversion of Traffic to El Paso Route

Unquestionably there was a difference in interest between
different parts of the Southern Pacific system, particularly between the Central Pacific or Ogden route, and the Southern
Pacific or El Paso route. When the Southern Pacific was first
completed to El Paso, the question was raised as to whether it
would be the policy of the management of the whole system to
divert all transcontinental freight via the southern route. In
a letter to a bureau of the United States Treasury Department,
Mr. Huntington observed that it would be necessary to continue to do a large part of the through business over the
Central Pacific in order that that road might be enabled to meet
its interest charges and the requirements of the government
indebtedness. The point was evidently regarded as one which
called for a decision as to policy. Mr. Huntington further
pointed out that it would be injudicious for the Southern
Pacific to push any advantage too strongly which it might
have, lest it provoke retaliatory action by other lines.[4]

---

[4] Report on the Internal Commerce of the United States (Treasury Department, 1884),
sup. cit.

The early practice of the Southern Pacific did not, however, altogether accord with this counsel of moderation, and the company seems not only to have been very active, but actually to have succeeded in capturing as much as 90 per cent of the New York–San Francisco business; also, while it did not permanently retain so large a share of the through freight which moved by rail, it continued to carry the major portion of the westbound traffic from the Atlantic seaboard to California until perhaps the year 1887.[5] Some of the freight which the Southern Pacific handled during this period was new business, but a considerable portion of it was taken from the Central Pacific.

There is more or less evidence that it was the practice of the Southern Pacific management to lay special emphasis upon the advantages of the southern route, in the attempt to divert as much business as possible to what was known as a 100 per cent line.   That shippers believed such a policy was being followed, is evident from statements which appeared in the public press.   It was currently asserted, for instance, that ticket and traveling agents of the Southern Pacific all over the state of California were instructed to use their best endeavors to induce passengers to move by way of the southern line instead of by way of Ogden.[6]   It was claimed that better time was made over the Southern Pacific than over the Central Pacific, and that freight shipments were more easily traced.

Speaking of westbound freight, a San Francisco merchant was quoted in 1896 as stating that the Southern Pacific delivered freight from New York to San Francisco in from twelve to twenty days.   Should the freight not come to hand promptly, officials of the company were said to be exceedingly careful to discover the causes of the delay and to see that the goods were pushed forward as rapidly as possible.   On the

[5] United States v. Southern Pacific, p. 155, testimony of Schumacher; p. 942, testimony of Chambers; pp. 1028–29, testimony of Spence.
[6] *San Francisco Examiner*, October 24, 1895.

other hand, if freight came via Chicago and Ogden, all the way from 18 to 28 days might be spent upon the journey, while information as to the causes of delay was difficult to obtain.[7]

Testimony of Employees and Officials

One may readily concede that complaints of the character referred to are to be accepted only with reservations; yet there is later information which bears out the substance of the charges in convincing fashion. When the Southern Pacific system was attacked in 1914 as a combination in restraint of trade, a great many railroad employees were put upon the stand, and testimony was secured which related not only to current policy, but also to practices which had been followed by members of the Southern Pacific staff for a number of years in the past.

It appears without substantial contradiction from the testimony in this case, that Southern Pacific, and even Central Pacific employees, solicited for the Sunset route before its combination with the Union Pacific in preference to the route via Ogden in order to obtain the long haul, even when the Sunset route was very roundabout. Mr. Connor, commercial agent of the Southern Pacific at Cincinnati from 1889 to 1901, testified that his office had directed its exclusive time and attention to securing traffic from California points for the New Orleans gateway. Shipments moving via Ogden he regarded as lost and reported them accordingly.[8] Mr. Sproule said that the same was true of the whole Central Freight Association territory, from Buffalo and Pittsburgh on the east, to Chicago and St. Louis on the west.[9]

Mr. Spence, director of traffic of the Southern Pacific Company, admitted that effort was made to send business to

---

[7] *San Francisco Examiner*, February 25, 1896.

[8] United States v. Southern Pacific, pp. 328, 338, testimony of Connor.

[9] *Ibid.*, p. 199, testimony of Sproule.

California via New Orleans when the point of origin was in territory east of a line drawn from Toledo through Indianapolis and Terre Haute to St. Louis.[10] Mr. Lovett thought that Southern Pacific solicitors even in Chicago did not work against the solicitation of lines leading to New Orleans, though acting independently they would solicit business via Ogden.[11] It is in the record, also, that Southern Pacific solicitors in 1914 sought freight from the Atlantic seaboard to Oregon and Nevada through the New Orleans gateway,[12] and that the great bulk of wool from western and central Nevada destined to the Atlantic seaboard actually moved west to Sacramento and then south and east over the Sunset line, instead of taking the direct route via Ogden.[13]

Complaints of Others

This direct testimony of Southern Pacific employees is in harmony with repeated assertions made by persons outside of the organization, and seems to indicate that some discrimination against the Central Pacific and in favor of the Southern Pacific on transcontinental business was encouraged by those in control of the Southern Pacific Company's affairs. As well informed a man as P. P. Shelby, traffic manager of the Union Pacific, declared in 1887 that he knew by conversation with shippers that the Central Pacific had diverted all the traffic they could control to the Sunset route ever since the Southern Pacific was completed, commencing in 1882. All kinds of merchandise had been diverted, especially such goods as canned fruits, canned fish, and wool. Asked whether the Union Pacific would carry 25 per cent more freight if the Central Pacific were separated from the Southern Pacific, Mr. Shelby qualified his state-

---

[10] *Ibid.*, p. 1034, testimony of Spence.   [11] *Ibid.*, p. 290, testimony of Lovett.
[12] *Ibid.*, p. 305, testimony of De Friest; p. 311, testimony of Johnson; p. 312, testimony of Hall.
[13] *Ibid.*, p. 219, testimony of Sproule; p. 152, testimony of Schumacher; p. 827, testimony of Kruttschnitt.

ment by saying that it was hard to answer the question. The Southern Pacific gave the Central Pacific a good deal of freight which that company would not have received were the two lines segregated. Had they been two independent lines, under independent management, the Southern Pacific would not have given the Central Pacific any freight at all.[14]

Similar charges were made by representatives of interests such as those of the English stockholders of the Central Pacific, who asserted that Mr. Huntington wished to ruin the Central Pacific, and dwelt upon the advantages of bankruptcy to a company from which the United States government was about to attempt to collect a debt. Knowing as we do that the Huntington-Stanford group shifted the weight of their investments from the Central to the Southern Pacific in the eighties, there is of course ground for suspicion that the diversion of freight, to which the evidence that has been quoted refers, was part of a carefully thought-out plan, and that more than traffic matters were involved.

Real Reasons for Traffic Diversion

Yet the truth of the matter probably is that while some diversion from the Central to the Southern route occurred, this diversion, although looked upon with equanimity by Mr. Huntington, was not part of an attack upon the Central Pacific, but may be explained by certain simple traffic considerations. There were at least two good reasons why an attempt should have been made to handle business from New York over the Southern Pacific rather than over the Central Pacific. The first reason was that it was more profitable for the Southern Pacific to take freight from New York by a route which it entirely controlled, than to divide the earnings on such business with the direct lines between New York and Ogden. The second reason was that the Southern Pacific could offer better

---

[14] United States Pacific Railway Commission, p. 2150, testimony of Shelby.

service on the Sunset route than over the Central Pacific because of the indifference of the lines east of Omaha. The Central Pacific business was done on a different classification from that in use in the East. Also, many classes of freight were taken at low rates because of water competition, so that the divisions accruing to eastern lines were very small, and their interest in the traffic correspondingly slight.

Finally, to the eastern roads the whole business was unimportant compared with the volume of other kinds of goods which they were handling. The result was that Mr. Stubbs, of the Southern Pacific, complained very vigorously that eastern lines neglected transcontinental business. It took four to six days he said, to get freight through the city of Chicago, and often thirty to thirty-five days to transport it from Omaha to New York. Freight had to be way-billed three times via Ogden as compared with one billing via El Paso. In fact, in 1885 and 1886 the trunk lines practically withdrew from the transcontinental business, and to this withdrawal should be attributed the large proportion of the traffic between San Francisco and New York which was handled by the Sunset route during these years.[15]

These two reasons, of which one still has force, and the other was important for a number of years, are sufficient to account for most of the diversions complained of, and it is not necessary to attribute additional motives to the Huntington management.

As a matter of fact, in spite of the traffic policy described, the gross earnings per mile of the Southern Pacific did not move very differently from those of the Central Pacific during the years from 1886 to 1895, when the data are distinguishable in the companies' reports. The advances and recessions in volume of traffic were not identical for the two companies

---

[15] United States Pacific Railway Commission, pp. 3304–6, 3362, testimony of Stubbs; pp. 357 2–73, testimony of Gray.

during these years, nor did they occur at exactly the same times, but the figures seem to offer no support to the charge that the prosperity of either company was being sacrificed.

It may also be observed that the policy of freight diversion was not confined to the period when the Central Pacific was negotiating with the government for the payment of its debt and with the English stockholders for the adjustment of their claims, nor to the years when the management of the Southern Pacific Company owned Southern Pacific shares and did not own a corresponding amount of the shares of the Central Pacific. In fact, as has been said, the policy of seeking to obtain the benefits of the long haul is still followed by the Southern Pacific Company, and its agents still take credit for sending freight all the way to New York by company lines, although the financial control of both the Southern and the Central Pacific has long been in one set of hands.

Traffic in Early Eighties

Like other systems in the United States, the earnings of the Southern and Central Pacific railroads fluctuated considerably from year to year. It has been pointed out in a previous chapter that during the period from 1870 to 1879 the rapid extension of the Southern Pacific in the South West, and the temporarily unproductive character of the new mileage built, well-nigh caused the bankruptcy of the entire concern. The associates were then saved by the completion of the Southern Pacific main line to The Needles, and by an improvement in general stock market conditions which enabled them to sell securities in New York. In 1885 the Central Pacific retired the greater part of a floating debt of $12,873,946 by an issue of bonds, and for the first time in many years was freed from what had always been a pressing danger.

In spite of this important relief, the years 1882, 1883, 1884, and 1885 were still years of considerable difficulty. Although the mileage of the system now increased but slowly, the revenue per mile declined. Thus the Central Pacific earned $9,449 per mile of line in 1881, $8,437 in 1882, $8,253 in 1883, and $7,496 in 1884. In three years gross earnings per mile dropped 21 per cent. This decline was due to a number of causes. The Central Pacific suffered greatly, for one thing, from the falling off in the tonnage supplied by the Nevada mines. Roads like the Eureka and Palisade, the Nevada Central, the Nevada and California, and the Virginia and Truckee railroads, which were at one time lucrative feeders to the Central Pacific main line, all showed a considerable decline in earnings and business between 1875 and 1885 because of the failure of the mines. The freight received at Palisade, the terminus of the Eureka and Palisade Railroad, declined 74 per cent between 1875 and 1888. The freight received at Battle Mountain, the terminus of the Nevada Central, fell off 78 per cent, while that arriving at Virginia City over the Virginia and Truckee Railroad dropped 86 per cent.

It was estimated that the shrinkage of traffic between 1876 and 1885 was not less than $2,000,000 per annum as compared with the period of highest prosperity of the Nevada country. The decrease was due in the first instance to the working out of the ore deposits, not only of the Comstock lode but of nearly all other camps within the states of Nevada and Utah west of Ogden which were tributary to the Central Pacific line. Following this, there was a large falling off in traffic, consisting of mining machinery and all kinds of supplies previously required by the miners at the mining camps, and also a large falling off in passenger travel as compared with the first and prosperous years of operation.[16]

Besides the loss of the Nevada mining traffic in the late seventies and early eighties, the Central Pacific also had to

---

[16] Frye-Davis Report (51st Congress, 1st Session, February 17, 1890, Senate Report No. 293, Serial No. 2703).

reckon with a certain loss of business by reason of the opening of transcontinental competing routes such as the Santa Fé in 1881 and the Northern Pacific in 1883. In the early part of the period the decline in business seems to have been due mainly to local conditions; in 1884, however, as was to be expected, a serious decrease in the earnings from through business occurred.

Later Earnings

As a contrast to the unsatisfactory character of the returns for the years 1883, 1884, and 1885, the reports of the companies show that, taking the Central Pacific–Southern Pacific system as a whole, the total earnings from 1885 to 1891 steadily increased, both in the aggregate and per mile of line. If we compare the condition of the system in 1891 with its condition in 1885, we find a progress which may be summarized as follows:

COMPARATIVE STATEMENT OF MILEAGE, CAPITALIZATION, EARNINGS, AND EXPENSES OF THE SOUTHERN PACIFIC SYSTEM, 1885,* 1886, AND 1891

Item	1885	1886	1891
Mileage operated	4,698	4,847	6,376
Capital stock	$171,036,160	$198,668,170	$264,375,066
Funded debt	158,970,716	181,041,680	205,621,373
Gross earnings	25,006,106	31,797,882	50,449,816
Operating expenses	12,149,824	18,514,656	31,163,612
Net earnings	12,856,282	13,283,226	19,286,214

* The figures of earnings for 1885 represent the results of from nine to ten months' operation only.

This was a satisfactory showing. The total mileage operated by the Southern Pacific Company and by the Southern Pacific Railroad, Northern Division, increased between 1885 and 1891 from 4,698 miles to 6,376 miles, not including the mileage of the steamship routes between New Orleans and Galveston and New York. The principal elements of new mileage added were certain lines in Oregon, including the property of the Oregon and California Railroad from Portland to the California state line (650 miles); a second road down the San Joaquin Valley on the west bank of the river (190 miles); and additional construction on the Coast Division (150 miles). Comparatively little was added during these years to the Central Pacific main line, or to the properties east of El Paso.

While the mileage operated thus increased by 1,678 miles, or 36 per cent, gross earnings became greater by the sum of $25,000,000, or approximately 100 per cent, and net earnings by $6,429,921, or about 50 per cent. This was accomplished with an increase in bonded indebtedness of only 30 per cent. The increase in stock outstanding was greater, it is true, than the increase in the funded debt, but the new stock issue did not increase the fixed charges of the road, and therefore in no way imperiled its solvency. In none of the figures cited are the so-called subsidy bonds issued by the United States government or the accrued interest upon the same included.

Decline Following 1893

Unfortunately, the progress of the Southern Pacific toward prosperity, which was so considerable between 1885 and 1891, was interrupted by the difficult commercial and industrial years between 1891 and 1897. The effect of world-wide depression upon American railroads is apparent when we observe that in the eastern part of the United States the gross earnings of companies like the New York Central fell off during this period from $21,000 per mile in 1892 to $18,000 per mile in 1897. The Pennsylvania lines west of Pittsburgh earned $44,210,000 in 1891 on a mileage of 3,502 miles. Six years later they hardly equaled this record on a mileage 500 miles greater. Even the protected system of the New York, New Haven and Hartford saw its gross earnings decline from $22,000 per mile in 1891 to $20,000 per mile in 1897.

It was scarcely to be expected that the relatively new system of the Southern Pacific would not suffer with the rest. The figures seem to show, however, that the Huntington lines suffered more than most eastern railroads from the depression in business following the panic of 1893. While it is true that the portion of the roads operated by the Southern Pacific Company which was known as the Atlantic system, comprising the lines east of El Paso, escaped with a decline of earnings from $7,700 per mile to $7,400, or only 43 per cent, the Pacific system, including the Central Pacific and the Southern Pacific Railroad of California, witnessed a decline in its returns from $8,000 per mile in 1891 to $6,400 per mile in 1897, or a loss of from five to six times as much in gross, and a still greater relative decline in net, receipts.

The following table shows the earnings and expenses of the Central Pacific Railroad per mile of road from 1885 to the reorganization of the company in 1898:

OPERATING RECEIPTS AND EXPENSES OF THE CENTRAL
PACIFIC RAILROAD OF CALIFORNIA, 1885-98 PER MILE
OF ROAD

Year	Gross Earnings	Operating Expenses	Net Earnings
1885	$ 8,383.26	$3,712.93	$4,670.33
1886	9,135.18	4,445.62	4,689.56
1887	10,092.27	5,394.48	4,697.79
1888	11,641.24	7,079.38	4,561.86
1889	11,416.92	7,178.13	4,238.79
1890	11,715.97	7,259.55	4,456.42
1891	12,224.76	6,771.95	5,452.81
1892	10,745.16	6,548.29	4,196.87
1893	10,488.89	6,267.71	4,221.18
1894	9,578.18	6,008.06	3,570.12
1895	9,534.31	5,990.94	3,543.37
1896	9,159.68	5,706.59	3,453.09
1897	4,270.75*	2,715.62*	1,555.13*
1898	11,595.87	6,769.00	4,826.87

* Six months only.

These figures show very clearly that the gross receipts of the Ogden route increased on the average per mile of road from 1885 to 1891, but that they fell off largely and persistently from 1891 to 1897. Indeed, the net earnings per mile each year from 1894 to 1897 inclusive, were less than those for any of the nine preceding years.

Suspension of Central Pacific Dividends

It seems very likely that this unusual falling off in the receipts of the Central Pacific Railroad Company is to be associated with the exceptionally disturbed traffic conditions on the Pacific Coast during the four or five years beginning in the latter part of 1891. These were the years when the Traffic Association of California was conducting its violent attack upon the Huntington interests. The period was also marked by the dissolution of the Transcontinental Association, and by the construction of the San Francisco and San Joaquin Valley Railroad. It was not to be expected that a campaign such as has been described in previous chapters would fail to have an influence upon the receipts of a company interested in business in, to, and from the state of California, so that a disproportionate decrease in Central Pacific earnings was not surprising. However this may be, the effect of the decline in earnings was to force the Central Pacific to stop the payment of dividends; and the cessation of dividends, together with other elements of uncertainty in the situation to which reference will be made, eventually caused the price of Central Pacific and of Southern Pacific stock to decline.[17]

---

[17] The dividends declared by the Central Pacific Railroad Company from 1861 to 1898 were as follows:

Year	Month	Per Cent	Amount
1873	September	3	$1,628,265
1874	August	5	2,713,775
1875	April	4	2,171,020
1875	October	6	3,256,530
1876	April	4	2,171,020
1876	October	4	2,171,020
1877	April	4	2,171,020
1877	October	4	2,171,020

Dividend Policy

In respect to dividends a word should be said here, enough at least to make clear that the whole dividend policy of the Central Pacific was a matter which provoked criticism, and that this criticism grew acute at the close of the period we are discussing. As a general matter it was charged that the Central Pacific had no business to pay any dividends at all while its indebtedness to the United States government remained uncanceled. It was further alleged, with more show of reason, that the dividends of the eighties were declared in order to assist the associates in disposing of Central Pacific stock in Europe, and not because there existed any surplus to which they could be properly and wisely charged. Finally, enemies of the company asserted, and showed ground for believing, that the dividends set forth in the annual reports of the Central Pacific to its stockholders did not represent all dividends actually declared; they asserted that, in addition, by special arrangement, considerable sums were paid out in unreported dividends, which may or may not have reached all holders of the stock.

It appeared in this connection that a gentleman named

Year	Month	Per Cent	Amount
1880	February	3	1,628,265
1880	August	3	1,778,265
1881	February	3	1,778,265
1881	August	3	1,778,265
1882	February	3	1,778,265
1882	August	3	1,778,265
1883	February	3	1,778,265
1883	August	3	1,778,265
1884	January	3	1,778,265
1888	February	1	672,755
1888	August	1	672,755
1889	February	1	672,755
1889	August	1	672,755
1890	February	1	672,755
1890	August	1	672,755
1891	February	1	672,755
1891	August	1	672,755
1892	February	1	672,755
1892	August	1	672,755
1893	February	1	672,755
1893	September	1	672,755

There were no dividends declared between September, 1893, and the reorganization of the Central Pacific in 1899.

Sir Rivers Wilson had come to the United States in 1894 as a representative of English shareholders.[18] Sir Rivers interviewed officers of the Central Pacific, inspected the property, and it was reported in the newspapers after his return to the East that he had arrived at a compromise with Mr. Huntington. The terms of the compromise were at first only vaguely understood, but the *London Economist,* in its issue of March 23, 1895, declared specifically that Mr. Huntington had undertaken to pay 1 per cent per annum in the shape of dividends until satisfactory legislation had been obtained for the adjustment of the Central Pacific's debt to the government, and that he had also agreed to pay 2 per cent per annum for two years after the debt question had been settled, during which time the shareholders would have opportunity to review their position and to consider effecting an arrangement of a more permanent character.

Mr. Huntington's attention was called to this statement of the *Economist,* but he made no denial of the facts stated. Three years later Mr. Huntington went further, and admitted that he had agreed with Sir Rivers Wilson to pay shareholders —all shareholders—an annual dividend of 1 per cent upon their stock.[19] It was understood that the money for the secret Central Pacific dividends was loaned to the Central Pacific by the Southern Pacific, although this detail was not authoritatively established.

Market Prices of Stock Shares

Neither the Central Pacific nor the Southern Pacific were ever investment properties under the Huntington régime, in the sense that a stable return could be expected by holders of their stock, or even in the sense that the selling price of their

---

[18] *San Francisco Bulletin,* November 20, 1894. Sir Rivers Wilson was ex-controller of the British National Debt Office.

[19] Testimony of Mr. Huntington before the California Railroad Commission, *San Francisco Examiner,* May 14, 1898.

shares remained reasonably uniform or ever reached a quotation in the neighborhood of par. Central Pacific stock sold at 34 in January, 1885. It rose to 51 in 1886, fluctuated principally between 26½ and 42 during the years from 1887 to 1892, and then proceeded to fall in value until in the spring of 1897 it was quoted on the New York Stock Exchange at the nominal figure of 7⅛ per share. The stock was ordinarily not traded in to any extent probably because so much of it was held abroad.

Southern Pacific stock was listed on the New York market in 1885, but as has been explained in a previous chapter, quotations on the shares were for several years artificial. In 1890 the stock sold mostly between 25 and 35. It declined slightly during the latter part of 1890 and the early part of 1891, but from September, 1891, to August, 1892, most of the sales were between 35 and 40. Beginning in 1893 the price of Southern Pacific stock began to decline. In 1894 it reached 17½, in 1895, 16¾; and in 1897 it touched the low point of 13½. After 1898 Central Pacific stock left the market, but Southern Pacific stock recovered to about 50 in the middle of 1901, at which approximate price 46 per cent of it was purchased by the Oregon Short Line.

It is not without interest that the fluctuations in the quotations of the stock of the Central Pacific were quite as extreme between 1885 and 1890 as were those of the Southern Pacific shares, although one stock was occasionally a dividend payer and the other was not, and that the Central Pacific stock was quoted at a distinctly lower figure between 1894 and 1898 than was the stock of its apparently more speculative associate. The reason is not to be found in the different natures of the properties represented by the two stocks, nor in any difference in operating conditions. It was plainly due to the gradually approaching maturity of the debt which the Central Pacific owed to the United States government, and to the complete uncertainty as to the effect which government action might have upon the solvency of the Central Pacific Railroad. So long as there seemed a possibility that the Central Pacific would be called upon to make good, in cash, an advance which by 1898 would amount to nearly $60,000,000—a sum which few persons believed that the Central Pacific would be able to pay—the stock certificates of this company could have only a speculative value.

The question of the best way to meet the huge obligation which had grown out of the assistance tendered to the Central Pacific Railroad by the federal government under the Pacific Railroad Acts of 1862 and 1864, was indeed the most important financial problem which the company had to solve after Mr. Stanford's death. The two following chapters will be devoted to an exposition of the points involved in this transaction, and to a description of the solution finally reached in the year 1898.

CHAPTER XX

THE THURMAN ACT

A Loan, Not a Subsidy

The original loan of the United States government to the Central and Western Pacific railroads amounted to $27,855,-680. The bonds which were issued to the companies were United States currency bonds, bearing 6 per cent interest, payable semiannually and maturing at the end of thirty years. They fell due therefore between 1895 and 1899. Some question has been raised as to whether these bonds were to be regarded as a loan or as a donation to the corporations which received them. Setting aside the fact that a loan at a critical moment may be almost as serviceable to the recipient as a gift, the evidence shows that the unquestionable purpose of Congress in 1862 and 1864 was that principal and interest of the bonds should be met by the railroads for the benefit of which they were issued. It follows that this bond issue constituted an advance to the Central and Western Pacific railroads, not a gift; a loan, not a donation. It was the contention of Mr. Huntington, indeed, that the very name "subsidy" was a misnomer. He said:

> The Central Pacific never got a subsidy; they got the loan of a small subsidy. The government loaned money at six per cent and they expected and did receive direct benefits from the time the road was built. It was not a subsidy in any way . . . A subsidy as I believe is where you give . . . For instance if you will build a railroad I will give you $10,000 as a subsidy; as to being a loan of money it is no such thing. It is only a business negotiation.[1]

---

[1] Huntington Manuscript, p. 91. On the general subject of the Thurman Act, see Davis, "History of the Union Pacific Railway," Ch. 4.

We must therefore recognize that the government advances to the Central Pacific did not constitute a subsidy in the ordinary meaning of that term. At the same time it should be observed that the Pacific railroads occupied a peculiarly advantageous position in respect to the loans which the government made to them. As will presently appear, although interest on this loan was charged, the companies were not obliged to pay a cent of this interest until the maturity of the bonds. This unusual concession was declared by the Supreme Court to be the necessary result of the absence of a precise stipulation to the contrary in the Acts of 1862 and 1864. The court said:

> It is one thing to be required to pay principal and interest when the bonds have reached maturity, and a wholly different thing to be required to pay the interest every six months, and the principal at the end of thirty years. The obligations are so different, that they cannot both grow out of the words employed, and it is necessary to superadd other words in order to include the payment of semiannual interest as it falls due.[2]

Payment of Simple Interest at Maturity

A second concession to the Pacific railroads was made when no interest on deferred interest payments was exacted. Ordinarily in such cases interest is compounded at intervals of six months. On a thirty-year loan of $27,855,680, issued under the conditions which characterized the subsidies to the Central and Western Pacific railroads, the difference between simple interest and interest compounded semiannually would be $113,-974,300. That is to say, simple interest would amount to $50,140,224 at the end of thirty years, while compound interest would equal the materially greater sum of $164,114,524. Put another way, the value in January, 1865, of the right to receive the principal of the government loan increased by simple interest according to the terms and at the dates contemplated by

---

[2] United States v. Union Pacific Railroad, 91 U. S. 72, 86 (1875).

the Acts of 1862 and 1864, was only $13,000,000. This was the value of the monetary consideration which the federal government accepted from the Central and Western Pacific railroads. On the other hand, the value of the advance made by the government to the same railroads as of the same date was $23,000,000, or a difference of $10,000,000. This computation assumes that government bonds were sold at par, and that the current rate of interest was 6 per cent. The difference indicated would be reduced if government bonds were assumed to have sold for less than par, and it would be increased were a higher rate of interest than 6 per cent used in the calculation. Discussions of the Acts of 1862 and 1864 usually fail to make clear that the government demanded simple interest only on its loan, but as a matter of fact this was a feature of the contract which was of substantial value to the beneficiary.

Claims for Indemnity

It was of course expected by Congress that the Pacific railroads would make adequate provisions during the life of the bonds to meet the interest and principal due at their maturity. Before discussing the disputes concerning the size and nature of the sinking funds which should have been erected, a few words may be said regarding certain equities to which the Stanford-Huntington group repeatedly alluded as constituting reasons for not paying the bonds at all. These equities may be briefly enumerated as follows:

The first equity was said to have arisen out of the loss which it was claimed the Central Pacific had sustained through failure to sell the bonds received by it from the government at par. This loss was estimated at $7,120,074, a sum which was raised by accrued interest up to the time of the maturity of the bonds to the very considerable figure of $19,936,206. According to Stanford, the government loan netted the company only 65 cents on the dollar. He said:

Indeed, if the company had taken advantage of the time allowed by Congress for the completion of the road, they could not only have sold the government bonds at par, but could also have disposed of their own first mortgage bonds at their face value, which would have been a net gain, over and above what was actually received, of $7,120,074, the interest on which for thirty years would have been $12,816,132, which would make an aggregate saving on the government bonds and the bonds issued by the company, principal and interest in round numbers, of about $40,000,000.[3]

In the second place the Central Pacific insisted that there should be credited to it a portion of the amount which the government saved in the transportation of government em-

---

[3] United States Pacific Railway Commission, p. 2529, testimony Leland Stanford. In order that the reader may have full data concerning the issue of the Government subsidy bonds, the following table of amounts and dates of issue is presented:

UNITED STATES SIX PER CENT CURRENCY BONDS ISSUED TO
CENTRAL PACIFIC RAILROAD COMPANY

Date Issued	Maturity of Bonds	Interest Commenced	Amount
May 12, 1865	Jan. 16, 1895	Jan. 16, 1865	$ 1,258,000
Aug. 14, "	" 16, "	Aug. 14, "	384,000
Oct. 16, "	" 16, "	Oct. 16, "	256,000
Dec. 11, "	" 16, "	Nov. 29, "	464,000
Mar. 6, 1866	" 1, 1896	Mar. 6, 1866	640,000
July 10, "	" 1, "	July 10, "	640,000
Oct. 31, "	" 1, "	Oct. 29, "	320,000
Jan. 15, 1867	" 1, 1897	Jan. 14, 1867	640,000
Oct. 25, "	" 1, "	Oct. 25, "	320,000
Dec. 12, "	" 1, "	Dec. 11, "	1,152,000
June 10, 1868	" 1, 1898	June 9, 1868	946,000
July 11, "	" 1, "	July 10, "	320,000
Aug. 5, "	" 1, "	Aug. 4, "	640,000
" 14, "	" 1, "	" 13, "	1,184,000
Sept. 12, "	" 1, "	Sept. 11, "	1,280,000
" 21, "	" 1, "	" 19, "	1,120,000
Oct. 13, "	" 1, "	Oct. 12, "	1,280,000
" 28, "	" 1, "	" 26, "	640,000
Nov. 5, "	" 1, "	Nov. 3, "	640,000
" 12, "	" 1, "	" 11, "	640,000
Dec. 5, "	" 1, "	Dec. 5, "	640,000
" 7, "	" 1, "	" 7, "	640,000
" 30, "	" 1, "	" 29, "	640,000
Jan. 15, 1869	" 1, 1899	Jan. 13, 1869	640,000
" 29, "	" 1, "	" 28, "	640,000
Feb. 17, "	" 1, "	Feb. 17, "	640,000
Mar. 2, "	" 1, "	" 17, "	1,066,000
" 3, "	" 1, "	Mar. 2, "	1,333,000
May 28, "	" 1, "	May 27, "	1,786,000
July 15, "	" 1, "	" 27, "	1,314,000
" 16, "	" 1, "	July 15, "	268,000
Dec. 7, "	" 1, "	" 16, "	1,510,000
Jan. 2, 1872	" 1, 1898	Nov. 28, 1868	4,120
Total..			$25,885,120

ployees and freight as a result of the rapid construction of its railroad. Under the terms of the Acts of 1862 and 1864, the Central Pacific and Union Pacific might have delayed completion of their road until July, 1876. As a matter of fact the through line from Sacramento to Ogden was opened in May, 1869. The consequent saving to the government was estimated at $47,763,178, of which the Central Pacific proportion was set at $21,971,062. A similar calculation laid before the United States Pacific Railway Commission in 1886 reached the conclusion that the total saving to the government up to January 1 of that year had reached the sum of $139,347,741 on the Union and Central Pacific combined. The basis for these estimates was found in a comparison of the rates which the government had paid for rail movement and the rates which it would have had to pay for ox team and mule team transportation.

Still a third claim was based upon an alleged loss of business consequent upon government subsidies to other transcontinental roads. The loss of earnings to the two roads from this cause was set at $37,000,000, of which the Central Pacific share was put at 46 per cent, or $17,000,000. Stanford did not deny that the government had a right in its discretion to aid other lines of railroad, but he took the position that if Congress found it in the interest of the country to do something which

UNITED STATES SIX PER CENT CURRENCY BONDS ISSUED TO WESTERN PACIFIC RAILROAD COMPANY

Date Issued	Maturity of Bonds	Interest Commenced	Amount
Jan. 24, 1867	Jan. 1, 1897	Jan. 26, 1867	$ 320,000
Sept. 1, 1869	" 1, 1899	Sept. 3, 1869	320,000
Oct. 29, "	" 1, "	Oct. 28, "	1,008,000
Jan. 27, 1870	" 1, "	Jan. 22, 1870	322,000
" 8, 1872	" 1, "	" 22, 1872	560
Total..			$1,970,560

Undoubtedly many of the bonds listed were disposed of at a considerable discount. Subsidy bonds to the :.mount of $4,922,000 had been issued by the government to the Central Pacific by October 25, 1866, and had been sold for $3,546,478. The subsidy bonds (currency sixes) were listed on the New York Stock Exchange, but there were few, if any, sales until 1868. Not a single transaction in these bonds was recorded for the year 1867. In 1869, however, the bonds went above par, the average sale price for the year being 108 1/8. (United States Pacific Railway Commission, pp. 4682-83.)

deprived the Central Pacific of the means of paying its debts, then it should compensate the Central Pacific for this action.[4]

No Basis for Claims

These three principal claims for indemnity were set up by officials of the Southern Pacific at one time or another as complete offsets to the obligations laid upon the company by the Acts of 1862 and 1864. Among minor equities should be mentioned also an alleged loss to the Southern Pacific by reason of the government's slowness in issuing patents to land. Another claim was based on a loss in respect to sinking fund investments of the company; and still another on the shipment of United States mails by other than bond-aided lines when the use of the latter was possible.

There was no real reason, however, why the government should have reduced its claims against the Pacific companies because of any of the equities mentioned. The administration certainly gave no guaranty in 1864 that the subsidy bonds would sell at par. The government offered the bonds for what they were worth, and the companies accepted them on that basis. Nor did the government at any time agree to preserve a monopoly of transcontinental business for the Central route, or to send its own freight over the Central and Union Pacific railroads to any greater extent than might prove convenient. On these points the facts are perfectly clear. It would seem clear, also, that the government was under no obligation to share with the companies any saving which it had made by reason of the early construction of the transcontinental line. The companies had built more rapidly than had been expected, it is true, but the construction was pushed in their own interest, not in that of the government, and gave rise to no proper claim

---

[4] United States Pacific Railway Commission, p. 275, testimony Leland Stanford; Report, pp. 91–95.

against the latter. The other points in the companies' contentions do not deserve special mention.

Sinking Fund Provisions

We may now return to the question of the government debt and its repayment. The Laws of 1862 and 1864 contained two provisions intended to enforce the original stipulation that principal and interest of the subsidy bonds should be paid by the beneficiaries. These laws required that 5 per cent of the net earnings of the Central Pacific after the completion of the road,[5] and second, that one-half of the compensation for services rendered to the government should be annually applied to the payment of interest and principal of the subsidy bonds until the whole amount was fully paid. It was then expected that these two sources of income would provide a fund sufficient to meet both principal and interest in full.[6]

This expectation was not, however, fulfilled. On the contrary, it was already apparent in the seventies that the amount which the companies would be called upon to repay was mounting up much more rapidly than the credits designed to meet it. Six per cent interest upon $27,855,680 of bonds called for an annual interest of $1,671,340.80. From 1867 to October 31, 1877, the one-half of transportation account for carrying mails, troops, supplies, etc., withheld by the government and credited to the Central Pacific sinking fund was only $1,423,555.74, or less than $200,000 a year.[7] The 5 per cent of net earnings account averaged $331,481 from 1872 to 1876.[8] The total annual payment by the Central and Western Pacific railroad

---

[5] The Supreme Court later held that the Central Pacific and Union Pacific railroads were completed on the 6th of November, 1869, in the sense that the companies became liable to pay over 5 per cent of their net earnings from this date. (99 U. S. 402, 449 [1878].)

[6] The Central Pacific Railroad Company in equitable account with the United States. A review of the testimony and exhibits presented before the Pacific Railway Commission, appointed according to the Act of Congress, approved March 3, 1887, by Roscoe Conkling and William D. Shipman of Counsel for the Central Pacific R. R. Co., New York, 1887.

[7] Report of the Secretary of the Interior, 1877, p. xxviii.

[8] Report of Mr. Thurman from the Committee on the Judiciary (45th Congress, 2d Session, March 4, 1878, Senate Report No. 111, p. 8).

companies, therefore, approximated $530,000, leaving a deficit of over $1,100,000 a year. At this rate it was not unreasonable to suppose that the Central Pacific would be much more heavily in debt to the government at the maturity of the bonds than it was at the time of their original issue.

Right of "Set-Off"

Alarmed at the probable failure of the sinking fund provisions, the Secretary of the Treasury, on advice of the Attorney-General, withheld from the Central Pacific Railroad *all* the compensation due it for services rendered to the government. The same action was taken with respect to the other bond-aided lines. This was clearly illegal, and Congress accordingly passed the Act of March 3, 1871, directing payment of the sums withheld.[9] On passage of the Act of 1871, the Secretary of the Treasury began to pay to the Central Pacific and to the other bond-aided companies, the 50 per cent of compensation for services rendered to the government which the statutes required. Since, however, there seemed to be a legitimate difference of opinion as to whether the government should continue to pay money to companies already heavily in debt to it, Congress proceeded two years later to pass the Act of March 3, 1873, which, in effect, remitted the whole controversy to the court.

The terms of the Act of 1873 were as follows:

> That the Secretary of the Treasury is directed to withhold all payments to any railroad company and its assigns, on account of freights or transportation, over their respective roads, of any kind, to the amount of payments made by the United States for interest upon bonds of the United States issued to any such company, and which shall not have been reimbursed together with the five per cent. of net earnings due and unapplied as provided by law; and any such company may bring suit in the court of claims to recover the price of such freight and transportation; and in such suit the right of such com-

9 16 United States Statutes 225 (1871).

pany to recover the same upon the law and the facts of the case shall be determined and also the rights of the United States upon the merits of all the points presented by it in answer thereto by them and either party to such suit may appeal to the Supreme Court; and both said courts shall give such cause or causes precedence of all other business.[10]

The intent of Congress in 1873 was that, in order to make a case, the Secretary of the Treasury should withhold the sums demanded by the bond-aided railroads including the Central Pacific, that the companies should sue, and that the court should then decide. In pursuance of this idea, the Union Pacific promptly brought suit against the government in the Court of Claims to recover the amount due from the United States for transportation of government passengers and property after deducting one-half of the amount as required by law. A decision being rendered in favor of the company, the United States appealed to the Supreme Court, where the judgment was affirmed.

The foundation of the government position was that the United States could legitimately offset the interest on subsidy bonds which it was paying currently against the sums due the bond-aided railroads for government transportation. The reply of the court was, first, that the general principles of "set-off" did not apply in the case at bar; and second, that the United States had no claim in any event because the law did not require the Union Pacific (and the same principles applied to other bond-aided railroads) to meet the interest charges on the government advances until the maturity of the bond.[11] A later case added the ruling that the United States had in the matter only the right of a creditor growing out of contract, and could not fall back upon its sovereign rights in order to protect its financial claim.[12]

---

[10] 17 United States Statutes 485, 508 (1873).
[11] United States v. Union Pacific Railroad Company, 91 U. S. 72 (1875).
[12] *Ibid.*, 98 U. S. 569 (1878).

Not only did the Supreme Court decide completely in favor of the companies in the important matter of "set-off," and in that relating to the date upon which the Pacific railroads became liable for the payment of accruing interest on the subsidy bonds, but it diminished also the sinking fund payments of the companies by holding that under existing legislation it was proper for the companies, in calculating net earnings, to deduct from gross earnings expenses incurred for enlarging and improving their property. The particular account involved was that of expenditure for station buildings, shops, and fixtures. Such expenditures are not ordinarily charged to operating expenses, and the court admitted that "theoretically" they should not be so charged. The practice was nevertheless justified on the ground of general policy, as likely to encourage a liberal application of earnings to improvements. The same decision also authorized the Central and the Union Pacific to deduct interest on first mortgage bonds from earnings before computing the 5 per cent of net earnings which was to be credited to the sinking fund. This ruling was defended as a legitimate consequence of the concession of priority to the first mortgage bonds.[13]

Need of Governmental Action

While Congress was considering ways and means for enforcing some adequate provision for the eventual repayment of the government's advance to the Pacific railroads, the Central Pacific declared dividends which amounted to no less than $18,453,670 in the five years from September 13, 1873, to October 1, 1877. In 1873, 3 per cent was declared; in 1874, 5 per cent; in 1875, 10 per cent; and in 1876 and 1877, 8 per cent. To see earnings divided among a group of financiers who were believed to be already overpaid, while the unpaid interest on the government subsidy bonds piled up, was all the more

---

[13] Union Pacific Railroad Company v. United States, 99 U. S. 402 (1878).

exasperating because of the apparent helplessness of Congress. Some action, however, was presently to be taken. In 1874 a bill was introduced in the Senate to alter and amend the Acts of 1862 and 1864 so as to safeguard the government equity. In 1876 Mr. Thurman, of Ohio, presented another bill, which was reintroduced in 1877, referred to the Committee on Judiciary, and ultimately reached the Senate in March, 1878. This bill ultimately became the Thurman Act of 1878.[14]

The situation as it appeared in 1878 was succinctly presented by Mr. Thurman on the floor of the Senate. The government's loan to the Central and Western Pacific amounted to $27,855,680. The interest upon that sum for thirty years would be $50,140,224, making a total of $77,995,904. The probable reimbursement from the 5 per cent of net earnings and the half of the transportation accounts would be about $15,000,-000, leaving probably due at the maturity of the government loan, should the laws remain unchanged, the sum of $62,995,-904, which, added to the amount that would probably be due from the Union Pacific, made an aggregate of $119,248,979.[15] To this amount there was also to be added in estimating the payments which the Central Pacific, Western Pacific, and Union Pacific would be called upon to make in the late nineties, the amount of the first mortgage bonds of the three companies, the lien of which was prior to the lien of the subsidy bonds.

It seemed manifest to Mr. Thurman in March, 1878, that the bare statement of the amount for which the government would be the creditor of the Pacific railroad companies ought to satisfy anyone that some step should be taken by Congress to secure the government from loss. This point of view was

---

[14] The Congressional history of the Thurman bill is as follows: Introduced, October 16, 1877, and referred to the Senate Committee on Judiciary (45th Congress, 1st Session, Congressional Record, Vol. 6. p. 58); reported back from Committee March 4, 1878 (45th Congress, 2d Session, *ibid.*, Vol. 7, p. 1445); debated in Senate March 12 to April 9 (*ibid.*, pp. 1688–2384); passed by Senate April 9 (*ibid.*, pp. 2779–90); approved by President, May 8 (*ibid.*, p. 3257).

[15] Speech of Senator Thurman of Ohio (45th Congress, 2d Session, March 12, 1878, Congressional Record, Vol. 7, p. 1690).

not seriously contested. Objection to any action there was, indeed, but not based on any denial of the assertion that the security of the government was becoming impaired.

Thurman Bill

On the basis of the admitted need, Mr. Thurman, in behalf of the Committee on the Judiciary of the United States Senate, made a series of concrete proposals. The essence of the Thurman plan was that the annual payments of the Pacific railroads for the eventual retirement of the government debt should be largely increased. It was contemplated that 5 per cent of the net earnings of these railroads, together with half of the sums due to the companies for government transportation, should continue to be applied to the retirement of the subsidy bonds. This annual appropriation Mr. Thurman estimated at $531,000. But it was now intended that in addition to this sum there should be retained by the government and credited to a sinking fund, the other half of the sums due to the companies for government transportation; proceeding still further, the Thurman bill provided that in case the whole of the government transportation accounts, added to the 5 per cent of net earnings, did not make a sum equal to 25 per cent of net earnings, then the Pacific railroads should pay into the sinking fund such sums not exceeding $1,200,000 for the Central Pacific and $850,000 for the Union Pacific, as would bring the companies' payment up to 25 per cent.

Textually, the section of the Thurman bill relating to the Central Pacific sinking fund read as follows:

Sec. 4. That there shall be carried to the credit of the said fund, on the first day of February in each year, the one-half of the compensation for service hereinbefore named, rendered for the Government by said Central Pacific Railroad Company, not applied in liquidation of interest; and, in addition thereto, the said company shall, on said day in each year, pay into the

Treasury, to the credit of said sinking fund the sum of one million, two hundred thousand dollars, or so much thereof as shall be necessary to make the five per centum of the net earnings of its said road payable to the United States under said act of eighteen hundred and sixty-two, and the whole sum earned by it as compensation for service rendered for the United States, together with the sum by this section required to be paid, amount in the aggregate to twenty-five per cent of the whole net earnings of said railroad company, ascertained and defined as hereinbefore provided, for the year ending on the thirty-first day of December next preceding.[16]

Mr. Thurman estimated the total payments which the Central Pacific would have to make under his bill at $1,900,000 annually, or substantially more than the accruing 6 per cent on the subsidy loans.[17]   In case earnings should be insufficient to meet interest charges on underlying first mortgage bonds after the deduction of 25 per cent, the Secretary of the Treasury was authorized to remit as much of the 25 per cent as might be necessary to avoid default.

Disappointing Results

From the point of view of the government, the clauses of the Thurman bill relating to the annual payments of the companies were of the first importance, because upon them depended the adequacy of the provision for the eventual cancellation of the government debt. As a matter of fact, the payments were less than Senator Thurman anticipated, because the earnings of the Pacific railroads proved disappointing. Instead of $1,900,-000 annually, the average contribution up to 1897 was only $629,690. In particular, the clauses requiring the companies to add to the sums earned from government transportation and that measured by 5 per cent of net earnings sufficient to bring the total up to 25 per cent of net earnings, were ineffective. In

---

[16] 20 United States Statutes 56 (1878).

[17] Report of Mr. Thurman from the Senate Committee on the Judiciary (45th Congress, 2d Session, March 4, 1878, Senate Report No. 111, Serial No. 1789).

but one year after 1883 was anything paid on this last account. Indeed, the earnings of the Central Pacific fell so low that the government transportation and 5 per cent accounts at times amounted to 50 per cent of net earnings without any addition from other sources.

It was assumed by some speakers on the Thurman bill in the Senate, that under the proposed plan the total contribution of the Pacific railroads toward the reduction of the government debt was to be paid into a sinking fund. This was not, however, the case, as a careful reading of the statement already made will make clear. Instead, the payments which these railroads had been making under the Acts of 1862 and 1864 were to be continued, and were to be credited directly to the railroad debt as before. The money was to be held in the United States Treasury, and no interest was to be allowed upon it.[18] It was only the balance, comprising the half of the payment due the companies for government transportation which they had received under the Act of 1864, and such additional payment, not exceeding $1,200,000 or $850,000 respectively, as would be necessary to bring the whole contribution of the companies under the proposed law up to 25 per cent of net earnings, which was credited to the sinking fund. The distinction is important, because the sums paid into the sinking fund earned compound interest,whereas the sums credited to bond and interest account earned no interest at all. That is to say, the contributions to the sinking fund were to be invested in government bonds, and the interest on these bonds was to be reinvested semiannually in the same security, but other payments merely gave rise to credits on the government books.

Sinking Fund Investments

The mention of the sinking fund leads naturally, however, to a reference to the provisions of the Thurman bill relating to

---

[18] Annual Report of the Commissioner of Railroads, 1882, p. 440.

sinking fund investments. Mr. Thurman proposed in 1878 that the sums credited to the Pacific railroads' sinking funds be used to purchase United States bonds, preferably 5 per cent bonds because other outstanding issues were either insufficient in amount or had only a short time to run. Up to June 30, 1897, about $6,000,000 were available for such purchases. But this limitation of the field of investment seriously crippled the earning power of the fund by requiring the purchase of securities of classes which either bore low rates of interest or which commanded considerable premiums in the market. The average premium paid by the Central Pacific up to 1883 was approximately 13 per cent.[19] In 1891 the Commissioner of Railroads reported that between the date of the creation of the sinking fund in 1878 and the date of his report, on June 30, 1891, the government had bought bonds with a par value of $6,138,800 for the Central Pacific, for which it had paid a premium of $1,110,409.62, or an average of 18 per cent. At times the premium paid had gone as high as 35 per cent,[20] and in the earlier years the payments on account of premiums materially exceeded the earnings of the sinking fund in the way of interest. This excess disappeared, of course, as the fund grew larger, but the absolute amount of the premium continued to grow.

The principal bonds in which the sinking funds were invested up to 1882 were the United States currency sixes, the 5 per cent funded loan of 1881, and the 4 per cent funded loan of 1907. In 1881 the funded fives matured and were continued at 3½ per cent. In 1882 the Treasurer of the United States exchanged these bonds for a new 3 per cent issue. Inasmuch as the bonds which bore the higher interest rates all commanded a premium, the actual yield of the fund up to 1886 was only from 2½ to 3 per cent. This condition was recognized as disadvantageous by all concerned. The Commissioner of Rail-

---

[19] Annual Report of the Commissioner of Railroads, 1883.
[20] See also the Brice Report (53d Congress, 3d Session, Senate Report No. 830, p. 17, Serial No. 3288).

roads declared in 1883 that it would require a century or more
at the rate provided in the Thurman Act to accumulate a fund
sufficient to discharge the railroad debt, with a strong probability that even then it could not be done.[21]   The Auditor of
Railroads in 1879, the Secretary of the Treasury in 1881, and
the Commissioner of Railroads, in various reports, all urged
that the field for investment of the sinking funds be widened, at
least to include the first mortgage bonds of the Pacific railroads.
Since the lien of these bonds was prior to that of the sinking
fund itself, it seemed appropriate to allow the Secretary of the
Treasury to buy them with sinking fund money.   The suggestion was adopted by Congress in 1887,[22] with the result that interest on the funds placed in this new investment amounted to
4.15 per cent.   This was a substantial increase from the 2½
or 3 per cent realized from government bonds, though still
less than the 6 per cent carried by the subsidy bonds themselves.[23]

Passage of Bill

The Thurman bill was carefully considered by the Senate
before its enactment, and may fairly be said to embody the best
judgment of Congress at the time of its enactment.   The final
vote in the Senate was taken on April 9, 1879.   Forty Senators

---

[21] Annual Report of the Commissioner of Railroads, 1883.
[22] 24 United States Statutes 488 (1887).
[23] Annual Report of the Treasurer of the United States, 1887, p. 28.
   Owing to the protests of the Pacific railroad companies at the low rates of interest
earned by the sinking funds, considerable amounts remained uninvested between 1882 and
1886.   The following table shows the cash uninvested in the Treasury to the credit of the
Central Pacific Railroad Company for a series of years:

Date	Amount
June 30, 1882	$ 527,886.53
" 30, 1883	844,652.13
" 30, 1884	1,089,159.75
" 30, 1885	2,020,900.13
Dec. 31, 1886	2,345,984.21
" 31, 1887	76,905.49
June 30, 1889	2,766.14

   No interest was earned on these uninvested balances.   After 1886, with the single exception of the year 1895, the uninvested portion of the sinking fund was negligible.   (Annual
Reports of the Commissioner of Railroads, 1882–89.)

voted for the bill, and twenty against it.[24] If paired votes for and against the act be included, the vote was forty-four to twenty-six. Twenty-seven Democrats voted for the bill, and six against it. Yet in spite of this strong Democratic party support and the opposition of Senators Blaine and Conkling, nearly as many Republicans went on record for the bill as voted or were paired against it. In the House there were but two votes against the bill compared with 243 in favor of it.[25]

In neither house was there marked party or sectional division. Doubtless the passage of the act was made easier by the general unpopularity of railroad enterprise in 1878, although adequate reasons for additional legislation undoubtedly existed. It was the period of the aftermath of the panic of 1873—the epoch of Granger legislation and railroad control bills, of revelations regarding rebates and construction frauds. Sentiment ran strongly against great railroad corporations. Railroads still had stalwart supporters, but it is putting it mildly to say that the presumption in doubtful cases was against them.

Feeling of Railroad Men

There is plenty of evidence, nevertheless, that railroad men felt very bitter that the Thurman bill should ever have been passed. Stanford declared that no act so destructive to private right had ever before been attempted in this country, and that only two examples of such atrocity could be found in English history; one being the suppression of the order of Templars in the time of Edward the Second, and the other, the suppression of the religious houses in the time of Henry the Eighth. Undoubtedly, also, the railroads were active in Congress in the

---

[24] 20 United States Statutes 56 (1878). On June 19, 1878, another act established the office of an "Auditor of Railroad Accounts" with authority to prescribe reports from subsidized railroads west, north, or south of the Missouri River, to examine books, and to furnish information to various government departments as it might be required. (20 United States Statutes 169, [1878].) Name changed to "Commissioner of Railroads" in 1881. (21 United States Statutes 381, 409 [1881].)

[25] 45th Congress, 2d Session, Congressional Record, pp. 2384, 2790. The House vote as given does not include pairs.

attempt to prevent the passage of the Thurman Act. The reader's attention has already been directed in a previous chapter to correspondence relating to the Thurman bill which passed between Huntington and Colton in 1877 and 1878. It will be recalled that in January, 1878, Huntington wrote that matters did not look well at Washington. He thought, however, that the railroad would not be much hurt, although "the boys are very hungry, and it will cost considerably to be saved." Some time before this, in May, 1877, Huntington wrote:

> We must have friends in Congress from the West Coast, as it is very important. I think that we can kill the open highway, and get a fair sinking fund bill by which we can get time beyond the maturity of the bonds that the Government loaned us, to pay the indebtedness.[26]

Again, in November, Huntington said:

> Some parties are making great efforts to pass a bill through Congress that will compel the Union Pacific and Central Pacific to pay large sums into a sinking fund, and I have some fears that such a bill will pass . . . The temper of Congress is not good and I fear we may be hurt.[27]

A letter from Colton dated March 5, 1878, reads:

> By the telegraph this morning in the papers I see outline of Thurman's Sinking Fund Bill, etc. It does seem as though the whole world, Courts and all, were determined to rob us.
>
> . . . .
>
> I know you are having a terrible struggle on that side, and think of you very often, but, Huntington, I see no way but to fight it out on these lines, and fight them inch by inch while we last; let's look to paying our debts, incurring no more, and stand by the wreck to the last. We can at least die game.[28]

When the Thurman bill passed the Senate, the correspondence took a still more gloomy turn. Huntington wrote Colton

---

[26] Colton case, p. 1770–71.   [27] Ibid., p. 1802, November 9, 1877.
[28] Ibid., argument of Hall McAllister, p. 248.

on April 19, 1878, that in his judgment the House would follow the Senate's lead. He had made some mistakes, of which the greatest was Gould's going to Washington. Colton replied, on April 29:

> We all agree with you that this Congress is simply a band of robbers. They were such a set of cowards they dare not go onto the highway and give the man they rob an even show with them, but went to Congress and did it through that channel. But Huntington, we will live to see many of these fellows come to grief. I trust the day will soon come that we can get in a shape that you can avoid going to Washington during a session of Congress. A few sessions like the present one and the last will wear you out . . .
>
> . . . .
>
> I think you will remember I wrote you once or twice that in my opinion Jay Gould would be a heavy load for us to carry in Washington or elsewhere, whenever we had connections with him that would affect our interests, on account of the general feeling against him. So I am not surprised to read what you say of him and the Funding bill, but it was a thing we could not help, as I understand it . . .
>
> . . . .
>
> I hope Congress will adjourn soon, and that you will be able to get out here as early as possible, for I want very much to see you again. There is much for us all to talk over and look after. I do not think you will find anyone to buy you out, nor do I want you to. I think we must stick to the wreck.[29]

---

[29] Colton case, argument of Hall McAllister, p. 249. Huntington never forgave Congress for having passed the Thurman bill. Years afterward he inserted the following comments in an autobiographical statement which he gave to the California historian, H. H. Bancroft:

"Senator Ransom voted for the Thurman bill. He came out and said 'Mr. Huntington, I voted for that bill. I knew I was wrong.' He said, 'I ought not to have done it.' Said I, 'Senator Ransom, I pity you.' Said he, 'What do you say?' Said I, 'Senator Ransom, I said and I repeat it for I do really pity you.' I turned on my heel and left him. Now there are a great many men in just that kind of a way; they don't dare to vote according to their convictions; they are afraid of what other people think of their acts. . . ."

. . . .

"I know old Thurman well. He expected to be President of the United States by passing the Thurman Act, but he was not honored of course. I don't believe he was in earnest. I don't believe he thought the Act was proper. It was a false contract. There was no warrant in law or equity. He turned demagogue for political purposes; . . . I think Thurman is a pretty good liar; lying was his best forte. He is an impressive speaker; he always seems to be so in earnest." (Huntington manuscript, p. 24–25, 76–77.)

It may throw some light upon the attitude of the Huntington group toward the Thur-

Letters such as those quoted display the state of mind of the Central Pacific associates during the months when the Thurman bill was under discussion. It was perhaps natural that they should have opposed sinking fund legislation, for this cut into the surplus which the Central Pacific would otherwise have had for dividends, and depressed the price of the railroad's securities. Nor, indeed, was it perfectly clear that the new legislation did not constitute a breach of the contract between the Pacific railroad companies and the government which could be deduced from the Acts of 1862 and 1864. The legislation in these acts had, it is true, reserved to subsequent Congresses the right of amendment and repeal, but it was uncertain, nevertheless, to what extent this right could properly be exercised. On this point a decision of the Supreme Court was had in 1878, upholding the constitutionality of the Thurman Law on broad grounds, but by a divided court.[30]

Charge Against Railroad

The unfortunate fact about the Thurman Act, however, was not that it excited the anger of representatives of the railroad companies to which it applied, but that it proved a failure in its primary purpose of providing for the eventual retirement of the subsidy bonds. But before summarizing the workings of the law in this respect, a word may be said regarding certain disputes which occurred in the course of its administration.

In February, 1881, Thomas French, Auditor of Railroads, made the charge that the Central Pacific was diverting business from the subsidized portions of its line to its leased properties in order to lessen the payments required under the Thurman

---

man Act to remember that the moneys in the sinking funds which the Central Pacific established for the retirement of its own mortgage securities were, at least in part, loaned to the Western Development Company, and used by this company in railroad building in southern California. This was, of course, an ideal arrangement from the point of view of Huntington and his friends.

[30] Sinking Fund Cases, 99 U. S. 700 (1878).

law. The basis for this charge, so far as reported, appeared to lie in the fact that the net earnings of the Central Pacific were decreasing, while those of the Union Pacific were going up. Mr. French suggested that the Pacific railroads be required to contribute up to 50 per cent of net earnings for retirement of the government debt, instead of up to 25 per cent as then required by the law.[31]

Mr. French's suggestion was not adopted, but the government subsequently advanced the claim that it had the right to retain all the compensation for service rendered to the government by the bond-aided companies without regard to the conditions of construction of particular sections of the road. The company took a different view of the matter, but in deference to an opinion of the Attorney-General on this point, the Secretary of the Treasury in 1884 withheld compensation on the entire mileage of the Pacific railroads pending an authoritative decision. The Supreme Court, however, ruled in favor of the companies,[32] and the sums withheld had to be paid over.

In subsequent years the earnings of the portions of the Central and Union Pacific which had received no bond subsidies were credited, in so far as they arose from government business, as a part of the 5 per cent of net earnings which these companies were required to apply to the eventual retirement of the government debt. This meant a considerable amount of bookkeeping, which was increased by other claims of the companies of which no detailed mention is here made. Indeed, when the final settlement was concluded between the Central Pacific and the government, credits to this one company were allowed by the United States to the amount of no less than $1,162,939.48.[33]

---

[31] Report of the Auditor of Railroad Accounts, 1881 (46th Congress, 3d Session, Exec. Doc. No. 87, Serial No. 1978). The same recommendation is contained in the Report of Commissioner of Railroads, 1894, p. 93.

[32] United States v. Central Pacific Railroad Company, 118 U. S. 235 (1886).

[33] 56th Congress, 2d Session, Senate Document No. 227, Serial No. 4043.

Definition of Net Earnings

In addition to the controversy over earnings on government transportation over non-bond-aided lines, there developed a second difference of opinion over the calculation of the net earnings of the Pacific railroads. It has already been observed that the Law of 1862, as interpreted by the Supreme Court, allowed the Pacific railroad companies to charge expenditures for additions and improvements to operating expenses, and thus to reduce their net earnings, upon the size of which the rate of provision for repayment of the government debt depended. The Central Pacific insisted that the same practice was legitimate under the Thurman law. But in this last-named legislation the wording of the clause relating to net earnings had been changed. In 1862 no definition of net earnings had been given. In 1878 it was provided that net earnings should be calculated "by deducting from the gross amount of their [the Pacific railroads'] earnings, respectively, the necessary expenses actually paid within the year in operating the same and keeping the same in a state of repair, and also the sums paid by them respectively within the year in discharge of interest on their first mortgage bonds." This was deliberately intended as an amendment of the Act of 1862. As Mr. Thurman told the Senate, it was his intention to leave the question of the nature of the net earnings, so far as the past was concerned, for the decision of the Supreme Court without any retroactive legislation at all, but to define net earnings for the future.

In spite of the apparently clear wording of the law, and the definite expression of the views of the Senate Committee on the Judiciary at the time the act was passed, the Central Pacific still maintained that it possessed the right to deduct expenditures for improvements and betterments from gross earnings, in the process of arriving at the figure of net earnings upon which its contributions toward the retirement of government indebtedness were in part based. A decision of the Court of Claims and another by the Supreme Court of the United States were necessary before this position was abandoned.[34]

Still other controversies arose between the Union Pacific and the United States government over earnings from the operation of the bridge across the Missouri River between Council Bluffs and Omaha, over receipts from the operation of Pullman cars, and over the payments by the Union and Central Pacific railroads to the Pacific Mail Steamship Company according to the terms of contracts described in a preceding chapter.[35]

Inadequacy of Law

The persistent disputes between the government and the railroad companies over the proper interpretation of the Thurman law made the administration of the statute difficult. The primary defect of the act, however, lay in the fact that the contributions which it compelled the companies to make were too small to provide for the retirement of the subsidy bonds with interest at their maturity. How far the ultimate provision under the law fell short of a proper accumulation may be seen from the table given in the next paragraph, in which the debits and credits on account of the government loan to the Central and Western Pacific railroads are given as of June 30, 1897, six months before the greater part of the subsidy bonds fell due.

According to the Commissioner of Railroads, the account between the United States and the Central Pacific Railroad stood on the 30th of June, 1897, as follows :[36]

---

[34] United States v. Central Pacific Railroad Company, 138 U. S. 84 (1891). See also Annual Report of the Commissioner of Railroads, 1883, p. 428 ff.

[35] 54th Congress, 2d Session, January 11, 1897, Senate Document No. 52, Serial No. 3469.

[36] Annual Report of the Commissioner of Railroads, 1897.

STATEMENT ON THE GOVERNMENT LOAN TO THE CENTRAL
AND WESTERN PACIFIC RAILROADS, AS OF JUNE 30, 1897

Debits:

Principal of subsidy bonds issued............	$27,855,680.00
Interest paid by the United States..........	47,954,139.78
Total debits	$75,809,819.78

Credits:

Applied to bond and interest account:

Transportation	$7,977,535.66
Cash	658,283.26

Applied to sinking fund account:

Transportation	5,027,848.71
Cash	633,992.48
Proceeds of sinking fund investments......	1,683,127.38
Total credits	$15,980,787.49

Balance of debt, June 30, 1897..............	$59,829,032.29
Excess of interest paid by the United States over all credits	$31,973,352.29

The reasons for the inadequacy of the Thurman law were, first, the failure of the net earnings of the Pacific railroads to increase as rapidly as had been expected, and second, the meager results of the sinking fund accumulations. Net earnings were disappointing because of general business conditions, especially after 1893, and because of competition from other transcontinental railroads. The accumulation of the Central Pacific sinking funds proceeded at a slower rate than had been anticipated, for reasons already given. Up to June 30, 1897, the table shows that the total proceeds of sinking fund investments by the Central Pacific Railroad had amounted to only $1,683,-127.28. When it is understood that this was less than a third of the sum which the moneys paid into the sinking fund would have earned if invested promptly and continuously at 6 per cent, the loss which resulted from the purchase of government bonds becomes evident.

After thirty years of contention and nineteen years of operation under the Thurman law, the accumulated reserve for the retirement of the subsidy bonds was less than $16,000,-000, of which only $7,300,000 was the result of the Thurman sinking fund. On June 30, 1897, the United States had actually paid out in interest on its bonds issued in aid of the Central Pacific Railroad, $31,000,000 more than had been provided against both the interest and the principal of the debt. Except to the extent of $7,300,000, the problem remained substantially as it had been presented in 1878.

CHAPTER XXI

FINAL SETTLEMENT OF THE CENTRAL PACIFIC INDEBTEDNESS TO THE GOVERNMENT

Refunding Proposals

It is the purpose of the present chapter to describe proposals for the settlement of the government's claims against the Central Pacific Railroad which were made between 1878 and the date of maturity of the subsidy bonds, and to explain in some detail the adjustment finally arrived at in 1899.

Soon after it became apparent that the Thurman law would not provide adequately for the retirement of the federal subsidy bonds at their maturity, agitation began for other and more stringent arrangements. As early as 1882, the Commissioner of Railroads suggested that the indebtedness of the Pacific railroads be changed from a running book account and that there be a settlement and actual delivery of interest-bearing bonds for the amount found to be due upon a convenient day, say July 1, 1883. On this day he proposed that the companies should deliver to the government 100 redemption bonds, each representing a hundredth part of the indebtedness. One bond was to fall due thereafter every six months, and interest was to accrue as before upon the unpaid bonds outstanding.[1]

Five years later the United States Pacific Railway Commission, in an important report, recommended also that the net indebtedness of the Central Pacific Railroad Company be ascertained as of a certain date—this time as of July 1, 1888—and that arrangements be made to fund the amount so determined into new railroad fifty-year 3 per cent bonds, which should be made a lien upon all the property which the Central

---

[1] Annual Report of the Commissioner of Railroads, 1882, p. 440.

Pacific owned or in which it had an interest.[2] Congress was not ready, however, to refund the Pacific railroad debts upon the terms proposed either by the Commissioner of Railroads or by this special body of experts.

The next official report was that issued by a select committee to which the United States Pacific Railway Commission report was referred. This committee report was known as the Frye-Davis report, from the names of the Senators who transmitted the sections dealing with the Union and Central Pacific railroads, respectively. The committee was instructed to, and did, personally examine the roads of the Union, Kansas, Central, and Western Pacific Railroad companies, together with that of the Central Branch Union Pacific. It further prepared a plan for refunding the Pacific railroad debt.

So far as the Central Pacific was concerned, the committee proposed that the company should pay its debt in seventy-five years from date, with interest at 2 per cent. In view of the serious financial condition of the company, and the alleged necessity of building several bridges and some additional mileage in California, 1 per cent of the 2 per cent was to be capitalized for ten years. During the first ten years the company's annual payment was thus to be from $600,000 to $650,000 per year; after that time it was to be about $1,400,000 annually. The Frye-Davis committee therefore required a smaller payment and contemplated a longer extension of time than did the United States Pacific Railway Commission. Like its predecessor, it demanded from the Central Pacific, as security, a mortgage on all the roads and property of every name and description which the Central Pacific possessed, including a mortgage on the whole road from four miles west of Ogden to San José. This mortgage was to include the lease of the Central Pacific to the Southern Pacific, and there was now in-

---

[2] United States Pacific Railway Commission Report, December 1, 1887 (50th Congress, 1st Session, Senate Executive Documents No. 51, Serial No. 2505).

serted a provision that the rental paid by the latter should never be less than the sums that the bill called for from the Central Pacific, thus making the Southern Pacific in effect a guarantor of the arrangement.[3]

Further Reports

In 1894 still another report was rendered, this time by James Reilly, of Pennsylvania, from the House Committee on Pacific Railroads. The report reviewed briefly the history of the relations between the Pacific railroads and the government. It was opposed to foreclosure. Instead, it suggested that the debt due to the United States be calculated as of January 1, 1895, and be funded into railroad 3 per cent bonds. The companies were then to begin paying on the debt at the rate of one-half of 1 per cent semiannually, for a period of ten years, commencing on the 1st of July, 1895. For the next period of ten years, three-quarters of 1 per cent was to be paid; for the next period 1 per cent; and so continuing that the railroad bonds, and therefore the principal of the debt, should be wiped out in fifty years. Meanwhile the railroads were to pay off their first mortgage bonds, leaving the new funding bonds a prior lien upon the property of the companies, including both the aided and the non-aided portions. Nothing was done with this report except to submit it.[4]

As the period when the greater part of the subsidy bonds were to mature approached, committee reports upon the Pacific railway debts multiplied. On the 28th of January, the Committee on Pacific Railroads submitted a long discussion through Senator Brice, of Ohio. The committee was opposed to government operation and pessimistic about the results of a foreclosure sale. It recommended that the subsidy bonds be re-

---

[3] Frye-Davis Report (51st Congress, 1st Session, February 17, 1890, Senate Report No. 293, Serial No. 2703). See also speech by Senator Frye, *ibid.*, Congressional Record, p. 1377 *ff.*

[4] Reilly Report (53d Congress, 2d Session, July 21, 1894, House Report No. 1290, Serial No. 3272).

funded for such a period and at such a rate of interest as should enable the companies, under ordinary circumstances and business conditions, to meet the current interest and a portion of the principal of the debt each year.

Powers Bill

On April 25, 1896, Mr. Powers, of Vermont, in behalf of the House Committee on Pacific Railroads, presented a bill and a report to accompany it. The House committee now definitely proposed that the Pacific railroad companies issue, and that the government accept, bonds equal in amount to the whole balance due the United States, and bearing interest at 2 per cent, payable semiannually. These bonds were to be secured by second mortgages, which were to embrace not only the subsidized parts of the Pacific railroads, but also all the other railroads, terminals, lands, and equipments belonging to the companies, to which the lien of the government did not then extend. It was provided that the companies should make annual payments on account of the principal of the bonds—smaller payments during the earlier, and larger payments during the later years—in such fashion that the debt would be repaid in about eighty-five years.

In addition to providing the government with the additional security which came from extending the lien of its second mortgage bonds, the Powers bill required, as one of the terms of the settlement, that the lease of the Central Pacific Railroad to the Southern Pacific Company should be so modified as to require, first, that the Southern Pacific Company guarantee the full payment of the obligations imposed upon the Central Pacific by the new legislation so long as it should remain lessee of the property; and second, that if the Southern Pacific Company should consent to the termination of the lease before the maturity of all instalments payable under the act, it should in that event guarantee the payment by the Central Pacific of

all required payments.   In case of any abrogation or termination of the lease, the principal of all bonds issued under the
act was, at the option of the President of the United States,
immediately to mature.[5]

The Powers bill was debated in the House of Representatives from January 7 to January 11, 1897. It was supported
by the friends of the railroad companies, doubtless because of
the long period over which the railroad debt was to be extended
and the low rates of interest on the refunding bonds. It was
opposed by anti-railroad men, and by those who thought the
bargain a bad one for the government from a business point
of view, and it was finally defeated because Congress was
unwilling to extend the government loan at 2 per cent for
eighty-five years until more convinced of the necessity of compromise.[6]

Additional Schemes

Four days after the submission of the Powers report and
its accompanying bill, a report was presented to the Senate by
Mr. Gear, of Iowa, which recommended the passage of a substantially identical statute.[7] Nothing was done with this report, nor with a suggestion which Mr. Gear made in January
that the whole matter be referred to a commission to be appointed for the purpose.

The submission of the Gear report brings the account of
the negotiations for the settlement of the Pacific railroads' indebtedness down to the spring of 1897. Four Congressional

---

[5] Powers Report (54th Congress, 1st Session, April 25, 1896, H. R. Report No. 1497,
Serial No. 3462).   The Powers bill also required the consent of the Southern Pacific to the
appropriation for payment of Central Pacific indebtedness, of the sum of $2,409,818.20,
which stood credited on the books of the United States Treasury to the Central Pacific for
services on non-aided lines.   The consent of the Southern Pacific was necessary for this
appropriation because a considerable portion of the amount in question had been adjudged
by the Court of Claims to be due to the Southern Pacific for the reason that the services for
which the sums mentioned were credited had been in large part performed by that company.

[6] The Powers bill was finally defeated—yeas, 103; nays, 168; not voting, 84. (54th
Congress, 2d Session, Congressional Record, p. 689.)

[7] Gear Report, 1896 (54th Congress, 1st Session, May 1, 1896, Senate Report No. 778,
Serial No. 3365; The House bill was numbered H. R. 8189; the Senate bill S. 2894).

committees had reported up to this time. Of these, two had recommended that the subsidy bonds be refunded at the rate of 3 per cent for fifty years, and two that they be refunded at the rate of 2 per cent for seventy-five years or more. All four had proposed an improvement of the government's security by extending the government lien to cover the non-aided portions of the Pacific railroads, and in addition to this the Reilly bill had provided that the government should secure a first lien upon the railroad property in question by paying off the underlying bonds.

It would be possible to lengthen the list of suggestions for the repayment of the subsidy bonds which were made during the eighties and the nineties, by including schemes elaborated by other persons than members of Congress and presented in other ways than through formal reports of Congressional committees to the legislature. This will not be done to any great extent because of limitations of time and space. While, however, the greater part of outside comment upon various pending refunding bills must be omitted, it is important to remember that the discussion outside of Congress, especially during the nineties, was quite as active as that within, and that it was conducted with great bitterness of feeling and freedom of expression. Indeed, the extreme contentions on either side are quite inadequately set forth in the Congressional debates.

Railroad Proposals

The general railroad position with respect to the repayment of the subsidy bonds was that the entire debt to the government should be remitted.[8] Failing this, the companies contended that the government should satisfy its claim by taking back a portion of the railroad land grant. If the United States should be indisposed to resume the land grant, then Mr. Stanford suggested that the government should take up all the liens

---

[8] United States Pacific Railway Commission, pp. 3589–90, letter from A. N. Towne.

on the Central Pacific Railroad prior to the subsidy bonds, and in lieu of them issue government bonds bearing interest at the rate of 2 per cent. The saving to the company, due to the reduction in the interest rate on first mortgage bonds from 6 to 2 per cent, would enable it to pay off its indebtedness to the government, sufficient time being given and a moderate rate of interest allowed.[9] In case even this settlement were rejected, it was proposed that the government refund the subsidy bonds by a new issue, running 100 or 125 years, and bearing interest at the rate of 2 per cent.[10]

In opposition to the railroad proposals, western shippers, who represented the extreme anti-railroad sentiment, violently objected to a refunding bill of any description. It was the belief of California men that a refunding bill would simply saddle the railroad debt upon the shipping public. For the railroad would make the necessary annual payments for interest and sinking fund from the proceeds of rates, which would necessarily be paid by the shipper. As able a man as John T. Doyle, of San Francisco, maintained, moreover, that refunding was unnecessary, because it would be found that the assets of the Central Pacific would be adequate on foreclosure sale to meet both its first and its second mortgage obligations. In saying this, Mr. Doyle relied upon the ability of the government to hold directors of the Central Pacific personally liable for misappropriation of funds, as well as upon alleged illegalities in the issue of first mortgage bonds, and upon the chance that the courts would consider the San Francisco terminals of the Western Pacific, together with other miscellaneous property, subject to the lien of the government mortgage, although the property was not "bond-aided" in a narrow sense.[11]

---

[9] Frye-Davis Report (51st Congress, 1st Session, February 17, 1890, Senate Report No. 293, p. 76, Serial No. 2703).

[10] *San Francisco Examiner*, February 18 and March 15, 1890.

[11] Memorial of the committee of fifty appointed at the San Francisco mass meeting of December 7, 1895.

Pacific Coast Agitation

As an example of the feeling in the West concerning the policy of refunding, particular reference may be made to expressions of opinion in the city of San Francisco. In May, 1894, a mass meeting of citizens of San Francisco elected a committee of three to proceed to Washington and to oppose the funding of the debt of the Central Pacific Railroad to the United States. In a memorial addressed to the Senate and House of Representatives, and designed to oppose the Huntington scheme of a long-time extension of the subsidy bonds at a low rate of interest, this committee said:

> In the name of the people of San Francisco, of California, and of the whole Pacific Coast, we protest against the acceptance by Congress of a plan which will keep more than $77,000,000 of the public's money from being paid to the United States Treasury, and which will secure in their present wrongful possession of that sum, besides promoting their other selfish and unpatriotic schemes, men who have for thirty years been wrecking a railroad, defrauding the Government, corrupting public morals, plundering and oppressing the people, and violating every principle of business probity, of law, right, justice, and public policy.

Another meeting, held in the Metropolitan Temple, in San Francisco, on June 19, 1894, called on the state conventions of both parties to introduce into their platform resolutions against the funding of the debt of the Central Pacific Railroad Company to the United States at the rate of 2 per cent per annum for one hundred years, at a rate of 4 per cent per annum for fifty years, or at any other percentage, or during any other period. Under the leadership of the eccentric Adolph Sutro, this meeting adopted an arraignment of the Southern Pacific which was almost inarticulate in its denunciation. It was charged that:

> This monopoly has spread a black cloud over the surface of the State. It has manœuvred through a large number of

corporations, of which the Southern Pacific Company of Kentucky is now the center. It has seduced and drawn into its service many prominent men, whose Americanism and integrity were not equal to their brains. It has antagonized the people, minimized immigration, choked enterprise, and, in this unrelenting attack, has used the supposed representatives of the people in each department of the government, Municipal, State, and National. It has controlled legislation, executive action and the administration of justice. It has discriminated in freights and fares and, at every station on its many thousands of miles of railroad, maintained a Custom House of its own.

This was followed on June 29 by a telegram, signed by Sutro and addressed to Grover Cleveland, advising the President that history would record him as the greatest benefactor of the American people if he would recommend the foreclosure of the mortgages on the Pacific railroads and the purchase of these railroads by the government at foreclosure sale. It was Sutro's idea that the government should hold the transcontinental lines as a great national highway, and permit all American railroads to run their locomotives and cars over it under payment of tolls to be regulated by the Treasury Department.

During the summer of 1894 the *San Francisco Examiner* circulated a petition against the Reilly funding bill, to which, by September 20, it was said that 194,663 names had been attached.[12] In January, 1895, both the Colorado and the California legislatures adopted resolutions opposing the refunding. In California there was not a dissenting vote. The same month another mass meeting was held in San Francisco, and in December, 1895, still another one followed, with the result that a committee of fifty was appointed, and a recommendation sent to the national government.

The San Francisco agitation in 1894 and 1895 was addressed to the comparatively moderate provisions of the

---

[12] *San Francisco Examiner*, September 21, 1894.

Reilly bill, proposing the refunding of the government debt for fifty years at 3 per cent. In 1896, when the more liberal Powers bill was under discussion, the agitation revived. At this time Mayor Sutro, of San Francisco, made an unsuccessful attempt to persuade the people of Kentucky to repeal the charter of the Southern Pacific Company. Although this particular move met with no success, a state anti-funding convention was held at the Metropolitan Temple in San Francisco on January 18, 1896, a new committee was appointed, and a new memorial was framed.

This memorial reiterated and reinforced most of the arguments presented in the memorial of the committee of fifty. It dwelt on the alleged frauds of the Central Pacific and Southern Pacific companies, the uncertainty as to the extent of the property of these corporations, and as to the validity of certain liens against them. The whole matter, the memorial urged, was distinctly one for judicial investigation. It urged that the government let foreclosure take its course. The Central Pacific should not be allowed to confirm possession of money it might have stolen. It was sound policy, the memorial agreed, to make sure that the company really had not enough to pay its debts, and to this end to see that transferred, withdrawn, and stolen assets were restored. Agitation along these same lines continued through 1896, and in January of the following year the legislature adopted a resolution opposing refunding and calling for foreclosure if necessary.[13]

Different Points of View

The fundamental difference between the sentiment in Congress in 1897 and that on the Pacific Coast was that the legislature at Washington addressed itself to Pacific railroad legislation with the object of recovering as much of the government's advances to the Pacific railroads as was possible under

---

[13] Laws of California, 1897, p. 581.   Joint Resolution, adopted January 8, 1897.

the circumstances. The gains sought were primarily financial. In California, on the other hand, public sentiment was more concerned with railroad service and railroad rates than with finance. And this was a principal reason for the insistence upon foreclosure and the equanimity with which government operation was regarded. That the difference between the two points of view was not more fully appreciated was doubtless because the necessity of shaping its arguments so as to influence Congress led the Pacific Coast to talk in terms of finance, even when they thought in terms of monopoly. So much must be understood in order that the animus behind the San Francisco agitation may be clear.

From the point of view of Congress, the weakness of the government's position in 1897 lay in the fact that its debt was secured by a second mortgage, and a mortgage which covered, at that, only a portion of the road. There seems to have been substantial unanimity of opinion among official representatives of the government after 1882 and 1883, that the bond-aided parts of the Pacific railroads would not bring at a forced sale a sufficient price to cover both the first and the second mortgage liens upon them. In fact, it was believed that if the Pacific railroad property should be put up at foreclosure sale, no bidder would appear except the Huntington-Stanford interest, and perhaps the Union Pacific Railway. Under these circumstances the price obtained was sure to be low, and it was not unlikely that the result of the sale would be to leave the railroad in the hands of its original owners free from all obligations to the government. "These very men whom you are now scolding about," said Mr. Powers, of Vermont, in 1897, "the very men who own the terminals and own these connecting lines are the only ones who can safely bid on the property, and probably they will be the only bidders. They would get the property at their own figures." [14]

---

[14] 54th Congress, 2d Session, January 7, 1897, Congressional Record, p. 559.

Stockholders' Liability

It is true that there were two possibilities that improved the government's position slightly. The first was found in the suggestion that directors or stockholders of the Central Pacific might in some way be held individually responsible for the debts of the company. If this could be done, the great wealth of the Stanford-Huntington group made the resource a substantial asset. It was pointed out by anti-railroad men that the Central Pacific was a California corporation, and that under California law each stockholder of a railroad corporation was liable, in proportion to the stock owned and held by him, for all its debts and liabilities. Moreover, the directors of the Central Pacific were said to be liable as directors because of the diversion of Central Pacific funds to the payment of dividends at a time when the company owed the government and its first mortgage bondholders large sums which it was unable to pay. In addition the directors were charged with illegal use of Central Pacific money in the construction of the Southern Pacific Railroad.

Unfortunately for the government, the United States Supreme Court squarely refused to entertain the notion that Central Pacific stockholders were individually liable for repayment of advances which the United States had made to that company. Individual liability depends upon express statutory prescription, and no word upon this point was to be found in the federal laws of 1862 and of 1864. While California railroad stockholders were undoubtedly personally liable to some degree for the debts of California corporations, yet the state law which established this liability was held not to apply to the debt due to the United States. The terms of liability as regards this debt were to be sought, according to the Supreme Court, in the Congressional enactment, and there only. It was said that any other ruling would not only lack solid legal foundation, but would have the unfortunate effect of imposing a heavier burden upon stockholders of the Central Pacific than upon those of the Union Pacific.[15]

Lien of Subsidy Bonds

A second possibility which might have strengthened the government's claim that the lien of the subsidy bonds might be held to extend to the non-bond-aided portions of the Central Pacific as well as to those portions for the construction of which the government had given aid. This was also the contention of Mr. Doyle, of San Francisco. The point was of the highest importance, because if it were denied, the government possessed a mortgage upon only the trunk lines of the Pacific railroads. It had no interest in, and could by foreclosure secure no control over any branches, or over the principal terminals. On the Central Pacific it could acquire by judicial sale only 860 miles from a total of 1,360, and on the Union Pacific 1,532 miles from a total of 7,944. The bond-aided portions of the Central Pacific reached neither Oakland nor San Francisco.[16]

In order to understand the relation of the subsidy bonds to the non-aided portions of the Central Pacific, it is necessary to refer for a moment to the terms of the Pacific railroad legislation. The clauses of the Act of 1862 which relate to the lien of the subsidy bonds of the Central Pacific were to be found in Section 5 of that law. They provided as follows, namely, that:

> ... the issue of said bonds and delivery to the company shall ipso facto constitute a first mortgage on the whole line of the railroad and telegraph, together with the rolling stock, fixtures and property of every kind and description, and in consideration of which said bonds may be issued; and on the refusal or failure of said company to redeem said bonds, or any part of them, when required so to do by the Secretary of

---

[15] United States v. Stanford, 161 U. S. 412 (1896). The United States sued the Stanford estate in this case for $15,237,000.

[16] See Annual Report of the Commissioner of Railroads, 1892, p. 141.

the Treasury, in accordance with the provisions of the act, the said road, with all the rights, functions, immunities, and appurtenances thereunto belonging, and also all lands granted to the said company by the United States, which, at the time of said default, shall remain in the ownership of the said company, may be taken possession of by the Secretary of the Treasury, for the use and benefit of the United States.[17]

By the Act of July 2, 1864, the lien of the subsidy bonds was subordinated to that of first mortgage bonds which the company was then authorized to issue, but no other change in the underlying security was made.[18]

The meaning of Section 5 of the Act of 1862, as amended, was considered by the United States Supreme Court in 1878 in a case brought against the Kansas Pacific Railway to recover 5 per cent of the net earnings of the Kansas Pacific, payment of which was required by Section 6 of the same act. In these matters the Kansas Pacific and the Central Pacific were subject to the same requirements. It appeared that the Kansas Pacific had received subsidy bonds for 393 15/16 miles of line, from the Missouri River to the hundredth meridian, but had actually constructed 637 miles, reaching as far west as Denver. The question arose as to whether the company was responsible to the government for 5 per cent of its net earnings on the whole mileage, or only for 5 per cent on 393 15/16 miles. Upon this point the Supreme Court ruled that "the subsidy bonds granted to the company, being granted only in respect to the original road, terminating at the hundredth meridian, are a lien on that portion only; and that the five per cent of the net earnings is only demandable on the net earnings of said portion." [19]

Provision in Thurman Law

The decision in the Kansas case clearly meant that the lien of the subsidy bonds authorized by the Act of 1862 did not

---

[17] 12 United States Statutes 489 (1862).   [18] 13 United States Statutes 356 (1864).
[19] United States v. Kansas Pacific Railway Company, 99 U. S. 455 (1878). See also United States v. Denver Pacific Railway Company, 99 U. S. 460 (1878).

extend to the non-bond-aided portions of the Central Pacific or to similar sections of any of the other Pacific railroads. This appears to be a conclusive answer to the later government argument, so far as the Act of 1862 is concerned. The legislation of 1862 was, however, amended in 1878, as we have seen in the previous chapter. Section 9 of the Thurman law read as follows:

> That all sums due to the United States from any of said companies respectively, whether payable presently or not, and all sums required to be paid to the United States or into the Treasury, or into said sinking fund under this act, or under the acts hereinbefore referred to, or otherwise, are hereby declared to be a lien upon all the property, estate, rights, and franchises of every description granted or conveyed by the United States to any of said companies respectively or jointly, and also upon all the estate and property, real, personal, and mixed, from whatever source derived, subject to any lawfully prior or paramount mortgage lien, or claim thereon.[20]

A comparison of the Thurman law with the Act of 1862 shows that the later law expressly extended the lien of the subsidy bonds to all Pacific railroad property "from whatever source derived," instead of limiting the lien to property "in consideration of which said bonds may be issued." It does not appear that this change was particularly considered in the debates on the Thurman bill. Mr. Thurman himself did not mention Section 9 in his opening address, and while members of the Senate discussed at length the power of Congress to alter, amend, or repeal the Act of 1862, they usually had in mind the sinking fund provisions of the Thurman law and not those relating to the lien of the subsidy bonds. The exception to this statement is to be found in a colloquy between Mr. Dawes, of Massachusetts, and Mr. Edmunds, of Vermont. Mr. Dawes called attention on April 3 to the sweeping nature

---

[20] 20 United States Statutes 56 (1878).

of the amendment contained in Section 9. He was of the opinion that in 1862 Congress never undertook to put a mortgage on anything except that which they granted to the railroad. Under the Thurman Act, however, he understood that all subsequently acquired property was also to be pledged, with the effect, Mr. Dawes added, that, among other results, all payment of dividends would become illegal.

To this criticism Senator Edmunds replied that the Act of 1862 already subjected all the property of the Pacific railroads to the lien of the subsidy bonds. It was the view of the Senator from Vermont that the words "in consideration of which said bonds may be issued" did not have the limiting effect in the Act of 1862 which Mr. Dawes ascribed to them, but rather that they conveyed the idea, with other words in the same clause, that the Secretary of the Treasury might from time to time issue bonds of the United States in consideration of the fact, which the law declared, that every particle of the property of the Pacific companies, real and personal, franchises, tolls, and everything else, were the security upon which the bonds were to be a lien.[21] Subsequent discussion did not serve to clear up the differences in interpretation brought out in the Congressional debate, but the later decision of the Supreme Court showed that, in the principal matter at issue, Mr. Dawes was right.

We may say with some confidence that the nature of the lien of the second mortgage subsidy bonds of the United States depended, under the Thurman Act, upon the power of Congress to alter, amend, and repeal the terms of the Acts of 1862 and 1864 in respect to the security provided for the government loan.

Court Decisions

Now on the question of the meaning of the "saving clause" in the Act of 1864, the courts had not in 1897, and still have

---

[21] 45th Congress, 2d Session, April 3, 1878, Congressional Record, p. 2229.

not, satisfactorily passed. That the clause did not authorize unlimited changes in the provisions of existing legislation was evident. The majority of the Supreme Court expressed the view in the sinking fund cases that the reserved power could not be used to undo what had already been done or to unmake contracts which had already been made, but that Congress could provide for what should be done in the future, and might even direct what preparation should be made for the due performance of contracts already entered into.[22] Under this interpretation the Supreme Court upheld the clauses in the Thurman law which required the Pacific railroads to pay certain moneys into a sinking fund.

The same court in 1895 decided that a federal act which required bond-aided railroads to operate their own telegraph lines was a legitimate amendment of the clause of the Act of 1862 which authorized these companies to enter into agreements with specified private corporations for the rendering of telegraph service.[23]

Again, in Menotti v. Dillon (1897), the court approved an amendment to the land-grant provisions of the Act of 1862 designed to quiet litigation in land cases in California;[24] and in Union Pacific v. Mason City and Fort Dodge, it sustained a law of 1871 which authorized the Union Pacific to issue bonds for the construction of a bridge across the Missouri River at Omaha, but required the company to permit the trains of all railroads terminating at the Missouri River at Omaha to use the new bridge up to a fair limit of its capacity and on payment of a reasonable compensation.[25]

None of these cases, however, can fairly be taken as precedents for so radical an alteration in a bargain made as would

---

[22] Sinking Fund Cases, 99 U. S. 700, 721.
[23] United States v. Union Pacific Railway Company and Western Union Telegraph Company, 160 U. S. 1 (1895).
[24] Menotti v. Dillon, 167 U. S. 703 (1897).
[25] Union Pacific Railroad Company v. Mason City and Fort Dodge Railroad Company, 199 U. S. 160 (1905).

have been produced by an extension of the lien of the subsidy bonds to non-aided portions of the Pacific railroads. On this precise point the nearest approach to a decision is found in a dictum growing out of litigation under the Thurman law with respect to the proper handling of compensation for government services. As explained in the previous chapter, the government contended at one time that all compensation for services rendered to the government by the Central Pacific Railroad should be paid into a sinking fund for the eventual retirement of the subsidy bonds or should be applied in liquidation of interest on these bonds, whether these services were rendered on bond-aided or on non-bond-aided portions of the company's lines. When this contention reached the Supreme Court it was rejected, on the ground that the Thurman Act, properly interpreted, applied only to the bond-aided lines.

The court went on to remark, moreover, that the construction which the government here sought to place upon the law would not only render the second section of the Thurman Act a breach of faith on the part of the United States, but would make it an invasion of the constitutional rights of the railroad company.[26] This indicates that the court would not have approved a law which clearly compelled the Central Pacific to turn over to the government the compensation for the transportation of government troops and supplies earned over sections of its lines which had not received a subsidy in government bonds. If this really represented the attitude of the court, then it seems still more unlikely that an attempt to extend the lien of subsidy bonds to these same non-bond-aided sections would have been sustained.

Critical Situation

It is reasonable to suppose that the repeated discussion of refunding plans in Washington was due to the fact that Con-

---

[26] United States v. Central Pacific Railroad Company, 118 U. S. 235 (1886).

gress was of the opinion that a rigid insistence by the government upon its legal rights would result in a minimum rather than a maximum recovery from the Pacific railroads. At the same time, the shrewder heads in the legislature were perhaps hopeful that results might be obtained by negotiation which could not be secured by legal proceedings. Hence the refusal to approve of any specific plan for the settlement of the debt.

In the year 1897 the pending maturity of the United States subsidy bonds made the situation too critical for action to be much further delayed. On March 4, 1897, the 54th Congress and the second administration of President Cleveland came to an end, and the administration of President McKinley began. A special session of Congress, called by the new President, convened on March 15. During this session Mr. Gear introduced a bill for the appointment of a commission to settle the debt of the Central Pacific and Western Pacific railroads to the government.[27] This bill failed to pass. In December, 1897, the first regular session of the 55th Congress convened. By this time the maturity of a large portion of the subsidy bonds was distant only a few weeks. That is to say, the bonds issued to the Central and Western Pacific railroads matured as follows:

January 16, 1895	$	2,362,000
" 1, 1896		1,600,000
" 1, 1897		2,432,000
" 1, 1898		10,614,120
" 1, 1899		10,847,560

About $2,000,000 of these bonds were held in the sinking fund established by the Thurman Act. These had naturally been canceled as they fell due. On December 21, 1896, moreover, most of the remaining bonds held by the government in the Central Pacific sinking fund had been sold and the proceeds applied to maturing indebtedness.[28]

[27] Gear Report, 1897, 55th Congress, 1st Session, April 8, 1897 (Senate Report No. 20, Serial No. 3569).

[28] Commercial and Financial Chronicle, Vol. 63, p. 1114.

These resources, together with the credits in the Central Pacific bond and interest account, had covered the demands upon the company up to January 1, 1898. Meanwhile coupons on the first mortgage bonds had been regularly paid, and arrangements had been made with first mortgage bondholders to extend the maturity of each instalment until January 1, 1898, at which date first mortgage bonds of the Central Pacific Railroad Company to the amount of $25,883,000 were to mature. First mortgage bonds of the Western Pacific Railroad, aggregating $1,970,000, matured on July 1, 1899. It was evident that all available Central Pacific resources would be exhausted by the 1st of January, 1898.

Negotiations Initiated

In the face of what amounted to a real crisis, involving not only the possibility of loss to the government, but also that of serious financial injury to private interests connected with the Pacific railroads, the initiative in seeking a compromise was now taken by the banking firm of James Speyer and Company, of New York, through which a large amount of Central Pacific securities had been marketed. Mr. Speyer felt responsibility in the matter because so many of his clients were involved. He later testified:

> I think it naturally suggested itself to us as bankers, having sold such a large amount of securities and the company being threatened with bankruptcy, we naturally sat up nights thinking how we could save it, because these bonds were all out, all over Europe, and stock too; and we tried to find some means to work it out so that these people would not lose their money. So that I think that originally when this debt came nearer and nearer, when it got so that it became a threatening thing to the Central Pacific security holders, we naturally began to look around to see how we could stave off receivership and bankruptcy.[29]

---

[29] United States v. Southern Pacific Company, pp. 1200–1201, testimony James Speyer.

There were also certain strategic considerations which had weight at this time.   These affected the dominant interests in the Southern Pacific particularly.   In spite of the apparently indifferent attitude of the Stanford-Huntington group, these gentlemen could not have been, and were not, blind to the fact that a receivership for the Central Pacific opened possibilities of disaster, not only for the Central Pacific itself, but also for the Southern Pacific, in which their main interest then lay. Such a receivership, if followed by a foreclosure sale, would have wiped out the last vestiges of the Stanford-Huntington stock holdings in the Central Pacific Railroad and would in all probability have eliminated also the lease of the Central Pacific to the Southern Pacific.   This suggested the possibility of a severe competition for Pacific Coast business, from which the Southern Pacific could scarcely have escaped unscathed. The whole future control of the railroad systems of the South West was clearly at stake.

It appears that Mr. Speyer took the matter up with Mr. Huntington,[30] probably early in 1898.   Mr. Huntington was receptive and the subject was then discussed with representatives of the government.   At an early stage in the negotiations President McKinley was consulted.   The matter was one deemed of great importance to the government; in fact, in January, 1898, the President directed the Attorney-General to give immediate attention to the Pacific railroad debts, to take every means necessary, and to spend as much money as should be needed in order to enforce the government's lien.[31]   In later proceedings Mr. Griggs, the Attorney-General, and Mr. Gage, Secretary of the Treasury, took an active part.   Mr. McKinley continued to follow the negotiations, and was about as well informed as any of the others as to how matters were getting on. Elihu Root was employed by the Attorney-General as special

---

[30] United States v. Southern Pacific Company, p. 1201, testimony James Speyer.
[31] *Ibid.*, p. 993, testimony John W. Griggs.

counsel.[32]   In short, the administration responded cordially to the initiative of the railroad and banking group.

Government Commission

While negotiations were going on, Congress passed the Act of July 7, 1897.   This act appointed the Secretary of the Treasury, the Secretary of the Interior, and the Attorney-General a commission with full power to settle the indebtedness to the government growing out of the issue of bonds in aid of the Central Pacific and Western Pacific bond-aided railroads.   The commission was required to submit any settlement made to the President for his approval, and it was forbidden to accept a less sum in settlement of the debt due the United States than the full amount of the principal and interest of the subsidy bonds.   It was empowered to grant an extension of time for repayment not exceeding ten years, at a rate of interest not less than 3 per cent, and to accept such security as might seem expedient.[33]   So far as the commission was concerned, this was Mr. Gear's proposal of the previous year.

It seems probable that negotiations had already reached an advanced stage before the Act of July 7 was passed.   Mr. Griggs was later of the impression that the act was drawn and passed to fit a tentative agreement which had already been made.[34]   If such were the case the willingness of Congress to entrust the matter to the executive branch of the government, after having once refused to do so, may be explained.   Possibly, also, the fact that the Union Pacific had been sold at foreclosure on November 1, 1897, for $58,448,223.75, a sum sufficient to cover the full amount of both first and second mortgage bonds, had weight.[35]

---

[32] United States v. Southern Pacific Company, p. 998, testimony John W. Griggs.

[33] 30 United States Statutes 652, 659 (1898).

[34] United States v. Southern Pacific Company, p. 994, testimony John W. Griggs.

[35] See Report of Attorney-General, 1897, pp. vi–vii; 1898, p. xv. The legislation described was inserted in the Deficiency Appropriation bill on motion of Mr. Gear. The provision requiring full payment within ten years was added on motion of Mr. White, of California. (55th Congress, 2d Session, June 29, 1898, Congressional Record, pp. 6464–65.)

The indebtedness of the Central and Western Pacific railroads to the United States government as of February 1, 1899, was $58,812,715.48. These figures were reached by adding thirty years' interest at 6 per cent to the original loan of $27,-855,680, and by deducting accumulated credits resulting either from the deposits in the sinking fund established by the Thurman law, or from the operation of the bond and interest account originating in the Acts of 1862 and 1864. Comparison of the figure of $58,812,715.48 with the slightly larger amount given in the previous chapter as of June 30, 1897, will show that during the intervening nineteen months the net amount of indebtedness had slightly decreased.

Plan of Settlement

In view of the impending maturity of large quantities of subsidy bonds, the first essential point in the negotiations between Mr. Speyer and the government was necessarily that more time should be allowed the Central Pacific for the payment of its debt. It was agreed that at least certain portions might be extended for as long as ten years. Mr. Speyer was of the opinion that, given this extension, the Central Pacific could repay its debt in full—a striking contrast to the former statements of Central Pacific Railroad men. By paying the debt in full was meant paying with interest on all delayed balances.[36]

In order to cover the matters just referred to, Mr. Speyer agreed in 1898 that the indebtedness of the Central Pacific to the government should be refunded into twenty notes of the railroad company, falling due one every six months, beginning August 1, 1899, and ending February 1, 1909. The notes were to carry interest at 3 per cent per annum, payable semiannually. Taken by itself, this offer was the most liberal that the railroad company had ever made. Yet it represented up to this point only a promise, without security. In order to provide secur-

---

[36] United States v. Southern Pacific Company, p. 1199, testimony James Speyer.

ity, Mr. Speyer proposed an additional arrangement, in two parts.

By the first part of the additional agreement, Speyer and Company undertook to purchase the four Central Pacific notes earliest in point of maturity, and to pay the face value thereof as soon as received from the government. This obligation of a reputable banking house to pay the substantial sum of $11,762,-543.12 was a valuable thing in itself, and materially increased the attractiveness of the whole plan from the government's point of view. In consideration for its advance, Speyer and Company received new first mortgage bonds of the Central Pacific Railroad, of an issue presently to be described. By the second part of the same arrangement, each note remaining in the hands of the government was to be secured by deposit of first refunding 4 per cent gold bonds of the Central Pacific equal in amount to the face of the note.[37]

It will, however, be asked how, in view of the outstanding capitalization of the Central Pacific, it was possible to offer a first mortgage security as collateral for the refunding notes. This was provided for by the further reorganization of the Central Pacific, and by the issue in particular of two new classes of bonds, of which the first was to be a 4 per cent, and the second a 3½ per cent issue, having a first and second mortgage lien, respectively, upon all property of which the Central Pacific was possessed.

Reorganization Proposal

On February 1, 1899, the outstanding debt of the Central Pacific Railroad consisted of the following issues:

Central Pacific Railroad of California, first mortgage bonds $25,881,000
Western Pacific Railroad Company, first mortgage bonds 2,735,000

[37] The exact amount of 4 per cent bonds to be deposited as security was $58,820,000.

Central Pacific Railroad Company (San Joaquin
    Valley branch), first mortgage bonds.......... $ 6,080,000
Central Pacific Railroad Company, land bonds.... 2,134,000
Central Pacific Railroad Company, 50-year 6 per
    cent bonds 56,000
Central Pacific Railroad Company 50-year 5 per
    cent bonds 10,245,000
California and Oregon Railroad Company, and
    Central Pacific Railroad Company, successor,
    first mortgage bonds......................... 10,340,000
                                                    ───────────
    Total $57,471,000

Under the proposed reorganization plan, the aggregate of
$57,471,000 of securities listed was to be retired in exchange
for $51,253,500 in new 4 per cent bonds, $13,695,000 in new
3½ per cent bonds, and $1,987,383.70 in cash. Generally
speaking, the outstanding first mortgage bonds were offered
par in new fours, with a slight bonus in new 3½ per cents.
Junior mortgages received 50 per cent in new fours, and from
70 to 90 per cent in new 3½ per cent securities. After the
retirement of outstanding first mortgages, the 4 per cent bond
issue was then to be increased further by the amount necessary
to provide the government with the collateral stipulated for in
the negotiations. Thus the government was set on a par with
outstanding first mortgage bondholders.

Here, however, was a real difficulty. It was plain that
while the old first mortgage bondholders might consent to the
retirement of the issues which they held by exchange for new
bonds, on the terms stated, they would yet hesitate to allow the
inflation of the first mortgage issue by putting out $58,000,000
first mortgage bonds over and above the amount of their holdings in order to satisfy a government claim hitherto secured
only by a second mortgage lien. It must be remembered that
the reorganization was a voluntary one, requiring for its success the free consent of all parties. Some additional consider-

tion had to be offered at this point in order to satisfy first mortgage bondholders. It was at this juncture that the Southern Pacific Company stepped in, with a guaranty on both the new 4 per cent and the new 3½ per cent issues. The additional security provided by this guaranty was without doubt an element contributing strongly to the successful carrying out of the proposed exchanges. At the same time the guaranty was received with favor by the government, because it increased the government's security as well as that possessed by former bondholders.

In subsequent years there was dispute as to how far the government relied on the Southern Pacific guaranty as an essential element in the security provided for the ultimate repayment of the government loan. Curiously enough, the fact of the guaranty was not mentioned in the original agreement of February 1, 1899, between the Central Pacific and the government, nor was it referred to in the report dated February 15, 1899, which the commissioners appointed to settle the Central Pacific indebtedness made to Congress, nor in the clauses of the refunding mortgage itself. But the testimony of all concerned is that the guaranty was understood to be a vital part of the agreement, and Attorney-General Griggs later went so far as to say that the Central Pacific bonds without the guaranty would not have been acceptable.[38]   When the bonds to which the government was entitled were delivered to the United States Treasury Department, they had indorsed on them in proper form the guaranty of the Southern Pacific Company.

Treatment of Stockholders

In addition to the promises for settlement of the government debt, mention should be made of the allowance made to Central Pacific stockholders in the reorganization plan, and of the provision for cash requirements.

---

[38] United States v. Southern Pacific Company, p. 1000, testimony Griggs.

Some provision for cash requirements is a necessary part of any reorganization plan. In the case of the Central Pacific and Western Pacific, the cash requirements consisted of $11,-762,543.12, which were needed to take up the first four notes issued to the government, and of $9,657,556.88 for new equipment, improvements, and other purposes of the new company, including expenses, commissions, compensation, and similar items incident to the reorganization. Speyer and Company, it will be recalled, had agreed to purchase the first four maturing notes issued to the government. The inclusion of the amount paid for these notes as a cash requirement of the Central Pacific was due to the fact that the money paid by the bankers for this purpose was regarded merely as a loan by the bankers to the railroad company. In all, the sum which it was necessary to raise amounted to $21,420,100. This money was raised by the sale to Speyer and Company, on behalf of a syndicate, of portions of the new 4 per cent and 3½ per cent issues aggregating $12,995,500, and by the issue of $12,000,000 of new preferred stock to the Southern Pacific in exchange for a like amount of that company's 4 per cent bonds. In addition, the Southern Pacific agreed to take up $8,000,000 additional preferred stock of the Central Pacific, as issued, upon the same terms.

As for the common stock of the Central Pacific Railroad, this was exchanged, dollar for dollar, for stock of the Central Pacific Railway Company (new corporation). Such an exchange was the best that stockholders could hope for. At the same time the Southern Pacific, here too, became a factor in the operation, by offering to issue its own stock, dollar for dollar, in exchange for the new stock of the Central Pacific Railway and to add thereto a bonus in the shape of Southern Pacific 4 per cent bonds to the extent of 25 per cent of the new stock issue.

Examination of the elaborate arrangements between the

Central Pacific, the government, and the Southern Pacific in 1899 shows that the last-named company participated in the reorganization plan which has been described to the following extent:

It became guarantor in respect of a bond issue
(new 4 per cent first mortgage) of........ $100,000,000
It became guarantor in respect of a bond issue
(new 3½ per cent second mortgage) of.... 25,000,000
It issued its own bonds for the purchase of
$12,000,000 of the preferred stock of the new
company, in the amount of................ 12,000,000
It agreed as and when required to purchase the
remaining $8,000,000 of the preferred stock
of the new company with bonds in the
amount of 8,000,000
It agreed to issue its bonds as part payment in
the purchase of $67,275,500 of the common
stock of the new Central Pacific Railway in
the amount of 16,819,000
It issued its own stock in partial payment for
$67,275,500 of the common stock of the new
Central Pacific Railway Company in the
amount of 67,275,500

Making a total of assumed liabilities of.. $229,094,500

This was a very substantial contribution for any third party to make to the success of a Central Pacific reorganization plan. True, the Southern Pacific received Central Pacific stock for its cash advance, but the value of this stock at the time was slight. The real consideration which counted with the Southern Pacific was the control of the Central Pacific system.

Execution of Agreement

In carrying out the proposed plan the commission named in the Act of July 7, 1897, reported to Congress under date of February 15, 1899, that an agreement had been reached, and

that the subsidy bonds were to be refunded into twenty notes of
$2,940,635.78 each.   On March 3, 1899, Congress authorized
the Secretary of the Treasury to sell the first four notes in order
that the agreement with Speyer and Company might be carried
out.[39]   These notes were already in the Secretary's hands.
They were duly purchased by the bankers named on March 10
of the same year.   During the summer of 1899, the Central
Pacific Railway was incorporated to succeed the former railroad company, and the various issues called for by the reorganization plan were put forth.   On February 1, 1909, the
last of the refunding notes matured and was duly paid.   The
divorce of the Central and Western Pacific companies from
the government was complete.

To anyone who has followed the long drawn-out discussions between the Central Pacific and the government, the speed
with which the final settlement was made and the favorable
terms which the government secured come as a distinct surprise.
Not once during the twenty years following the passage of the
Thurman Act had it been suggested that the Central Pacific
could meet principal and interest of the government loan on
condition only that it be granted an average extension of five
years on its indebtedness with interest at 3 per cent on delayed
payments.   The result was properly regarded as a triumph for
the administration.

In a measure, also, the settlement justifies in a general way
the entire policy of the administration with respect to the issue
of subsidy bonds to the Central and Western Pacific Railroad
companies.   These subsidy bonds were issued originally for a
well-considered purpose.   The purpose was accomplished, and
repayment of the loan was secured without important delay.
From a business point of view the operation was therefore a
distinct success.   Doubtless there were disadvantages connected with the policy.   Such were the many disputes between

---

[39] 30 United States Statutes 1214, 1245 (1899).

railroad and government, which hampered the railroad in its later development, and occupied the time and energy of public men. Such, also, was the apparent consent which the government yielded to the permanent consolidation of the Central and Southern Pacific companies by its acceptance of the reorganization of 1899. The final price paid by the public was larger than is sometimes appreciated. But the final gain was also very large.

CHAPTER XXII

THE SOUTHERN PACIFIC MERGER CASES

New Era

There is no question that the final separation of the finances of the Central Pacific from those of the United States government was a matter of very great importance to both parties. The direct result was to place the federal government outside the Central Pacific instead of inside it. Instead of holding the dual relation of creditor and regulating body, Congress now stood as regards the Central Pacific in the same position as with respect to every other railroad in the United States—without interest in the company's internal finance, but free to act in the interests of the consuming, shipping, and investing public. This was an immense advantage, both from the point of view of the government and from that of the railroad itself.

The Central Pacific reorganization of 1899, moreover, not only accomplished a desirable change in the external relations of the Huntington lines, but it also brought about a change in the relations between the Central Pacific Railroad and the Southern Pacific Company which was of considerable significance. It will be recalled that from 1885 to the time of the reorganization of the Central Pacific in 1899, these relations had rested upon a leasehold interest only. The insecurity of such a connection had been brought forcibly to the atttention of the Southern Pacific management during the course of the reorganization proceedings. But as a result of the participation of the Southern Pacific in the reorganization which made possible the repayment of the government debt, that company became possessed of the ownership of the entire outstanding Central Pacific common and preferred stock. While such ownership still lacked the completeness which would have followed the assumption of direct title to the Central Pacific road-bed and rolling stock, it was considered satisfactory, and certainly was an improvement from the Southern Pacific's point of view over anything which had gone before.

Separated from all financial connection with the government and with its parts joined together by the double tie of leasehold and stock control, the Central Pacific–Southern Pacific system, on the conclusion of the Central Pacific reorganization of 1899, entered upon a new era which contained possibilities of new policies, and of a sounder and more profitable development than it had yet known. There was, too, one additional circumstance which made it easy for the stockholders of the Southern Pacific in 1900 to embark upon new policies —namely, the death of Mr. Huntington. Of the original associates, Huntington was the last survivor. Mark Hopkins had died in 1878, Charles Crocker in 1888, and Stanford in 1893. For ten years, at least, Huntington had been the active manager of the Southern Pacific properties. Personally, he never owned so much as 50 per cent of the Southern Pacific stock outstanding,[1] but by virtue of the support of the Crocker and the Hopkins interests, he exercised almost undisputed control. Huntington had reached the ripe age of seventy-nine years in 1900, and his death was not unexpected. The effect was none the less great, however, for the passing of Mr. Huntington meant the removal of the last of the men to whom the integrity and independence of the Central and Southern Pacific companies were matters of personal pride.

Purchase of Control by Union Pacific

It was the death of Mr. Huntington, to repeat, which now made possible a very important change in the relations which

---

[1] At his death in August, 1900, Huntington owned 37 1/2 per cent of the stock of the Southern Pacific Company.

the Central Pacific and the Union Pacific railroads bore to each other. While the Union and the Central Pacific roads both owed their existence to the same federal legislation, and while they had been close business associates for over thirty years by virtue of geographical necessity, both had uncompromisingly maintained their independence. Neither Jay Gould, who was long influential in Union Pacific affairs, nor Huntington himself, were men who cared to form part of organizations which they could not control. Moreover, Huntington distrusted Gould. He once wrote Colton that Gould had scared the Kansas Pacific people so that they had let him, Gould, get into bed with them. For his part, he did not intend to follow the Kansas Pacific example. Gould might frighten him so that he would leave the bed, but never so that he would share it. After Gould's death in 1890, the same disinclination to combine persisted. The Huntington group was now powerful, and still unwilling to enter a combination which it could not control. The record shows that proposals were made. The Union Pacific, dependent upon the Central Pacific for direct connection with San Francisco, and fearful lest at Mr. Huntington's death his Southern Pacific stock should fall into unfriendly hands, offered to purchase his shares, or, failing in this, to conclude a permanent alliance. To this offer Mr. Huntington remained indifferent.

Huntington died, however, in August, 1900, leaving his Southern Pacific stock to his widow and nephew in the proportion of two-thirds and one-third, respectively; and both, as had been anticipated, proved willing to dispose of their holdings. Negotiations were carried to completion in February, 1901. Four hundred and seventy-five thousand shares were purchased from the Huntingtons and from Edwin Hawley, the late financier's most intimate business associate, while enough was secured from other parties through Kuhn, Loeb and Company to make an aggregate of 677,700 shares, at an average price of 50.6146. Market quotations were then in the neighborhood of 45. On February 4, Kuhn, Loeb and Company engaged to deliver to the Union Pacific one month later 72,300 additional shares at the same price, plus 4 per cent interest from February 11, bringing the company's holdings up to 750,000 shares.

This, in Mr. Harriman's opinion, was sufficient for control. A year or two later an attempt to force the Southern Pacific to pay in dividends earnings which its managers thought should be expended in improvements led the Union Pacific to acquire 150,000 additional shares. In January, 1910, purchases were renewed for the last time, in view of pending legislation in Congress which promised to make the possession of an absolute majority of Southern Pacific stock desirable; but these purchases ceased after 74,000 shares had been obtained, and 50,000 of these shares were subsequently sold. This concluded the episode. On June 30, 1911, the Union Pacific through the Oregon Short Line owned 1,266,500 shares of Southern Pacific common, or 46 per cent of all outstanding stock— sufficient to give undisputed control.

Harriman System

This purchase by the Union Pacific of a controlling interest in the stock of the Southern Pacific, made the latter a partner in a railroad system of about 18,500 miles, stretching from Omaha, Kansas City, and New Orleans on the east, to Los Angeles, San Francisco, and Portland on the west, and, by means of the Morgan Steamship Line, reaching New York. In addition, the Union Pacific owned a majority of stock in the Pacific Mail Steamship Company, which carried freight and passengers from the Pacific Coast to the Orient and to Panama. Of the total mileage west of the Mississippi-Missouri River and south of the Northern Pacific Railroad, the Harriman management controlled 19 per cent. Finally, through stock ownership in the Illinois Central, the Chicago and Alton, and other lines, and by contract with the San Pedro, Los Angeles, and Salt Lake, it possessed in varying degree influence over connecting and competing roads.

Undoubtedly its association with the Union Pacific increased the prestige of the Southern Pacific Company at the time when the merger took place. The association involved, however, serious dangers, for it placed the credit and the earning power of the Southern Pacific at the disposal of Mr. Harriman for speculative projects in eastern fields, and also it ran counter to a national policy opposed to great accumulations of capital under single control which was presently to become clearly defined. It is true that public hostility toward big business seemed unimportant in 1901 when the Union Pacific and the Southern Pacific first combined, yet the attitude of the courts toward monopoly became a matter for serious consideration by the latter in 1911, ten years after the original merger had taken place, when the federal government attacked the Union Pacific–Southern Pacific consolidation as a combination in restraint of trade under the terms of the Sherman Anti-Trust Act of 1890. A brief discussion of the issues of this extremely important lawsuit is therefore necessary.

There was perhaps some ground for conflicting views with respect to the motive which had induced the Harriman interests to seek control of the Southern Pacific. The obvious explanation of the operation was that the Union Pacific desired to increase its power in the South West. It was stoutly maintained by Mr. Kahn, of Kuhn, Loeb and Company, however, that the desire to control the Southern Pacific line from San Francisco to El Paso was not a motive in the transaction. The necessity of buying the Sunset route, he said, was considered an obstacle and a deterring feature. If a way could have been found to secure the Central Pacific alone, it would have been preferred at the time. The possible reduction of competition was not even considered at any of the meetings of the executive committee at which the subject was brought up. Speaking of the Southern Pacific, Mr. Kahn declared:

> We knew it would require a great deal of money to be spent on it, we knew it added thousands of miles to the burden of administration and management. We were very anxious that the Union Pacific should receive as much of the administrative ability and of the railroad genius of Mr. Harriman as it was possible for him to give it, and we were rather disinclined to put upon him any more burden than was necessary to the best development of the Union Pacific; and therefore we, individually, felt that if the Southern Pacific could be separated, keeping only the Central Pacific and the north and south lines in California, and getting rid of the southern part of the Southern Pacific, we would be getting rid of a nuisance.[2]

Arguments of Railroad Counsel

The contention of the Union Pacific Railroad in 1911 was that the consolidation of the Union Pacific and Southern Pacific properties was legal under the Sherman law irrespective of motive, because the two systems were not competing, and that the government was unable to interfere in any case because the consolidation took place through the means of a purchase of stock instead of by contract or agreement between the railroad corporations concerned. On this last point the railroad also argued that, as a matter of law, ownership by one railroad of another's stock did not constitute control unless a clear majority was held. Control, said counsel, is a matter of power. A minority may direct the operation of a railroad because the majority has confidence in it, but this is lawful. The argument applied to the Southern Pacific case because it was known that

---

[2] Full information with respect to the Union Pacific-Southern Pacific merger case is to be found in the record and briefs submitted to the Supreme Court. The testimony and exhibits in this case fill thirteen volumes, and constitute an important addition to the source material on railroad transportation. The case is discussed in detail in Daggett, "The Decision on the Union Pacific Merger," in *Quarterly Journal of Economics*, February, 1913, and in another article by the same author, entitled "Later Developments in the Union Pacific Merger Case" (*ibid.*, August, 1914).

the Union Pacific possessed only a minority interest in the first-named company.

Apart from this, counsel contended that a purchase of stock was a thing which the federal government could not control, for the reason that the acquisition or disposition of property was not commercial intercourse. "If any citizen should step into a broker's office on Broadway, New York, buy some stock in the Pennsylvania Railroad, pay for it, put the certificates in his pocket, and walk out, would he, or the broker, or the broker's principal, be engaged in commercial intercourse between nations and parts of nations? . . . Would a state corporation buying those certificates be in any different situation from an individual purchaser, if the State of its domicile had endowed it with corporate power to buy stock?"

Moreover, to continue the argument, though purchases of stock were subject to federal law, they would violate no provisions of the Sherman Act. A purchase or sale is not a contract in restraint of trade, for a contract is executory, implying something yet to be done; while a sale is executed, completed when made and because it is made. Nor is a contract in restraint of trade necessarily unlawful. It must be undue, that is, not entered into with the legitimate purpose of reasonably forwarding personal interest and developing trade. The same may be said of an attempt to monopolize. Every act of competition tends to drive competitors out of business, but competition is legal, in the absence of fraud or duress. It follows that an individual may buy out a competitor, and then another competitor, and so on, and a corporation may do the same thing. "It is evident," said Mr. Dunne's brief, "fraudulent, intimidating, coercive, and other like wrongful and unlawful methods apart —that here we touch a fundamental principle of the freedom to buy and sell, of the legal right of the individual in respect to his own property."

Government's Contention of Previous Competition

The arguments of railroad counsel in defense of the Union Pacific–Southern Pacific merger rested predominantly, although not wholly, upon points of law such as have been mentioned. Fundamental as some of these were, the main interest in the case for the ordinary student will be found in the elaborate analysis of the competitive relations between the Southern Pacific and the Union Pacific which the government developed in the course of its argument. So far as the writer is aware, no record has ever been presented to any court in which the nature and extent of the competition between two great railroad systems has been so thoroughly discussed.

In establishing the fact that competition had been active between the Southern Pacific and the Union Pacific before the merger of the two companies in 1901, the government insisted upon the fact that the Central and Southern Pacific managers had continuously diverted all the traffic which they could control to the Sunset route so long as they remained independent of Union Pacific dictation.[3] The government examined no less than seventy witnesses—shippers, Southern Pacific employees and ex-employees, and representatives of independent railroad lines. Among those who testified were Mr. Hawley, for nineteen years eastern agent of the Southern Pacific and afterwards a financier of prominence; Messrs. Stubbs, Spence, and Munroe, of the traffic department of the Southern Pacific; Paul Morton, one-time vice-president of the Equitable Life Assurance Company; Mr. Jeffery, president of the Denver and Rio Grande; and Mr. Hannaford, in charge of traffic on the Northern Pacific.

Substantially all these witnesses testified that traffic from the Atlantic seaboard could move to the Pacific Coast either via the Morgan Steamship Line to New Orleans and thence over the Sunset route of the Southern Pacific to San Francisco, or

---

3 This question of the diversion of business from the central route has been discussed in Chapter XX.

Map showing mileage owned in 1913 by the Central Pacific Railway
and the Southern Pacific Railroad.

via the trunk lines and their connections to Omaha, thence over
the Union Pacific to Ogden and over the Central Pacific to the
coast. Although the Southern Pacific was interested in both
of these routes, it secured all the revenues from freight moving
via the Sunset route, and only 30.1 per cent of the total revenue
from freight delivered to it by the Union Pacific at Ogden.
In consequence, it used its best efforts to influence freight to
travel by the southern line.

The government showed by the evidence of shippers that
freight was actually solicited in competition between the two
Pacific companies. The Southern Pacific, it appeared, took
traffic at New York rates from as far west as Buffalo and
Pittsburgh, not including those cities, and from as far south as
Norfolk. Not only this, but the Union Pacific was not altogether restricted to the route via Ogden. By diverting freight
at Granger and sending it north to Portland over the Oregon
Short Line and the Oregon Railroad and Navigation Company,
it could affect the transcontinental rate in two ways. In the
first place, it was physically possible for traffic to move from
Portland to San Francisco by boat; and in the second place, a
slight reduction in the rate to Portland compelled a cut to every
Pacific terminal point in order to maintain these different cities
in the same relative position for the distribution of eastern
goods. As Mr. Stubbs expressed it, "Let the rate be cut on the
Great Northern, and it goes down to the Gulf of California."

Mention may also be made of the route via the Isthmus of
Panama, in which the Southern Pacific had an interest by virtue
of its control of a steamship line from San Francisco to Panama. The business was not large, but in so far as any moved
this way it was in competition with the rail lines via Ogden.

Competition between Other Points

In addition to competition between the Southern Pacific and
the Union Pacific on business between the Pacific Coast and

points east of the Missouri River, the government succeeded in showing the existence of competition between the Atlantic seaboard and Colorado and Utah common points. A good many sheep wintered in the desert west of Salt Lake, and in the spring moved to the summer ranges in Idaho where they were sheared. The railroad near which the shearing took place secured the outbound wool, and for this reason the Union Pacific, Southern Pacific, and Rio Grande Western offered every attraction possible in order to influence the movement of the flocks. The Union Pacific for instance, at one time paid a head tax which Wyoming levied on all sheep brought into that state. The Oregon Short Line purchased salt on behalf of the sheep owners, carried it to Idaho, and collected the purchase price only when the salt was delivered. In the same way there was competition in respect to cattle and horses which wintered in southern Idaho and northern Nevada and moved east in the spring.

In return for the wool, cattle, hides, etc., shipped east, there were brought in shipments of miscellaneous merchandise, dry goods, machinery, and the like. When the Union Pacific handled the business, the freight moved from New York to Norfolk or Newport News, thence by rail to Omaha and over the Union Pacific lines to destination. When the Southern Pacific took it, the freight went by Southern Pacific steamers to New Orleans or Galveston, and thence over railroads controlled by the company to Fort Worth, Texas, where it was given to connecting lines for delivery at destination. The rate was the same either way, but the rivalry between soliciting agencies was intense.

Still again, there was competition between Portland and Utah and Colorado common points, including certain points in Nevada. Portland enjoys a fairly direct route over the Oregon Railroad and Navigation Company's tracks to Huntington, and from there over the Oregon Short Line to Granger, a few miles east of Ogden. The Southern Pacific runs south from Portland to Roseville, near Sacramento, and thence east through California, Nevada, and Utah to Ogden. The distance over the one route is 945.3 miles, and over the other 1,487.3 miles. The Roseville route has nearly twice the rise and fall of the route via Huntington, while the curvature also is greater. In a calculation made by Mr. Kruttschnitt, he estimated that the direct line haul was equivalent to 3,498 miles of straight level track, but that the haul via Roseville was equivalent to 6,164 such miles. The evidence nevertheless showed that some business, especially lumber, had moved the long way round before 1901. Traffic had also moved via the Oregon Short Line and Central Pacific to points as far west of Ogden as Wells, Nevada. How much all this amounted to was not clearly shown—at best it was probably not a great deal. After the consolidation of the Union Pacific and Southern Pacific in 1902, through rates with the Oregon Railroad and Navigation Company via the Shasta route were discontinued and competition ceased.

Other kinds of competition included competition for traffic between San Francisco and Portland, between San Francisco and points in Montana and Idaho, and competition for Oriental traffic destined to points in the United States east of the Missouri River. In short, the voluminous evidence thus summarized showed that active competition had existed of almost every conceivable kind. There had been competition of parallel routes between the same termini, of parallel or roundabout routes between different termini, of roundabout routes entirely controlled by the competing lines, of the routes in which the Union Pacific and Southern Pacific were links only in chains of connecting and independent roads, and finally there had been competition in cases where one competitor had to rely upon the other for a greater or less proportion of the haul.

Dissolution of Merger

This demonstration that the Union Pacific and the Southern Pacific had competed with each other before the merger of 1901, followed by easily secured evidence that the competition had ceased after the merger, was sufficient to persuade the Supreme Court to grant the government a decree, in spite of the protests of the defendant railroads.[4]   The effect upon the Southern Pacific was of course important.   A drastic reorganization of the affairs of the company was called for in order to take the Southern Pacific out of the control of the Union Pacific and to re-establish the conditions of the Huntington régime.   Such a reorganization presently occurred.   While the details of this transaction are not of present significance, it may be said, in brief, that after several abortive attempts the Union Pacific disposed of all its Southern Pacific stock under a reorganization plan dated May, 1913, delivering some of this stock to the Pennsylvania Railroad in exchange for stocks of the Baltimore and Ohio Railroad, and selling the rest to the general public.[5]   Henceforth the rail lines of the Southern Pacific were not to reach east of New Orleans and of Ogden.

Attack on Control of Central Pacific

When the United States Supreme Court declared that the Union and Southern Pacific systems must be separated, it merely restored the latter to a condition of independence.   The United States Department of Justice was of opinion, however, that the logic of the decision went further than this, and, encouraged by its preliminary success, it took the dramatic step of attempting to separate the Southern Pacific and the

---

[4] United States v. Union Pacific Railroad Company, 226 U. S. 61, 470 (1912, 1913).

[5] Preferential subscription rights were given to Union Pacific and Oregon Short Line Railroad Company stockholders, on condition that these last-named individuals divest themselves of their ownership of Union Pacific and Oregon Short Line shares before actually receiving their Southern Pacific certificates.   See Daggett, "Later Developments in the Union Pacific Merger Case," *sup. cit.*

Central Pacific companies by the application of the same principles which had torn the Southern Pacific and the Union Pacific apart. The new suit was known as the United States v. Southern Pacific Company, and, like the old, was brought under the Sherman law.[6]

The principal points in the case of the United States v. the Southern Pacific Company were as follows. A glance at the accompanying map will show that the Central Pacific Railroad, from Ogden to Sacramento, and the Western Pacific, from Sacramento to Oakland, were in practical effect but the western end of a route of which the Union Pacific formed the eastern part. So far as competition was concerned, all parts of the route were on a parity. If the Union Pacific competed with the Southern Pacific when it hauled eastern freight from Omaha to Ogden, the Central Pacific did likewise when it hauled the same freight from Ogden to Sacramento. If it would promote competition to place the Southern Pacific and the Union Pacific in separate hands, the same could be said of the Central Pacific and its southern neighbor. So much is reasonably clear even from a cursory examination of the facts.

In at least two important respects, however, the relations between the Southern Pacific and the Central Pacific differed from those between the Southern Pacific and the Union Pacific. These points were emphasized in the briefs of counsel, and formed the basis of the companies' defense. Unlike the Union Pacific, the Southern Pacific had obtained control of the stock of the Central Pacific at a time when and under circumstances in which the federal government was an interested party. If the details of the reorganization of 1898 are recalled, it will be remembered that the government then accepted notes in satis-

---

[6] This was the second suit of the same nature. In July, 1894, Richard Olney, United States Attorney-General, filed a bill in the United States District Court at Los Angeles to dissolve the Southern Pacific combination. In 1894, as in 1915, it was charged that the consolidation of the Southern Pacific and the Central Pacific companies was illegal under the Sherman law. The Olney suit was later withdrawn.

faction of its claims against the Central Pacific which were secured by mortgage bonds carrying a Southern Pacific guaranty. This guaranty, in turn, was offered by the guaranteeing company as one element in a series of transactions which included the acquisition of Central Pacific stock by the Southern Pacific in exchange for the latter's own stock certificates. The implications of this episode were mentioned when the transaction was described. While it certainly gave no permission to the Southern Pacific to violate the Sherman or any other law as a consideration for assisting the Central Pacific to pay its debts, the government did lay itself open to the charge of having at one time approved and enjoyed the fruits of a transaction of which it later complained.

The more important distinction between the later and the earlier merger cases in which the Southern Pacific was involved, lay in the circumstances that the combination of the Union Pacific and the Southern Pacific had been a recent matter, while the relations between the Central Pacific and the Southern Pacific had begun almost as soon as the latter corporation had been organized. In discussing the construction of the Southern Pacific, the remark has been made that the two enterprises were originally but different manifestations of the activities of a single group of men. The first statement in the brief of Mr. Herrin, chief counsel for the defense in the Central Pacific case, was similarly that: "This case does not involve any combination of competitive units, or any combination at all, for the Southern Pacific and Central Pacific lines were projected and built and have been operated since their organization as one property." [7] These two characterizations indicate a difference of considerable significance between the Union Pacific and the Central Pacific cases.

---

[7] United States of America v. Southern Pacific Company. The record and briefs in the case of the United States v. the Southern Pacific are as extensive as those submitted in the Union Pacific merger case. No attempt will be made to give detailed references to accompany the summary account presented in the remainder of this chapter.

Final Decision Doubtful

It must be pointed out, nevertheless, that in spite of the long and close association between the Central and the Southern Pacific railroads, there were certain features in this controversy which made it difficult to forecast the final decision of the Supreme Court of the United States. Counsel for the railroad company in the Union Pacific case dwelt much upon legal technicalities. But in the Southern Pacific case the forms were all opposed to the company's contentions. For one reason or another, doubtless largely for political effect, the associates had always scrupulously insisted upon the separate identity of the two companies concerned. The corporations had been made to appear to deal with each other at arm's length, and there had even been much discussion of the relative profitableness to each of the contracts concluded between them.

Nor was the matter one of form alone, as we have seen in earlier chapters of this study. While the construction of both roads was financed by the same parties, after 1880 the associates disposed of the greater part of their Central Pacific holdings. The Southern Pacific and the Central Pacific were still held together by lease relations, it is true, but they then became separate, not merely in organization but also in ownership. The separate ownership continued until 1899, when the new arrangements were made to undo which the government brought suit. It followed that counsel for the defendant railroads were in the position of defending a combination of legally distinct corporations, owned by different parties, with no connection between them save through the minority holdings of individual stockholders and through the very arrangements of which complaint was made. As an answer to this indictment, the circumstance that the same parties had found their profit in building each of the defendant lines could hardly be given weight, nor was the fact that the original consolidation antedated the Sherman law important.

The suit of the United States v. Southern Pacific Company was argued before the circuit judges of the Eighth Circuit sitting at St. Louis in December, 1915. The decision of a majority of this court was rendered in March, 1917, and was unfavorable to the government's contention.[8] The grounds of this opinion were not brought out with complete distinctness, but two judges held that there had never been a "natural and existing competition" in interstate commerce between the Southern Pacific and the Central Pacific. Nearly half of the text of the decision, moreover, was devoted to a description of the financial settlement of 1899, in which Congress appeared to have treated the control of the Central Pacific by the Southern Pacific as consistent with the statutes of the United States. Judge Carland dissented from the conclusions of his colleagues in a carefully prepared opinion. The case was appealed, and after full oral argument, was submitted to the Supreme Court on April 19, 1921. An early decision is expected. Meanwhile, the continued close relations between the Central Pacific and the Southern Pacific are approved by public sentiment upon the Pacific Coast, while the continuance for the present of common control of the two companies certainly avoids many practical difficulties.

[8] United States v. Southern Pacific Company, 239 Fed. 998 (1917).

CHAPTER XXIII

OIL AND TIMBER LAND LITIGATION

Oil Land Ownership

The discussion in the previous chapter dealt with litigation under the Sherman law which checked the absorption of the Southern Pacific by the Union Pacific system and profoundly altered the relations of these two companies to each other. Our narrative will close with the mention of two other suits or groups of suits which concerned, the one, the possession of certain oil properties in southern California, and the other, the administration of lands—mainly timber lands—granted to the Oregon and California Railroad in the North by federal legislation of 1866 and 1869. The Southern Pacific Company took part in both of these controversies as a principal interested party.

The oil lands which until recently belonged to the Southern Pacific Railroad lay principally in the West San Joaquin fields in southern California. They covered an area of between 160,-000 and 170,000 acres. In 1917, a committee of the California State Council of Defense estimated that the Southern Pacific and its subsidiary companies controlled 26.4 per cent of the total output of the state, although much of the oil so controlled was not produced upon the company's own land. The actual production of oil by the Southern Pacific Company in June, 1918,[1] was 49,679 barrels out of 282,672 barrels of production by all companies in the state, or a little less than 18 per cent.[2] No later statistics of production by companies have been made public. In June, 1920, however, the Southern Pacific Land

---

[1] Including the output of the Associated Oil Company.
[2] Third Annual Report of the State Oil and Gas Supervisor of California, 1917-18.

Company owned 19.38 per cent of all the proven oil land in California, and in addition the Southern Pacific Company held a controlling interest in the Associated Oil Company, also a large producer.

Unquestionably the Southern Pacific oil lands are valuable. A witness in one of the recent cases testified that he had told Mr. Huntington in 1893 that the railroad oil lands were worth more than the entire Southern Pacific Railroad, while it is common report that the value of the properties may run into the hundreds of millions of dollars. All this is, moreover, recent. The discovery of oil in large quantities was first made in southern California in the Kern River field, near Bakersfield, in the spring of 1899. This was followed by discoveries in the so-called McKittrick and Sunset fields, and by an oil boom of extraordinary proportions. In so far as the railroad owns oil lands, it has therefore recently secured an unearned increment which is not only of great size, but of a character entirely unanticipated by legislators of earlier days. This has given rise to controversy, in which the government has questioned the railroad title.

The peculiarity of the oil land litigation, and the reason why the federal government is involved, is found in the fact that the railroad land is mostly land-grant land, lying within the limits laid down by the Act of 1866 from which the Southern Pacific Railroad took its life. It follows from this that the railroad title was affected by certain reservations in the land-grant legislation, such as that of exempting mineral lands from the operation of the grants. The government offered to convey certain land to the railroad free of charge when it undertook to stimulate railroad building in California, but it did not include mineral land in this offer, except coal land and iron land. Not only this, but the exception of mineral lands was repeated in the patents later issued by the Department of the Interior, and in such patents the words, "excluding and excepting all mineral lands should any such be found in the tracts aforesaid," were used, making the exemption apply to future discoveries as well as to discoveries occurring before the patents were issued. Evidently the legislature and the land office intended to limit the donations to the Southern Pacific by excluding unknown and immeasurable increments of value in so far as this might be done. Coal and iron were left, for the reason that these minerals were intimately connected with the construction and operation of the road.

Test Case

In 1910, one Edmund Burke filed a bill in equity in the Circuit Court of the United States for the Southern District of California, in which he challenged the title of the railroad to oil lands in an area covering five sections in Fresno County, California. This was a test case. Disregarding minor points, the larger questions at issue were the following:

The first question was as to whether or not oil was a mineral. The plaintiff said that it was a mineral, the defendant said that it was not. If oil was a mineral, then the railroad could not obtain title under the land-grant laws to land which was known to contain oil at the time the patent was applied for. If oil was not a mineral, there was no limitation. Now matters of definition always cause trouble. The word "mineral" is sometimes associated with metallic ores, a notion which would not include a resultant from the decomposition of organic matter such as California petroleum. Indeed, the Secretary of the Interior once held that the word "mineral" embraced only the more precious metals, such as gold, silver, cinnabar, etc., although on rehearing this view was rejected. Common usage includes more than the metallic ores, and the courts have considered as mineral such articles as clay, coal, and marble, and even deposits such as guano.[3] When the matter was presented to it, the

---

[3] For a full discussion of this and kindred subjects, see Lindley on Mines, ed. 3.

United States Supreme Court followed common usage and held that petroleum was a mineral.[4]

The second point had to do with the effect of a patent. It was shown that the Southern Pacific had received patents as early as 1892 to lands which ultimately proved to contain petroleum, and there was dispute as to whether this subsequent discovery invalidated title to property once patented. On this point, fortunately, the law was clear. Quoting the Supreme Court:

> The settled course of decision . . . has been that the character of land is a question for the Land Department, the same as the qualifications of the applicant and his performance of the acts upon which the right to receive the title depends, and . . . [that] when a patent issues it is to be taken upon a collateral attack, as affording conclusive evidence of the nonmineral character of the land and of the regularity of the acts and proceedings resulting in its issue, and upon a direct attack, as affording such presumptive evidence as to require plain and convincing proof to overcome it.

The Supreme Court therefore held that the Southern Pacific was secure in its possession of lands to which it held patent, unless fraud could be shown, and this irrespective of any saving clause in the patent itself, and without regard to the nature of the investigation by which the Land Office had originally satisfied itself as to the character of the land.[5]

Elk Hills Suit

The effect of the rulings of the Supreme Court in the test case of Burke v. Southern Pacific was not only to cause the dismissal of the pending suit, but to make it evident that the government must show fraud on the part of the railroad company before the company's title could be disturbed. The hold-

---

[4] Burke v. Southern Pacific, 234 U. S. 669 (1914).

[5] *Ibid.*, pp. 691–92. See also Roberts v. Southern Pacific Company, 186 Fed. 934 (1911).

ing of the court that oil lands were mineral lands was, however, an important victory for the government. It was under these circumstances that the federal government instituted a fresh series of suits. Of these, one suit called in question the title of the Southern Pacific to some 6,109 acres of land in the Elk Hills region of southern California, held under a patent issued December 12, 1904. The other suits attacked the legality of the railroad's possession of substantially all its remaining oil lands, obtained at various dates from 1892 to 1902. The value of the lands involved in the second proceedings was estimated by the government as in excess of $421,000,000. Counsel alleged that the company's land agents, Messrs. Eberlein and Madden, had accompanied the lists, which they had submitted to the government for patenting, with affidavits stating that the lands were not mineral lands, although both agents knew at the time the patents were applied for that the lands in question contained oil. This charge, if substantiated, amounted to a showing of fraud. In both cases the government sought to show that the presence of oil upon the lands sought was a matter of common knowledge, and that there was reason to believe that the company was fully cognizant of the facts.

Most of the sensational testimony taken in the oil land cases appeared in the so-called Elk Hills case. Mr. Eberlein here figured as the land agent for the Southern Pacific. Omitting again all relatively unimportant detail, it appeared that Mr. Eberlein had filed an affidavit with the Land Office in November, 1903, in which he swore to two pertinent facts: first, that he had caused the lands for which the railroad applied to be carefully examined by the agents and employees of the company as to their mineral or agricultural character; and second, that to the best of his knowledge and belief, none of the lands returned in the list were mineral lands. These statements had been repeated in September, 1904, when a substitute list was filed.

In the face of these sworn assertions, the United States Supreme Court later found that Mr. Eberlein had not examined the lands in question, nor had he caused them to be examined by others. Indeed, Eberlein had even objected to the examination of the lands. He had protested verbally to Judge Cornish, vice-president of the Southern Pacific Company against examination, and to Mr. Markham, its general manager, and in 1908 he had summed up his repeated objections by writing to the assistant land agent of the company as follows:

> The examination of our S. P. lands not yet patented by our oil experts must be stopped as information that they may obtain or give as to mineral character prior to patent will forever prevent our getting title . . . Mr. Dumble (the company's geologist) and his men should not be furnished by us with any data whatever except as to *patented* lands. For reasons above given such information will be embarrassing to them and us and may make them witnesses against this company in mineral contests hereafter.[6]

The most that can be said for such an epistle is that it indicated an anxiety to keep within the letter of the law.

Government Victory and Defeat

Besides falsely swearing that he had made an examination of the lands involved in the Elk Hills case, Mr. Eberlein made the positive statement in his affidavit that none of the lands covered by his application were mineral lands, in so far as he was informed. Now in this matter it is clear that the evidence before Mr. Eberlein, such as it was, pointed to a mineral and not to a non-mineral content of the land in question. This evidence consisted primarily in the results of work of Southern Pacific geologists in the general region of which the Elk Hills were a part, and in the presence there of a certain number of

---

[6] Southern Pacific v. United States, in the United States Circuit Court of Appeals for the Ninth Circuit (Brief of United States, Appellee, pp. 364–65).

producing wells. It is on record that in 1902 the Southern
Pacific withdrew from sale many of its patented lands which
surrounded or were adjacent to the land in controversy "because they were in or near oil territory." The following year
the company decided to lease such of its lands as were considered valuable for oil purposes to a subsidiary company—the
Kern Trading and Oil Company. The proposed lease was laid
before Eberlein in August, 1904. He at once objected. In a
letter to C. H. Markham, general manager of the Southern
Pacific Company and second vice-president of the Southern
Pacific Railroad Company, Eberlein set forth (September 10,
1904) the reasons for his opposition in these words:

> In addition to this there is a very urgent reason for de-
> laying the execution of these papers. We have selected a large
> body of lands interspersed with the lands sought to be conveyed
> by this lease and which we have represented as non-mineral in
> character. Should the existence of this lease become known,
> it would go a long way toward establishing the mineral charac-
> ter of the lands referred to and which are still unpatented.[7]

A similar letter addressed the week before to Judge Cornish
in New York contained arguments of a similar nature. The
protests were heeded, and the leases of lands in the McKittrick
and Coalinga districts were held up. It was recognized, moreover, that the matter was a delicate one, and the papers relating
to the proposed leases were placed in a special and private file
separate from the general file of the land department of the
railroad company. Summing up the evidence in the case, the
United States Supreme Court later observed that the natural, if
not the only, conclusion from the facts was that in pressing the
selection the officers of the railroad company were not acting
in good faith, but were attempting to obtain the patent by representing that the lands (covered by the Elk Hills litigation)

---

[7] *Ibid.*, p. 363.

were not mineral when they believed the fact was otherwise.[8] The decree of the United States Supreme Court requiring the cancellation of the railroad patents to the 6,000 acres of land in the Elk Hills district was given on November 17, 1919.

Three months before this Supreme Court decision, Judge Bledsoe, in the District Court for the Southern District of California, dismissed a suit challenging title to some 165,000 acres of land in the oil territory on the west side of the San Joaquin Valley.[9]   This suit represented a consolidation of the oil land suits other than those included in the Elk Hills case. Perhaps 156,000 of the acres under litigation were claimed by the railroad.   Cases are seldom alike, and the Bledsoe case differed from the Elk Hills controversy in several important details.   In this case, for example, it appeared that the railroad had sold lands in the disputed territory at agricultural prices—a policy which it presumably would not have followed had it believed that these lands had mineral value.   There was also lacking much of the direct evidence which had helped to demonstrate the fact that Mr. Eberlein had distorted the truth in his representations to the government.   On the other hand, the refusal of Judge Bledsoe to believe that men like the general manager of the Southern Pacific, its land agent, and its vice-president would lend themselves to fraud, is less impressive after a perusal of the Elk Hills material.   The government has announced that it will not appeal from Judge Bledsoe's ruling—a decision which, on the face of things, appears to be a mistake.

Sale of Oil Lands

The most recent development in connection with the Southern Pacific oil lands is associated with the organization of the Pacific Oil Company.   The formation of this company was

---

[8] United States v. Southern Pacific Company, 251 U. S. 1 (1919).   The decision of the Circuit Court of Appeals, which was favorable to the railroad, is reported in 249 Fed. 785 (1918).

[9] United States v. Southern Pacific, 260 Fed. 511 (1919).   See also *ibid.*, 225 Fed. 197 (1915).

announced in March, 1921. It purchased from the Southern
Pacific Land Company, for the sum of $43,750,000, about
259,000 acres of lands in California, most of which were
proven oil lands, and 200,690 shares (50.48 per cent) of the
capital stock of the Associated Oil Company. This was the
whole of the Southern Pacific interest in the oil fields. The
Southern Pacific Company provided the funds for the purchase
by subscribing to 3,500,000 shares of the Pacific Oil Company
at $15 per share, but the railroad disposed of its newly acquired
shares by extending to holders of its own stock the right to
purchase Pacific Oil stock at $15 per share, one share of stock
of the new company for each share of the Southern Pacific
Company stock so held. This transaction will transfer the
ownership of the railroad oil lands from the Southern Pacific
Company to the stockholders of that company as fast as the
subscription rights are taken up. Commenting on the plan for
the separation of the oil and railroad properties, President
Sproule observed that the plan was simply responsive to the
spirit of the times. It seems likely, however, that it will have
the additional result of preventing further action tending to
disturb the railroad title. The president of the Pacific Oil
Company is Mr. Shoup and its directors are men of influence
in the East.[10]

Timber Land Grant

This summary discussion of the oil land litigation in California brings us to the last of the great cases with which the
Southern Pacific has, in recent years, been concerned, namely,
to the dispute between the federal government and the Oregon
and California Railroad over the administration of timber
lands in Oregon. By the Act of July 25, 1866,[11] Congress

---

[10] The annual report of the Southern Pacific Company for the year ending December
31, 1920, contained the statement that Southern Pacific Company stockholders or their
assigns had purchased an aggregate of 3,414,604 shares of Pacific Oil Company stock, thus
leaving 85,395 shares still in possession of the company.

[11] 14 United States Statutes 239 (1866).

authorized the California and Oregon Railroad to build a railroad and telegraph line in the state of California from a point on the Central Pacific in the Sacramento Valley to the northern boundry of the state. The same act empowered "such company, organized under the laws of Oregon, as that state should designate," to construct a railroad from Portland, Oregon, to a junction with the California and Oregon upon the Oregon-California boundary line. The legislature granted to the company mentioned a right-of-way, and in addition ten alternate sections of public land on each side of its track.

At the time Congress acted, there was no company in Oregon in condition to become the beneficiary of the grant. In 1867, however, the Oregon Central Railroad Company of Salem was incorporated, and the following year this railroad received the needed legislative designation. It appears that there was some dispute between the Oregon Central of Salem and another organization known simply as the Oregon Central Railroad Company, and that the doubt as to which of these two was entitled to receive the granted lands in Oregon delayed the filing of the necessary formal assent to the terms of the Congressional Act of 1866. In 1869, therefore, Congress extended the time for the filing of the required assent.[12]

At the time this privilege was accorded, however, Congress introduced an important limitation to its previous action, by providing that the lands granted by the Act of 1866 should be sold to actual settlers only, in quantities not greater than 160 acres to one purchaser, and for a price not exceeding $2.50 per acre. So amended, the Act of 1866 was accepted by the Oregon Central, and on March 16, 1870, the rights acquired were assigned to the Oregon and California Railroad. In 1887, the Oregon and California was absorbed by the Southern Pacific.

As a result of the legislation described, the Oregon and California Railroad Company received a total grant estimated

---

[12] 16 United States Statutes 47 (1869).

at 3,821,902 acres, which it held subject to the requirement that
it should dispose of the property to actual settlers, in small lots,
at prices not exceeding $2.50 per acre. Now the simple facts
with regard to the company's administration of this estate are
that it did not limit the price which it charged to $2.50 per acre,
that it took no pains to ascertain whether or not, purchasers of
its lands were actual settlers, and that it sold in whatever quantities were convenient from the point of view of revenue. Between 1894 and 1903, to take the period when the company
neglected its obligations most grossly, there were sales at prices
ranging from $5 to $40 an acre, and in amounts which in one
instance reached the figure of 45,000 acres to a single purchaser. Out of 820,000 acres sold during this period, approximately 370,000 were sold to 38 purchasers in quantities
exceeding 2,000 acres to each purchaser, and at prices higher
than $2.50. These sales, according to the Supreme Court,
were to persons other than actual settlers, and for other purposes than settlement. On January 1, 1903, the company
reached the climax of its disobedience to law by withdrawing all
of its lands from sale and refusing to accept offers for any of
them, asserting that they were timber lands and unsuitable for
settlement. In 1911 there were 2,360,492.81 acres unsold, of
which 2,075,616.45 had been patented. Only a comparatively
small part of the grant, that is to say, had been disposed of.

Land Rebought by Government

It is somewhat amazing that so clear a violation of the
terms under which the Oregon and California held its land
grant should have passed unchallenged. Nor can the obstinacy
of the company's defense fail to excite surprise. When the
Attorney-General of the United States sought to have the
Oregon and California grant declared forfeit [13] because of the

---

[13] See Joint Resolution No. 18, 35 United States Statutes 571 (1908), instructing the
Attorney-General to institute certain suits.

company's disregard of the terms of the law, it proved necessary to litigate for eight years, to take seventeen volumes of
testimony, to consider 2,500 pages of briefs, and to obtain three
court decisions and the enactment of a new law before the matter could be finally set at rest. It is unnecessary to go into the
elaborate record, or the arguments by which counsel sought to
demonstrate that the restrictive provisions of the Act of 1869
were beyond the power of Congress to enact, or to discuss the
contentions that breaches of the law had been condoned and
that the covenants were not in any case enforceable. The case
was considered by the Circuit Court of the United States for
the District of Oregon in 1911,[14] and by the Supreme Court of
the United States in 1915.[15] Both courts pronounced the restriction on the alienation of Oregon and California lands binding.

The controversy was at last settled by a new Act of June
9, 1916, in which Congress resumed possession of the unsold
lands appertaining to the grant, while appropriating the sum
of $2.50 an acre for these lands as a payment to the railroad
company.[16]

Under the terms of the act, the Secretary of the Interior
was directed to ascertain the exact number of acres of land
patented to the railroad company, and the number of acres of
unpatented land which the company was entitled to receive in
the future according to the original grants. The Secretary was
then to calculate the value of all this land at $2.50 per acre,
and to pay over the amount so ascertained to the railroad company from time to time from the proceeds of future sales of the
lands or of the timber upon it, after deducting from the valuation the amounts already received by the railroad and by its
predecessors in interest. The intent was clearly to allow to

---

14 United States v. Oregon and California Railroad Company, 186 Fed. 861 (1911).
15 Oregon and California Railroad Company v. United States, 238 U. S. 393 (1915).
16 39 United States Statutes 218, Ch. 137 (1916).

the railroad $2.50 per acre of the original grant, no more and no less, taking full account of the sums already received by the company. The constitutionality of the law was later upheld by the Supreme Court.[17]

---

[17] Oregon and California Railroad Company v. United States, 243 U. S. 549 (1917). Suit was brought by the United States in 1917, in accordance with the law, seeking to offset against the compensation of $2.50 per acre due the company for the unsold lands, moneys received by the company, in excess of $2.50 per acre, by reason of past sales, leases, and otherwise, as well as taxes levied since the forfeiture decision and voluntarily paid by the federal government to the state of Oregon. This case was ready for trial in 1921 and will probably be soon heard and decided.

CHAPTER XXIV

FINAL REMARKS

Character of Associates

It is to be regretted that the oil, land, and timber litigation of recent years has once more presented the Southern Pacific in the light of a corporation more heedful of its own financial interests than of the requirements of public policy or of a high ethical code. In all fairness to the company, it should be said that this controversy does not truly represent its attitude at the present time. Stanford and Huntington are dead, and their properties are in other hands. The great railroad system which they left, controlled by leaders who are responsive to new policies, is in general no longer a profit-making device in the hands of a small group of men, but instead is a powerful machine for the promotion of industry and commerce on the Pacific Coast.

Our narrative will now close with a few words of summary and conclusion.

The purpose of the writer in presenting the story of the Southern Pacific has been to throw light upon the problems encountered by the most important railroad upon the Pacific Coast, and to characterize and interpret the policies adopted by that railroad and by the men who governed it.

The writer's view with regard to the so-called Southern Pacific associates, Stanford, Huntington, Mark Hopkins, and Crocker, is that they were rough, vigorous, and grasping men, tenacious of rights to property once acquired, kind-hearted within the circle of their families and intimate friends, but narrow in vision, uneducated, and inexpert in the details of railroad operation, and uninformed in all that related to ques-

454

tions of public policy. Huntington alone, while rough and selfish as the others, showed important constructive capacity in the railroad field. The strength of the associates lay in their courage and persistence, in their loyalty to each other in business matters, in their readiness to attract and to support able men whose views did not differ too greatly from their own, and in a native shrewdness which, in Huntington at least, reached to a superlative degree.

Achievements of Group

The reputation of the Huntington group rests upon the fact that within fifty years they built up an organization operating 11,152 miles of lines and earning an operating revenue in a single year of no less than $282,000,000. A statement like this is quickly made. The significance of it comes home, however, only to those who understand the difficulties of successful management of great corporations and who appreciate the multitude of decisions as to policy which must have been, on the whole, soundly made, at least from the point of view of the corporation itself, in order to achieve such a success.

Doubtless most of the details of the Southern Pacific management were necessarily handled by subordinates. It is unlikely, for instance, that the associates had much to do with the construction of railroad rates in the West, with the negotiation of special contracts with California shippers, or with agreements with the Pacific Mail. The contribution of the owners was here the appointment of competent men at liberal salaries to attend to matters which they did not understand or for other reasons were not able to handle themselves. The credit for general direction and support of the policies adopted, however, belongs to the associates even in these matters, when credit is due, just as responsibility for errors properly falls upon them.

Principles of Operation

There are three principles relating to the operation of these railroad properties which the author feels that he can attribute with some confidence to Huntington and his friends. The first of these was that the Southern Pacific enterprise should remain under the associates' control and free from eastern entanglements. The second was that railroad monopoly in California was essential to a satisfactory railroad profit, and that the utmost possible profit should be exacted when monopoly power had been attained; and the third was that regulation by public bodies was in all respects objectionable, although public grants were considered to be legitimate sources of revenue.

Looked at in a comprehensive way, the history of the Southern Pacific may be said to have centered in the application of these principles to the solution of a series of problems, of which the final disposition of the Southern Pacific oil and timber lands was the last. These problems, to name them consecutively, included the construction of the original Central Pacific and Southern Pacific railroads; the establishment of these companies as going concerns with opportunity for prosperity and power; and the adoption by the associates of policies with respect to government regulation, with respect to rates, and with respect to relations with competing lines. They included also the negotiation of a plan of settlement with the federal government under which the financial assistance tendered to the companies in their younger days was repaid, and the railroad stood forth free of unusual responsibility and devoid of special privilege. At a later date the merger of the Southern Pacific with the Union Pacific represented an additional adventure, although one which was never part of Huntington's plan; and still another episode, the oil and timber litigation just described, was concerned with a forced liquidation of interests of which Huntington had known and approved.

Two Eras in Company's History

Grouped in a somewhat different way, but with the same essential point of view, the history of the Southern Pacific may be divided into two parts, the one ending and the other beginning in or about the year 1883. Before 1883, the Huntington group was primarily interested in construction from Sacramento to Ogden in order to obtain the benefit of the federal subsidy, and in construction in southern California, New Mexico, and Arizona, in order to prevent the building of an independent competing line. In this period, also, steps were taken to crush the competition of certain local enterprises in California. After 1883, or more accurately, after 1879, the attention of the associates was concentrated upon the establishment of their credit, the resistance to the threatened regulation by the state of their properties in California, and upon the competition of the newly created transcontinental railroad lines and the water routes from the Pacific to the Atlantic Coast. The second of these dangers led them into local politics, and the third resulted not only in a variety of agreements with competitors, but also caused the Southern Pacific to modify its rate structures and to subsidize potential competitors upon the sea. Still later came the necessity of repaying the loans which the Central Pacific had received from the federal government at the time of the construction of its road and the new relations with the Union Pacific under the Harriman régime. The oil and timber litigation, though falling within the second period, represented the closing up of grants received in the first.

In solving all the problems presented in the course of the Southern Pacific's career, the associates followed consistently the three fundamental principles laid down in a preceding paragraph whenever the principles were applicable and the circumstances permitted of a deliberate choice. The only striking variation from them occurred when the Union Pacific was allowed to obtain a controlling interest in Southern Pacific stock—a transaction which occurred after Huntington's death and one for which the associates were not responsible.

The Charge against Associates

The weakness in the position of the Huntington group lay in the fact that their insistence upon monopolistic control of railroads in the state of California and their resistance to government regulation, ran counter to public policies of a most fundamental kind. A further ground for incisive criticism is properly found in the methods which the associates adopted in their business and political campaigns. It is not sufficient to declare that Huntington and Stanford merely imitated practices which they found about them. There is reason to believe that the Southern Pacific associates lowered the standard of business ethics of their time. The reader who has examined the data submitted in preceding pages will need no specification of this charge. In finance, in politics, in questions of rates, and in their relations with public bodies, the associates were indifferent to standards of private and public conduct, which alone can bring trust and confidence into business relations. The great material achievements of the Huntington group were marred by the moral and spiritual defects of its members.

Public's Present Favorable Attitude

This narrative closes without consideration of the part which the Southern Pacific played in the war of 1914-1918, and without detailed analysis of the present position of the company or of its prospects for the future. As a matter of fact, the tendency today is for individual systems to be assimilated into the national railroad net through governmental regulation of rates, of wages, and of many details of operation, so that elaborate discussion of the affairs of single companies has lost much of the interest which it once possessed. The future of the Southern Pacific will depend more on the outcome of national policies with respect to the support and control of railroads in all parts of the country, than it will on the success of the strategy of any group of railroad men.

For good or bad the pioneer days are over. Public opinion in California is now well disposed toward the Southern Pacific in marked contrast to the attitude of earlier days. Probably the change is in part due to the efficiency of the technical staff of the company and to the excellence of its service as compared with other roads. Probably also the recent enforced separation of the Union Pacific and the Southern Pacific has on the whole strengthened the latter by relieving it of the unpopularity which would have followed long-continued outside control, while the completeness of public authority over rates through state and federal commissions has removed still another cause of discontent. In spite of past errors the Southern Pacific now looks forward to a long and prosperous career and to a popularity properly the result of the loyal and efficient service of a great body of official employees.

INDEX

461

PROPERTY OF
DAVID O. McKAY LIBRARY
BYU-IDAHO
REXBURG ID 83460-0405